The Bollywood Reader

The Bollywood Reader

Edited by Rajinder Dudrah and Jigna Desai

 Open University Press

Open University Press
McGraw-Hill Education
McGraw-Hill House
Shoppenhangers Road
Maidenhead
Berkshire
England
SL6 2QL

email: enquiries@openup.co.uk
world wide web: www.openup.co.uk

and Two Penn Plaza, New York, NY 10121—2289, USA

First published 2008

A catalogue record of this book is available from the British Library

ISBN-13: 978-0-33-522212-4 (pb) 978-0-33-522213-1 (hb)
ISBN-10: 0-33-522212-9 (pb) 0-33-522213-7 (hb)

Typeset by Kerrypress, Luton, Bedfordshire
Printed by in the UK by Bell and Bain Ltd, Glasgow

The **McGraw·Hill** Companies

Contents

PART 3
Bollywood abroad and beyond

Contributors

Sumita Chakravarty: Associate Professor of Culture and Media, New School for General Studies, New York, USA

Nicholas B. Dirks: Professor of Anthropology and History, Columbia University, USA

Sangita Gopal: Assistant Professor of English, University of Oregon, USA

Lalitha Gopalan: Associate Professor of Radio-Television-Film, University of Texas – Austin, USA

Nitin Govil: Assistant Professor of Communication, University of California – San Diego, USA

Brian Larkin: Associate Professor of Anthropology, Barnard College, New York, USA

Monika Mehta: Assistant Professor of English, State University of New York – Binghamton University, USA

Vijay Mishra: Professor of English and Comparative Literature, Murdoch University, Australia

Ashis Nandy: Senior Honorary Fellow at the Centre for the Study of Developing Societies – Delhi, India

Sheila J. Nayar: Associate Professor of English and Communication Studies, Greensboro College, USA

Manjunath Pendakur: Professor and Dean in the College of Mass Communication and Media Arts, Southern Illinois University, USA

Madhava Prasad: Professor of Film and Cultural Studies in the Centre for European Studies, Central Institute of English and Foreign Languages – Hyderabad, India

Amit Rai: Associate Professor of English, Florida State University, USA

Ashish Rajadhyaksha: Senior Fellow of the Centre for the Study of Culture and Society – Bangalore, India

Parama Roy: Assistant Professor of English, University of California – Davis, USA

Biswarup Sen: Visiting Assistant Professor of English, University of Oregon, USA

Rosie Thomas: Reader in Art and Media Practice, University of Westminster, UK

Patricia Uberoi: Professor in Social Change and Development at the Institute of Economic Growth – Delhi, India

Acknowledgements

Rajinder Dudrah and Jigna Desai would like to thank Chris Cudmore (the original Commissioning Editor of this Reader) and also Jack Fray and colleagues at Open University Press for their invaluable work and assistance on this book. Thank you also to all of our contributors.

Rajinder would like to thank: Mum, Dad, sisters, brothers, and nieces and nephews, all for being unflinching supporters of my academic work and pursuits. Thanks for always listening, critiquing and contributing to my ideas. I dedicate this book to my sisters Balvinder and Pinky, my two favourite accomplices to watch a Bollywood film on the big screen with. A special nod of gratitude is owed to my undergraduate and postgraduate students over recent years at the University of Manchester where I teach my courses on popular Hindi cinema – you all keep me on my toes in a good way. Professor Sue Harper – my undergraduate Film and Cultural Studies guru – your pedagogy and intellectual advice has been an immense boon, even today. My work colleagues, Professor Viv Gardner, Professor Maggie Gale, Dr Susan Rutherford, Professor Tony Jackson and Dr Aleksandar Dundjerovic have often been providers of gems of suggestions and cross-references from their own respective research and teaching. And thank you Jigna for being a pleasure to work with and to discuss all ideas Bollywood for the Reader.

Jigna would like to thank: my parents Harish and Naina Desai, my brother Rakesh, and my sister Seema for their generous love and encouragement. I am especially grateful for the many hours of labour, childcare and sustenance, not to mention the steady supply of DVDs, that you all provide. I dedicate this book to my brother, whose courage never ceases to amaze me. Thanks to Rohan and Khayaal, whose endless activities make sure that my days are jam-packed, but more rewarding than I could have ever imagined. To Ruskin, who slogs through film after film with me, I owe my deepest gratitude; your unflagging and unequivocal support, love, and humour sustain me day after day. Thank you Sue Hunt for all of those extra trips to the Midwest – they make all of our lives richer and better. Diane Detournay has repeatedly proven that I may leave dozens of detailed tasks in her competent hands and that they will be shepherded to completion. And Rajinder, I can say that you exemplify what is best in a colleague – collegiality, warmth, inspiration, intellectual rigour and patience. Thank you.

Publisher's acknowledgements

The editors and publisher wish to thank the following for permission to use copyright material:

Thomas, R. (1985) 'Indian Cinema: Pleasures and Popularity', *Screen*, 26(3–4): 116–30. Reproduced with kind permission.

Mishra, V. (1985) 'Towards a Theoretical Critique of Bombay Cinema', *Screen*, 26(3–4): 133–46. Reproduced with kind permission.

Prasad, M. (2000) 'The Economics of Ideology: Popular Film Form and Mode of Production', in M. Prasad, *Ideology of the Hindi Film: A Historical Construction*. New Delhi: Oxford University Press. Reproduced by permission of Oxford University Press India, New Delhi.

Pendakur, M. (2003) 'In the Throes of Change: Exhibition, Production and Distribution', in M. Pendakur, *Indian Popular Cinema: Industry, Ideology and Consciousness*. Cresskill, NJ: Hampton Press. Reprinted with the permission of the publisher.

Nandy, A. (1998) 'Introduction: Indian Popular Cinema as a Slum's Eye View of Politics', in A. Nandy, *The Secret Politics of our Desires: Innocence, Culpability and Indian Popular Cinema*. London: Zed Books. Reproduced with kind permission.

Chakravarty, S. 'The National-Heroic Image: Masculinity and Masquerade', in S. Chakravarty, *National Identity in Indian Popular Cinema, 1947–1987*, © 1993. By permission of the University of Texas Press.

Gopalan, L. (1997) 'Avenging Women in Indian Cinema', *Screen*, 38(1): 42–59. Reproduced with kind permission.

Roy, P. (1998) 'Figuring Mother India: The Case of Nargis', in P. Roy, *Indian Traffic: Identities in Question in Colonial and Postcolonial India*. Berkeley, CA: University of California Press.

Mehta, M. (2001) 'What is Behind Film Censorship? The *Khalnayak* Debates', *Jouvert*, 5(3).

Dirks, N. B. (1996) 'The Home and the Nation: Consuming Culture and Politics in *Roja*', in C. Pinney and R. Dwyer (eds) *Pleasure and the Nation: The History,*

Politics and Consumption of Public Culture in India. New Delhi: Oxford University Press. Reproduced by permission of Oxford University Press India, New Delhi.

Nayar, S. J. (2004) 'Invisible Representation: The Oral Contours of a National Popular Cinema', *Film Quarterly*, 57(3): 13–23. Reproduced with kind permission of the University of California Press.

Uberoi, P. (2001) 'Imagining the Family: An Ethnography of Viewing *Hum Aapke Hain Kaun*', in C. Pinney and R. Dwyer (eds) *Pleasure and the Nation: The History, Politics and Consumption of Public Culture in India.* New Delhi; Oxford University Press India.

Rajadhyaksha, A. (2003) 'The "Bollywoodization" of Indian Cinema: Cultural Nationalism in a Global Arena', *Inter-Asia Cultural Studies*, 4(1): 25–39.

Govil, N. (2006) 'Bollywood and the Frictions of Global Mobility', in D. Thussu (ed.) *Media on the Move: Global Flow and Contra-Flow.* London: Routledge, pp. 84–97. Reproduced by permission of Taylor & Francis Books UK.

Larkin, B. (2003) 'Itineries of Indian Cinema: African Videos, Bollywood, and Global Media', in E. Shohat and R. Stam (eds) *Multiculturalism, Postcoloniality, and Transnational Media.* New Brunswick, NJ: Rutgers University Press, pp. 170–92, © 2003 by Rutgers, the State University. Reprinted by permission of Rutgers University Press.

Desai, J. (2004) '"Ever Since You've Discovered the Video, I've had no Peace"': Diasporic Spectators Talk Back to Bollywood *Masala*', in J. Desai, *Beyond Bollywood: The Cultural Politics of South Asian Diasporic Film.* New York: Routledge.

Dudrah, R. (2005) 'Queer as *Desis*: Secret Politics of Gender and Sexuality in Bollywood Films in Diasporic Urban Ethnoscapes', in R. Dudrah, *Bollywood: Sociology Goes to the Movies.* London: Sage.

Every effort has been made to trace the copyright holders but if any have been inadvertently overlooked the publisher will be pleased to make the necessary arrangement at the first opportunity.

1

The essential Bollywood
by Jigna Desai and Rajinder Dudrah

Introduction

While longstanding, scholarship on Indian cinema has seen a recent proliferation, one that suggests that scholars globally are taking film and media in India seriously. Two epistemic obstacles may have prevented scholarship from previously flourishing. The first is the hegemony of Western and Hollywood cinemas in media, film, and cultural studies. The second is the dismissal of popular film culture in Indian scholarship. With the rise of postcolonial and transnational scholarship, more global attention has focused on Bollywood and other Indian film cultures attempting to 'provincialize' Hollywood. Even scholarship in India which, at times, was dismissive of popular films as Technicolor fantasies catering to the masses, has undergone a revolution with the works of scholars such as Rosie Thomas, Ashis Nandy, Ravi Vasudevan, Ashish Rajadhyaksha, and Madhava Prasad in the last few decades. Now one of the largest film industries in the world with an audience that exceeds any other globally, Indian cinema and media have become significant areas of academic enquiry in India and abroad.

It is only since the mid-1980s that scholarly attention has been paid to these films as significant cultural texts. This reader collects key essays that introduce major paradigms of theorizing and analysing this significant cinema. 'Bollywood' – once a tongue-in-cheek term used by the English-language media in India – has become the dominant globally recognized term to refer to Bombay's (Mumbai's) prolific Hindi-Urdu language culture industry and cinema. Characterized by music and dance numbers, melodrama, lavish production and an emphasis on stars and spectacle, Bollywood films have met with box-office success and enthusiastic audiences both nationally within India and globally. This book provides a guide to the cultural, social and political significance of recent Hindi cinema, outlining the history and structure of the Bombay film industry, and its impact on global popular culture.

While various narratives exist for the origin and history of the term Bollywood, Madhava Prasad (2003), proposing an imperial history, argues that it should be traced back to the older term Tollywood used by an American producer referring to the Tollygunge area of Calcutta/Kolkata in the 1930s. Over time, the term

Bollywood has come to be used interchangeably with and replaced others such as Bombay/Mumbai cinema or popular Hindi cinema that marked films as regionally and linguistically specific. The use of the term Bollywood has increasingly been used to refer to the now globalized Mumbai's Hindi film culture industry. Ashish Rajadhyaksha (see Reading 15) posits that Bollywood may refer to a mode of production, a way of producing culture within a national and global context that is inextricably linked to the Indian nation-state and the postcolonial economy of liberalization. Hence, the term itself is by no means ubiquitous or universal in its usage. Bollywood is now synonymous for most viewers outside of India, at least, with national Indian cinema. (While Indian filmmakers have produced films in over thirty languages, only the very largest audiences support major regional industries including Hindi, Tamil, Telegu, Bengali, and Malayalam.)

Recent arguments by stars, directors and scholars reveal the schisms in perspectives around the term. Its critics charge that it overshadows and erases the diversity of other regional cinemas within India, privileging one particular region and language over others; that it is a poor second cousin to Hollywood, marking commercial Indian film industry as a derivative and mimic of its Western counterpart; and that it refers to the increasing globalization and diasporization of the film industry and its attendant industries (e.g. fashion, music, advertising, performances and media) which are proving to be more profitable than the films themselves. Madhava Prasad (2003) asks us to consider why we use the term Bollywood and what it might mean to us:

> Is it meant to suggest that the cinema is imitative and therefore deserves to be rechristened to highlight this derivativeness? Or is it in fact the opposite: an attempt to indicate a difference internal to the dominant idiom, a variation that is related to but distinct from the globally hegemonic Hollywood? Is it Indian cinema's way of signifying its difference or is it (inter)national film journalism and scholarship's way of reinscribing the difference that Indian cinema represents within an articulated model of global hegemony and resistance?
>
> (Prasad 2003)

The name Bollywood, he suggests, begs a comparison. It implicitly demands that we set Hollywood the standard and place all other cinemas as derivative and secondary. Buried in the contention over the term is an epistemological question. Within much scholarship, Indian cinemas are immediately read within Eurocentric hermeneutics. Of course, it is not the name Bollywood alone that evokes these interpretative strategies and comparisons. Scholars writing on non-Western cinema, in general, have had to wrestle with Eurocentric frameworks that implicitly see Europe and North America, not simply as the sites of emergence of film, but as the sites from which all cinema development and progress must be measured and understood. Hence, non-Western cinemas have been evaluated in the shadow of European cinematic aesthetics, forms and epistemologies. Within these rubrics, popular Indian films, and especially Bollywood, are poor imitations of art, evincing a lack of social realism, and merely spectacles of music, fantastical settings, melodrama, and glittery aesthetics. Though understood as always lagging and lacking, we may discover that Bollywood media and Indian cinemas may be and do something else entirely.

In the last few decades, scholars have reassessed these positions that dismiss popular culture and films and have advocated for new theoretical and methodological approaches to Indian cinemas. Some intellectual approaches to Indian cinema work with Western film studies but do not subsume Indian film studies into paradigms based on Hollywood production and forms. For example, Sumita Chakravarty (Reading 7) employs structuralist film theory to discuss how Hindi film interpollates a spectator into the nation through a communal mode of address. This reader features some of the most important scholarship in Indian film studies overturning previous paradigms and reframing central concerns. How do we work against readings of Hindi and other Indian cinemas that reproduce the West as the natural cradle and crucible of film as well as film and media studies? How do we work against several decades of discourses that have dismissed popular Hindi cinema as merely entertainment or *time pass* for the illiterate masses? How do we study this contemporary phenomenon that is Bollywood? How do we locate Bollywood within cinema and media studies? These questions resonate and repeat within the scholarship on Indian films, from early discussions which seek to contextually read Indian films as sites of pleasure and popularity to more recent contentions over the term Bollywood and its increasing transnationalism. We offer here an engagement with Bollywood that addresses and works around and through the issues that return repeatedly in studying Bollywood.

Long before Bollywood there were Indian cinemas

It would be easy to trace some seamless linear trajectory from *Raja Harishchandra* (1913) and *Alam Ara* (1931) to the Bollywood remake of *Sholay* (1975) as *Ram Gopal Verma Ki Aag* (2007). However, in creating such a seamless history, one must ask with what narrative would these films be linked; what use would we make of the films and other media that exist in archive; how would one narrate the fragments and gaps in that film archive; what would this historiography narrate that would neither support colonial nor national historiographies; how can we avoid a teleology of film and other media that evokes some culturalist explanation of cinema's success in India using Bollywood as its exemplar; in other words, what does it mean to provide a history of film in India? Like historiographies of India, historiographies of Indian cinemas raise similar concerns and theoretical dilemmas. While providing some information to guide the reader about the emergence and development of film in India here, we seek to avoid creating such a historiography of film and strive to present a more critical understanding of the project of film historiography and its relationship to Bollywood.

General historiographical accounts of cinema in India often refer to the emergence of individual films, technological developments, directors/auteurs, studios and performers as evidence of Indian cinema's and Bollywood's history. This desire to use such materials and elements to create and justify a unified, coherent, and traceable history suggests the need for a specifically national culture and cinema that is also inherently coherent. Most frequently, these histories would be written implicitly to mirror those of Western films going from silent to talkies, discussing auteurs and the studio mode of production, possibly ending in the current arena of global Hollywood. (While our discussion below encompasses several of these topics, it is not to trace a simple history, but to understand to examine a few key moments, developments, and disjunctures that are critical to the discussions within the reader's essays.) Film histories struggling against such Eurocentrism, often endeavour to prove that their cinemas, like their nations, have a history that is traceable in some way. Other accounts of Indian film focus on the significant economic, political, social and legal processes and discourses that impact modes of production, distribution and reception, pointing out their imbrications with colonialism, nationalism and capitalism. In the discussion below, we provide a brief narration of some of the complex factors that are significant to the study and understanding of the emergence and rise of Bollywood as a culture industry.

Within colonial epistemologies, technologies, such as film, are always thought of as arriving late to India, and therefore, of having delayed histories. But within seven months of the Lumière Brothers introducing film to Paris in December 1895, it had arrived in Mumbai on its way to Australia in July 1896. (The exhibition in India was not unique and part of an almost simultaneous eruption globally including in Russia, South Africa, China, Europe and Australia.) As Barnouw and Krishnaswamy (1980) and others have described, exhibitions were immensely popular in Mumbai with repeated extensions of the shows. While early audiences tended to be predominantly British, it was not long before Indian viewers sought to exhibit, distribute and/or create their own films. Within that year, the first camera had been imported to India and documentary footage of a wrestling match in Mumbai was sent to London for processing by Bhatavdekar. Hence, Indian filmmaking began soon after the technology was introduced to the subcontinent in 1896. In these early years, many saw the moment as opportune and sought to capitalize on the possibilities offered by the entrance of this new medium. Many show people, moving from indoor theatres to outdoors in large tents and fields, began importing, making and touring with an ensemble of imported and domestic shorts making film more widely available. Within these early circuits of distribution and exhibition, these shows travelled far and wide not only in India, but also to other parts of South Asia, Southeast Asia and Africa. Of the several hundred silent films made during the early decades, very few actually survived. As Neepa Majumdar (2007) argues in her reading of three silent documentaries sponsored by the British colonial project, how we read the archived films can complicate rather than fortify the notion of Indian film.

Filmmakers in India did quickly deploy the medium for their own purposes – mimicking and absorbing other as well as producing their own visualities, auralities, and hapticities. It is clearly evident that Indian cinemas are rich in intertextuality as they make reference to and rework the styles, forms, aesthetics and/or semiotics of a wide variety of cultural forms including Parsi theatre, religious epics such as the *Mahabharata*, song and dance, oral performance and drama. Scholars have argued strongly for analyses of cinema that look to Indian cultural forms and practices (such as the darsanic gaze for understanding spectatorship and *rasa* theories for understanding body, affect and aesthetics) that reflect grounded and historical understandings of the medium within the larger context of Indian cultural production.

Similarly, one might seek to reframe the charges of plagiarism that are lobbied against Bollywood's borrowings from other cinemas (e.g. from Hollywood, Hong Kong, Chinese, Japanese, Korean, or Soviet cinemas) in its remakes of famous films such as *A Star is Born* as *Abhimaan* (Pride, 1973, dir. Hrishikesh Mukherjee) or the Korean film *Oldboy* as *Zinda* (Alive, 2006, dir. Sanjay Gupta). The use of early film for mytho-religious narratives is usually cited as evidence of the indigenization of the medium. *Pundalik* (Saint Pundalik, 1912, dir. P.R. Tipnis), was probably India's first feature film that was religious and mythological in its content. Supposedly inspired by seeing *The Life of Christ*, Dhundiraj Govind Phalke (also known as Dadasaheb Phalke) is most credited with being a founder of Indian cinema and producing the first full feature length (over 3500 feet) mythological *Raja Harishchandra* in 1913 for commercial release. The film starred all men as working within the growing film industry was not deemed respectable work for women. Catering to Indian audiences fluent with Hindu stories and mythologies, Phalke's first and subsequent films were thought to have wooed and wowed audiences with its familiar narratives while simultaneously fostering new identificatory and gazing practices and formulating new genres. This kind of appropriation is not unique to Indian films (e.g. the spaghetti westerns of Sergei Leone). *Sholay* (Embers, 1975, dir. Ramesh Sippy), one of the most successful films in Indian film history, clearly borrows from sources as widespread as Sergei Leone, Akira Kurosawa, John Ford and Sam Peckinpah. This omnivorous and elastic appetite of Bollywood might be better understood as a strategy of accommodation, indigenization and hybridity as well as of a strong sense of cinephilia than simple copying. In the case of *Sholay*, the film produces a subgenre now known as the curry Western, a form that contributes to the multiple global remakings of the Western in general.

Lest one think that the only proper way to read Indian cinema is via copies of the West, Hindu epics, *rasa* theories, or narratives of tradition, we must emphasize that Indian cinema has been heavily invested in the production of modernity as well. As one can see in the example of the curry Western above, Indian cinema participates in a social and political economy that strongly emphasizes the location of the modern within Indian society. Hence, representations of and contestations over the modern girl, modern family, or the modern nation are not only common but also de rigueur. To cite another example, by the 1920s and 1930s, women had entered the silent film industry and had become part of the popular culture as starlets. The 'modern girl' was a particular onscreen and offscreen star persona that achieved major fandom through not only the films themselves but also attendant media and paraphernalia such as postcards, magazines, and pictures. These women, such as the famous Salochana, often had short hair, wore make-up and Western clothes, and were sexy, as well as racially and religiously ambiguous (Ramamurthy 2006: 200). Hence, the film and visual cultures became spaces producing and linked to the desire for modernization within the context of a loose and expansive understanding of 'India'. Ramamurthy argues that as the 1940s approached a different understanding and formation of 'Indian' became dominant and began to replace this earlier, perhaps more fluid moment. One may argue that these contestations over what constitutes Indian (in terms of religion, race, gender, region, etc.) have a longstanding history within film and public cultures.

Perhaps the greatest increase in demand for *Indian* films came with the arrival of sound. Silent films had the benefit of being portable in that they crossed linguistic borders fairly easily. The development of sound and talkies complicated the accessibility of the film. It also created the ability to localize film to its regional, cultural and vernacular audiences. Until the rise of the talkies and the subsequent rise in vernacular Indian language films, many of the films viewed during the silent period were primarily American in origin. Early Indian silent films were predominantly made in Mumbai and Kolkata, but also in places such as Nasik and Hyderabad, thus, perhaps creating the possibilities for regional cinemas to emerge in multiple locations. Thus, while we think of cinema as a *national* form, there is good reason to question this assumption and instead investigate how films become a national cinema.

Additionally, with the rise of sound and talkies, films made in various languages, often accompanied by extended musical soundtracks, became increasingly popular. *Alam Ara* (1931, dir. Ardeshir Irani), is usually credited with being India's first sound film featuring seven songs. The significance of song as well as language has been critical to the popularity of much of Indian cinema and to the form of Hindi cinema itself. The development of Hindi cinema with its interruptions of song and dance sequences is cited as a critical feature distinguishing it from other cinemas (Gopalan 2002); it is often also cited as an impediment to serious cinema as well as the most significant marker of Bollywood and Indian cinema's difference from other cinemas. Consequently, the film industry in Mumbai has been critically linked to the music industry as well. We return to the issues of music, genre, and relationship of media below.

The question of colonialism, nationalism, and the rise of cinema in India is not a simple one. Scholars such as Roy Armes have remarked that India is a unique case globally as it has the 'only major film industry to emerge under colonialism' (Armes 1987: 111). The significance of colonialism and the anticolonial nationalism to the development of film cannot be overstated. However, rather than frame colonial power as simply repressive, that is framing cinema censorship as repression, negation and erasure, reading through a framework in which colonial power is productive of and imbricated with Indian cinema, framing censorship as a productive tension between the colonial authorities and indigenous creative forces, is more fruitful (cf. Jaikumar 2006). Similarly, we would not want to propose that independence merely ushered in a golden age of cinema in which the medium, the nation-state and the masses were all aligned through the production and consumption of cinema which expressed and represented something inherently Indian. As our discussion of silent films of the 1930s indicates, it is possible to see the 1940s and the rise of the independence movement as actually producing a more narrow and rigid understanding of the category of India and Indian.

In general, the flourishing of film in India did not go unnoticed by colonial powers, which saw the potential of film to be an incendiary and dangerous medium for the independence movement or other insurgencies. The attempt to regulate and protect the technology and medium through legal codes produced multiple discourses and material consequences. Scholars of early film and legal history have commented that the colonial administration paternally saw the Indian viewer of films generally as illiterate and immature, therefore, in need of 'protection' around moral issues, namely race, religion, sexuality and politics. Hence, there were, at some time or another, limitations on the representations of the degradation of women or rape, torture of whites or blacks, white people drunk, uprisings, and the destruction of religious sites. This protection extended in several directions, attempting to prevent any anticolonial sentiments, offensive images of whites (especially women and interraciality) and offensive images of Indians. On one side, in order to preserve the superiority of the white colonial rulers, the authorities wanted to ensure that whites did not appear as buffoons or in degraded roles or that (successful) resistance to colonialism was not depicted. Anxieties about sexuality and race were more generally part of colonial anxiety about the peril of white women and interracial desire, in particular. As scholars have argued, these early censorship codes about race, gender and sexuality have had long-term repercussions on postcolonial cinema in India. As suggested above, the censorship extended beyond films made by Indian filmmakers. The prohibition against depictions of brown and black peoples that might offend Indian viewers and therefore further destabilize colonial powers was a critical part of the British censor code. Interestingly, it is British and American films that were the objects of anxiety and the object of regulation, remark Bhowmik (1995), Vasudev (1978) and Pendakur (2003). This indicates early on that Indian audiences were still consuming global productions, albeit marked along class and cultural capital lines (see Kaul 1998: 22–37; Jaikumar 2006: 41–64).

Studies have argued that the period of Indian cinema under British colonial rule, leading up to the talkies (post-1930s) and independence (post-1947) was one where we can witness the vexed relationship of the State to cinematic entertainment, the formation of the studio system, and the arrival of a Hindi-Urdu lingua franca which was to hold a hegemonic sway over the national cinema-going populace, representing Hindi cinema from Mumbai as 'the' cinema of India globally (Maitra 1995; Majumdar 1995; Kaul 1998; Jaikumar 2006). Citizenship and modernity through cinema's colonial and postcolonial history is telling of a refracted and, at times, ad-hoc relationship between film producers, artistes, audiences and the State.

Only recently, in its hundred-year plus history, has Indian cinema been granted official industry status by the Indian government in 2001. Hitherto, the workings of the cinematic industry can best be characterized as a series of trades, sometimes partly organized through official agencies and at most times not. Under the colonial moment, cinema was an issue worth keeping an eye on not least because of the growth of nationalism as a movement in India and the increasing waning of colonial authority within the country, as well as overseas. However, its management was often at odds with policy recommendations or actual needs in terms of harnessing a nascent industry. For instance, in 1927 the government of India (under the British Empire) set up the Cinematograph Committee to consider the perceived dangers of exhibiting too many Western films (i.e. American and British ones). Its recommendations went further than simply curtailing the number of imperial films for it claimed that the production of Indian films should be encouraged. To this effect, it went on to suggest measures that included the opening up of a new Department of Cinema; a new government film library to highlight the educational value of films; the building of a governmental film finance fund to aid producers with loans; and to launch a government plan to encourage the building of cinema halls (much needed at the time). The Committee also recommended the abolition of all import duty on raw film (a source of revenue for the State) in order to encourage the production of Indian films. The Committee was also in favour of a modified quota plan requiring Indian theatres, with some exceptions, to show a minimum percentage of Indian films. The colonial government ignored these recommendations of the Committee (Majumdar 1995: 298).

Censorship as a form of State control was also effective only up to a point under colonial authority. In an attempt to achieve a hegemonic balance between being in charge and appearing to be tolerant masters, the State was unable to foresee nor manage the pleasures that Indian audiences were gleaning from indigenously produced and directed films. Pre-independence films that were mythological and historical in scope and nature included villains and socio-political trials and tribulations which were read by audiences as a symptom of British foreign occupation (see *The Peacock Screen*, 1991); the films also included motifs and icons that were read as representative of the Congress Party and/or the independence movement (e.g. the use of the wheel in motion or the handloom from variations of the Indian national, political flag).

Even with independence in 1947, cinema was not fully fostered by the State. Cinema and its primary product, film, then, has been an ill-managed affair by the State until official industry status, where a momentum of change has begun (see below). Colonial and post-independence governments have held a relationship in terms of producing maximum taxes for themselves without procuring towards cinematic infrastructural support and development. Entertainment tax accrued from ticket sales and cinema exhibitions were implemented under colonial authority and gradually more than doubled by governments after independence. The imposition of high taxes on cinema exhibition was fuelled by a perception on the part of the State regarding cinema's role as a producer of vice. Even in the successive five-year developmental plans after India's independence in 1947, the State fostered a rudimentary affinity with cinema, barely managing to mention it seriously, if it all. Furthermore, the State's attempts to discourage the dominance of film and film music were also ultimately unsuccessful. For a period of time that All India Radio (AIR) prohibited the broadcasting of film music, listeners sought out alternative channels such as Radio Ceylon that capitalized on these omissions.

Prasad (2000: 29–51) has noted how Indian film production has been operating as a capitalist vehicle without a State capitalist infrastructure supporting it, unlike in other industries. Film producers themselves were not without blame for the lack of professional and infrastructural development of Indian cinema. In the run up to independence and after, discussions were held between Indian filmmakers and the State with a view of setting up official departments and agencies to oversee the running of cinema as a formally recognized industry with State intervention and controlled film production. The notion of control over almost every aspect of the production to distribution process made producers uncomfortable; not wanting to relinquish their autonomy in terms of filmmaking practices and, moreover, neither their freedom to accrue financial revenue for productions from various sources, including black money. As such a flexible and creative textual aesthetic form emerged (albeit one not wholly professionally organized), which allowed producers and directors to make Indian films by drawing from previous incarnations of popular cultural story-telling ranging from religious and mythic ideologies, the classical, folk and Parsi theatres that incorporated pre-modern and modern oral and visual cultures, to reworkings of Hollywood and other international cinematic referents and stories.

While a studio system emerged and existed from the 1920s to 1950s in India (although the full vertical integrated production, distribution and exhibition monopoly as in the classical Hollywood studio period was achieved by only a very few studios, see Reading 3 by Mishra and Reading 4 by Prasad), the post-independence period witnessed the rise of the independent producer who lured the actor away from the studio contract to emerge as an autonomous commodity in his or her own right as a star. This star phenomenon is incredibly significant and as Parama Roy (Reading 9) points out how intertextual Readings of the film text and star persona can account for extra-diegetic aspects of national popular culture and politics such as Hindutva and communalism. Roy focuses on Muslim actress Nargis, her performance as and in *Mother India*, and her relationship to highly visible Hindu figures ranging from her husband co-actor Sunil Dutt to former prime minister Indira Gandhi. As a star persona, Amitabh Bachchan's popularity in India has been unmatched in the Indian film industry. Bachchan's angry young man persona in cinema in the 1970s garnered him a national following. In 1982, while working on the film *Coolie* (1983, dir. Manmohan Desai), Bachchan sustained nearly fatal injuries; stories of fans praying for his health and offering to sacrifice or donate their own limbs in order to save him abounded in the media. Though Bachchan's stardom suffered a great deal in the next decade, he was able to make a successful transition to television to revitalize his career and then return to films soon after; his son Abhishek also entered into acting and then married one of the premier stars of Bollywood, Aishwarya Rai. This establishing of family legacies has created dynasties within the film industry that continue the star system. This commercially driven star system, one where male actors continue to be paid more than their female counterparts, became cemented as a primary mode of operation through which Indian cinema, and Bollywood in particular, continues to conceive of films from inception through to post-production. The generic form within which these different yet related elements of the pre- and post-independence characteristics of popular Indian cinema congealed best was, perhaps, the *Masala* film.

Despite or perhaps because of these adverse circumstances in relationship to the State, cinema has flourished within India. This period after independence in

1947 until about 1961 has often nostalgically been referred to as the golden or classic age of Bombay cinema and the height of refining of the *Masala* film. During this period the films of stars such as Raj Kapoor and Nargis became household names with films such as *Awaara* (The Vagabond/Tramp, 1951, dir. Raj Kapoor) and *Mother India* (1957, dir. Mehboob Khan). The popularity of these films extended not only throughout various regions within India, but also through other parts of South Asia, the USSR, China, Africa, Fiji and Western Asia (or the Middle East). Hence while we speak of the globalization of the Indian film industry as a recent phenomenon, the internationalization of Indian films occurs much earlier through parts of the non-Western world. Additionally, Indian cinema received recognition from the West with the inclusion of Satyajit Ray's films, especially the Apu trilogy and *Pather Panchali* (Song of the Little Road, 1955), within the category of world cinema, hence as a form of art cinema, in contrast to the more commercial and popular cinema associated with Bollywood and the *Masala*. As mentioned earlier, this distinction between serious art cinema and popular films for the masses deferred much scholarly discussion of Hindi cinema within cinema and media studies.

Genre: a mixture of *Masalas*

Different explanations exist for understanding the genres of Bollywood cinema. While some are dismissive, characterizing them as apolitical, cultural confusion or formulas, others mark them as specifically Indian referring to them as *Masalas* – as in a mixture of spices, or read through an understanding of the political economy of the postcolonial nation-state as All-Inclusives or even All-Action Films. All of these comment on the combination of elements that appear with the elastic and changing form. While to many Western viewers, Bollywood suggests some static genre that characterizes all Indian film, genre classification is a tricky business. Working against the notion of some simplistic culturalist explanation that sees these all-encompassing forms as naturalized, scholars have painstakingly examined the genre from various angles (see amongst others, Someswar Bhowmik (1995) on genres in pre- and post-independence India, Madhava Prasad (2000) on the ideology of genres, and Lalitha Gopalan (2002) on action genres).

Earlier critiques dismissed popular films for their encompassing form – they were too unrealistic and far too escapist and melodramatic, not least in the song and dance omnibus form (see Reading 2 by Thomas and Reading 12 by Gopal and Sen). Often invested in social realist narratives, detractors of popular Hindi cinema have read the form as providing 'mere entertainment' or 'timepass', in contrast to the serious film of art, parallel or even middle cinema, foreclosing the possibility of social and political engagement within the *Masala* film form. The development of what has been called middle, art and parallel cinema is one that is relevant and overlapping with that of popular Hindi cinema. The boundaries between these categories would certainly have to be considered porous as the films of director Mani Ratnam, for example, might be seen as crossovers not only from Tamil cinema but also into both art and popular cinema.

Song and dance sequences within the *Masala* film have often been considered a key characteristic of the all-encompassing genre. While the inclusion of song and dance sequences is critical to defining the genre of *Masala*, it is also the element which viewers invested in social realism have difficulty accepting as it is seen as rather extraneous constructions of the 'real'. Alternative understandings of the function of song and dance sequences (such as the spaces of fantasy and the imaginary disrupting the limitations of the narrative) have been offered by various scholars such as Gopal and Sen (see Reading 12). Moreover, that song and dance sequences enable and incorporate multiple forms of performance and viewing within the film, for example non-normative or transgressive sexualities within the context of courtesan dance scenes or same-sex desire or intimacy, has engendered conversations among scholars about the ways in which these previously ignored components of the film require much more serious attention.

The song and dance sequences have also been key to the production and consumption of the films themselves as well. Yash Chopra in the 1970s developed the trademark motif of setting these sequences in foreign locations, such as Switzerland. These settings, perhaps standing in for the place of Kashmir in the Indian imaginary or creating a tourist gaze of the foreign for Indian viewers' consumption, also practically assisted directors in getting actors to make commitments to being physically present on location at their scheduled times. As film production itself is a fragmented and complicated process within the industry for many reasons, including the fact that actors often work on multiple films simultaneously, that films are made without scripts, and that actors sometimes do not appear according to shooting schedules, the opportunity to whisk away these prized commodities in foreign locations and therefore sequester them from other projects was a clever method of extracting labour as needed. The songs (which are usually sung not by the actors but rather by playback singers) are highly valuable commodities within their own right. The portability and mobility of song and dance sequences outside of the film itself into other forms of media (radio, video, television, digital media, live performance, etc.) is an important aspect of not only the success of the film, but also a critical aspect of the development of media and cultural technologies in South Asia that has quickly globalized.

Despite the variety of subgenres (including the historical, the family social, the gangster/underworld, and the courtesan), Bollywood is inevitably characterized primarily as a musical genre with a fixed form. *Masala* films are often the ones mistaken to represent all Bollywood films as formulaic or 'the same' in uninformed commentaries on Indian and popular Hindi cinema. This type of film was actually anticipated in the late 1960s by a type of B movie called Stunt Films which were rather like the American Zorro or Marvelman serials (Johnson 1987: 2) or like Hong Kong action films. *Masala* films are often packed with glamour and have been especially popular with the urban working class. They may be seen to represent the hopes and anxieties of the everyman and woman in a fast changing world. The angry young man series of films of the 1970s starring Amitabh Bachchan, such as *Deewar* (The Wall, 1975, dir. Yash Chopra) and *Muqaddar Ka Sikandar* (King of Destiny, 1978, dir. Prakash Mehra), are good examples of the *Masala* genre. *Masala* films draw on all aspects of Indian popular culture for their formulae. In a loosely knit story one can see big city underworld crime, martial arts fights scenes with exaggerated hitting noises – 'dishum, dishum', car stunts, sexy cabaret, elaborate dance sequences with dozens of extras, comedy, romance and family melodrama. The appeal of these films is spectacle, melodrama and affect, and everything is designed to give maximum impact. The producers are challenged by the audience to continually think up something more spectacular, more imaginative, and sometimes even more bizarre, with which to assault the senses. At their worst *Masala* films are kitsch rubbish but at their best they are enthralling entertainment that has the audiences reeling with laughter and tears from one minute to the next.

During the 1990s, All-Action films suffered a blow themselves in terms of the decline in audience attendance and takings at the box office in India. As a case in point *Salaakhen* (Barrier, 1998, dir. Guddu Dhanoa) was produced at a cost of Rs 8 million but made a loss of Rs 3.5 million. *Kabhi na Kabhi* (Sooner or Later, 1998, dir. Priyadarshan) was made at Rs 5.5 million but made a staggering loss of Rs 4 million. For decades the *Masala* movie was thought to be a guaranteed success to recover production costs and boost profits. This is no longer the case as when romantic films like *Hum Aapke Hain Koun?* (Who Am I To You?) and *Dilwale Dulhaniya Le Jayenge* (The Braveheart Will Take the Bride) were released in the mid-1990s, they inspired a feel-good factor which brought back urban middle-class cinema audiences in India and across the diaspora in large numbers; this was after the slump in attendance figures caused by competition from video and non-terrestrial media for middle-class viewers in particular. These films removed almost all the conflict and trauma from the narratives, instead focusing on the anxieties of achieving and fulfilling romantic couplings and the displays of ample consumption. Audiences began to slacken away from the tried and tested formulas of the *Masala* films. The period of the late 1990s, then, saw film teams associated with All-Action films as redirecting their energies and finances towards more rounded family entertainers, consisting of a more palatable blend of romance and consumption, and peppered with action only when required according to the script. The genre of the historical and anti-Pakistani films have continued to provide some space for action, along with the continued valorization of a certain brawny masculinity that is less central to the romance films. Male stars like Akshay Kumar, Sunil Shetty and Sunny Deol have also undergone a transformation in recent years from their young, hard men screen personas to believable heroes with more credible causes to defend (Dudrah 2006: 178–9).

The *Masala* film is perhaps the genre often banked on and hoped by filmmakers to make their fortunes at the box office due to its immediate recognition and perceived sale-ability with audiences. Even so, a number of other genres can be identified within Indian cinema, namely Mythologicals or Devotional films that recounted or reworked epic stories from the *Ramayana* or the *Mahabharata* as well as other religious traditions within the South Asian subcontinent. Historical Films were particularly pertinent in the pre-1947 independence period, where a focus on actual Indian historical figures was laden with messages about foreign British rule. Social Films or Topicals were often social-conscious evoking melodramas that engaged with the hopes, ideals and broken promises of

India as it emerged as a young independent nation, post-1947; many of these are considered to be part of parallel, art or middle cinema, as well as part of Bollywood. Muslim Socials are best considered as a subgenre of the social films; these were popular in the 1960s and inspired by stories from Urdu love poetry whose appeal crossed religious boundaries. Romantic films depict the universal boy-meets-girl love story and the numerous socio-cultural obstacles they face along the way. Non-resident Indian or NRI films are on the ascendancy since the mid-1990s that represent the relationship of the overseas Indians to the homeland through the particular lens of Bollywood cinema. Horror or Supernatural Films consist of elements of Indian superstitions, folklores, and divine or semi-divine interventions against evil and demonic acts. Collectively, these several genres operate in a broad and connected sense. Rather than consign them as rigid generic definitions, these taxonomies are best considered as hybrid forms, sometimes borrowing from one another, sometimes quoting each other and frequently blending together. For example, it would not be odd for a *Masala* film to consist of elements from any or all of the genres above or vice versa (see Dudrah 2006: 175–80).

As official industry status is well underway post-1998, some filmmakers have become eager to identify and promote genres of commercial Hindi films through formats more familiar to international audiences of Hollywood genres. Heightened modes of publicity and easy viewer identification of films are increasingly becoming the norm in the contemporary moment as Bollywood cinema in particular ventures global; not only vying for traditional South Asian viewers but more so hoping for newer Western (i.e. non-diasporic South Asian) audiences too. This is now part and parcel of what Rajadhyaksha has termed the 'Bollywoodization of the Indian cinema' (see Reading 15). The various initiatives in process in the post-official industry climate also raise its fair share of socio-political possibilities and concerns.

Official industry status

May 1998 marked the inception of formal State acknowledgement and liberalization of Indian cinema as an industry. This was a long and drawn out process brokered by cinema industry stalwarts and State officials, led by then Information and Broadcasting Minister, Sushma Swaraj (Indian Express 1998). Three years later in 2001, Indian cinema was formally accorded industry status (MacGregor 2006). This has led to the possibilities for filmmakers to seek co-production possibilities from new sources of income both in and beyond India (see Dudrah 2006: 141–66). Until this time, the finance for the production of Bollywood films came from a number of sources, including production houses under the studio system present from the 1930s to the 1950s, independent producers and directors, business entrepreneurs attracted by the glamour of the entertainment industries, kith and kin networks from within the film industry, and even, as has been widely alleged, through money related to the criminal underworld (on the history of Bollywood's lead up to official film industry status, see Ganti 2004: 43–52). The formal liberalization of cinema since the late 1990s has allowed it to benefit from actual rewards in the form of lower production charges, tax benefits, and for filmmakers to accumulate production finance from banks and other corporate financial institutions, thereby according it an important and legitimate economic and symbolic status. Part of this move by the State can be understood within the context of wanting to consolidate India's growth across all industry sectors as a potential global economic super power, heralded of late by many economists overseas as well as in the country itself. Within this framework, cinema then is to be supported and developed as a marker of Indian success in the international market place of goods, where Bollywood films compete with Hollywood ones at box offices around the world.

However, since the announcement of Bollywood as an official industry and its increasing liberalization, filmmakers have been split on whether financing from banks and other corporate institutions is a truly productive venture. Press reports from the national and international Indian media have indicated a discord at national conventions in India that have brought together filmmakers, corporate managers and trade and entertainment ministers to discuss the possible futures for financing in the cinema industry. Financial institutions consider filmmaking, and in particular popular Hindi filmmaking, as very risky business, given the number of high failure to low success ratios of films at the box office. Subsequently, funding from financial institutions comes with a number of conditions attached. Banks and financial institutions have asked the film industry to form a corporate culture akin to professional businesses and to prepare bankable scripts in order to get funding. The unorganized and high-risk nature of the film industry (where often no date is set for completion on most films before production commences and where fiscal losses are very high), has made corporate financiers nervous about releasing capital. Corporate financiers are more in favour of risk formula assessments in order to guard against potential losses to their investments and are seeking what they consider safe investment ventures, such as television channels and exhibition infrastructures like the growing number of multiplex cinemas across urban India which have predictable cash flows. Targeting NRI and/or urban audiences has become a consistent strategy by which producers seek to gain returns on the films either through the power of the dollar and pound or through the growing middle-class multiplex audience in India. Film merchandising and product endorsements (e.g. Pepsi and Coca Cola) along the lines of indirect advertising inherent in contemporary Hollywood cinema is also being encouraged as additional revenue for films, thereby allowing corporate financiers such as banks to be more comfortable about venturing into debt financing for filmmakers (Dudrah 2006: 149).

Such demands have met with mixed responses from the filmmakers themselves. On the one hand there is the view by some that the entertainment business is one of individuality and ad-hoc collaborative creativity. Filmmakers such as Shekhar Kapur and Yash Chopra have gone on record claiming that the corporatization of filmmaking will damage the creative culture of commercial filmmaking in India, and that to accord this cultural production as a higher risk than any other business is a false alarm. While on the other hand filmmakers such as Shyam

Benegal and Mani Ratnam favour funding by corporate institutions and banks. They believe that this will lead to new routes for funding in terms of co-production possibilities. It appears then that a debate is in motion among filmmakers, financiers and the state regarding whether to keep filmmaking as a flexible creative activity, or to manage that creativity alongside enterprise governance (Dudrah 2006: 150).

Furthermore, the Indian government, urged on by Indian film and media production companies, is seeking to formalize co-production treaties with other countries such as Britain, Italy and Canada. Indian producers are keen to market their films with crossover appeals among international audiences with an eye on maximizing their profits and this makes having co-production treaties with other countries all the more important. With co-production treaties companies can explore the advantage of hiring foreign talent and using their technology to make quality films at competitive costs and to market and distribute them globally. The move towards securing co-production treaties can be further understood in the context of the fast growing Indian media sectors, and amidst the expansion of South Asian consumer culture in recent years that has also caught the attention of global media companies and foreign investors to the South Asian subcontinent (Dudrah 2006: 150–1). Moreover, there have been Bollywood spin-offs in English made by Indian and diasporic filmmakers that are often partly financed by foreign capital and/or involve co-productions; these films (e.g. Kaizad Gustad's *Bombay Boys* and Mira Nair's *Monsoon Wedding*) may be considered part of Bollywood (Desai 2004).

Indian cinema has also ventured into diversifying its co-productions in the area of three-dimensional animation feature films. With the success of the animated film *Hanuman* (2005, dir. V.G. Samant and Milind Ukey), based on the stories of the Hindu Monkey God, which appealed to Indian and its diasporic audiences, a new market niche is being explored by leading Indian media production companies alongside traditional commercial films. Yashraj Films Ltd have teamed up with Walt Disney Studios on *Roadside Romeo*, a cartoon based *Masala* production starring a dog, due for release in the summer of 2008. Like its US animated feature counterparts, *Roadside Romeo*'s lead character voices will be provided by A-list Bollywood stars Saif Ali Khan and Kareena Kapoor and is being directed by junior actor turned director Jugal Hunsraj. In another example, Mumbai-based Graphiti Multimedia, led by Ram Mohan, is developing two animation films that are being produced by Turner, a Time Warner Company and by Anubhav Sinha, the director of the 2007 Bollywood film *Cash* (see Sapre 2007). In another related instance, reports have claimed that over a third of the digital and animation special effects in the Christmas 2007 fantasy blockbuster release, *The Golden Compass* (dir. Chris Weitz), co-produced by the USA and UK under the New Line Cinema banner, were realized by a team of 100-plus artists working at the Mumbai studios of special effects specialists, Rhythm & Hues (Parthasarathy 2008). Such skills, in use within the Indian media and entertainment industries, are evidently in demand globally. However, what remains to be seen is whether the possibilities listed above under the aegis of the post-industry status in Indian cinema, reap benefits that are equitable and sustainable for all those involved; or whether they increasingly become part and parcel of a neo-liberal global media economy in which production and post-production skills and requirements are outsourced to countries like India for maximum profits alone, due to the cheaper rupee against the dollar.

Organization

In part, *The Bollywood Reader* examines the historical evolution of the scholarship on modern Hindi cinema in India, with an emphasis on understanding the interplay between cinema and colonialism, nationalism and globalization. More specifically, the readings attend to issues of capitalism, nationalism, Orientalism and modernity through their understandings of race, class, gender and sexuality, religion and politics as depicted in Indian popular films. In general, the readings focus on the film industry, cinema and Indian media in relation to current social and political issues, including the role of Bollywood in the public culture of India and its diasporas. In doing so, the readings seek to understand the relation between popular culture and the political economy and social imaginary of the nation-state. The readings also raise a variety of issues specific to the medium itself, including but not limited to the development of particular genres, narrative forms, and exegetic and diegetic elements including musical and dance numbers as well as questions of spectatorship, audience and institutional formations. In addition to including some of the existing key scholarship in the area, the reader has original and new contributions (by Sangita Gopal and Biswarup Sen, and Amit Rai) that have been written specifically for the publication. Where the symbol '[...]' appears in the readings, this indicates where some text has been omitted.

The reader is divided into three main parts. Part 1 introduces canonical essays in theorizing the significance and meaning of Hindi cinema historically. These readings include early arguments forwarding the cinema as an object worthy of study and articulate different approaches to interpreting the significance of the films and understanding the development of the film industry. Part 2 looks at more recent (often postcolonial) scholarship that builds on the earlier theoretical paradigms forwarding more specific and nuanced frameworks focusing on significant absences in or reworkings of the earlier literature. Part 3 expands the discussion to concentrate on both the national and transnational aspects of Bollywood. It is here that we have chosen readings that explore the significance of specific and critical issues within cinema studies including an emphasis on gender, sexuality, religion, and the nation. It also interrogates how this cinema has created a global presence in a variety of locations including North America, the UK and West Africa.

References

Armes, R. (1987) *Third World Film Making and the West.* Berkeley, CA: University of California Press.

Barnouw, E. and S. Krishnaswamy (1980) *Indian Film*, 2nd edition. New York: Oxford University Press.

Bhowmik, S. (1995) *Indian Cinema, Colonial Contours.* Calcutta: Papyrus.

Desai, J. (2004) *Beyond Bollywood: The Cultural Politics of South Asian Diasporic Film*. New York: Routledge.

Dudrah, R. (2006) *Bollywood: Sociology Goes to the Movies*. New Delhi: Sage.

Ganti, T. (2004) *Bollywood: A Guidebook to Indian Cinema*. New York: Routledge.

Gopalan, L. (2002) *Cinema of Interruptions: Action Genres in Contemporary Indian Cinema*. London: British Film Institute.

Indian Express (1998) 'Bollywood Corp gets a fillip', www.indianexpress.com/res/web/pIe/ie/daily/19981219/35350574.html, originally published on 19 December 1998, date accessed 7 January 2008.

Jaikumar, P. (2006) *Cinema at the End of Empire*. Durham, NC: Duke University Press.

Johnson, E. (1987) *Bombay Talkies: Posters of the Indian Cinema*. Birmingham: West Midlands Area Museum Service Travelling Exhibition, Birmingham Central Library.

Kaul, G. (1998) *Cinema and the Indian Freedom Struggle*. New Delhi: Sterling.

MacGregor, J. (2006) 'Bollywood seduces the West', www.netribution.co.uk/2/content/view/283/182/, originally published on 19 March 2006, date accessed 7 January 2008.

Maitra, P. (1995) 'Cinema and state', in P. Maitra (ed.) *100 Years of Cinema*. Calcutta: Basumati.

Majumdar, D. (1995) 'Indian film industry', in P. Maitra (ed.) *100 Years of Cinema*. Calcutta: Basumati.

Majumdar, N. (2007) 'Film fragments, documentary history, and colonial Indian cinema', *Canadian Journal of Film Studies* 16(1): 63–79.

Parthasarathy, A. (2008) 'Indian hands behind Hollywood's The Golden Compass fantasy', on www.hindu.com/2008/01/06/stories/2008010655971100.htm, originally published on 6 January 2008, date accessed 7 January 2008.

Pendakur, M. (2003) *Indian Popular Cinema: Industry, Ideology, and Consciousness*. Cresskill, NJ: Hampton Press.

Prasad, M. (2000) *Ideology of the Hindi Film: A Historical Construction*. New Delhi: Oxford University Press.

Prasad, M. (2003) 'This thing called Bollywood', *Seminar Magazine* 525: May, www.india-seminar.com/2003/525/525%20madhava%20prasad.htm, originally published May 2003, accessed 2 January 2008.

Ramamurthy, P. (2006) 'The modern girl in the interwar years: interracial intimacies, international competition, and historical eclipsing', *Women's Studies Quarterly* (1–2): 197–226.

Sapre, O. (2007) 'Big budget animation from Bollywood in' 08', http://economictimes.indiatimes.com/News/News_By_Industry/Media__Entertainment_/Entertainment/Big_budget_animation_from_Bollywood_in_08/articleshow/msid-2560324,curpg-2.cms, originally published on 22 November 2007, date accessed 7 January 2008.

The Peacock Screen (1991) Three part documentary on popular Indian Cinema, director Mahmood Jamal. Channel 4 Television, London, UK.

Vasudev, A. (1978) *Liberty and License in Indian Cinema*. New Delhi: Vikas.

PART 1
Theoretical frameworks

2

Indian cinema: pleasures and popularity
by Rosie Thomas

The pseudo-intellectuals here try to copy Westerners. We think we're better than Westerners – they can't make films for the Indian audience.

– Bombay film-maker

Discussion of Indian popular cinema as 'other' cinema is immediately problematic. There is no disputing that, within the context of First World culture and society, this cinema has always been marginalised, if not ignored completely. It has been defined primarily through its 'otherness' or 'difference' from First World cinema, and consumption of it in the West, whether by Asians or non-Asians, is something of an assertion: one has chosen to view an 'alternative' type of cinema. However, this is a cinema which, in the Indian context, is an over-ridingly dominant, mainstream form, and is itself opposed by an 'Other': the 'new', 'parallel', 'art' (or often simply 'other') cinema which ranges from the work of Satyajit Ray, Shyam Benegal and various regional film-makers, to Mani Kaul's 'avant-garde' or Anand Patwardhan's 'agitational' political practice. In these terms Indian popular cinema is neither alternative nor a minority form. Moreover, in a global context, by virtue of its sheer volume of output, the Indian entertainment cinema still dominates world film production, and its films are distributed throughout large areas of the Third World (including non-Hindustani-speaking areas and even parts of the Soviet Union), where they are frequently consumed more avidly than both Hollywood and indigenous 'alternative' or political cinemas. Such preference suggests that these films are seen to be offering something positively different from Hollywood, and in fact, largely because it has always had its own vast distribution markets, Indian cinema has, throughout its long history,[1] evolved as a form which has resisted the cultural imperialism of Hollywood. This is not, of course, to say that it has been 'uninfluenced' by Hollywood: the form has undergone continual change and there has been both inspiration and assimilation from Hollywood and elsewhere, but thematically and structurally, Indian cinema has remained remarkably distinctive.

Corresponding to this diversity of contexts, each constructing Indian popular cinema as a different object, has been considerable confusion of critical and evaluative perspectives. This article will examine the ways in which this cinema has been discussed by critics in India and abroad, and will suggest that, as a first step, the terms of reference of the Indian popular cinema itself should be brought into the picture. It attempts to do this, using material from discussions with Bombay film-makers[2] about what, for them, constitutes 'good' and 'bad' Hindi cinema in the 1970s and '80s.[3] Points will be illustrated through the example of one very popular, and at the time of release generally lauded, film, *Naseeb* (1981 *Destiny*),[4] whose producer/director, Manmohan Desai, is Bombay's most consistently commercially successful film-maker. It will be suggested that, while First World critical evaluation outside these terms of reference is, at best, irrelevant and also often racist, to impose a theoretical framework developed in the West – particularly one concerned with examining textual operations and the mechanisms of pleasure – does allow useful questions to be asked, as well as opening up the ethnocentrism of these debates.

The most striking aspect of First World discourse on Indian popular cinema must be its arrogant silence. Until home video killed the market in the '80s, the films had been in regular distribution in Britain for over 30 years, yet ghettoised in immigrant areas, unseen and unspoken by most non-Asians. Even in 1980, when the first Bombay film (*Amar Akbar Anthony*) was shown on British television, it passed more or less unnoticed: the BBC not only programmed it early one Sunday morning, without even troubling to list it with other films on the *Radio Times* film preview page, but pruned it of all its songs and much narrative, including most of the first two reels, which are, not surprisingly, crucial to making any sense of the film. Although the situation has begun to change over the past two years, largely through the initiative of Channel Four's two seasons of Indian entertainment cinema, the traditional attitude remains one of complacent ignorance. Clichés abound: the films are regularly said to be nightmarishly lengthy, second-rate copies of Hollywood trash, to be dismissed with patronising amusement or facetious quips. British television documentaries have a long tradition in perpetuating these attitudes, for the baroque surface of the Hindi film, particularly if taken out of context, makes for automatic comedy. Even *Time Out*'s TV section recently announced *Gunga Jumna* (a classic of Indian cinema, but obviously unpreviewed) with the smug throwaway: 'Sounds turgid, but who knows?'.[5]

Where popular Indian films have been taken at all seriously, it has either been to subject them to impertinent criticism according to the canons of dominant Western film-making:

> **Mother India** *is a rambling tale of personal woe, narrated episodically in unsuitably pretty Technicolour.*[6]

or to congratulate them patronisingly:

> *All told, a disarmingly enthusiastic piece of Eastern spectacle, exaggerated in presentation and acting, exotic, and yet charmingly naive … .*[7]

They have generally been looked at as 'a stupendous curiosity' – even the '50s, as an ethnographic lesson, a way to:

... get to close grips with a handful of (India's) inhabitants. That Indians make the same faces as we do when they fall in love astounds me beyond measure ... .[8]

But the most general theme since the 1960s has been unfavourable comparison with the Indian art cinema:

It all goes to prove once again that Satyajit Ray is the exception who proves the rule of Indian film-making.[9]

As Indian art cinema is comparatively well known and enthusiastically received in the West, and much conforms to conventions made familiar within European art cinema, Western audience assumptions about filmic form can remain unchallenged. In fact, the art films serve mostly to confirm the 'inadequacy' of popular cinema to match what are presumed to be universal standards of 'good' cinema – and even of 'art'. Western critics are perhaps not completely to blame, for they take their cues from the Indian upper-middle class intelligentsia and government cultural bodies, who have a long tradition of conniving at this denunciation and somewhat ironically, themselves insist on evaluating the popular films according to the canons of European and Hollywood film-making. One commonly hears complaints about the films' 'lack of realism', about the preposterous 'singing and dancing and running round trees', and that the films are 'all the same' and simply 'copy Hollywood'. To dislike such films is, of course, their privilege. What is disturbing is the tone of defensive apology to the West and the shamefaced disavowal of what is undoubtedly a central feature of modern Indian culture. Thus, for example, Satish Bahadur, comparing popular cinema unfavourably with Satyajit Ray's *Pather Panchali* (which 'was a work of art ... an organic form'), refers to its 'immaturity' and asserts:

The heavily painted men and women with exaggerated theatrical gestures and speech, the artificial-looking houses and huts and the painted trees and skies in the films of this tradition are less truthful statements of the reality of India ... .[10]

Even Rangoonwalla, who has devoted considerable energy to compiling much of the published material available on Indian cinema, dismisses the work of the 1970s as 'a very dark period, with a silly absurd kind of escapism rearing its head,'[11] and he is tolerant of popular cinema only if it attempts 'sensible themes'.

One of the central platforms for this kind of criticism is the English language 'quality' press. Week after week, the Indian *Sunday Times* and *Sunday Express* produce jokey review columns which score easy points off the apparent inanities of Hindi cinema. Typical is a *Sunday Times* feature entitled 'Not Only Vulgar but Imitative', which skims through all the critical clichés: absurd stories, poor imitations of Hollywood, lack of originality, and finally the myth of a golden age – of the *1960s* (sic) — when commercial films were 'gentle, warm-hearted, innocent'. Most significant is the fact that the article appeared – by no coincidence – in precisely the week that Bombay was full of Western delegates to the annual film festival. It makes no bones about its intended audience, to whom it defers:

not surprisingly the West cares little for these films. All that they stand for is exotica, vulgarity and absurdity ... [12]

Naseeb was, of course, received within this tradition. The *Sunday Express* review was captioned: 'Mindless Boring Melange', and, for example, described a central scene – in fact one that was spectacularly self-parodic, in which many top stars and film-makers make 'Guest Appearances' at a party – as:

> a 'homage' to ... all those who have, in the past thirty years, brought the Hindi film down to its present state of total garish mediocrity. In fact, the film encapsulates the entire history of our sub-standard 'entertainment' – elephantine capers ... the manufactured emotion, the brutalism in talk and acting, the utterly 'gauche' dances ... [13]

The tone is echoed throughout the popular English-language (hence middle-class) press, and even among regular (middle-class) film-goers there appears to be huge resistance to admitting to finding pleasure in the form. Thus letters to film gossip magazines ran:

> Want to make **Naseeb?** Don't bother about a story or screenplay. You can do without both. Instead rope in almost the entire industry ... Throw in the entire works: revolving restaurant, London locales, and outfits which even a five year old would be embarrassed to wear to a fancy dress competition. Now, sit back, relax, and watch the cash pour in. [14]

> Manmohan Desai's concept of entertainment still revolves around the lost and found theme, with a lot of improbabilities and inanities thrown in ... But how long can such films continue to click at the box-office? Soon audiences are bound to come to their senses. [15]

There are also, of course, more serious and considered critical positions within India, notably of the politically conscious who argue, quite cogently, that Hindi cinema is capitalist, sexist, exploitative, 'escapist' mystification, politically and aesthetically reactionary, and moreover that its control of distribution networks blocks opportunities for more radical practitioners. It should, of course, be remembered that what may be pertinent criticism within India may be irrelevant – or racist – in the West, and apparently similar criticisms may have different meanings, uses and effects in different contexts. However, two central objections to all the criticisms do stand out. One is the insistence on evaluating Hindi cinema in terms of film-making practices which it has itself rejected, a blanket refusal to allow its own terms of reference to be heard. The second is the reluctance to acknowledge and deal with the fact that Hindi cinema clearly gives enormous pleasure to vast pan-Indian (and Third World) audiences. In view of this, such supercilious criticism does no more than wish the films away. Dismissing them as 'escapism' neither explains them in any useful way, nor offers any basis for political strategy, for it allows no space for questions about the specifics of the audiences' relationship to their so-called 'escapist' fare. What seems to be needed is an analysis which takes seriously both the films and the pleasures they offer, and which attempts to unravel their mode of operation.

Clearly, a body of 'film theory' developed in the West may mislead if it is used to squash Hindi cinema into Western film-making categories, particularly if it brutalises or denies the meanings and understandings of participants. Thus, for example, Hollywood genre classification is quite inappropriate to Hindi cinema and, although almost every Hindi film contains elements of the 'musical', 'comedy' and 'melodrama', to refer to the films in any of these ways imposes a significant distortion. Certainly no Indian film-maker would normally use such classifications. Important distinctions are marked instead by terms such as 'social', 'family social', 'devotional', 'stunt' or even 'multi-starrer' (terms hard to gloss quickly for a Western readership). However, the *concept* of genre, in its broadest sense – as structuring principles of expectation and convention, around which individual films mark repetitions and differences[16] – does appear to be potentially useful in opening up questions about Hindi cinema's distinctive form. In the first place, it moves immediately beyond the tired rantings about Hindi cinema's 'repetitiveness' and 'lack of originality' – although, on this point, some of the Bombay film-makers are in fact many steps ahead of their so-called 'intellectual' critics:

> *People seem to like the same thing again and again, so I repeat it ... but you always have to give them something different too ... There can be no such thing as a 'formula film' – if there were, everybody would be making nothing but hits ...* [17]

Secondly, it points to questions about narrative structure, modes of address and conventions of verisimilitude that, at the least, help organise description which can take Indian cinema's own terms of reference into account and from which further questions about spectatorship and pleasure become possible. The rest of this article attempts to illustrate such an approach.

Contrary to common 'intellectual' assumptions within India, the Indian mass audience is ruthlessly discriminating: over 85 per cent of films released in the last two years have not made profits,[18] and these have included films with the biggest budgets and most publicity 'hype'. There is a clear sense among audiences of 'good' and 'bad' films, and the film-makers, committed as they are to 'pleasing' audiences, make it their business to understand, and internalise, these assessments. While the yardstick of commercial success is of course central – for film-makers a 'good' film is ultimately one that makes money – they do also have a working model of (what they believe to be) the essential ingredients of a 'good' film and the 'right' way to put these together. This model evolves largely through the informal, but obsessive, post-mortems which follow films whose box-office careers confound expectations, and is undergoing continual, if gradual, redefinition and refinement.

Bombay film-makers repeatedly stress that they are aiming to make films which differ in both format and content from Western films, that there is a definite skill to making films for the Indian audience, that this audience has specific needs and expectations, and that to compare Hindi films to those of the West, or of the Indian 'art' cinema, is irrelevant. Their statements imply both a sense of the tyranny of this audience and a recognition of the importance of a class link between film-maker and audience. The example of the barely educated Mehboob Khan, whose cult classic *Mother India* (1957) still draws full houses today, is often cited proudly – buttressed by assertions that his film is 'of our soil', 'full of real Indian emotions' – and by that token inaccessible to the emotionally retarded, if not totally cold-blooded, West.[19]

Whatever the critics' clichés may suggest, no successful Bombay film-maker ever simply 'copies' Western films. Of course, most borrow openly both story ideas and sometimes complete sequences from foreign cinemas, but borrowings must always be integrated with Indian film-making conventions if the film is to work with the Indian audience: no close copy of Hollywood has ever been a hit.[20] Film-makers say that the essence of 'Indianisation' lies in: (1) the way that the storyline is developed; (2) the crucial necessity for 'emotion' (Western films are often referred to as 'cold'); and (3) the skilful blending and integration of songs, dances, fights and other 'entertainment values' within the body of the film. There is also the more obvious 'Indianisation' of values and other content, including reference to aspects of Indian life with which audiences will identify, particularly religion and patriotism. It is, for example, generally believed that science fiction would be outside the cultural reference of the Indian audience, and censorship restrictions mean that films about war, or overtly about national or international politics, risk being banned.

The film-makers' terms of reference often emerge most clearly when discussing a film which is judged a 'failure'. A trade press review[21] of *Desh Premee* (1982 *Patriot*), one of Manmohan Desai's few unsuccessful films, is particularly revealing.

> **Desh Premee** has all the ingredients that make a film a hit, yet every aspect is markedly defective. Firstly, the story has a plot and incidents but the narration is so unskilled that it does not sustain interest. There is no grip to the story. The situations are neither melodramatic, nor do they occur spontaneously, but look forced and contrived. Secondly, the music side is not as strong as the film demands. All songs are good average, but not one song can be declared a superhit. Thirdly, emotional appeal is lacking. Although there are a few scenes which try to arouse feelings, they fail to hit their objective. Fourthly, production values are average, considering the producer. The traditional grandeur of Manmohan Desai is missing, as are technical values.
>
> **Desh Premee** has no sex appeal. The romantic part is too short. Comedy scenes and melodramatic scenes are missing … [My precis: the stars' roles are not properly justified … . several appear for too short a time … action, thrills and background music are only average …]
>
> Several of the scenes look like repetitions from many old hits and there is no dose of originality in the film … Although every formula film is basically unrealistic and far from the truths of life, everything can still be presented with acceptable realism and logic. But in this film there are several 'unbelievables' even with normal cinematic licence granted. This is not expected from any seasoned film-maker.[22]

Particularly interesting is the order in which defects are listed: the screenplay is recognised to be crucial, the music (i.e. the songs) of almost equal importance, 'emotional appeal' a significant third, and fourth are production values, or expensive spectacle. A 'dose of originality' and 'acceptable realism and logic' are additional points of general importance. Big stars are a decided advantage (viz. 'the ingredients that make a film a hit'), but cannot in themselves save a film – particularly if not exploited adequately, and in contrast, *Naseeb* on its release had been particularly praised for 'Assembling the biggest starcast ever (and) ... justifying each and all of them.'[23]

Two themes emerge from this review: firstly that of the expected narrative movement and mode of address, and secondly, the question of verisimilitude.

Narrative

Indian film-makers often insist that screenplay and direction are crucial and the storyline only the crudest vehicle from which to wring 'emotion' and onto which to append spectacle.

> *It's much more difficult to write a screenplay for **Naseeb** than for a Western or 'art' film, where you have a straight storyline. A commercial Hindi film has to have sub-plots and gags, and keep its audience involved with no story or logic.*[24]

The assertion that Hindi films have 'no story' is sometimes confusing to those unfamiliar with the genre. 'Who cares who gets the story credits? Everyone knows our films have no stories', and, in fact, the story credits are often farmed out to accommodating friends or relatives for 'tax adjustment' purposes. However, Hindi cinema has by no means broken the hallowed bounds of narrative convention, and the most immediately striking thing about *Naseeb* is the fiendishly complex convolutions of this multi-stranded and very long succession of events, which neverthless culminate in an exemplarily neat resolution. What is meant by 'no story' is, first, that the storyline will be almost totally predictable to the Indian audience, being a repetition, or rather, an unmistakable transformation, of many other Hindi films, and second, that it will be recognised by them as a 'ridiculous' pretext for spectacle and emotion. Films which really have 'no story' (i.e. non-narrative), or are 'just a slice of life', or have the comparatively single-stranded narratives of many contemporary Western films, are considered unlikely to be successful.

> *The difference between Hindi and Western films is like that between an epic and a short story.*[25]

Not only is a film expected to be two-and-a-half to three hours long, but it is usual for the plot to span at least two generations, ('beginning with the main protagonists' births or childhoods and jumping twenty or so years often in a single shot) to the action of the present. There is of course good evidence that Hindi films have evolved from village traditions of epic narration, and the dramas and the characters, as well as the structure, of the mythological epics are regularly and openly drawn upon. Film-makers often insist that: 'Every film can be traced back to these stories', and even that 'There are only two stories in the world, the *Ramayana* and the *Mahabharat*.'[26] In fact, it is the form and movement of the narrative that tends to distinguish the Hindi film, the crux of this seeing that the balance between narrative development and spectacular or emotional excess is rather different. [...]

Verisimilitude

Beyond the basic suspension of disbelief on which cinema depends, any genre evolves and institutionalises its own conventions, which allow credibility to become unproblematic within certain parameters.[26, 27] Compared with the conventions of much Western cinema, Hindi films appear to have patently preposterous narratives, overblown dialogue (frequently evaluated by film-makers on whether or not it is 'clap-worthy'), exaggeratedly stylised acting, and to show disregard for psychological characterisation, history, geography, and even, sometimes, camera placement rules.[28]

Tolerance of overt phantasy has always been high in Hindi cinema, with little need to anchor the material in what Western conventions might recognise as a discourse of 'realism', and slippage between registers does not have to be marked or rationalised. The most obvious example is the song sequences, which are much less commonly 'justified' within the story (for example, introduced as stage performances by the fictional characters) than in Hollywood musicals. Hindi film songs are usually tightly integrated, through words and mood, within the *flow* of the film – 'In my films, if you miss a song, you have missed an important link between one part of the narration and the next'[29] – and misguided attempts to doctor Hindi films for Western audiences by cutting out the songs are always fatal. However, the song sequences (often also dream sequences) do permit excesses of phantasy which are more problematic elsewhere in the film, for they specifically allow that continuities of time and place be disregarded, that heroines may change saris between shots and the scenery skip continents between verses, whenever the interests of spectacle or mood require it. [...]

The spectator

It would appear that the spectator-subject of Hindi cinema is positioned rather differently from that of much Western cinema. In fact, even on the most overt level, Indian cinema audience behaviour is distinctive: involvement in the films is intense and audiences clap, sing, recite familiar dialogue with the actors, throw coins at the screen (in appreciation of spectacle), 'tut tut' at emotionally moving scenes, cry openly and laugh and jeer knowingly. Moreover, it is expected that audiences will see a film they like several times, and so-called 'repeat value' is deliberately built into a production by the film-makers, who believe that the keys to this are primarily the stars, music, spectacle, emotion and dialogue – this last having a greater significance than in Western cinema.[30]

What seems to emerge in Hindi cinema is an emphasis on emotion and spectacle rather than tight narrative, on *how* things will happen rather than *what* will happen next, on a succession of modes rather than linear denouement, on familiarity and repeated viewings rather than 'originality' and novelty, on a moral disordering to be (temporarily) resolved rather than an enigma to be solved. The spectator is addressed and moved through the films primarily via affect, although this is structured and contained by narratives whose power and insistence derives from their very familiarity, coupled with the fact that they are deeply rooted (in the psyche and in traditional mythology).

Whether, and how, one can relate the 'spectator-subject' of the films to the Indian 'social audience'[31] is not immediately clear, although certain comparisons with other discourses within India through which subjectivity is lived are suggestive. For example, it has been suggested[32] that Hindu caste, kinship and religious 'ideologies', in particular beliefs in destiny and *Karma,* position a decentred, less individuated social subject. One can also point to specific cultural traditions of performance and entertainment which must be of direct relevance, notably the forms on which early cinema drew, from the performances of the professional story-tellers and village dramatisations of the mythological epics, to the excesses of spectacle ('vulgar' and 'garish' according to contemporary critics) of the late nineteenth and early twentieth century Urdu Parsee theatre with its indulgent adaptations of Shakespeare and Victorian melodrama. Beyond this, one must remember that Sanskrit philosophy boasts a coherent theory of aesthetics which bears no relation to Aristotelian aesthetics and, rejecting the unities of time and place and the dramatic development of narrative, the theory of *rasa* (flavours/moods) is concerned with moving the spectator through the text in an ordered succession of modes of affect (*rasa*), by means of highly stylised devices. All Indian classical drama, dance and music draw on this aesthetic.

Of course, most present-day film-makers make no conscious reference to this heritage and, for example, the privileging of spectacle and music can be accounted for in many other ways, not least the pragmatic one that, to make money, the films need to appeal across wide linguistic and cultural divides within India itself. 'Tradition' cannot be used to provide too neat an 'explanation' of the present form – apart from anything else, Indian cultural 'tradition' is a heterogeneous assimilation of Sanskritic, Islamic, Judeo-Christian and many other influences, and could be selectively drawn upon to 'explain' almost any present form. Moreover, invoking tradition also holds dangers of uncritically romanticising the present form as exotically 'other' and ignoring its diverse influences and constant evolution. Its role should rather be seen as one of a framework of terms of reference within which certain developments have been stifled, others allowed to evolve unproblematically, and which can be used to throw light on the different possibilities of forms of address which might be expected or tolerated by an Indian audience.

This article has attempted to examine Indian popular cinema's 'terms of reference' by placing it within a number of contexts: primarily that of the film-makers' own descriptions of their films and generic expectations, but also briefly that of audiences, and of earlier and co-existing cultural forms and traditions. There is, of course, the problem of the infinite regress of context: no description of conditions and discourses could ever be 'adequate' to contextualising Indian cinema. But any criticism which ignores the specificity of the textual operations and pleasures of Indian popular cinema will remain caught up in the confusion and condescension which marked British responses to the London release of *Aan* in 1952:

> But having proved themselves masters of every cliché in the Western cinema, its remarkable producers should have a look around home and make an Indian film.[33]

Notes

1 The first Indian feature film, a mythological, D. G. Phalke's *Raja Harischandra*, was released in 1913.

2 This refers here primarily to those employed in the film industry as producers, directors, writers and distributors.

3 Films produced in the Hindustani language (and primarily in Bombay) account for less than 20% of pan-Indian film production. However, they alone are distributed throughout the country and, having the biggest budgets, stars and hence prestige, influence almost all regional language film-making.

4 *Naseeb*'s box-office returns rank with those of three other films as the highest of 1981. It is one of the most expensive 'multistarrers' ever produced in India (distribution rights sold for a little over £2 million in total).

5 Geoff Andrew in *Time Out*, August 2–8, 1984.

6 James Green, in the *Observer*, March 26, 1961, referring to *Mother India*.

7 'ER' in the *Monthly Film Bulletin*, September 1952, vol 19 no 224, referring to *Aan*.

8 Virginia Graham in *The Spectator*, July 18, 1952, referring to *Aan*.

9 *Monthly Film Bulletin*, August 1963, vol 30 no 355, referring to *Gunga Jumna*.

10 A Vasudev and P Lenglet (eds) *Indian Superbazaar*, Vikas, Delhi, 1983, p 112.

11 F Rangoonwalla, *Indian Cinema Past and Present*, Clarion, Delhi, 1983.

12 Khalid Mohamed in *Times of India*, 'Sunday Review', January 8, 1984.

13 *Sunday Express*, May 3, 1981.

14 Iqbal Masud in *Cine Blitz*, July 1981.

15 *Star and Style*, November 13, 1981.

16 Stephen Neale, *Genre*, London, British Film Institute, 1980.

17 Manmohan Desai, in interview with the author, May 1981.

18 *Trade Guide*, January 5, 1985. Video piracy has had a particularly harsh effect on the Bombay film industry. However, even in the late '70s it is alleged that only 10% of releases made 'sizeable' profits (*Report of the Working Group on National Film Policy*, Ministry of Information and Broadcasting, May 1980, p 17).

19 It has, in fact, been generally well received in the West and is the only Indian film ever to have won an Oscar nomination (Best Foreign Film, 1958).

20 Where European and Hollywood cinemas have drawn upon literary traditions for their story ideas, Hindi cinema has primarily looked to other films for basic

stories to adapt. Inspiration from Hollywood is often integrated with storylines from the Indian mythological epics, e.g. a recent proposal 'for a cross between *The Omen* and the *Mahabharat*'. The only virtual frame-to-frame remakes of Hollywood films (*Khoon Khoon* of *Dirty Harry* and *Manoranjan* of *Irma La Douce*) flopped disastrously. So did *Man Pasand*, based closely on *My Fair Lady*, a failure which the BBC ignored in its dismissive documentary on the film in 1982.

21 There are two weekly Bombay trade papers, *Trade Guide* and *Film Information*. Their reviews are generally respected in the film industry (unlike all other press reviews, especially the Sunday critics') and do in fact have a good record in predicting subsequent box-office performance.

22 *Trade Guide*, Special Edition, April 2, 1982 (with slight stylistic adaptations).

23 *Trade Guide*, May 3, 1981.

24 K K Shukla, screenplay writer of *Naseeb*, in interview with the author, April 1981.

25 Javed Akhtar, screenplay writer, in interview with the author, February 1981.

26 The two key mythological epics of India.

27 Stephan Neole, Op. at.

28 Camera placement rules can be disregarded, particularly in action (fight) scenes, which seem to be allowed something of the non-continuity conventions of song sequences.

29 Raj Kapoor, film-maker, in interview on *Visions*, Channel Four, February 1983.

30 Audiences often talk of dialogue as a central draw, and books and records of film dialogue sell sometimes better than collections of film music.

31 Annette Kuhn, 'Women's Genres', *Screen*, January-February 1984, vol 25 no 1, p 23.

32 L Dumont, *Homo Hierarchicals*, London, Weidenfeld and Nicolson, 1979.

33 is footnote 32 above.

3

Towards a theoretical critique of Bombay cinema

by Vijay Mishra

Any discussion of films from a relatively alien culture – 'relatively' and 'alien' in Britain at any rate would have very different meanings than, say, in Australia – involves a certain element of redundancy. At the risk of sounding somewhat tedious, I will go over some of the propositions which I develop at some length later. My basic argument is relatively straightforward and requires no major theoretical apparatus for its enunciation. I read Bombay Film (capitalised, 'Film' and 'Cinema' are used interchangeably throughout this paper) as a form which is homologous with the narrative paradigm established over two millennia ago in the Sanskrit epics, namely the *Mahabharata* and the *Ramayana* (hereinafter cited collectively as *MBh/Rama* and individually in full). Bombay films may, therefore, be seen as transformations of the narrative structures which may be discovered in these epics. Their influence, however, is not limited to narrative form alone. Since these epics were also ideological tools for the expansion of structures of belief endorsed by the ruling classes, there is also a significant way in which the Bombay Film legitimates its own existence through a re-inscription of its values into those of the *MBh/Rama*.

Beyond narrative authority and ideological control the question of transmission must also be considered. For these epics were orally transmitted and had their basis in folklore and ritual. They were, in short, an organic part of Indian culture, versions of which were quickly translated into vernacular languages and re-presented as their own.[1] This oral transmission (and transmutation) of the epics also meant that the epics quickly lost their links with an original, ur-text, becoming instead a heterogeneous collection of narratives/texts to which the mystified categories of 'original or primary text' or of 'source and ultimate meaning' could not be easily applied without considerable distortion. Yet the structure of the individual accretions (which may be read as 'texts' in their own right) did not disrupt the normative rules of the major narrative whose beginnings and ends were fixed. In the case of the *Mahabharata* it begins in general terms with the tale of

Samtanu and ends with Yuddhisthira's return to the higher heavens; in the case of the *Ramayana* it begins with Rama's birth and ends with Sita's return to Mother Earth.

Yet my use of the term 'heterogeneity' acquires a distinctively oral resonance when it comes to the actual production and re-presentation of episodes from the epic.[2] Each 'presentation' was an individual 'moment' with the vitual collapse of the discrete identities of singer and audience. Each 'presentation' as a 'moment' could be endlessly repeated with a variation in theme here or (more rarely) a metrical twist somewhere else. Meaningful only in terms of the major narrative syntagm of the epic and almost gratuitously repetitive, the 'moment' may be seen as a 'perpetual metonymy',[3] a play on a pre-existent totality, a confirmation, in a way, of the spectator's (and the subject's) desire to repeat.

Bombay Films too are moments of a grand narrative: each individual movie is a 'play' on the discursive practices which make up the 'other', unseen, movie as one massive unit. In short, the Bombay Film is one massive system with a series (incomplete) of specific actualisations. But the Bombay Cinema is also a pan-Indian social reality with a potential audience of something like 400 million. Produced in what is gradually becoming a distinctively Bombay Hindi, it is feverishly followed by enthusiastic Indians from every social class from Bombay to Calcutta, from Srinagar to Colombo. Overseas, this cinema is viewed on video, in the theatres, by yet another 4 million expatriate Indians.[4] Made unabashedly for popular consumption, it is perhaps the single most powerful cultural artefact of modern India: no change can take place without its tacit approval.

It is true that like any art form Bombay Cinema has produced its moments of 'otherness', its deconstructive forms which, for the purposes of this paper, I must ignore. Having quickly bracketed the subversive moments within the dominant form, I return to Bombay Film based on the 'song and dance' formula. And indeed this form may be deemed a genre in its own right. So what we have in fact is not simply one 'super' narrative but also one dominant genre whose rules are to be discovered in films from Phalke's *Raja Harischandra* (1913)[5] to the latest block-buster from Bombay. Yet like any genre, a close examination of its various actualisations shows degrees and levels of self-reflexivity, an awareness, almost parodistic at times, of its own 'artificial totality'. Occasionally such self-consciousness throws up movies, ostensibly written in the dominant code, which destabilise the presumed monolithic totality of the genre. It is in them that a degree of contestation of form occurs and in movies such as *Aadharshila* (1981), *Chakra* (1980), *Manthan* (1981) and even *Bhavna* (1984), such contestation, dialogically, foregrounds the dominant genre as the 'other'. With these preliminary remarks, I should now like to return to the precursor text: the *MBh/Rama* as the great code of Bombay Cinema.

The precursor text

Both the *Mahabharata* and the *Ramayana* belong to a pan-Indian meta-text and may be grouped collectively. And like the epic meta-text, Bombay Cinema too may be read as a palimpsest capable of endless expansion and repetition and like a palimpsest always betraying its compositional form – the previous inscriptions are always visible upon close inspection. On the basis of such a conflation, I should like to claim that the *MBh/Rama* is finally a crucial 'founder of [Indian] discursivity'.[6] For, after all, it should be remembered that the Bombay Film is only one of many discursive practices which 'embed' themselves into the *MBh/Rama*. Narrative forms as varied as the *mathnavis*, the Indian bourgeois novel and Indian folk theatre retrieve the rules of their own formation from the *MBh/Rama*.[7]

To support this claim we must examine the precise nature of the *MBh/Rama* discourse. I propose to do that by examining two verses from the *Mahabharata* and the *Ramayana* respectively. My aim is in fact to demonstrate how the precise rules even of filmic narrative are firmly embedded in passages as short as these. Furthermore, they demonstrate the themes of desire, *dharma* (Law), order and revenge which characterise Bombay films.

> *sa taya saha samgamya bharyaya kurunandana*
> *panduh paramadharmatma yuyuje kaladharmana*[8]

> (*In the [enchanting] embrace of his wife he, Panda, the joy of the Kurus, the foremost, upholder of **dharma**, was united with the Law of Time.*)

This is the description of Pandu's death in the *Mahabharata*. Pandu, brother of blind Dhritarastra, was condemned to suffer sexual abstinence all his life. Of his two wives Kunti had to cohabit with various demigods to produce three of his sons (Yudhisthira, Bhimasena and Arjuna), while Madri, his second wife, bore her children of the *ashvins* (the 'Horses'). Pandu, however, comes to his death because one strangely exciting day he finds the enchanting beauty of his wife Madri irresistible and ravishes her. As the malediction had combined sex with death, Pandu quickly dies as a consequence of his passion.

There is clearly a play on desire here: desire as both for the 'Other' (that is sex) or for the Self (that is preservation). But at a more fundamental level of discourse, the language itself is heavily marked by an excessive use of parataxis (without, that is, any grammatical signs of coordination or subordination). Pandu is described twice: once as *kurunandana* (the joy of the house of Kurus) and again as *paramadharmatma* (the foremost upholder of Law/*dharma*). There is no real subordination of these compounds to the subject; they belong co-extensively with Pandu. Similarly, death is opposed, both metrically and semantically, to *paramadharmatma* with the use of a parallel compound *kaladharmana* (the Law/*dharma* of Time/Death). The epic clearly wishes to bring the two kinds of *dharma* together but the form of representation adopted implicates a virtually continuous chain of referents. They are, in short, metonymic as the signifiers lack that total referentiality, the organic conflation of the signifier and the signified, found in metaphorical discourse. This descriptive system – a system marked by a high degree of parataxis and metonymy – is central to the discourse of the Bombay Film as well.

There is a further case of deferral which should be examined. The passive form *yuyuje* ('was joined') and the unnecessarily repetitive *samgamya* ('in the embrace') mark a certain periphrastic detachment, a whole discourse of allusion, evasion and suggestion which again seems almost 'culture specific'. I must, however, accept the all too obvious linguistic fact that the middle voice in which *yuyuje* is inflected is a common feature of Sanskrit, and passive formations generally are not unusual. But the jump from syntax to meaning – that the passive and, by extension, the instrumental case imply a culture of deferral and allusion, 'the actor as acted upon and not acting' – should not be read as an academic quirk. The passive, demonstrably, governs filmic representation too. For it is the mode of discursivity itself rather than a continuous series of narrative displacement and/or extension which constitutes the essential structure of the Bombay Film.

te vayam dharmavibhrastam svadharme sthithah
bharatajnanam purakruya nigrihnimo yathavidihi[9]

(*In following* **dharma** *according to the dictates of Bharata, we punish evildoers as prescribed by Law.*)

Our second verse is from the episode which deals with the slaying of Bali, one of the more contentious episodes in the entire *Ramayana*. The question at issue here is fundamentally moral for, in death, Bali accuses Rama of dishonouring his own codes of *dharma*. In short, as Bali carefully argues, he was ignobly killed by Rama and this must surely be interpreted not only as cowardly but as *adharmika* (non-dharmic) by the world at large. Rama's answers reinforce the significance of order, the importance of an orderly transmission of power so that the ideology of caste and hierarchy remains intact. Not surprisingly, it is the signifier *dharma* again, the Law, which is given surplus value, is over-semanticised, given a degree of 'supervalency' in fact. Rama justifies his killing of Bali by invoking the 'permissibility' of his action within the Law (*dharma*). Under these conditions we punish (*nigrihnimah*) evil-doers; under these conditions, too, vengeance may be taken, killing may indeed be deemed rightful, even 'holy'.

The Bombay Film is firmly embedded in this mode of discursivity. To read the Bombay Film necessitates an initial understanding of this practice even when in many instances the practice itself has been significantly transformed. But our insights into Bombay Cinema will remain partial if we do not develop adequate hermeneutic models, themselves offshoots of a massive tradition of meta-textual commentaries on the epics, with which to read them. It is only then that we can re-insert Bombay Cinema into a continuous Indian cultural formation: the political democracy which, according to Benjamin, is heralded by the cinema needs no more articulate confirmation than Bombay Film.[10]

The Bombay film as a problem in genealogy

A useful starting point for an examination of the importance of genealogy in both the epics and in Bombay Cinema is, naturally, a filmic version of the epic. Genealogy is, after all, a fundamental feature of Indian culture, the orderly transmission of genes being so very crucial to the maintaining of caste and hierarchy: blood must never be polluted. Yet the epics do, in their own way, probe ways in which this patrilineal transmission of authority may be subverted. In the case of Pandu, who in fact fathered none of his children, the priestly commentators simply moved this very ordinary fact out of its historical context and transmuted it into the genealogy of demi-gods. In the absence of the Father – in the *MBh*/*Rama* he is either blind or impotent or languishes for a banished son – it is naturally the Mother who becomes dominant. That this happens in the film version of the epic (*Mahabharata* 1967) is not unusual given that Kunti, the Mother, is the only real genealogical anchor for the Pandavas in the epic.[11]

But the valorisation of the Mother and the foregrounding of a particular constellation, of familial relationships in terms of the Mother (and not the Father) is fundamental to Bombay Cinema. In the film *Mahabharat*, this fetishisation of the category 'Mother' acquires considerable force. Upon the return of the Pandava brothers, the film pauses to highlight, dramatically, the Mother's directive to share whatever the brothers, singly or collectively, had won. As she is inside praying, she does not know that the object of this directive is Draupadi, the woman Arjuna had won at the *svayamvara* ('betrothal'). The Mother's word as Law and the Mother as the 'origin' of all genealogical secrets is further shown in Kunti's final request to Karna (her son born of the Sun-god before she married Pandu) to save her five 'legitimate' sons in the great battle of Kuruksetra. The image of Mother-as-beggar is a reversal of Mother-as-word and is carefully counterpointed in the film. But the filmic mode consistently neutralises any suggestion of illegitimacy through a highly developed (though necessarily predictable) system of evasions. We get a version of the same genealogical problematic in one of the best-known Bombay films Raj Kapoor's *Awara* (1951) where two kinds of structures may be found. The first is the epic structure of banishment: a wife is banished by a wealthy lawyer because he thinks she was defiled by the leader of a gang of dacoits who had kidnapped her on their honeymoon. The second is the whole question of patrimony as the lawyer refuses to recognise his wife's son as his own.

Together with the backdrop of Sita's banishment by Rama, the whole issue of 'fatherhood' is constantly replayed in Bombay Cinema. The answers which are invariably put forward always confirm the orderly nature of the genealogical transmission. Raj's father in *Awara* too finally acknowledges Raj to be his own son. At another level, genealogy often becomes 'Karmic', a continuous *mise-en-abyme* (receding mirror image), an endless series of reversals and 'cyclical detours'. In a film like *Mai tulsi teri agana ki* (1975) we find one of the more common instances of this genealogical reversal. The mother of one of the half-brothers in this film is a prostitute but it is her son who finally saves the family name from disgrace. The entry of the 'prostitute' again is important for us as it creates yet another category (especially if the prostitute is mother too) with which the Bombay Film feels terribly uncomfortable. We apply the same notion of 'indirection' or 'evasion' we found at the level of discourse itself. The filmic prostitute is thus a prostitute as yet 'undefiled', one who escapes from the clutches of a matronly, plumpish, pimp just before her fate can be sealed that night. There is, therefore, a hint of that virginal purity which, in retrospect, makes her as perfect a mother as any. The central issue again is thus resolved not through specific instances of social 'determinations' but through an entry into a prescribed, formal system of abstraction. The half-brother's 'goodness' is ontologically given – his mother was, after all, not a real prostitute.

The moment genealogy enters particular social formations, the Bombay Film begins to feel terribly uneasy and rarely does it actually face up to the *reality* of an illegitimate child in a family. Genealogy affirms equilibrium, the return to orderly transmission of genes: genealogy, that is, defined at its crudest. In *Zanjeer* (1973) genealogy is shifted to the level of the Imaginary and exists only through specular identifications established by the viewing subject. Both Vijay, the hero, and Mala, the knife-grinder whom Vijay brings home, have no genealogical antecedents in the text. Both are, in this context, floating signifiers for whom genealogy must be re-constructed – and genealogy, as the *MBh/Rama* affirms, does not exist outside connections by blood. Now it may be that *Zanjeer* wishes to free the hero and heroine from the shackles of genealogical bondage so that, as free agents, their actions (*karma*) and their obligations to the Moral Law (*dharma*) are placed in considerable relief. This is a legitimate argument and one, I am sure, the narrative endorses. Yet the freedom from genealogical constraints so given, enables realignments of the crucial filmic subjects with the viewing subject. Through a pre-symbolic form of identification, the viewer then re-constructs the very freedom that genealogy denies him in the Real so that genealogy now becomes a re-construction, a question of plenitude and lack, and not a given in the text.

These films often end up re-placing, re-focusing emphasis, rather than radically challenging the narrative authority of the precursor text, the *MBh/Rama*. Recent Bombay films like *Artha* (1983) face up to the whole basis of genealogy (and its over-valuation in Indian society generally) by stressing the strain on genealogical expectations placed by extra-marital affairs, divorce, second marriage and so on. There is perhaps a relatively large tradition of filmic contestations of this kind in the Bombay Film but generally even filmic narrative cannot handle the dis-economies created in any major shifting of basic Hindu social categories: a man/woman is either a Renouncer or a Man-of-the-World.

The renouncer and the man-of-the-world

'There are two kinds of men in Hindu India', wrote Louis Dumont over twenty years ago, 'those that live in the world and those that have renounced it'.[12] The opposition between *nivritti* ('renunciation') and *pravritti* ('worldliness') constitutes a major epistemological shift in Hindu thought which survives, in its various forms, to this day. Needless to say, its ramifications in the Bombay Film too are considerable. A crucial filmic text with which I should like to develop my argument is *Zanjeer*. Here the opposition of *nivritti* and *pravritti* is re-worked at various levels. A first distinction may be made between the villains who are all men-of-the-world and the hero's 'jail-bird' father who upon hearing about the cause of his daughter's death during the period of his imprisonment (she died because the bootlegging company for which he worked had flooded the market with worthless pharmaceutical drugs) immediately renounces his erstwhile collaborators. He and his wife are, therefore, shot. His son escapes injury and is brought up in another household. He may be no more than the 'outsider' but cultural specificities would dictate the reception of this 'outsider' as someone who situates himself outside the modern, bourgeois expression of *pravritti*. *Nivritti* is given another twist when the hero in *Zanjeer* is forced out of the police force because he is mistakenly suspected of bribery (the villains are responsible for this) and must, therefore, fight from outside the establishment. The heroine too, who is initially presented as a *churiwalla*, the 'knife-grinder', has no immediate relatives. The ironic potential of this is enormous for a prostitute in Hindi may be called *chappan-churi* ('fifty-six knives'). The third 'renouncer' in this triad is a Pathan who is won over by the hero because he, the Pathan, begins to respect Vijay as his equal in martial arts (a mixture of Bruce Lee and the street fighter). Yet the movie moves towards espousing a median between *nivritti* and *pravritti*, both of which through their symbolic representation by the hero's world and the villain's world respectively are shown to be excesses. In other words, the filmic narrative opts for a gentle balance situated right in the midst of the hero who becomes an exemplar of this mediation.

Any significant archaeology of the 'renouncer' in Bombay film would necessitate an analysis of two character-types. The first is the hero 'estranged', one whose higher sense of duty requires a radical act of estrangement from the woman he loves.[13] All popular Bombay actors must do this and all we have to do is construct a syntagm of actors of the past thirty or so years to demonstrate this: Dilip Kumar blinds himself after he has actually seen for himself that Nargis does not recognise him in *Deedar*. Both Raj Kapoor and Devanand in films like *Mera nam joker* and *Bambai ka babu* respectively lose the women they love. Raj Kapoor loses all three of them, perhaps a neat projection of the many loves in his own real life. In *Sangam* the renouncer is Rajendra Kumar, the hero's friend (whose girl he too loves) and an actor who thoroughly enjoyed roles oozing with melancholy and self-pity. Of the more recent matinee idols Rajesh Khanna was, for a while, constantly in a state of *vipralambha* or 'estrangement' (*Amar prem*, *Amardeep*, *Daag*, etc) and Amitabh Bacchan too in an interesting movie like *Silsila* (1982) sacrifices his love for duty towards another woman. We can only hint at these because the issue really involves an intricate set of signifiers which are produced through popular demand and media publicity. In Hindi one speaks of the *bicara* complex, the complex of self-pity (or, more positively, a version of 'the tragic sense') which produces a melancholic individual capable of singing some highly sentimental songs.

The second character-type is clearly the Mother. The archetypal Mother is Nargis of *Mother India* (1957). The filmic Mother often renounces everything for the sake of her husband or son. A husband may abuse her, a son may leave her (which sons do not do all that often) but she remains steadfast, the ultimate beacon that guides erratic ships to safety. So when a Mother renounces her own son (which is rare) or her husband (which is rarer still) the sheer emotional weight of all this is enormous. So Kunti's plea for the lives of her 'five legitimate sons' in the *Mahabharata* also implies an act of monumental renunciation – Karna must die as a consequence. Similarly, Nargis must shoot her son Birju (Sunil Dutt) in *Mother India* because her son had subverted codes that transcend filial obligations, codes indeed of *dharma* itself. The moment she shoots her son dead, she is canonised, becomes, in short, a super-mother, that terrible renouncer who is at once Mother and Kali. It is a prospect that the Bombay Film often tries to avoid either through the simultaneous death of the Mother and son or through some other form of 'indirection'.[14]

Mother India also problematises the role of hero-as-renouncer as Birju's radical renunciation is not so much an act of personal retreat from the affairs of the world but a revolutionary onslaught on the very structures that support and buttress the man-of-the-world: the feudal orders of Indian peasant society. He revolts against a system that perpetuates inequities and traps the Indian peasant into eternal servitude. But his error is that he wishes to abduct and ravish the landlord's daughter as an act of vengeance. It is here that the biological Mother whose duty is to her son becomes Durga or Bhavani, upholder of *dharma*, the codes that maintain Hinduism. In such situations, the Bombay film feels happier with a hero whose Mother is dead so that some codes may be subverted without the fear of a Mother's wrath. *Zanjeer* and *Silsila* both either negate or down-play the Mother, and the Mother in *Awara* too must not be allowed to face up to the consequences of her son's profligacy and vagabondage.

More recently in movies like *Artha* which perhaps only marginally belong to the genre of Bombay Film, a more radical shift in representation of the Mother may be detected. *Artha* in fact proposes to alter the Bombay 'frame of reference' with regard to the Mother by proposing the category Woman, a fact which in many ways comes closer to the original dramatisation of women in the epics – Satyavati, Lunti and even Sita are Women first and Mothers only subsequently. Of course, they have not been received in this fashion by Indian culture, especially as the semiotic system of *dharma* has denied Mother-as-Woman an independent voice. One need only remember that a wife is always called a *dharmapatni* (the wife of *dharma*).

The dharmic text

At one crucial level the precursor text of the Bombay Film is the *MBh/Rama* as a treatise on *dharma*. The term *dharma* covers a wide semantic field including morality, religion, duty, justice, virtue and so on and so forth. The ideology of *dharma* is variously manipulated by the filmic text. The film version of the epic, for instance, reads *dharma* extensively as a religious code which gains its significance from Krishna himself. This happens quite naturally because so many commentators have tried to give the *Mahabharata* a textual status indistinguishable from other religious texts. A more radical example of this is the *Ramayana* which, through its many vernacular versions, has almost become a *dharmashastra* (a Bible). I should like to interpret *dharma* a bit more loosely here so as to accommodate the varying degrees of political adjustment that the Bombay Film has had to make over the years. But insofar as the 'cultural specificity' of the Bombay Film is concerned, it resides squarely in its appropriation/distortion/

confusion of essentially dharmic categories and this, I have argued, is the crucial hermeneutic model for the study of the Bombay Film.

One of the invariables, however, is the way in which *dharma* is finally read as fidelity to its, the film industry's own, conception of what constitutes a stable bourgeois world-order. Behind the rhetoric of *dharma*, whether it is the rationale of the Mother's shooting of Birju or the ritualistic purification of a prostitute in a temple before the hero can marry her as in B R Chopra's *Sadhana* (1959), lies a naked ideological motive. I suspect that this has to do as much with the survival of particular kinds of script-writers, producers, directors, singers, musicians and so forth as with the truth value of *dharma* itself. In making the essential conflict a dharmic one, the forms of resolution become quite naturally pre-textual and hence, in a curious way, a justification for the film industry's own existence: the film too, finally, has a matrix enshrined in all Indian texts.

Dharma then is both the impetus and a screen that hides the blatant inconsistencies inherent at all levels in the filmic text. What it hides, furthermore, are the very processes of monopoly and exploitation which produce the text. The illusory unity of the text achieved sometimes through an excessive demonstration of the grammar of *dharma* (as in *Swami*) is no more than a systematic ploy aimed at avoiding a degree of self-consciousness about the filmic 'act/labour' in these movies. These are the features which movies like *Artha* and *Aadharshila* propose to deconstruct. This may be the beginning of a massive deconstruction of the hermeneutic models I have advanced in this paper too.

The parallel text

The 'reader' of the filmic text has two large sub-texts which must be handled simultaneously. The first is the epic text, the text that has accrued around the *MBh/Rama*. This text is crucial both in terms of the forms of discursive practices employed by the films and in terms of the hermeneutic models into which it positions itself. The hierarchy of models (from dharmic perhaps to genealogical) raised in this paper may, therefore, be legitimately superimposed upon the filmic text. The second sub-text is a parallel text which may be called the 'actor-text' or to give it a useful Hindi equivalent, the *Kalakar-shastra*. In other words, what now must be probed, albeit very generally, is the concept of actor as a text.

I would like to explore this concept of the 'parallel text' through the figure of the Bombay actor Amitabh Bacchan, whose film career spans fifteen years (1969–1984). In the wake of the Rajiv Gandhi brand of Indian populism, Bacchan, like a number of other Bombay Cinema actors and actresses (Sunil Dutt, Vijayanthimala, etc) is now a Congress Party parliamentarian. He made his impact on the Bombay screen around 1970 with his portrayal of the doctor of a terminal cancer patient. The film was *Anand* in which the central role was played by Rajesh Khanna, for a brief period India's most popular movie star.[15] There are a large number of biographical facts – real and apocryphal – which add to the Indian response to these actors – their marriages, love affairs, etc – but invoking them here would simply complicate our already difficult sub-text.

In *Anand*, Amitabh Bacchan has a supporting role which he fulfils with considerable tact and involvement. A curious comment (perhaps the author's anyway but perhaps suggested by Bacchan) is of not inconsiderable interest to us. As a doctor he tends people living in city ghettos but casually remarks, on one occasion, the impossible job of a doctor in India if every death is inevitably followed by at least another birth. Heroes don't say this in Indian cinema – but then the doctor is not the hero of *Anand*. Still, the movie begins to counterpoint Rajesh Khanna with his *bicara*-complex and Amitabh Bacchan with all the marks of a hero in rebellion. The rebellious figure is not unusual in Bombay Cinema; both K L Saigal and Raj Kapoor had defied some of the basic codes of Indian society. In *Awara*, for instance, Raj Kapoor had in fact used the urban *gunda* (the 'hooligan' associated with the Indian metropolis) to positive effect. Thus Amitabh Bacchan was already inscribing himself into the actor-text of a 'deviant'/'disruptive' tradition in films. It was a minor tradition (the tradition of Karna), not greatly at odds with the 'Rama hero', which occasionally reminded audiences of a certain subversive element which has always been present in Indian narrative.

My interest in Amitabh Bacchan arises straight out of this. I read him as a 'sub-text' which destabilises the 'positive' continuities we have detected in filmic discourse. But the 'sub-text' becomes a fully-fledged parallel text and displaces the filmic text itself: the actor becomes the film. The recent brouhaha over Amitabh's accident on the set of a movie (*Coolie*), which led to Indira Gandhi's visit to the hospital, a blind child's offer of his life in place of the actor's and urban billboards proclaiming 'God is Great Amit is Back', has all the marks of a 'narrative' in its own right. The crucial filmic text in his career was, however, *Zanjeer* and I should like to return to that movie now.

The immediate antecedents of *Zanjeer* are films on the theme of revenge such as *Baradari* and *Samrat*. In a way the narratives of both the *Mahabharata* and the *Ramayana* too may be read as propelled by a need for vengeance: the Pandavas seek vengeance because they are cheated, their 'wife' Draupadi ridiculed; Rama because Ravana 'ravishes' Sita. The moral justification for revenge goes back to Rama's words to the dying Bali. Yet *Zanjeer* internalises 'revenge' through a dream-text which dominates the entire work. It is true that this fills no more than a few frames of the film, but it is a highly polysemic dream-text. I have briefly commented on its filmic antecedents. It is important to recall also the importance of the *ashvamedha* ('horse sacrifice') and the *ashvins* ('the twin-horse headed gods') generally in Indian consciousness and their centrality in Indian mythology. There is also, however, a much more complex role of the horse which we have not touched upon but which surfaces in the filmic text through a quite fascinating series of signifiers of castration and/or potency. For the play with the phallus of the horse in the *ashvamedha* is crucial to a more comprehensive understanding of the highly ambiguous horse symbology in Indian culture.

In *Zanjeer*, as we point out in a forthcoming study of this movie,[16] the first representation of the '*ashva* nightmare' is a twice repeated shot of the horseman crossing the frame left to right. This is a slightly unusual form of 'Bombay representation' because the Bombay Film normally codifies such sequences through repeat zooms as in the 'flash visions' of Rishi Kapoor in *Karz* (1980). For us the significance of the shot is as a motif in the movie which alludes to the 'charm' on the villain's bracelet on the night on which he slaughters the hero's parents. As a child, the hero saw this from the closet where he was hiding. Moreover, this may be considered as a narrative 'event' unifying the revenge narrative of the film through the kinds of multiple signification we have suggested in this paper, i.e., the inter-text of Bombay movies with horsemen and, more significantly, the various transformations of the horse in Indian mythology.

More importantly, though, this 'event' could be related to the concept of the parallel text. From *Zanjeer* onwards – and *Zanjeer* now pushes the actor Amitabh Bacchan forward through a highly symbolic conjunction of actor and the 'symbolic horse' – Amitabh Bacchan becomes a complex 'text' in his own right, sanctioned by mythology and responding to a need for rebelliousness in the restless Indian lower middle classes (the target population; of the Indian film industry as a whole). It becomes readily obvious that any number of Amitabh Bacchan films – *Sat Hindustani, Barsat ki ek rat, Adalat, Hera pheri, Lavaris, Imam dharam, Khun pasina, Silsila, Shakti, Inquilab, Coolie, Sharabi, Naseeb*, etc – may be read through a sub-text called 'Amitabh Bacchan', constructed in turn through the dual process of the 'materiality' of filmic production, and audience reception. In all these movies the filmic subjects get subsumed by a larger than life text. The 'authority' and the 'author' of these films, if these terms may be read as 'a principle of grouping of discourses, conceived as the unity and origin of their meanings, as the focus of their coherence'[17] rather than as the physical 'originator' of the text (as 'screenplay writer', 'director', etc), are therefore to be located squarely at the interface of 'actor as text' and the Bombay Film as the complex discourse this paper has outlined. Once one projects this version of the 'authority of the text', one may also advance, parallel to the narrative inter-texts, a concept of 'actor inter-text'. In *Zanjeer,* and for Bombay Cinema generally, this 'actor inter-text' is essential to an understanding of the total reception of the movie – the fact that there is also an ideal Indian reader of the filmic text too.

Conclusion

Any theoretical critique of Bombay Cinema must begin with a systematic analysis of the grand Indian meta-text and 'founder of [Indian] discursivity', namely the *MBh/Rama*. This pre-requisite is not just an intellectual ploy, it is the 'minimal' starting point for a systematic analysis of this massive cultural artefact. No grammar of the Bombay Film can be established with any certainty nor will it stand up to close scrutiny unless the basic structure of this meta-text is firmly grasped. Beyond this the exercise becomes purely interpretative and here I have suggested 'received' ways in which this cinema may be tackled. These interpretative models open up ways in which the genre itself may be finally deconstructed. Yet every text, every genre, every cultural form also has its own history of reception, its own 'moments' of struggle and contestation and these 'moments' too require intensive treatment. This article has made some significant gestures towards them, especially insofar as it has given some primacy to a whole new 'parallel text' which must be constructed.

Ultimately, however, the presumed totality of the genre can be no more than illusory. Already movies like *Artha, Mandi, Masoon* etc, throw up age-old contradictions which require redress. They gradually begin to fragment the culture's cherished assumptions about order, sexuality and so on. The departures from the normative rules of an imperialistic discourse in such movies are adequate warning that the collapse of the genre may not be too far away. The margins gradually begin to acquire prominence, the absences a presence, the silences a voice: that which had been marginalised begins to assert itself. If a critique of the Bombay Film is going to be successful it must now pay as much attention not simply to the rules of the discourse (my initial contention) but also to the 'other' that this very discourse very conveniently silenced.

Notes

1 See Kamil Bulke, *Ram-katha,* Prayag, Hindi Parisad, 1959, for a comprehensive account of the many versions of the *Ramayana*. Chief among them are Tulsidas' *Ramcaritamanasa* (Avadhi), Kamban's *Ramayana* (Tamil) and Krittivas Ojha's Bengali version.
2 I am indebted to A B Lord, *The Singer of Tales,* Cambridge, Mass, Harvard University Press, 1960, for a theory of oral poetics.
3 I borrow this term from Stephen Heath, *Questions of Cinema,* London, Macmillan, 1981, p 13.
4 See *India: A Reference Manual,* Delhi, Ministry of Information and Broadcasting, 1950–1982.
5 For the title of films I have adopted Bombay Cinema's own somewhat idiosyncratic but remarkably uniform orthography. Sanskrit transliterations have not been supplied with diacritical marks.
6 Michel Foucault, 'What is an Author?' in J V Harari (ed), *Textual Strategies,* London, Methuen, 1980, pp 141–160.
7 A number of these *mathnavis* were used by Homi Wadia during the '30s, '40s and '50s. Films like *Alibaba aur uske chalis chor, Aladin aur uska jadavi chirag, Husn ka chor* and many others were immensely popular. Among the Indian bourgeois novels may be mentioned B Bannerjee's *Pather Panchali,* Premchand's *Godan,* Phaneshvar Nath Renu's *Maila Acal* and Mulk Raj Anand's *Untouchable.*
8 *Mahabharata,* Poona Critical Edition, I, 116.12.
9 Y Drivedi and L Jha (eds), *Ramayana,* Varanasi, 1967, IV, 18.11.
10 Walter Benjamin, 'The Work of Art in the Age of Mechanical Reproduction', in *Illuminations,* (Hannah Arendt ed), London, Collins/Fontana Books, 1973.
11 Used as absolute terms both Father and Mother begin with capital letters throughout.
12 Louis Dumont, 'World Renunciation in Indian Religions', *Contributions to Indian Sociology,* IV, 1960, pp 33–62.

13 The erotic, wrote the Sanskrit aesthetician Mammata, is of two types: love in union and love in separation. See Mammata, *Kavya prakashah* (Acarya Vishveshvara ed), Varanasi, 1960, 4.29.

14 It is interesting to note that in the Bombay Film the Mother is hardly ever around when a hero (or supporting hero) dies or leaves home for good. In *Sangam* (1964) there is no reference to Gopal's Mother before he shoots himself and in Gurudatt's *Pyasa* (1957) the poet's Mother dies before he leaves home with the prostitute Gulabo. *Lavaris, Shakti* and many more may be added to this list.

15 See K A Abbas, *I am not an Island: An Experiment in Autobiography*, New Delhi, Vikas Publishing House, 1977, pp 485ff, for an interesting account of Amitabh Bacchan.

16 Vijay Mishra, Peter Jeffery, Brian Shoesmith, 'Zanjeer and Bombay Film', work-in-progress, Murdoch University.

17 Michel Foucault, 'The Order of Discourse', in Robert Young (ed), *Untying the Text*, London, Routledge and Kegan Paul, 1981, p 48.

4

The economics of ideology: popular film form and mode of production
by Madhava Prasad

There is a good deal of writing on the economics of the film industry, some of it by professional economists.[1] This constitutes a valuable body of information on the sources of finance, the roles of various agents (producers, distributors, exhibitors) in the industry, the relations of power and dependency that develop between these agents as a reflection of their relative financial position, the revenues accruing to the government from the industry, the avenues for legitimate and reliable finance, etc. When we place these details alongside the actual cultural content of the films, the ideologies they circulate, there are, however, some questions that arise that have so far remained unaddressed. These questions are neither strictly economic, like the ones just described, nor purely cultural, but belong to a border area between them, overlapping with both. This is the area with which this chapter is concerned: the point at which political, economic and ideological instances intersect.

The film-maker Kumar Shahani has remarked: 'The biggest problem seems to be that we are working within a capitalist framework and we do not have a capitalist infrastructure. It is all run on highly speculative lines, on some systems of trading and circulation of money' (Rizvi and Amlad 1980: 13). Shahani's remark points to an extremely vital link between the mode of organization of the industry and the opportunities for experimentation afforded by that industry. Thus to focus on economic questions relating to the industry is not simply to 'flesh out' the background to cultural production but to uncover the nature of the nexus between economic, ideological and political forces that shape the conditions of possibility of cultural production in India.

In exploring this area, our point of departure will be the dominant textual form of the popular Hindi cinema, the form that has enjoyed pre-eminence in the Bombay film industry for nearly four decades. It is a form that would be familiar to anyone who has watched even a small number of the Bombay films. Even in other languages, especially in films from the south, the same textual form serves to organize the cinematic spectacle to a large extent. In the last few years, the industry has been undergoing changes which may lead to mutations of this form, or the introduction of new ones, but as yet the form associated with what I will call the feudal family romance has by no means exhausted itself.

Let us try to define this form. A definition of form, as opposed to a description of content, should be such as to account for, among other things, the narrative structure, the organization of elements within the structure, the means employed to carry the narrative forward from one stage to the next and those by which narrative closure is achieved.

The feudal family romance employs a narrative structure that goes back to the 'romances' that preceded the advent of modern realist fiction in the capitalist west.[2] The romance was typically a tale of love and adventure, in which a high-born figure, usually a prince, underwent trials that tested his courage and at the end of which he would return to inherit the father's position and to marry. This narrative structure occurs, not in its original form, but in the form that it acquired in popular theatre, where the entertainment programme would include the narrative interspersed with other elements like the comic routine, music and dance, etc. It was the Parsi theatre that first popularized this form in India. Indian cinema, however, did not adopt this form straightaway. It could not possibly do so in the silent era, but even after the introduction of sound, the adoption of this form was a gradual process. It stabilized roughly during the 1950s, and was to remain unchallenged until the beginning of the 1970s, when new elements were introduced, without, however, completely discarding the old form.

At its most stable, this form included a version of the romance narrative, a comedy track, an average of six songs per film, as well as a range of familiar character types. Narrative closure usually consisted in the restoration of a threatened moral/social order by the hero. This form was flexible enough to include a wide range of contingent elements, including references to topical issues, and propaganda for the government's social welfare measures (to please the censors). Thus, it should not be thought of as being necessarily and completely a bearer of feudal values, even though the overall narrative form derived from romances of the feudal era.

However, Bombay, as well as other centres of film-making have also witnessed campaigns against this form even during the period of its dominance, in favour of 'realism', a term which was defined in a variety of ways. For people in the industry who were dissatisfied with the dominant form, the model to emulate was Hollywood: in periodicals like *Screen* and *Filmfare*, film-makers would confess to a preference for films that were realistic and justify their own inability to make such films by blaming the poor taste of the audience. Whenever big-budget films failed, leading to a crisis, the press would repeat its advice: the audience has rejected the old *masala* film, it wants realistic, authentic stories, not songs and dances. Film-makers were urged to work with a ready script and adhere to short, tight schedules. Producers would try, every few years, to unite and impose order on the industry's functioning, to regulate the work schedules of stars, to co-operate in reducing the duplication of themes, etc.

In spite of this recurring effort, the so-called 'formula film' held on to its position of pre-eminence. The question that arises therefore is how and why this form was able to dominate the scene for so long. In this chapter, we will investigate this question primarily from the economic angle.

Before proceeding with the analysis, I will set down for convenience, the general conclusions the study arrives at:

(i) As regards the production sector, I will argue that the mode of production in the Hindi film industry is characterized by fragmentation of the production apparatus, subordination of the production process to a moment of the self-valorization of merchant capital, the consequent externality of capital to the production process, the resistance of the rentier class of exhibitors to the expansionist drive of the logic of the market, and the functional centrality of the distributor-financier to the entire process of film-making.

(ii) The Hindi film industry has adopted what Marx calls the 'heterogeneous form of manufacture' in which the whole is assembled from parts produced separately by specialists, rather than being centralized around the processing of a given material, as in serial or organic manufacture. This is of significance to the status of the 'story' in the Hindi film.

(iii) There is evidence of an ongoing struggle between two broadly defined tendencies within the industry, one committed to an ideological mission in keeping with the goals of the postcolonial state's controlled capitalist development and aspiring to the achievement of a homogenized national culture, the other moored in a pre-capitalist culture, employing a patchwork of consumerist and pre-capitalist ideologies and determined to maintain its hold over the production process from the outside. In this context the role of the state as the primary agent of capitalist development becomes crucial. The unfolding of the struggle between these two contending forces has involved appeals for particular forms of state intervention, a campaign for realism and melodrama, and concerted efforts to establish the production sector on an independent basis. It is a struggle, in other words, to effect an adequation of the political, economic and ideological instances.

In the run-up to independence, a section of the industry expected that the government of free India would recognize the potential that cinema held as a medium of mass education and would give it the same encouragement that was envisaged for other industries. It was felt that a modernizing nation would need a modern, cultural institution to undertake the requisite ideological tasks. In 1945, five producers from Bombay, Calcutta, Lahore and Madras undertook an expedition to Europe and America to study the conditions of the film industries there. Their report (*Report of the Indian Film Industry's Mission to Europe and America*, nd) was full of admiration for western efficiency, and concluded with suggestions that would be repeated by industry spokespersons for decades to come. Government support was sought for establishing the industry on a 'stable and progressive foundation'. The state was urged to supply finance, to launch the indigenous manufacture of raw film and equipment, to start a film council and a film institute (which had been proposed before but had been squashed in the Legislative assembly just before the publication of the report); and lastly, a 'Central Film

Academy and Research Institute' was proposed to 'combat ... anti-Indian propaganda vehemently carried on abroad especially in the United States before and during the last war' (*Mission*: 59–60).

The report projected the industry as a partner in the about-to-be independent country's campaign to modernize and project a good image abroad. This was in conformity with the model of socio-economic progress that was emerging as the chosen path for India, and was embodied in Nehruvian socialism. Among others this consisted of a combination of measures to develop indigenous capital, to enable it by protection and other state-initiated economic measures to consolidate itself, while launching a social programme of progressive education, the gradual emancipation of the population into an awareness of the rights and responsibilities of social democracy. But the Nehruvian state did not do for the film industry what it was committed to doing for other industries. Nehru himself had remarked that the film industry was not a priority for the new nation,[3] causing considerable anxiety in industry circles. Despite attempts to portray the industry as sharing the government's (and in particular Nehru's) views about the role of cinema, and the assertion that it was the state's duty, in a capitalist society, to develop entertainment facilities, nothing concrete materialized.

The need to establish film-making as an industry was emphasized by Phalke[4] earlier in the century and continues to be a recurrent motif in debates on the future of Indian cinema. To gain 'industry status' is to acquire legitimacy in the eyes of the state, to be accorded the privileges of a successful native industrial venture. In practical terms such a recognition would translate into availability of institutional finance and a collaborative approach on the government's part.

It is not as if the state was unaware of the uses of cinema as a tool of mass education. Building on the existing infrastructure for colonial propaganda film production, the Films Division expanded into a gigantic machine producing newsreels and documentaries for screening in commercial theatres and other places. This was also a source of revenue, since a small fee was charged for each screening. Thus the state policy conformed with the imperative of reproduction of conditions of formal subsumption. The industry's demand was for initiatives that would enable a transformation of the prevailing film aesthetic. The state's response was to impose a parasitical propaganda element on every screening, which was meant to take care of education in modernity, leaving the form of the feature itself untouched.

Following the Film Enquiry Committee report, however, a Film Finance Corporation (FFC) was set up in 1960. With a budget that was too small to earn it a major role in the industry, the FFC gave out insufficient loans to producers who consequently ended up with incomplete films and unrepayable loans. Later, a revised policy of financing low-budget, non-commercial films was implemented, inaugurating the era of the 'new cinema,' which will be discussed later on. As far as the mainstream cinema was concerned, the FFC brought about no change in the existing state – industry relations. The institution that was expected to change this state of affairs was the Film Council, also recommended by the Film Enquiry Committee (FEC) report. Without the 'political' alliance between the state and the industry that the Film Council would have represented, the economic intervention via the FFC was ineffectual. However, though the industry as a whole clamoured for the economic assistance promised by the FFC, only a few producers were willing to enter into an institutional alliance with the state that would impose obligations on both parties.

Similar ideas for government – industry co-operation had been floated even before independence. Fazalbhoy's review reports for instance, that the Indian Motion Picture Congress of 1939 was envisaged as a permanent body that would function as a 'central organisation' of the industry as recommended previously by the 1927 ICC report (Fazalbhoy nd: 84–5). This central body was, in the eyes of its proponents, a symbol of the will to lead the film sector into the industrial era, of the industry's self-image as a national institution with developmental responsibilities (ibid: 96–7). The 1951 *Report of the Film Enquiry Committee* (FEC *Report*), reviving the idea, observed:

> On the organizational side we would recommend that early steps should be taken to set up a statutory Film Council of India as the central authority to superintend and regulate the film industry, to act as its guide; friend and philosopher, and to advise the Central and State governments in regard to various matters connected with the production, distribution and exhibition of films. Such a Council, we envisage, will give the industry the necessary stimulus and inspiration to regulate its affairs on healthy and constructive lines, ensure that organizationally it functions in an efficient and businesslike manner, ensure professional conduct and discipline in its various branches and enforce standards of quality which would make the film a cultural agent and an instrument of healthy entertainment ([Patil] 1951: 187–8).

The Council had to *regulate* the industry without *controlling* it. It was to have statutory powers and the authority to institute research projects, training institutions, a 'story bureau', a casting bureau, a production code administration on the lines of the one in America, etc. (ibid: 189–94).

This measure came up for consideration frequently and was blocked each time by the resistance of a large section who claimed that control rather than benign regulation was the government's real motive. Throughout the fifties, sixties and the early seventies, the idea of a Council was discussed in the film press, with a mounting sense of urgency as the Indira Gandhi regime unfolded its 'socialist' agenda. Support for the idea came from established film-makers like V. Shantaram, Raj Kapoor, Satyajit Ray, Mohan Segal, etc. and from the technicians' and cineworkers' unions which stood to gain from a well-organized industry. It is possible that some of those who openly supported the idea were motivated by a fear of displeasing the government. Opponents of the plan were people with a more traditional business approach like Sunderlal Nahata, Chandulal Shah and lastly, J. Om Prakash, who as elected head of the Film Federation of India, warned his membership that they would have to achieve internal unity in order to ward off the threat of a Film Council.[5]

Clearly, the long-term benefits that might accrue from a stable infrastructure were not very attractive to those whose interests were best served by preserving the anarchic backward capitalism that reigned in the industry. Behind the stated fear of government control was a real apprehension of having to forego the benefits of a substantial inflow of black money. It became clear in the course of this conflict between the supporters and opponents of the proposal, that the industry was not ready for a transformation of the prevailing relations of production and power. That the proposal came to nothing is not surprising: even its supporters were not ready to make a crusade of it. Their reluctance was reinforced by fears that the Indira Gandhi regime was contemplating radical measures like nationalization and licensing of producers. In 1980, the *Report of the Working Group on National Film Policy* (NFP *Report*) dismissed the Council idea as ill-advised and instead recommended 'indirect' measures to improve quality ([Karanth] 1980: 20).[6] Nevertheless, while it lasted, the idea of a Film Council served as a measure of the changing relations between government and industry. It became the focus of a discourse of industrial advancement tied to the project to develop a new, bourgeois aesthetic, a developmental vision of cultural production and state-backed capitalist growth.

The organization of production

The film texts that reach us as finished products are made possible, not only by 'cultural' factors, but also by the mode of production that prevails in the industry, and in the society in which that industry operates. Janet Staiger (1985), who has done an exhaustive study of the Hollywood mode of production, begins by asserting that the socio-economic 'base' does not enjoy any privileged role as determinant in the emergence of technology and ideological forms, as Jean-Louis Comolli (1993) had argued. Instead, following John Ellis (1992) and Geoffrey Nowell-Smith, she regards the conditions of film practice – ideological, economic, political and technological – as 'a series of histories' constituting 'the terrain of possibilities' (Staiger 1985: 87–8).

Staiger argues that we cannot simply assume that the 'group style' that dominated Hollywood film-making was made possible by historical conditions extraneous to it. It is equally possible that certain production practices were adopted *because* they were the best for the particular style of film-making that the industry desired (ibid: 88). Staiger is right in rejecting the economic determinism implied by the argument that the style is just a reflection of the adopted mode of production. However, she does not take up the same question in a larger context: that is to say, do the socio-economic conditions prevailing in the society as a whole have anything to do with the choice of style and form?

Staiger identifies a series of 'systems of production', i.e. the modes of combination of the 'factors of production' in the Hollywood film industry. She traces the ways in which the labour force, the means of production, and financing combine in different ways to constitute in different periods of film history, specific 'systems of production' organized around the central function of a particular skilled member of the firm: the 'cameraman' system of production, the director system, the 'director-unit' system and so on (ibid: 85–153, 309–64).

In order to determine what systems of production may be in operation in Bombay, it is necessary to first understand the relations between the different sectors of the film industry and the way production is organized within the network formed by these sectors.

The FEC report of 1951 notes that unlike the concentration of production in the hands of a few concerns in Hollywood, 'India is distinguished by a plethora of producers' ([Patil 1951:]64). The figures cited show the extent of fragmentation:

Table 1 A Plethora of Producers

Year	Films	Producers	Maximum films by a single producer
1939	167	94	9
1940	171	102	7
1946	200	151	–
1947	283	214	7
1948	264	211	6

Source: Report of the Film Enquiry Committee, [Patil] 1951: 64, 323–4

The average number of films made per producer was highest in 1939 at less than two. By 1948 the average had dropped to just over one film per producer. Not only were there a large number of producers turning out one or two films a year, but a significant number of them were 'newcomer independents' afflicted by a high rate of 'infant mortality'.

The production sector of the industry can thus be divided into two broad segments consisting of a tiny group of 'established' producers and a large number of independents. This has been the general trend at least since 1939, that is to say, before India was drawn into the war effort. Y.A. Fazalbhoy's *Review* (nd) published soon after the 1939 Indian Motion Picture Congress that was held in Bombay, shows that under-capitalization was very much the norm even in the 'studio era', thus reducing the importance of the break that was attributed (by Barnouw and Krishnaswamy (1980), for instance) to an influx of black money that lured stars away from the studios during the Second World War years.

To begin with, Fazalbhoy traces the entry of independent producers to the early thirties when the arrival of sound suddenly freed the Indian language film from competition with imported films and led to its undisputed leadership and a vast expansion of its market. Thus,

> every qualified and unqualified man rushed into film production and over four hundred pictures were made in some of the earlier years. Very soon came a glut in the market and a number of studios and producing companies closed down because their products could not be sold profitably. The industry has not yet recovered from the depression that came in the train of these successive disasters (*Review*, nd).

He concludes with the now familiar prescription that organization 'on more scientific principles' and 'better facilities for finance' could alone prevent the high rate of failure of the production companies.

The Indian producer, according to Fazalbhoy,

> is usually satisfied if he can take one picture in hand at a time and follow it up to its end through many months of hard labor. The economies in overhead expenditure that come from producing a number of pictures at a time have necessarily to be sacrificed (ibid).

Establishing the industry on a firm capitalist basis, with high capital investment and mass production were seen to be crucial but the industry's 'internal organization' was too weak to achieve this and thus could not attract the support of the government and the public.

> If the extremely small units of the present day succeed in expanding sufficiently to ensure economic working or if they merge into larger units, they can not only get sufficient financial support, but also secure such an important voice in commercial matters that governmental authorities, will scarcely be able to ignore them (ibid: 7).

Related to these symptoms of economic disorder and fragmentation is the question of how the individual film itself is put together: Studio facilities being limited, the lack of pre-planning adds to delays and necessitates last minute improvisations (Fazalbhoy *Review*: 10–11). Dialogue, role development and even the story's line of progression were being decided during the production. The NFP report, published in 1980, did not see any change in this regard ([Karanth 1980:] 17). Thus, while a large number of films are produced every year, there is no 'mass production' in the strict sense of the term. The importance of this detail will make itself felt as we proceed.

The studios, an important cornerstone of the film industry, were in a position of unquestioned dominance in the 1930s, when the film world was 'beginning to have the look of an organized industry' (Barnouw and Krishnaswamy 1980: 117). Why were they then unable to hold on to their position of strength when it was challenged by the independent newcomers? As it is usually understood, the strategy of the newcomers was based on a shrewd calculation of the role of the star in the success of a film. The stars, whose incomes in the studios were moderate, were lured away with the offer of huge sums, thus drawing the studios into a competition from which they never recovered: The elevation of the stars to the status of independent values, capable of a sort of self-valorization, upset the control over the production process which had enabled the studios to maintain their methods and (non)disciplines of work. This was also the occasion for the entry of 'black money' into the industry. The newcomers, backed by the tainted surpluses of blackmarketeers (later they would be joined by smugglers), offered a part of the high payment to the stars in the form of unaccounted money, which would be 'tax-free'. During the last years of British rule, this practice was even regarded as a patriotic act (ibid: 127).

But there is another reason for the loss of dominance: although the studios were large well-organized production centres, they functioned on what Barnouw and Krishnaswamy call the 'one-big-family' principle. 'The big companies of the 1930s, like the Phalke company before them, seemed to be extensions of the joint family system. Many of the companies had, in fact, clusters of relatives' (ibid: 117). Thus, these companies were functioning in a market economy, producing commodities for mass distribution, but the production relations were based on kinship loyalties.

From the trends noted above it would be reasonable to conclude that the transformation wrought by the influx of independent producers intensified rather than caused the dispersed mode of functioning of the industry. The independent producer was at best a small-scale capitalist entrepreneur who could depend on the availability of low-wage casual labour and freelance acting talent with enormous wage differences between the stars, the 'character actors' and the 'extras' and could rent all the requisite technical services and equipment. The star, who was previously only one of the more important units of congealed value (or 'symbolic capital') to go into the product, now became the primary source of value.

A separate distribution sector for the Indian film industry was a late development. In the silent era, when Indian films formed only a small segment of the total films exhibited in the country, only imports were put on the market by distributors. A distribution sector for Indian films only emerged with the birth of the talkies and an increase in Indian language film production. Distribution and exhibition are the two sectors of the entire process that are widely acknowledged to be the most profitable. The proliferation of small and short-lived production companies with no fixed capital and limited working capital has meant that the distributors' profits have emerged as one of the main sources of finance for film production.[7] The separate existence and the relation of dependence between the distribution and production sectors ensures that capital remains permanently dissociated from the production sector which it subordinated to its own self-valorization. Capitalist enterprise is still in its emergent form here and for all practical purposes remains a system akin to the 'putting out system' of early capitalism, where production is subservient to distributors' capital which is advanced to producers, the product then belonging to the financier.

Film distribution was not the main occupation of those who entered the business. Most of them were moneylenders who turned distributors in order to recover their money:

> The chief characteristic of distribution in India is that to a great extent the firms handling the work are merely departments of financing houses ... . Since the returns from a picture will be recovered only after it is in the market for some time the studio must have sufficient funds to carry on its activities. The financiers who stepped-in with this help took as security the returns from the picture and in the majority of cases retained the distribution with themselves ... (Fazalbhoy Review: 28–9).

The 'minimum guarantee system', which is supposed to assure the producer a minimum return on each film, is also not as favourable to producers as it appears.

The amount that is fixed as the minimum guarantee in this transaction is usually the amount loaned by the distributor to the producer during the making of the film. As a result the producer often gets no revenue from a film after production because the minimum return has already been given in the form of loans. It was also in the distributors' interest 'to see that returns from pictures are not so excessive as to enable the producer to pay them off' (ibid: 48).

The exhibition sector's role in this scenario largely complements that of the distributor. In the first place, distributors, to secure their long-term interests, establish control over theatres. A syndicate of distributors has been in operation in Bombay, monopolizing the theatres. The rise of the multi-starrer, and the saturation release strategy led to rental increases which reinforced the monopoly of a few distribution houses ([Karanth 1980:] 24). Theatres were scarce in any case because of unfriendly construction rules. Even when new ones were constructed all over India during the seventies after the rules were relaxed, demand continued to exceed supply in densely-populated cities.

There also emerged an intermediary class of 'theatre contractors' who booked theatres and sold time to distributors at higher prices. The logic of the industry also gave rise to the staging of 'fake jubilees' in some centres to create a good impression on audiences in late-release centres. In 1957, *Filmfare* decided to focus on the 'exhibition racket'. The sharp rise in rentals – between 1955 and 1957 according to the magazine, the average rental went up by Rs 700 in the case of small and second-run theatres and by Rs 2000 in the case of first-run houses – was the most tangible index of what was seen as a racket involving various forms of deceit.[8] In 1972, echoing the Indira Gandhi government's slogan of 'Garibi Hatao', a *Filmfare* editorial entitled 'Zamindari Hatao' returned to the question of the black money hoards of the exhibitors and the exorbitant rentals. It pointed out that even foreign film theatres demanded black money payments when they screened Hindi films. It wondered how long the 'socialist government' would tolerate such 'antisocial' activities. The title pointed to the links between theatre owners and a more traditional, British-created form of landlordism. The government, which had recently proclaimed its commitment to ending feudal practices was called upon to smash the power of theatre owners and bring them into the modern capitalist economy as rationally-functioning entrepreneurs.

This brief account of the economic structure of the Bombay film industry demonstrates the dominance of merchant capital and the fragmentation and heteronomy of the production sector. [...]

Notes

1 [...] R. D. Jain. (1960), M.A. Oommen and K.V. Joseph (1991), Manjunath Pendakur (1990), Someswar Bhowmik (1986); reports of the inquiry commissions appointed by government are also a good source of such information and analysis.

2 See McKeon (1987) for a detailed discussion of the romance form as precursor of the novel.

3 *Filmfare,* 28 November 1952, p. 5

4 See the translations of Phalke's writings published by the National Film Archives of which a selection has been reprinted in *Continuum* 2.1 (1988/89) 51–73. Especially significant is the fact that Phalke conceived of Indian cinema as part of the Swadeshi campaign to develop indigenous industry. For a further discussion of Phalke and Swadeshi, see A. Rajadhyaksha, 'The Phalke Era', *JAI* (1987).

5 *Screen,* 12 July 1968, p. 1; 19 July 1968, p. 13; 14 February 1969, p. 1; 16 May 1969, p. 1; 23 May 1969, p. 8; 14 November 1969, p. 1; 14 August 1970, p. 1; 23 October 1970, p. 1.

   Also *Filmfare,* 4 April 1952, p. 4; 27 May 1955; 6 January 1956, p. 5; 3 February 1956, p. 3; 17 February 1956, p. 3; 25 May 1956, p. 19; 16 October 1964; 30 October 1964, p. 5; 17 January 1969, p. 7; 11 April 1969, p. 5; 4 July 1969, pp. 27, 29, 31; 1 August 1969, p. 23; 5 December 1969, p. 7; 16 January 1970, p. 7; 28 August 1970, p. 5; 11 September 1970, p. 5; 17 December 1971, p. 7; 2 May 1975, p. 9.

6 B.K. Karanjia, as editor of *Filmfare* and the FFC chair, had championed the proposal, revived the idea in a 1987 article and harked back to the regulation vs. control debate. However, the advent of television, the liberalization measures of the Congress regimes, a new culture of vigorous middle-class consumerism and the industry's scramble to survive in a competitive environment had meanwhile so transformed the scene that the idea of state-supported capitalist growth seemed distinctly odd.

7 Note that financing of production by distributors is by no means a peculiar feature of the Indian scene. This was commonly the practice in Hollywood and elsewhere. What is important is the industry's status in relation to that sector.

8 *Filmfare,* 24 May 1957, p. 3

References

Barnouw, Erik and S. Krishnaswamy (1980) *Indian Film.* 2nd edition. New York: Oxford University Press.

Bhowmik, Someswar (1986) 'The State of the Indian Film Industry', *Splice* 2, July: 31–7.

Comolli, Jean-Louis (1993) 'Technology and Ideology' in Bill Nichols (ed) *Movies and Methods.* Vol. 2. Calcutta: Seagull.

Ellis, John (1992) 'Stars as a Cinematic Phenomenon' in Gerald Mast [, Marshall Cohen and Leo Braudy] (eds) *Film Theory and Criticism.* [4th edition]. New York: Oxford University Press.

Fazalbhoy, Y.A. (nd) *The Indian Film: A Review.* Bombay: Bombay Radio Press.

Jain, Rikhab Dass (1960) *The Economic Aspects of the Film Industry in India.* Delhi: Atma Ram.

[Karanth, K.S. (1980) *Report of the Working Group on National Film Policy.* New Delhi: Government of India Press.]

McKeon, Michael (1987) *The Origins of the English Novel 1400–1700.* Baltimore: Johns Hopkins.

Oommen, M.A. and K.V. Joseph (1991) *Economics of Indian Cinema*. New Delhi: Oxford and IBH Publishing.

[Patil, S.K. (1951) *Report of the Film Enquiry Committee*. New Delhi: Government of India Press.]

Pendakur, Manjunath (1990) 'The Indian Film Industry' in John Lent (ed) *The Asian Film Industry*. London: Christopher Helm.

Report of the Indian Film Industry's Mission to Europe and America. Bombay: Avanti Prakashan, nd.

Rizvi, Ahmed and Parag R. Amlad (1980) 'Is There a New Cinema Movement?', *Cinema Vision India 1.3*, July.

Staiger, Janet (1985) 'The Hollywood Mode of Production to 1930' and 'The Hollywood Mode of Production, 1930–60' in [David Bordwell, Janet Staiger and Kristin Thompson] *The Classical Hollywood Cinema: Film Style and Mode of Production to 1960*. New York: Columbia University Press.

5

In the throes of change: exhibition, production and distribution
by Manjunath Pendakur

During World War II the cinema-going habit spread much further and faster among the population following a greater purchasing power among all classes, particularly the poor and lower middle-classes ... Within three months of decontrol (of wartime raw stock rationing) over 100 new producers entered the field, attracted by the prospects held out by the industry ... Within three years of the end of the War, the leadership of the industry had changed hands from established producers to a variety of successors. Leading "stars," exacting "financiers" and calculating distributors and exhibitors forged ahead ... Film production, a combination of art, industry and showmanship, became in substantial measure the recourse of deluded aspirants to easy riches ... Yet such is the glamour of quick and substantial returns which a comparatively small number of producers secure ... that the industry has shown no signs of suffering from lack of new entrepreneurs who are prepared to gamble for high stakes, often at the cost of both the taste of the public and the prosperity of the industry.

(Film Enquiry Committee, [Patil] 1951)

The post-war boom and its impact on the structure and policies in the Indian film industry are captured well by this quote. The principal forces that were set in motion – the collapse of the studio system,[1] the parallel rise of unintegrated production companies and the star system, and the emergence of unaccounted money – shaped the film economy in interesting ways. This "black money,"[2] an important source of capital for the film industry, would eventually invite all kinds of antisocial elements into the film business with some serious consequences to which I return later in the chapter. This chapter examines the three principal sectors of the film industry – exhibition, production, and distribution – to sketch the contours of India's film industry.

Systematic data on the feature film industry are not gathered by any organization in the industry or the government. The Central Board of Film Certification, the National Film Development Corporation, the various film chambers of commerce, unions, national and other trade associations, and the Reserve Bank of India are the institutional sources of data, whereas *Screen, Filmfare*, and *Trade Guide* are some of the magazines that publish trade-related information. A researcher has to piece together these disparate sources of data and attempt to arrive at an understanding of the complexities of this industry.

Available statistics clearly testify to the film industry's mammoth size and importance. It is the ninth largest industry in the country, employing directly or indirectly some 6 million people in production, distribution, and exhibition. The Film Enquiry Committee in 1951 had estimated investment in studios and laboratories at Rs. 60 million, theaters at 260 million, working capital in production at 30 million, and in distribution at 60 million, which came to a total of 410 million rupees (Oomen & Joseph, 1981). One estimate placed the total investment in all sectors of the industry for 1978 at Rs. 7,200 million (Dharap, 1979). By 1998, the industry had grown by more than eight times to an estimated Rs. 60,000 million (Aiyar & Chopra, 1998). In 2001, the Federation of Indian Chambers of Commerce and Industry estimated the size of the entertainment industry at about Rs. 96 billion and projected its growth to about Rs. 286 billion by 2005. Estimates regarding investments in the film sector, however, varied wildly from Rs. 10–13 billion in 2001. Films remain the cornerstone of the entertainment industry in India and drive investment and potential for profits in other related industries.

Exhibition

According to an official estimate, 13 million tickets are sold every day in the approximately 13,000 theaters nationwide, but the actual theatrical attendance may be around 26 million a day. It is practically impossible to obtain exact figures for box office collections in India because theater operators engage in massive deception in order to avoid taxes. According to one theater operator, tax evasion is so rampant in small and medium-sized towns that if a theater sells 1,000 tickets, not even 100 are reported to the tax authorities. Often, theater owners underreport the number of shows per day to swallow the entire box office, thereby cheating both the government and the distributor (Venkanna, *personal communication*, 1997). The distribution representatives who are supposed to watch over the exhibitors collude with them by taking bribes and, as such, except in the cities where the distributors maintain offices, it is difficult for them to get accurate ticket sale data. Taking into account the fact that one third of theaters in the country are in rural areas where underreporting of ticket sales is pervasive, it is reasonable to estimate that at least twice as many tickets are sold in the country compared to the 13 million reported.

Distributors classify theaters based on their location and grossing capacity. Generally speaking, big cities such as Bombay, Delhi, Calcutta, Bangalore, Madras, and Hyderabad are classified as "A" centers; medium-sized cities with populations over 100,000 are "B" centers, and small towns are "C" centers. [...]

Touring cinemas are unique to India. They are a rural phenomenon where a combination of lack of investment, licensing, and other bureaucratic hassles discourage the construction of new theaters. Made up of bamboo walls and thatched roofs, touring theaters operate only in the off-rain season because a heavy storm could wipe out the structure. Furthermore, poor road conditions or even nonexistence of roads in some parts of the country make it nearly impossible for people to visit a theater during the monsoons.

Table 2.1 [...] provides an overall historical picture of the exhibition sector of the industry. Several important issues stand out in terms of the development of this sector. If 1948 is used as a benchmark, as it is a year after independence from Britain, and the number of theaters in every decade is compared, a clear pattern of growth of cinemas emerges. Between 1948 and 1997, the number of theaters in the country more than quadrupled, from 3,003 to 12,772. That is a sizeable growth considering India's backward economy and the relative poverty of the majority of its people. New theater construction, however, has lagged behind the relative growth in population. There are numerous reasons for such a state of affairs including the high land prices in urban centers after 1975 and the capital-intensive nature of theater construction. [...]

Table 2.1. Growth of Cinemas in India

Year	Permanent	Touring	Total
1921	—	—	148
1922	—	—	171
1923	—	—	188
1924	—	—	219
1925	—	—	286
1926	—	—	309
1927	309	37	346
1928	241	34	275
1938	1,213	444	1,657
1948	2,095	908	3,003
1950	2,394	844	3,238
1952–53	2,660	688	3,348
1953–54	2,653	797	3,450
1954–55	2,700	800	3,500
1955–56	2,780	875	3,655
1956–57	2,897	980	3,877
1957–58	2,918	1,088	4,006
1958–59	2,999	1,219	4,218
1959–60	3,082	1,273	4,355
1960–61	3,174	1,325	4,499

Year	Permanent	Touring	Total
1961–62	3,579	1,241	4,820
1962–63	3,593	1,345	4,938
1963–64	3,688	1,428	5,116
1964–65	3,837	1,452	5,289
1965–66	3,808	1,639	5,447
1966–67	3,890	1,739	5,629
1967–68	4,021	1,882	5,903
1968–69	4,232	2,029	6,261
1969–70	4,255	2,286	6,541
1970–71	4,482	2,505	6,987
1971–72	4,590	2,711	7,301
1972–73	4,787	2,801	7,588
1973–74	5,304	2,932	8,236
1974–75	5,468	3,266	8,734
1975–76	5,650	3,367	9,017
1976–77	5,845	3,322	9,167
1977–78	6,030	3,521	9,551
1978–79	6,216	3,744	9,960
1979–80	6,405	4,157	10,562
1980–81	6,667	4,146	10,813
1981–82	6,991	4,248	11,239
1982–83	7,172	4,580	11,752
1985–86	7,703	4,641	12,344
1996–97	—	—	12,772

Source: For 1921–82, see Dharap (1985). For 1985 and 1997, Films Division, Government of India, Bombay.

Production

India's prolific film output is in the range of 800 to 1,000 feature films yearly, which exceeds production in any country in the world. Studios located in Bombay, Madras, Hyderabad, Bangalore, Bhubaneswar, Calcutta, Mysore, and Trivandrum, contribute to that total. Data from the Central Board of Film Certification are useful in examining the broad patterns of production in the country, although they are limited to pictures that are completed. There may be several pictures a year that never reach the completion stage and no organization seems to keep track of such films. Table [2.2] lists feature films and shorts certified for selected years from 1931. Film production has clearly been growing over the years. Although the big jump is seen between the 1930s and 1940s, the industry's nascent years, there was noticeable growth every 10 years. Between 1951 and 1989, the number of films produced grew by a remarkable 71%. It peaked in 1990 with 948 feature films, declined a bit but crossed the threshold of 1,000 films in the year 2001.

A remarkable aspect of Indian cinema is that full-length feature films are made in more than 20 languages. Since the introduction of talkies in 1931, Indian audiences have demanded motion pictures in their own languages and dialects, the result of which is clearly seen in Table 2.5. Features are produced even in languages spoken by relatively small numbers of people limited to parts of a state (e.g., Konkani, Tulu, Bodo, Haryanvi). There were nine features in English as well. This characteristic makes Indian cinema uniquely regional. In cultural terms, language has worked like a shield, a sort of a protective barrier, thereby making indigenous films very competitive to imported films. The phenomenon of dependence on foreign, particularly U.S. films, found in some other parts of the world is not the case with Indian movie-going audiences. The result is, historically speaking, that an estimated 93% of screentime is occupied by regional language films. [...]

Table [2.2]. Indian and Foreign Films Censored in Selected Years

Year	Features			Shorts			Total
	Indian	Foreign	sub Total	Indian	Foreign	sub Total	
1931	28	NA	NA	NA	NA	NA	NA
1941	166	NA	NA	NA	NA	NA	NA
1951	219	320	539	831	2,638	3,469	4,008
1955	287	281	568	498	1,697	2,195	2,763
1960	324	165	489	29	1,457	2,086	2,575
1965	326	200	526	912	1,290	2,202	2,728
1970	396	176	572	1,210	1,078	2,288	2,860
1975	475	102	577	1,220	994	2,214	2,791
1980	742	159	901	1,381	1,660	3,041	3,942
1985	912	128	1,040	1,533	692	2,225	3,265
1989	781	139	920	1,240	419	1,659	2,078
1990	948	NA	NA	NA	NA	NA	
1995	795	220		850	NA	NA	
1996	683	139		934	NA	NA	
1997	697	191		895	272		
1998	693	180		934	365		

Source: For 1931 and 1941 see Dharap (1985, pp. 253–254). For years 1995–1998, see Ministry of Information & Broadcasting [...] For the other years, Central Board of Film Certification, Bombay.

Distribution

Within the commercial cinema, the rate of success is quite limited. Unlike the U.S. film industry where supply is controlled by a handful of oligopolistic corporations with monopoly power,[3] hundreds of Indian producers compete for markets. Some vertically integrated production – distribution companies, all privately held (AVM, Prasad, Annapurna), do make films, but they may not distribute their own pictures nationwide due to the high costs involved. According to Manmohan Shetty, the partner of Ad Labs in Bombay, a major release consisting of 300 prints was estimated to cost approximately Rs. 6 million in print costs (at Rs. 20,000 a print) and an equal amount in publicity expenses (Shetty, *personal communication*, 1984), all of which have nearly doubled in the 1990s. Given the enormity of risks in film distribution, national distribution companies do not exist, but territorial ones are common. As the bulk of the films are made by fly-by-night operators, they simply look for a quick sale to a territorial distributor to recoup their investment. In many a case of box office disaster, as Mitra (1985, p. 166) points out "the men involved have gone bankrupt, pawned the last piece of their wives' jewellery, attempted suicide, gone insane or found refuge in the bottle," but new producers keep arriving.[4] An important factor that seems to drive new investment in film production and distribution is the underground economy in India, which some claim is as large or bigger than the regular economy.

The country is divided into five territories for the purposes of distribution of feature films: south, north, Bombay and the western region, Delhi and Uttar Pradesh, and the eastern region. The foreign market is a separate territory. In the 1980s, a multistarrer, big budget extravaganza in Hindi may have been sold for Rs. 10–12 million per territory. The 1990s were on an entirely different scale. *Daud*, released in August 1997, starring Sanjay Dutt and Urmila Matondkar with A. R. Rahman's music, was reportedly sold for Rs. 20 million per territory, supposedly the highest amount shelled out by distributors at the time for any film (Box Office, 1997, p. 9).

Markets abroad were counted as one single territory for many years because sale of pictures was channeled through a government agency – the National Film Development Corporation. Theatrical markets abroad declined rapidly since the advent of videocassettes in the 1980s as data presented in Tables [2.3 and 2.4] indicate. Although the theatrical revenues were lost by more than half between 1981 and 1988, revenues from sale of rights to video markets outside the country have grown. Marketing Indian films abroad was done poorly by both the privately owned distribution companies and the public sector undertakings. There are many intervening factors for this lackluster performance, not the least of which is ineffective state intervention. [...]

Table [2.3]. Total Export Revenues 1979 Through February 1989 Value of
Canalized Exports
(*Rs in Lakhs*)[a]

Year	Theatrical/TV Rights	Video Rights	Export of Recorded Videocassettes from Seepz[b]	Total
1954	97.13	—	—	97.13
1960	175.89	—	—	175.89
1970	586.00	—	—	586.00
1979–80	1,214.64	—	—	1,214.64
1980–81	1,507.43	—	—	1,507.43
1981–82	1,454.98	16.25	889.00	2,360.23
1982–83	1,150.70	103.00	736.00	1,989.70
1983–84	967.67	185.07	387.00	1,539.74
1984–85	693.85	155.76	386.00	1,235.61
1985–86	618.28	99.58	445.00	1,162.86
1986–87	572.18	146.24	332.00	1,050.12
1987–88	730.68	176.06	221.00	1,127.74
1988–89	606.44	298.19	232.51	1,137.15

[a]A lakh is equivalent to 100,000.
[b]Tax free export zone.
Source: For 1954–1970, see Oomen and Joseph (1981, p. 26). For other years,
National Film Development Corporation, Bombay.

Films are typically sold on the basis of a flat sale, percentage deal, or pre-sale basis
with an advance toward the box office gross. The big budget Hindi films command
the highest price, currently ranging around Rs.10–20 million per territory in India.
Foreign markets are an additional, but increasingly important source of revenue.
As banks generally have been reluctant to invest in film production, producers
often rely on pre-sale to distributors to raise finances, thereby indirectly handing
creative control over production to the distributor. In cases where such pre-sale
cannot be arranged, a producer may borrow funds at high rates of interest (often at
40%–60%) to complete a film (Tripathy, 1989).

Table [2.4].   Number of Films Sold and Revenue from Key Export Markets for Indian Films (1988)

Country	No. of Films	Revenue (Rupees)
Arabian Gulf	179	24,349,000
USSR	18	9,811,000
Indonesia	41	9,484,000
Sri Lanka	30	2,588,000
Burma	17	2,463,000
UK & Ireland	67	2,286,000
Morocco	36	2,031,000
Jordan	28	1,814,000
Fiji Islands	29	1,785,000
Singapore	27	1,642,000
Mauritius	61	1,632,000
Sudan	31	1,288,000
Tanzania	28	1,281,000
Maldives	27	1,214,000
Kenya	22	1,086,000
Malaysia	33	808,000
Yemen, Djibouti, Sanna	13	761,000
West Indies	13	590,000
South/Latin America	12	524,000
Gambia	11	536,000
Nigeria	10	451,000
Liberia	10	331,000

Source: National Film Development Corporation, Bombay.

Pre-sale of pictures to raise production funds is also done by selling ancillary rights, particularly audio rights. The audiocassette market grew exponentially with the proliferation of cassette tape recorders (called "two-in-ones" because they combined a radio with a cassette recorder) since the early 1970s. Gulshan Kumar, the founder of Super Cassette Industries (SCI), started the T-series that used a loophole in the copyright law to reproduce previously recorded music and legally avoid paying royalty to the copyright holder. SCI flooded the market with cheaply produced cassettes and created a new network of dealers and wholesalers to reach into the rural towns, hitherto untapped by its competitors. Kumar's bold initiative and entrepreneurial zeal shook up the stodgy, old record companies like the Gramaphone Company of India (with their famous HMV label). This boom in the cassette market encouraged the growth and easy availability of other popular musical forms such as devotional songs, Hari Kathas, puja tapes, light entertainment music, and even folk music.[5] By the 1990s, this cassette market had grown into an oligopoly from which investment for production could be drawn by two ways. Cassette manufacturers and record companies became producers of films and could also be counted on for buying the audio rights of other pictures. These revenues are considerable for Hindi cinema and one could presume similar development in the regional film industries as well. For example, Gulshan Kumar bought the audio rights of Yash Chopra's *Dil To Paagal Hai* for Rs. 50 million, a record by industry standards. Time, another audio company, bought the rights to *Krishna* for Rs. 10 million for each territory. UTV, a newcomer to the scene, reportedly bought the audio rights of Feroz Khan's *Prem Aggan* for approximately Rs. 35 million (Mahadevan, 1997). Such investment from the audio industry may have contributed to cost escalation in production, but by 1997, it was generally acknowledged that profits from the audio rights had fallen off by about 50% due to competition from television programs that rely on feature film songs (Mahadevan, 1997). Growth of audiocassette sales picked up quickly to a remarkable level. Approximately 400 million audiocassettes were sold in India in 1999, 10% of them outside the country. RPG International, the overseas arm of HMV, raked in Rs. 200 million in 1997–1998, up from Rs. 90 million the year before. Sony Music sold 400,000 units (cassettes and music digital disks) of *Kuch Kuch Hota Hai* (Hindi, 1997) and A. R. Rahman's *Vande Mataram,* a music album celebrating the 50th anniversary of India's independence from Britain (Kohli, 1999). [...]

Global markets

Indian popular cinema historically has been exported to countries where Indians and other South Asians had migrated during the British colonial rule. After World War II, the trail blazers into the global markets were Mehboob Khan, Raj Kapoor, and V. Shantaram. They were able to get an occasional picture released at a regular theater in London and New York. Raj Kapoor's glittering success with Russian audiences is well known when he broke into that market with his film *Awara* (Hindi, 1951) which was dubbed into Russian and released all over the then Soviet Union. Mehboob Khan also succeeded in establishing a distribution agreement with Alexander Korda, a major distributor-exhibitor for *Aan* (Hindi, 1952) for the United Kingdom and other parts of Europe. It was subtitled in 17 different languages and marketed in more than 28 countries bringing in revenues of approximately Rs. 773,060 (Reuben, 1994). India's art cinema, particularly that of Satyajit Ray, Mrinal Sen, and Shyam Benegal still gets an occasional screening in the college and commercial theatrical circuits in the United States and Canada. This historic record, sparse it is, is not something that can be characterized as commercial success as the available data here show.

What is remarkable, however, is the lasting impression that Indian cinema has left on worldwide audiences. In my nearly 20 years of teaching at Northwestern University, I have met several African, Arab, and even some Latin American students whose conversations began with how wonderful a particular film was. They would recall songs and dances and comment on the beauty of Indian actresses. South African audiences, Black and Indian, saw imports from India at segregated theaters throughout the apartheid period. Young people from West Africa studying at Northwestern told me that they would see every Indian film even if it was not dubbed into local languages or subtitled. They seemed to know how to see and understand India's popular cinema. This is an area of research that is still unexplored, and it could be fascinating in terms of aesthetics and cross cultural communication. In Africa, if there is any competition to Hollywood imports, it is not from the British or French films but films imported from India. Although market potential existed all along with both the diaspora audiences and others, exploitation of global markets by Indian producers and distributors was not all that glorious for decades (see Table [2.3]). [...]

Ancillary markets

Revenues from ancillary markets within the country (videocassette, television, audio, etc.) grew rapidly in their first 10 years of existence. According to one newspaper report (*Prajavani*, 1986), the video market consisted of an estimated 40,000 retail outlets, 15,000 buses equipped with video, 20,000 video parlors, and 11,000 hotels with video. In 1986, the estimated turnover in this market was in the range of Rs. 1.5 billion and by 1991 it appears to have grown considerably to Rs. 7 billion ("The booming video market," 1991). Reportedly, Rs. 4 billion of that business was concentrated in the Bombay market.

Given that the cost of a videocassette recorder (VCR) is still too high for most families in India, only some middle class and many upper middle-class households, primarily in urban areas, have VCRs. An estimated 1 million households have VCRs, and video distributors claim that they have penetrated only about 15% of the potential market within the country. Sell-through or outright sale of tapes to individual collectors is still limited. The sale of 25,000 cassettes to video retailers, who will in turn make a dozen copies of the original, is considered a success ("The booming video market," 1991). On an average, only 10,000 to 15,000 cassettes are sold nationally to video retailers. The other retailers, perhaps numbering 30,000, buy pirated copies. Brand new releases cost Rs. 150–180 and even less when the demand dies down (Shankaran, 1991).

In the 1980s, producers hesitated to exploit the video markets, believing that video releases would keep audiences home. The current trend, however, is to extract revenues out of the growing market. Manmohan Desai, who made *Ganga, Jamuna, Saraswati* (1988), was reported to have sold the video rights of the film for an estimated Rs. 4 million and some 50,000 cassettes were released in India while the film played in theaters. As pirated copies of the new releases circulate, no matter what, Desai's strategy to take in as much revenue up front from the video market worked. In 1991, Raj Kapoor's *Henna* and Subhash Ghai's *Saudagar* were claimed to have been sold for Rs. 6.5 million to Rs. 7.5 million (Shankaran, 1991). These are, however, extraordinary cases because of the high status of the directors and production "values" in the films. On an average, video rights in the country fetched about Rs. 2 million.

The quality of dubbed cassettes was very poor as the video wholesalers in India and abroad did not pay much attention to signal quality. Introduction of laser disks in the late 1980s, at least in the international markets, could have provided additional revenues from individual collectors of films abroad. Production and marketing of laser disks was done rather poorly and a good opportunity was missed. Sony introduced a lesser quality technology called video CD in India in 1996–1997. The growing number of homes with DVD in the U.S.-Canada, however, has resulted in Indian films being available in that better quality format. Between 1998 and 2001, the demand for DVDs of Indian movies grew rapidly and major Indian distributors expanded their inventory from 15–20 titles to 15,000 titles. Video was clearly on the way out. At the same time, the demand for theatrical release of Indian films also grew at such a pace that even Hollywood began to pay attention to Indian popular cinema. Typical big budget extravaganzas with major stars began to be released simultaneously on 55–60 screens in 35–40 cities across North America. While Hindi cinema dominated the screens with four or five new releases every month, Tamil films were not far behind.

Another development was the practice of placing advertisements in videos by Indian film producers. A well-publicized film, produced as a blockbuster, would be released on video with commercial breaks every 10 minutes. This is a lesson that the producers seem to have learned from the U.S. broadcasting industry. *Saudagar* (Hindi, 1991), a big budget picture directed by Subhash Ghai, received such a release. The film was so saturated with commercial breaks that it had to be placed on two videocassettes. The producer was believed to have charged $10,000 to the video distributor in the United States for placing these advertisements in his film (Gandhi, *personal communication*, 1991). [...]

Underworld dons and racketeers

An international network of thugs connecting Bombay, Karachi, and Dubai has come to dominate Hindi film production and distribution. The relationship between the film industry and the underworld is laced with cases of extortion, murder, exile, extravagant lifestyles, glitzy parties with stars, and millions of dollars of unaccounted money being laundered through the movie industry. India's news media have covered the nexus between the underworld and the film industry extensively since the lid broke wide open with the murder of Gulshan Kumar in 1997. In December 2000, the Bombay police released audio recordings of cellular phone conversations between Nazim Rizvi and a don in Dubai. The recording revealed names and illegal practices that are punishable under the Maharashtra Control of Organized Crime Act (Raval & Chopra, 2001). The floodgate of information on the interconnections between filmmaking and the mafia opened and it became quickly apparent that the problem was far more serious than any one had imagined. It led to the sensational arrest of Bharat Shah, a major film financier and the king of the country's diamond trade, for alleged mafia involvement and racketeering.

One of the key reasons for mafia involvement in the film business is that the Indian government did not recognize film as a legitimate "industry" until 1998, which meant that institutional financing was not available to producers, distributors, exhibitors, or any business connected with film. Some banks have ventured into financing films, especially if the producer could put up a collateral toward the loan. Institutional financing is available only in those states that have set up incentive mechanisms to boost production and other related enterprises in their own turf. In Karnataka and Andhra Pradesh, which instituted certain support mechanisms to help develop a local film industry, the resources allocated are never enough, whether it is for infrastructural development (studios, labs, importation of equipment, and so on) or grants for starting filmmakers or even bridge financing.[6] In the absence of such needed measures, producers have historically resorted to raising the money from private investors who come primarily from construction, jewelry, and assorted trades. Given the glamour and glitz associated with film, it is quite common to find all sorts of investors to get involved in this business. When producers are desperate to complete a picture into which they have sunk huge sums of money, they are often willing to pay usurious rates of interest (36%–40%) to an investor. Not only are there such high returns in lending money to film producers, but unaccounted money can be put to use in an industry where stars and others usually get paid in cash and receipts are issued only for a fraction of the total amount involved.

Another significant reason for the mafia involvement in the film industry may have come about when desperate producers sought help from the dons to obtain shooting dates with stars who are in high demand. Rizvi and others seem to have been involved in such criminal conspiracy and attempted murder against Rakesh Roshan, a major producer in Bombay and his son, Hrithik, a heartthrob of the Hindi film audience (Joseph, 2000). Shah Rukh Khan, another major star, confirmed that he received threatening calls from the mafiosi for 4 years and had kept the police informed of those events ("I've been receiving threats," 2001).

Evidence of "black money" in the Indian economy is not new but its size and significance have grown since the 1970s to gain the dubious status of a parallel economy. In the 1997–1998 national budget, the finance minister introduced the Voluntary Disclosure of Income Scheme, basically an amnesty program allowing tax evaders to come forward. It met with such huge success and surprised everyone including the news media by bringing in 400,000 persons who owned up to undisclosed assets amounting to Rs. 330 billion. The revenue netted by the government amounted to Rs. 100.5 billion. In a nation of some 300 million working people, it is reported that the number of persons who file income tax returns is about 1.2 million, which is negligibly small. What the amnesty program revealed clearly was that those who came forward to pay represented just the tip of the iceberg of the parallel economy ("Luring blackmoney," 1998, p. 12). Real estate tycoons, diamond merchants, industrialists, and even petty traders loaded with unaccounted money have found it relatively easy to invest in film production and distribution.

Every few years, the income tax authorities conduct raids on major film personalities and find unaccounted money, gold, diamonds, and other assets buried in all sorts of odd spaces in their lavishly furnished houses. None of the culprits has been charged with or jailed for any criminal offense. In fact, no one seems to bother about why none of them has been punished by the concerned government authorities. Such an episode took place in Bombay in December 1996, when the income tax authorities recovered about Rs. 160.5 million from the undeclared assets of major film stars. The government seized certain assets from the residences and offices of the following leading film industry people: Shah Rukh Khan, Rs. 15 million; Madhuri Dixit and her secretary Rakesh Nath, Rs. 41.7 million; Karishma Kapoor, Rs. 1.9 million; Sunil Shetty, Rs. 5 million; Ajay Devgan, Rs. 12 million; Veeru Devgan, Rs. 2.7 million; Anu Malik, Rs. 15 million; K.C. Bokadia, Rs. 9 million; David Dhawan, Rs. 15 million; Morani Brothers, Rs. 11.7 million; Mahesh Bhatt, Rs. 6 million; Kumar Shanu, Rs. 2 million; Firoz Nadiadwala, Rs. 16 million; and others 12 million (Pachouly, 1997). Such an atmosphere in the country when the laws are flouted by the rich and powerful can only encourage more criminal activity. It is not surprising then to find pirates, thieves, criminals, and underworld dons attempting their hand in the film industry.

It was widely known that Haji Mastan, an underworld don in Bombay, attempted to invest in film production in the 1970s. No investigations were conducted and neither was there any concern expressed by the government or the industry regarding such involvement by undesirable elements of Indian society. For various reasons, Mastan did not make film production a priority business according to the press reports of this period. The situation appears to have changed quite dramatically since the 1980s. Not only were films made with funds from the underworld with its vast connection to trade in the Gulf countries, but film stars, producers, and others participated in this wholeheartedly or unquestioningly. Film stars socializing with well-known mafia types were splashed in fanzines and no police investigations were launched. Everything came to a head and the dam of information broke in August 1997 when Gulshan Kumar, a multimillionaire who owned the music conglomerate firm SCI, was gunned down in broad daylight in Bombay.

Kumar's murder focused the media's attention on the nexus between the industry and the underworld. It is a story that could not be hushed up anymore as there are many privately controlled television channels now and generally people's curiosity about film stars and other personalities is insatiable. The clues were visible for all to see sometime ago. For example, Divya Bharati, a rising star in Hindi cinema, was reported to have committed suicide in 1993, with speculation that she or her husband had dealings with Ibrahim Dawood, a Bombay-mafia don operating out of Karachi, Pakistan and Dubai. If anyone in the industry had reliable information on this tragic death, they certainly did not come forward with it. Another important fissure in the industry occurred when Sanjay Dutt, a leading male star was arrested in 1993 under the Terrorist and Disruptive Activities (Prevention) Act.[7]

The 1993 bomb blasts in Bombay exposed the connection between the film industry and the underworld. Sanjay Dutt was arrested by the police for allegedly storing five AK-47 machine guns in his house, the possession of which is illegal in the country. While the highly publicized case meandered through the special courts, no inquiry was conducted by the government regarding the underworld's involvement in the film industry.

Ibrahim Dawood, a major don from Karachi, entered the Bombay film scene in the 1980s. He started throwing lavish parties in India and abroad to cultivate the glitterati. Stars flew to Dubai and other cities to entertain Dawood's friends and enjoy themselves. Dawood and other dons also started putting money into Hindi film productions with big budgets. Unheard of people became producers overnight. Hanif Kadawala and Samir Lakdawala, both well-known video pirates, were made film producers by Dawood. Sudhakar Bokade, a former Air India cargo handler, Mukesh Duggal, a small garments trader, and Dinesh Patel, a clothes-shop owner, also launched big budget films with stars such as Dilip Kumar and Sanjay Dutt. According to one estimate, underworld money funded as much as 40% of Mumbai's films in the 1990s (Koppikar, 1997).

Investors usually attempt to influence the content of the films as well. Not only did Hindi cinema go through a major shift in the 1980s in its looks, but smugglers and other such villains became larger than life, a position usually reserved for the hero. There were other pressures on the movie industry from the underworld. Director Partho Ghosh reported receiving a few calls from Delhi demanding that he change the name of his film, *Mustafa* (apparently Prophet Muhammad's name). The title was changed to *Ghulam-e-Mustafa* (Koppikar, 1997).

For various reasons, the underworld investors have turned to extortion and murder. The real estate industry, another lucrative source for profits in a city like Bombay, went into a slump in the 1990s and many speculate that may have been another reason for this change in business tactics. The movie industry personalities are considered "soft targets" by the underworld because underworld bosses know which film industry person has the illegal funds and where they may be hidden.

In an interview with V. Shankar Aiyar, associate editor of *India Today*, Abu Salem, a close associate of Dawood, denied that the cold-bloded murder of Gulshan Kumar was done by his men. When asked if his gang is involved in extortion of the film industry people, Salem replied, "No, no. We have excellent relations with many film wallahs. If we want to kill, we kill. We've done that many times. But Gulshan was among our good friends. It's all political" (Koppikar, 1997, p. 22). To a question about extortion from several leading film personalities including Rajiv Rai and Subhash Ghai, two leading producers and directors of Hindi films, Salem replied, "I had sent my boys only to speak to Rajiv. If we wanted to, we could have killed him and his guard." Rai was spared in an attack that took place near his office in Bombay. Aiyar posed the question, "But Bollywood claims it has no ties with the underworld?" Salem emphatically stated, *"Sabke bain* [All of them have]. You give me your number and name the person. I will have him talk to you." Aiyar probed him further, "Are you involved in funding the film industry?" Abu Salem replied, "I am not going to answer that. It is known to bade bhai [elder brother, Dawood] and, he doesn't tell me about his investments. I am just a small pawn" (Koppikar, 1997, p. 22).

If these reports are accurate, Abu Salem clearly confirmed the link between the underworld dons and the film industry. The scenario that has been reported in the press is that Gulshan Kumar was on notice by Dawood to part with Rs. 10 million. Apparently Kumar had paid one installment and refused to pay more. On August 5, Kumar had come from Delhi to Bombay. He received a phone call that day in which the caller demanded some money. On August 8, there was another phone call which was witnessed by his younger brother, Darshan Kumar. "They said if you haven't yet informed the Mumbai[8] Police then you obviously are not taking us seriously. And you better take us seriously." Gulshan's apparent reply to the caller was, "I am doing my *dharma* [duty]; you do yours." The calls stopped but Kumar was hunted down and killed in broad daylight on August 12 (Koppikar, 1997). [...]

Notes

1   For a detailed account of the rise and fall of the studio system see (Garga, 1996).

2   I am aware of the racial connotations of this term and am noting it here to ensure that the reader sees the context of its usage in India. [...]

3   Issues relating to the structure of the U.S. film industry after World War II have been extensively researched by Wasko (1995), Pendakur (1990), and Guback (1969). For pre-war years, the best work was done by Huettig (1948). [...]

4   One producer, who had made 11 features, told me that he lost Rs. 5 million between 1972 and 1985 (personal communication, 1984).

5   Hari Katha is a story-telling form that was popular in rural India. Steeped in the oral tradition, one itinerant narrator, usually a male, performed stories from the two great epics combining songs and dialogue. These performances occurred late at night in the temple or some public space. He was paid by donations collected at each performance. Their popularity with all age groups was considerable but cinema and television have cut into these kinds of leisure activities. These Hari Kathas, however, survive on audiocassettes and many middle-class, Hindu households buy such cassettes and listen to them on festival days. [...]

6   Also known as completion money in the business, it is the gap between the funds raised by a producer and what is actually needed to complete the picture.

7   This draconian law came under serious criticism for how it was abused by the authorities. Finally, the law was allowed to lapse in 1995 and the central government has proposed the Prevention of Terrorism Bill, 2000 which will force journalists to reveal any information they may have on "terrorist activities" and punish them if they refuse to cooperate. If the bill is passed with this provision, it could seriously impinge on the rights and freedoms enjoyed by the media in India (Mitta, 2000).

8   Bombay became Mumbai; Calcutta got changed to Kolkota; Trivandrum became Tiruvananthapuram, and Madras was rechristened as Chennai. Political parties make the false claim that such renaming infuses national pride.

References

Aiyar, S. V. and Chopra, A (1998) *Film Industry. Waiting for Action*, www.india-today.com/itoday/2051998/biz.html, May 25, retrieved August 10, 2001.

Box Office (1997) *Screen*, August 29.

Dharap, B.V. (1979) *Indian Films 1977 & 1978*. Pune: Motion Picture Enterprises.

Dharap, B.V. (1985) *Indian Films 1983*. Pune: National Film Archive of India.

Garga, B.D. (1996) *So Many Cinemas. The Motion Picture in India*. Mumbai: Eminence Designs Pvt. Ltd.

Guback, T.H. (1969) *The International Film Industry: Western Europe and America since 1945*. Bloomington: Indiana University Press.

Huettig, M.D. (1948) *Economic Control of the Motion Picture Industry: A Study in Industrial Organization*. Philadelphia: University of Pennsylvania Press.

'I've been receiving threats for four years: Shah Rukh' (2001) www.rediff.com/news/2001/feb/26shah1.htm, February 26, retrieved August 8, 2001.

Joseph, M. (2000) 'Scenes of the Mafia'. *Outlook*, December 25.

Kohli, V. (1999) 'Look, here's a booming market!', www.businessworldindia.com/archive/99027/mktg1.htm, February 7, retrieved July 27, 2000.

Koppikar, S. (1997) 'Murder in Mumbai'. *India Today*, August 25.

'Luring blackmoney' (1998) Editorial. *The Hindu*, January 8, 12.

Mahadevan, S. (1997) 'Swing high swing low'. *Filmfare*, 124–126.

Mitra, S. (1985) 'Cinema. The fading glitter'. *India Today*, December 31.

Mitta, M. (2000) 'TADA Mark II threatens media', www.expressindia.com/ie/daily/2000529/ina29023.html, May 28, retrieved July 16, 2001.

Oomen, M.A. and Joseph, K.V. (1981) *Economics of Film Industry in India*. Gurgaon: Academic Press.

Pachouly, M. (1997) 'I-T dept recovers Rs.16.5 cr from film stars'. *Mid-Day*, September 13, 1.

[Patil, S.K. (1951) *Report of the Film Enquiry Committee*. New Delhi: Government of India Press.]

Pendakur, M. (1990) *Canadian Dreams and American Control: The Political Economy of the Canadian Film Industry*. Detroit: Wayne State University Press.

Prajavani (1986) *Bangalore*, January 31.

Raval, S. and A. Chopra (2001) 'Bollywood body blow'. *India Today*, 23–28.

Reuben, B. (1994) *Mehboob ... India's DeMille: The First Biography*. New Delhi: Indus.

Shankaran, J. (1991) 'Pros and cons of video trade'. *Screen*, October 25, 21–22.

Tripathy, S. (1989) 'Ganga Jamuna Saraswathi. Formula Failure'. *India Today*, January 31.

Wasko, J. (1995) *Hollywood in the Information Age*. Austin: University of Texas Press.

6

Introduction: Indian popular cinema as a slum's eye view of politics
by Ashis Nandy

Mahmood Jamal's charming documentary on Indian popular cinema, *Peacock Screen,* and the official report, *Mass Media in India 1992,* compiled by India's Ministry of Information and Broadcasting, both tell us that on an average day, India releases more than two-and-a-half feature films, produced by the world's largest film industry, and sees some 15 million people throng the country's 13,002 cinema halls.[1] As if this were not enough, these films are an important cultural presence from Russia to North Africa and from the Caribbean to Fiji. Operating in a country with an average per capita income of about US$330 a year, one of the lowest in the world, this is no mean feat for an industry that few in India take seriously, except as a revenue earner. Even other Indian industrialists are dismissive towards the film producers; none of India's more respected chambers of commerce would like to be caught with a film-maker among its office bearers.

What does this immensely successful but slighted industrial product stand for, politically and culturally? Does it have anything to say about the fate of popular culture in societies transiting from older modes of cultural self-expression to a more impersonal, centrally controlled, mass culture? This [chapter] gives possible answers. The answers presume that the Indian commercial cinema, to be commercially viable, must try to span the host of cultural diversities and epochs the society lives with, and that effort has a logic of its own.

The logic accepts that the product called Indian popular cinema has undergone change. It is very different today from the pioneering days of Dadasaheb Phalke or Phalkemuni, as Christopher Byrski affectionately calls him to underscore the continuity between classical Sanskrit plays and Bombay cinema.[2] It is different even from the days of Bombay Talkies, New Theatres, Raj Kapoor and Guru Dutt. In the industry itself, I understand, thoughtful persons talk of the earlier years as an age of innocence. By which they mean, I presume, that the heritage has to be remembered and respected, not emulated. What has that loss of innocence entailed? That story cannot be told without involving one other actor of the kind Indian popular cinema has rarely handled comfortably and self-consciously: the politics of culture in India and, for that matter, the whole of South Asia.

Once the role of that other politics is accepted, the right metaphor for the Indian popular cinema, alias conventional, commercial or Bombay cinema, turns out to be the urban slum. Ratnakar Tripathy, who first suggested the metaphor to me, seemed to hold that both cinema and the slum in India showed the same impassioned negotiation with everyday survival, combined with the same intense effort to forget that negotiation, the same mix of the comic and the tragic, spiced with elements borrowed indiscriminately from the classical and the folk, the East and the West. However, there is at least one other sense in which the metaphor of the slum seems apt: the popular cinema is the slum's point of view of Indian politics and society and, for that matter, the world. There is in both of them the same stress on lower-middle-class sensibilities and on the informal, not-terribly-tacit theories of politics and society the class uses and the same ability to shock the *haute bourgeoisie* with the directness, vigour and crudity of these theories.

The slum here means exactly what architect and social activist Jai Sen means when he speaks of the 'unintended city' – the city that was never a part of the formal 'master plan' but was always implicit in it.[3] The official city cannot survive without its unintended self, but it cannot own up to that self either. For that other city consists of a huge mass of technically and officially discarded 'obsolete' citizens who form the underground of a modern city. They provide the energy – literally the cheap labour – that propels both the engine of civic life in a Third World society and the ambitions of its modernizing élite.

The discarded, obsolete population that inhabits the unintended city is a constant embarrassment to the rest of their urbane brethren – in the way that the concerns and style of popular cinema are often an embarrassment to the devotees of art films and high culture.[4] These discards show the same cussed unwillingness to bow out of history and the same obstinate ability to return and 'illegitimately' occupy a large space in the public domain, geographically and psychologically.

Are inhabitants of the unintended city the passive objects or tools of history they are often made out to be? Are they only an urban proletariat waiting to be organized into a new political formation? Or are they the makers of their own destiny [...]? Is the apparent obsolescence of the unintended city merely a camouflage that hides a crucial repressed, disowned self of a modernizing society? Is the shock many 'enlightened' Indians claim to feel when facing the aesthetics of the slum, the shock of seeing one's own face in a convex mirror, which distorts but does so in one specific way, according to the strict laws of optics?

Before grappling with these strange questions, a word on the political and social contours of the slum. Nearly half of metropolitan India today lives in slums, as if anticipating a world in which, according to environmentalist Edward Gold-smith, more than half of humanity will live in slums in another two decades. There is nothing particularly strange about this; the slum is often the first visible marker of modernization in Third World society. In both Bombay and Calcutta, the slum-dwellers are in a clear majority; if their present rates and patterns of growth continue, both cities will become 80 per cent slum by the year 2010. However, even in cities where they constitute a small minority, the slum-dwellers loom large on the urban consciousness as a dark, ominous, ill-understood, unmanageable presence. For the slum, whatever its socio-economic status, has now come close to the heart of India's urban, middle-class consciousness. It now sets the tone of India's political culture, even if as a negative utopia or dystopia. About 25 per cent of all Indians now live in urban settlements and they are directly exposed to the urban-industrial world and the media network that supports its cultural style, pan-Indian homogeneity and global connection. These Indians live with the standard nightmares of the middle classes the world over, of which the fear of the slum is one.

Twenty-five per cent may not sound particularly impressive, but in absolute terms it is enormous. It amounts to more than 225 million people, larger than all except four countries in the world. It is larger than the population of each of the neighbouring countries of India, of which many Indians choose to live in mortal fear. Even if we take 175 million as a conservative estimate of the size of India's urban middle class, it is three times the size of the population of Britain, which once ruled India, with an industrial base larger than Britain's. With this size go greater skills in entering and coping with the modern institutions and a growing ability to influence the country's mainstream culture of politics.

Things could not be otherwise, given the definitions of state, nationalism, national security, secular statecraft, professional expertise, civil society and development the country has opted for. The entire ideology of the Indian state is so formatted and customized that it is bound to make more sense – and give political advantages – to those better acquainted with the urban-industrial world and modern economic and political institutions. The rest are supposed to either painstakingly train themselves to enter that world or cope with the ideology from the outside as best as they can. In a plebiscitary democracy threatening to become a psephocracy, numbers count; and though in the last six decades rural India has arrived politically, even the cause of rural India has now to be processed through the urban middle-class consciousness. Some of the most powerful public figures with inelastic support bases or vote banks have not exercised real power or controlled the course of political events because they have undervalued the middle-class culture of public life. They have managed, within a short time, to offend the intelligentsia and the bureaucracy and to alienate the media, and in the process lose their legitimacy and political manoeuvrability.[5]

This veto exercised by the public sensibilities of a minority has ensured the Indian middle class a disproportionate access to state power [since 1978] and has pushed the culture of Indian politics in directions that would have been unthinkable earlier. The class now gives a sustainable base to the emerging mass culture of politics in the country and, to do so, has redrawn the map of the popular culture mainly created by the class itself in the pre-war years. Structurally, this sustainable base mostly consists of the more numerous lower-middle class, exposed to modern media, pan-Indian politics and the global market. It is the class that has closest links with the slum and lives with the fear of slipping into a slum or never getting out of it.

The definition of the middle class used here is obviously more political-cultural than economic or social. It does not conform to the standard textbook definitions of the class. We are talking of a social stratum that lives with hopes of breaking into the upper echelons of society and provides a political base and the power of numbers to the upper-middle class, which in turn, unlike the upper-middle classes in some other societies, maintains continuities with the lower-middle class in political and cultural tastes. The Indian upper-middle class may have some of the economic features of an élite, but it has not tried to distance itself from the culture of the lower-middle class. Much of India's upper-middle class is simply a lower-middle class with more money. More important, such a class is not big enough in size to influence the political process by itself; it has to carry the lower-middle class with it. This has not proved difficult. The lower-middle class is shot through with fears of demotion to the proletariat and lives with the anxieties associated with that fear and with the standard hopes and ambitions of the middle class. It cherishes its political-cultural links with the upper-middle class. It is willing to be led.

One must read the political and cultural self-expression of the slum against the backdrop of this political-cultural closure. The language of the slum in India is the lower-middle-class reading of the culture of the *haute bourgeoisie* into which it breaks in fantasy, memories of a peasant or rural past serving as a pastoral 'paradise' from which it has been banished, fears about the urban-industrial jungle into which it feels it has already strayed, and anxieties about the 'amoral' frame of modern life into which it fears it might any day slip. It is a psychological existence at the margins of at least two utopias, one of them located – as with all utopias – in the future and the other paradoxically in the past. Everything else – the reactive grandiloquence, the stylized idiom, the conventions and mannerisms of self-expression we see in Indian commercial cinema and increasingly in Indian politics – follows from these mediations. The slum in India is not so much the enforced abode of the industrial proletariat or the urban poor, atomized and massified. It is an entity that territorializes the transition from the village to the city, from the East to the West, and from the popular-as-the-folk to the popular-as-the-massified. The slum is where the margins of lower-middle-class consciousness are finally defined.

If there is a tacit overall political argument in this analysis, it is that the passions of, and the self-expressions identified with, the lower-middle class – for that matter, the middle class as a whole – now constitute the ideological locus of Indian politics. This social sector is now capable of sustaining large-scale, ambitious political and aesthetic initiatives that were beyond its capability [in the 1970s]. On the other hand, it has lost some of its earlier élan and creativity which came from being a minority experimenting with new ideas, forms of self-expression and modes of dissent the traditional élite could not risk exploring.

If the middle class plays a role in Indian society and politics disproportionate to its size, so do popular films. These films, it is true, are seen by a wide cross-section of people, and their appeal is certainly not sectoral. But they are produced, conceived and executed within the middle-class culture, more specifically within the confines of the lower-middle-class sensitivities we have discussed. In fact, they are threatening to turn both the folk and the classical into second-order presences (the way the immensely successful television serials on the Ramayana and the Mahabharata now influence the frame for interpreting the epics for a large number of Indians) and, today, even the global mass culture enters the subcontinent filtered through the same middle-class sensitivities epitomized by the commercial cinema. It is in this sense that the popular cinema represents the low-brow version of the values, ambitions and anxieties of Indians who are caught between two cultures, two lifestyles, and two visions of a desirable society.[6]

To return to our metaphor, the urban slum consists of people who are uprooted and partially decultured, people who have moved out of traditions and have been forced to loosen their caste and community ties. That does not mean that the slum has no access to cultural traditions. Often the resilience of cultures is seen in the most dramatic fashion in the urban slum. Two processes are central to an understanding of this resilience.

First, the slum recreates the remembered village in a new guise and resurrects the old community ties in new forms. Even traditional faiths, piety and kinship ties survive in slums, wearing disguises paradoxically supplied by their own massified versions.[7] The slum may even have its version of classicism. It is not what classicism should be according to the classicists, but what classicism often is, when bowdlerized and converted into its popular version for easy digestion and saleability in a mass market.

Second, the slum creates its own culture out of the experiences of the slum itself: out of the close encounters between the different time periods and diverse cultures telescoped into the slum; out of the impact of 'strange' communities, ethnicities and world-views on the individual; and out of interactions with the alien world of impersonal institutions that have begun to penetrate even the more sleepy South Asian communities.

Both processes are conspicuous in the popular film – the remembered village and the compacted heterogeneity of stranger-neighbours, with the former often providing a frame to cope with the latter. That is why the popular film ideally has to have everything – from the classical to the folk, from the sublime to the ridiculous, and from the terribly modern to the incorrigibly traditional, from the plots within plots that never get resolved to the cameo roles and stereotypical characters that never get developed. Such films cannot usually have a clear-cut story line or a single sequence of events, as in, say, the dramatic, event-based, popular films of Hollywood or even Hong Kong. An average, 'normal', Bombay film has to be, to the extent possible, everything to everyone. It has to cut across the myriad ethnicities and lifestyles of India and even of the world that impinges on India. The popular film *is* low-brow, modernizing India in all its complexity, sophistry, naiveté and vulgarity. Studying popular film *is* studying Indian modernity at its rawest, its crudities laid bare by the fate of traditions in contemporary life and arts. Above all, it is studying caricatures of ourselves – social and political analysts negotiating the country's past and present – located not at the centre, studying others, as we like to see ourselves, but at the peripheries, standing as spectators and looking at others studying themselves and us. The popular cinema may be what the middle class, left to itself, might have done to itself and to India, but it is also the disowned self of modern India returning in a fantastic or monstrous form to haunt modern India.

Does this mean that the popular film threatens India's cultural élite by confronting them with the underside of their own dreams? Does it inadvertently mock this élite's vision of a desirable society by taking it seriously and standing it on its head? The answers to both these questions may well be 'yes'.

The politics of popular cinema is not a hermeneutic puzzle, nor is it enticingly tacit. It does not require sophisticated analytic schemes of the kind that an Indian postmodernist might cherish. It is often vulgarly blatant. But it is never trivial, not even when it is expressed in films that are trivial. Witness for instance the way the politician as a character has entered the popular cinema during the last decade as a *khadi*-wearing villain. As one box-office hit after another shows, the politician-as-villain today is not merely a counterpoint to the hero-as-the-anti-hero who repels many film analysts, disgusted with the surfeit of violence and sex in cinema [...]. He is also the counterpoint to the less violent, more androgynous heroes who once represented for the Westernized Indians everything that was wrong with Mother India. The early model of the hero survives, but increasingly as a nostalgic moral presence in a world dominated by their new, street-smart, ultra-violent incarnations. In film after film, it is the politician-as-villain who pushes the innocent *Devdas*-like hero into a life of crime and violence, into his new incarnation as an anti-hero. In film after film, characters close to the earlier model of the hero are unable to cope with the new villains, who have entered the popular cinema and, presumably, Indian life. Elsewhere, I have tried to show how the same problem is sometimes posed in popular Indian cinema through what for such cinema is the evergreen device of a double.[8] The hero who is non-violent and innocent, having a culturally rooted moral self and a sense of limits, is shown incapable of handling his problems, which have to be solved by his lookalike, an exteriorized projection of his self who usually happens to be a ruthless, hyper-masculine industrialist of violence.

The trajectory of Amitabh Bachchan's life in almost every one of his popular films recapitulates the life of the Indian cinema – its movement from the days of Dilip Kumar, Raj Kapoor and Dev Anand to that of Bachchan. It is not a coarse simplification to say that in a typical Bachchan film, the hero begins his life in the first reel as a Dilip Kumar or a Raj Kapoor – as, for that matter, any of the more innocent, ethical, visionary heroes of yesteryear – and ends up midway in the narrative as none other than Bachchan himself.[9] The anti-hero, when he turns against the villain, also turns against the 'passive', 'effeminate', ineffective hero and, if I may add, against the popularly perceived cause of the decline and collapse of the imagined world of pastoral innocence and moral incorruptibility. To invoke the well-known psycho-analytic formulation of an ego defence, he turns against a self that has become identified with failure and impotency. Perhaps this is not merely true of the life-cycle of the heroes Bachchan portrays in his more violent films, but also his real-life career in films. He *has* moved from playing the role of the quiet, well-behaved but effete hero, in films that were but minor successes, to his triumphant portrayals of angry, violent vigilantes functioning at the margins of the society. Ontogeny, as the biologists say, replicates phylogeny.[10]

In a parallel development, the villain has become more handsome, polished, erotically attractive, modern and in full control of himself. Villainy is his not-so-secret self; it is kept only formally a secret. The decline of politics in India and that of the moral status of the politician – living in a world of local toughs available on

hire, trade-union gangsters, violent college elections, corrupt police, petty smugglers – were captured in Indian popular cinema long before they became the
subjects of heated debate in the columns of newspapers and among political
scientists.[...]

The glorification of vigilantism in cinema has come not simply because the
politician-as-villain symbolizes the decline of politics and the subversion of the
judiciary, the law-enforcing agencies and the state itself – the trust in them was
never remarkably high among the wily Indians – but because the communities in
South Asia have begun to come apart. The individual is being increasingly left
stranded, with only his or her own tattered moral self, and the fantasies of a secret
self represented by the vigilantism of the hero as the anti-hero-turned-superman.

Like all politics, however, the politics of popular cinema, too, is the art of the
possible. Despite the growing emphasis on individual evil and heroism, it cannot
cater to only that sector of the society to which these themes appeal. It has to be, as
I have said, all things to all people. It has to simultaneously reaffirm values that go
against such individuation of good and evil. Perhaps here lies one of popular
cinema's durable ties with 'eternal India'. Many years ago, A. L. Basham noticed in
his *A Cultural History of India* the continuity between classical Sanskrit plays and
contemporary films. And more recently Byrski has shown how such continuities
are worked out in a specific context by comparing Kalidas's *Abhigyan Shakuntalam*
and Raj Kapoor's *Satyam, Shivam, Sundaram*.[11] Such continuities may or may not
exemplify the deployment of the traditional *rasa* theory (classical poetics governing
Sanskritic poetry and theatre) in a modern cinematic context; they must, while
bringing in elements of modernity in Indian concepts of good and evil, simultaneously rebel against such importation. Perhaps even the presence of all the nine
prescribed *rasas* of classical poetics comes in as a technology of checks and
counterchecks that contends against every excess. The ultimate remedy of a trendy
'pathology' within the popular cinema is not changes in fashion, of the kind
available within a mass market, but the seeds of 'self-destruction' the trend or
genre carries within itself.

Thus, a decade of sweet romance and chocolate-pie heroes is followed by a
decade of revenge-seeking, thin-lipped, homicidal heroes. They, too, in due course
yield place to a new trend of, say, teenage romances featuring fresh actors and
actresses or a new mythological mode defined by, say, brand new goddesses who
seem fully attuned to the psychological demands of urban India.[12] For after a
particular level of awareness has been 'mobilized' for the box office by a particular
genre, fatigue or boredom sets in and other levels have to be mobilized to sustain
interest in the product.

Often the balance is restored within the film itself. Sometimes violence is
neutralized by comic interludes or by the inclusion of a more comic version of the
violence. In *Appu Raja*, while a life-and-death battle rages, one associate of the
hero tickles into submission a member of the enemy gang. In *Kishen Kanhaiya* the
villains, at the end of all the violence, seem to make fun of their own humiliation.
In *Don*, while the hero and the villain fight their climactic battle towards the end,
the hero – none other than the much-maligned retailer of violence, Bachchan –
stops midway to ask permission from the villain to eat a *paan* before resuming the

life-and-death struggle. In *Naseeb*, a climactic scene of violence is also the final choreography of a film that is a carnival – as if the audience were being reminded in a Brechtian manner that the depicted violence is only a pretence. Likewise with sexuality. The heroine who is a cabaret dancer by profession is usually doubly submissive as a daughter-in-law and out-mothers her sisters-in-law when it comes to the younger generation of the joint family.

To return to our defining metaphor for one last time: the slum may or may not be ugly, it may or may not symbolize absurdity, but it always has a story to tell about the state of the vitality, creativity and moral dynamism of the society that defines the relationship between the slum and suburbia. That story can take many forms. The slum can be read as the past of the suburbia or as an alternative to or decline from it. It can even be romanticized and invested with the vision of a desirable society or a lost utopia, as Sai Paranjape's *Katha*, Saeed Mirza's *Raju Ban Gaya Gentleman* and the television serial *Nukkad* come so close to doing. That vision is often built on the slum's capacity to recreate a community, sometimes even an entire village with its own distinctive lifestyle. Obviously, a mimic village is never quite like the original one, but the reconstruction can be an impressive cultural enterprise. It tells not so much the history of the slum as the past it tries to remember or pines for, its self-created myths of origin and visions of the future, its adaptive strategies, the politics of culture that shapes it while it desperately tries to incorporate aspects of alien cultures that could be more charitable to the surviving fragments of a community-based culture.

The legitimacy of popular cinema in India is based on a similar set of equations. Such cinema is both a 'romantic' attempt to reconstitute an increasingly imaginary village, and a dialogue with the compacted heterogeneity of urban-industrial India. The attempt challenges the way the problem of cultural invasion through popular films has sometimes been posed by the social scientists and film critics. The local, the small-scale and the vernacular are not merely being *supplanted* by an urban, individualistic, aggressively Western, global mass culture leading to a more homogenized society; the former are also being repackaged or *retooled* into mass-compatible forms and made available to the first generation of the culturally uprooted inhabitants of the new world into which the uprooted are entering. That is why such threats to traditions have provoked so little resistance till now.

A corollary of this repackaging is the strangely familiar world that the popular films conjure up for the shamelessly rustic and the blatantly cosmopolitan. This familiarity is built on a well-honed psychological technique: creating a lovable or at least tolerable strangeness by projecting predictable elements of a once-known world on to the strange and the distant. (Exactly in the manner in which Steven Spielberg's high-tech *Star Wars* series turns out to be, on a less than close scrutiny, a repolished version of old-style westerns. The empire does strike back!) Without the familiarity, the strangeness would have been fearsome, perhaps even incapacitating. Once this projection is shared by the viewers and the strangeness is reinterpreted as part of ancient continuities, the strange – in this instance, the modern world – continues to arouse anxieties, but these anxieties do not become debilitating; they can be contained and channelled along more acceptable paths.

Put differently, popular cinema creates a space for the global, the unitary and the homogenizing, but does so in terms of a principle of plurality grounded in traditions. As a result, the homogenization such cinema promotes is not a unilinear movement from diversity to uniformity, but a multi-layered affair with the global mass culture which itself takes weird new forms as a result.

Our story till now reaffirms the obvious – that all visions, fantasies and nightmares have their politics, and the popular in Indian cinema, even when it seems least political, is a major political statement. But the story also deals with the less obvious: it claims that popular cinema not merely shapes and is shaped by politics, it constitutes the language for a new form of politics. Formal social sciences have not yet thrown up analytic categories appropriate for the form, and normal politics cannot wait for the social sciences to do so. Consequently, there has emerged a different kind of continuity between such cinema and the culture of Indian politics. The former serves as a poor man's political scientist working in tandem with the astrologer on the one hand, and the political activist on the other. Its focus is on the key concerns of some of the most articulate, vibrant and volatile sectors of the Indian electorate today. On this plane, such cinema can be seen as what some less articulate Indians might reveal of their political and social experiences to the psychoanalyst after putting the latter on the couch.

Despite the charisma that 'masses' as an abstract entity have come to enjoy in the last hundred years or so, thanks to what Edward Shils calls the dispersal of the charisma previously concentrated in the monarch or the ruling élite, the political idiom of the 'lower classes', as opposed to their politics, continues to sound meaningless, dangerous or sick. In fact, most well-wishers of these classes like to serve as the latter's mouthpieces in the belief that they use the wrong language to interpret their predicament.[13] Indian popular cinema suggests that the language, though sometimes garbled, is not insane, and sometimes can even be moving. For it is after all only a distorted history of our own desires, lived out by others who acknowledge them. That is why the most absurd moments of popular cinema often can be its most poignant.

Such a language can survive as an exotica in an old society with relatively intact traditions and community ties, and as a marker of transitory times in a society where modern technology and media have become hegemonic. In neither case can it have any intrinsic legitimacy, aesthetic or social. In a society where traditions and community ties are relatively intact, popular culture of the kind the Bombay films typify is not really that popular after all; it has to compete with the predominant presence of a wide variety of folk culture. On the other hand, the 'magical' powers of mass culture in a fully modernized society come from the breakdown of communities and the decline of traditions and from the substitutes for such communities and traditions ventured by the mass media with the help of modern technology. Until now, Indian popular cinema has refused to cede that magicality to mass media, though it is coming closer to doing so. Nor has it tried to be a typical mass media though in recent years it has borrowed heavily from the genre.

This may be simply a long-winded way of returning to the proposition that in South Asia, and perhaps in much of Asia and Africa, mass culture and popular culture do not fully overlap. Elements of mass culture, disembedded from their global context, can become popular (e.g. denims and cola drinks). But that by itself means little; for these elements have to be processed through the local popular culture which provides, exactly for that purpose, an indigenously forged bicultural sieve. The Indian cinema not only does this processing on behalf of a vulnerable section of the Indian population, it also has a built-in plurality that tends to subvert mass culture even when seemingly adapting to it passively.

This has another implication. If Indian popular cinema has to be seen as a struggle against the massified, it must also be seen as a battle over categories – between those that represent the global and the fully marketized, in tune with India's now almost fully institutionalized official ideology of the state, and those who by default represent the culturally self-confident but low-brow multicultural-ism in which the country has invested an important part of its genius during the last hundred years or so, both as a means of survival in our times and as a technology of self-creation with an extended range of options. The popular in Indian cinema cannot be the classical – art cinema exists for that – or folk, of which there is as yet no dearth in India. [...]

This [chapter] invites the reader to use it as a means of thinking about cinema and the politics of cultures in South Asia in less conventional ways, unencumbered by formal film theory and trendy hermeneutics of the kind that, for reasons of academic correctness, sucks all life from one of the most vigorous expressions of the selfhood of the Indian caught between the old and the new, the inner and the outer, the local and the global. [...]

Notes

1 *Peacock Screen* (London: BBC Channel 4, 1996), director Mahmood Jamal, script Firdous Ali; *Mass Media in India:* 1992 (New Delhi: Publications Division, Ministry of Information and Broadcasting, 1993), pp. 157, 198.

2 M. Christopher Byrski, 'Bombay Philum – the Kaliyugi Avatara of Sanskrit Drama', *Pushpanjali*, November 1980, 4, pp. 111–18.

3 Jai P. Sen, 'The Unintended City', *Seminar,* April 1976, 200, pp. 33–40.

4 Strangely, the slum seems to be less of an embarrassment to the rural Indians. They perhaps know the slum better as a standard pathway for those who migrate from what has become for them the stifling primordiality of the village, to what has become for everyone the impersonal charm of urban anonymity.

5 This part of the story has been told in more detail in Ashis Nandy, 'The Political Culture of the Indian State', *Daedalus*, Fall 1989, 118(4).

6 Ashis Nandy, 'An Intelligent Critic's Guide to Indian Cinema', in *The Savage Freud and Other Essays in Possible and Retrievable Selves* (New Delhi: Oxford University Press, [1995]).

7 One example are the new versions of faith available in packaged form in the modern sector for those anxious about their wavering faith within; for instance the Hindutva movement that has caught the imagination of a significant section of urban, semi-Westernized Hindus and, appropriately enough, expa-triate Hindus, has much less to do with Hinduism than with middle-class expectations from politics.

8 Nandy, 'An Intelligent Critic's Guide to Indian Cinema'. Two questions
   remain: Shall we now see a decline in the number of films with the theme of
   the double, given that the hero has begun to incorporate the double within
   himself? Or shall we see a revival of the double after a decent interval, given
   that the idea of the double-in-the-hero has begun to go stale?

9 For the moment I am, of course, ignoring the parallel shift from heroes who
   start as criminals, to become law-abiding citizens, to heroes who start as
   innocent migrants lost in a heartless city and end up as criminalized vigilantes.

10 Two distinguished scholars, one an anthropologist and the other a philosopher
   and historian, have recently argued that the decline of the hero in Indian
   popular films faithfully mirrors the decline of Indian public life. See Akbar S.
   Ahmed, 'Bombay Films: The Cinema as Metaphor for Indian Society and
   Politics', *Modern Asian Studies*, May 1992, 26(2), pp. 289–320; and Ziauddin
   Sardar, 'Dilip Kumar Made Me Do It', see Chapter 2 of *The Secret Politics of
   our Desires*.

   While agreeing with the overall thrust of their argument, one must recognize
   the scope of the global crisis in public life and democratic politics precipitated
   by full-blown 'modern rationality'. The hero is what he is, not by choice, but
   because he cannot be otherwise in the world he lives in. That is the main
   difference between violence in these films and in those of, say, Hollywood. The
   changing life-cycle of the film hero is located within that rationality. As a
   well-known critic of Western modernity, Sardar, who shows little sympathy for
   the new 'hard', modern face of the hero in Indian films, should have
   appreciated this part of the story.

   The point I am trying to make is beautifully [...] [made in] the film
   Mashaal, in which an elderly couple played by a famous hero and a heroine of
   earlier years, Dilip Kumar and Waheeda Rehman, are caught in a heartless
   megalopolis. The wife, injured and facing death, is carried by the morally
   upright, law-abiding husband in the dead of the night through the deserted
   streets of Bombay, where he tries to stop a passing car to take his wife to a
   hospital. But nobody stops while he screams in anguish, 'Brother, stop the
   car', and no one ever opens a window of the tall apartments lining the street.
   Dilip in bitter frustation throws a stone at one of the multi-storeyed buildings.
   No one responds to that desperate gesture either. [...]

11 Byrski, 'Bombay Philum – the Kaliyugi Avatara of Sanskrit Drama'.

12 Veena Das, 'Jai Santoshi Ma', *India International Centre Quarterly*, 9(1), 1981.

13 The rural and the traditional, it is true, are no longer dirty words, as they were
   in many of the major schools of nineteenth-century social knowledge, including the major dissenting visions. Environmental concerns and the growing
   discomfort with urban industrialism in recent decades have changed the
   intellectual culture in this respect. The wisdom of the peasant and the shaman
   is a trendy concern today. But this revaluation does not cover those who have
   one foot in the village and the other in the city. They seem neither authenti-
   cally traditional nor genuinely modern, and are therefore a hybrid worse than
   both. Popular cinema originates from that liminal world; it is bound to arouse
   ambivalent feelings.

7

The national-heroic image: masculinity and masquerade
by Sumita Chakravarty

> The body is not a static phenomenon, but a mode of intentionality, a directional force and mode of desire. As a condition of access to the world, a body is being comported beyond itself, sustaining a necessary reference to the world and, thus, never a self-identical natural entity. The body is lived and experienced as the context and medium for all human strivings … . the body is always involved in the quest to realize possibilities.
>
> —Judith Butler, "Sex and Gender"

In an article on Latin American fiction written some years ago, critic Jean Franco describes how its discourse of nationalism constructs images of the male as active and of the female as passive and private. If the feminine is associated with immobility and hence "territoriality," masculine creativity becomes the agency whereby heterogeneous elements in Latin American culture are valorized as a sign of carnivalesque pluralism.[1] A similar though historically and culturally distinct effort at incorporating heterogeneity and reveling in it is evident in Indian commercial cinema in terms of the male body as the interface of multiple regional, class, and religious identities and texts. The male hero as the center and source of narrative meaning is "resemanticized" into a mode of instability and the dispersion of meaning. Forms of disguise, impersonation, and masquerade are the visual means that serve to render this move from the natural to the acculturated body, allowing the spectator means of recognition of his/her social world within the world of the film through the hero's "play" with the signifiers of dress, accent, and gesture. This distinct tendency within the Bombay film to both identify and nullify marks of (intercultural) difference in a wide variety of textual situations allows national identity to surface as so many styles of the flesh.

Whether as a dominant theme played out through the use of the double and/or various forms of disguise, as in *Hum Dono* (*The Two of Us,* 1961), *Mera Naam Joker* (*My Name Is Joker,* 1967), *Naya Din Nayi Raat* (*New Day New Night,* 1974), *Chinatown* (1962), and *Johnny Mera Naam* (*My Name is Johnny,* 1970), or as a visual motif in particular sequences, as in *An Evening in Paris* (1967), *Love in Tokyo* (1966), *Amar Akbar Anthony* (1977), and *Desh Premee* (*Patriot*, 1982), or as a narrative element in romantic comedy, such as *Padosan* (*Neighbour*, 1968), or *Chupke Chupke* (*Quietly, Quietly*, 1975), or *Victoria No. 203* (1972), the Bombay film has been obsessively concerned with the "enigma" of (male) subjectivity and the need for the disavowal of fixed notions of identity. In a society where the social markers of identity are so well-defined, where caste, creed, region, and education all translate into distinctive visual emblems (the Brahmin's mark on the forehead and sacred thread, the Bengali versus the Gujarati woman's style of wearing a saree, the Sikh's turban – the list goes on), where to give one's name is (usually) also to reveal one's caste and regional background, it is small wonder that the popular film engages with the question of identity at various levels of articulation. Critics have usually pointed out one or other of several tendencies whereby the Bombay film "fails" to identify its characters. Thus Ashis Nandy tells us that the Hindi film hero "will simply be Mr. Rakesh or Mr. Raj or Mr. Ashok – surnameless and, thus, regionless, casteless, ethnically non-identifiable and ultimately ahistorical. He is in this sense an archetype, a representation of cultural concerns which, if given a specific historical setting, would become less forceful, less black-and-white, and thus less communicative."[2] While this observation is generally true, the film text is usually less unambiguous than such a view suggests, and visual codes function to "situate" the hero, at least broadly as either Hindu or Muslim, upper class or poor, educated or not, Westernized or not. Also, Vijay Mishra, Peter Jeffery, and Brian Shoesmith's notion of "the actor as parallel text," of "the actor as text in his own right," addresses the issue of stardom and how star quality and presence working *within* films construct processes of identification and continuity of spectatorial response.[3] One might add that this continuity of recognition and response hinges on the notion of authenticity, on how filmic transformations metonymically evoke the actor's "real" personality and conduct. Amitabh Bachchan and Rekha's off-screen romance, for instance, affects our reading of their on-screen performance, creating textual gaps or openings through extratextual awareness. Along the same lines, although Amitabh Bachchan has been cast in every working-class role imaginable (in addition to portraying a Hindu, Muslim, and Christian), one does not forget his actual class and caste affiliation. Rather, this knowledge is used to judge how he measured up to the expected behavior patterns associated with each group that are themselves textually constructed and lodged in the popular mind through repetition.

How, then, can one reconcile these contradictory impulses within the average Bombay film? In particular, how do recurrent uses of disguise and masquerade define masculinity and heroism in Indian mass culture? How are particular scenarios constructed that mediate between private longings (of romance and family life) and public social roles? What are the possibilities of male impersonation? Psychoanalytically informed accounts of the masquerade have stressed its relationship to femininity.[4] Marjorie Garber's recent book, *Vested Interests*, also a study of forms of masquerade and cross-dressing in popular culture, sees them primarily as expressions of the blurring of gender boundaries.[5] In film criticism as well, attention has been focused on how women spectators are positioned in relation to the screen.[6] The masquerade's carnivalesque possibilities and the significance of the *male* body as it presents itself as a social-semiotic field have been less systematically studied. But as James Naremore, in his book *Acting in the Cinema,* writes, "Clearly films depend on a form of communication whereby meanings are *acted out;* the experience of watching them involves not only a pleasure in storytelling but also a delight in bodies and expressive movement, an enjoyment of familiar performing skills, and an interest in players as 'real persons.'"[7] Naremore's excellent study of the rhetoric of screen acting, his emphasis on the visual aspects of film performances, is important for our purposes, since so much of the effectivity of the performative codes of the Bombay cinema depends on the audience's complicity with the multiple roles adopted (and gaily abandoned) by the actor.

Nevertheless, it is worth stressing that the notion of disguise and masquerade in relation to the cinema is rarely discussed. In a sense, this is understandable, since "acting" denotes a kind of artifice, and disguise, when used in the cinema, is generally taken as a plot device or as an embellishment of the mise-en-scène. Charles Affron's view may be cited here as representative: "Coated with layers of makeup that obliterate blemish and dissymmetry, modeled by a miraculous array of lights, located and relocated by the giddy succession of frames, the stars capriciously play with life and subject it to a range of fictions from preposterous to profound."[8] Contrarily, when masks are studied as social and cultural myths and artifacts, as in Joseph Campbell's *The Hero with a Thousand Faces*[9] or David Napier's book[10] on the facial mask, attention is devoted solely to its traditions of use in drama and in ritual events, but no mention is made of film. The latter's technological base and naturalistic conventions would seem to render it "alien" to the essentially symbolic function of masks and masquerades in traditional forms of representation and validation of group existence. However, as Robert Ezra Park, in the context of symbolic interactionism, reminds us, there is a more fundamental aspect to masking:

> It is probably no mere historical accident that the word person, in its first meaning, is a mask. It is rather a recognition of the fact that everyone is always and everywhere, more or less consciously, playing a role ... It is in these roles that we know each other; it is in these roles that we know ourselves ...

> In a sense, and in so far as the mask represents the conception we have formed of ourselves – the role we are striving to live up to – this mask is our truer self, the self we would like to be.[11]

The mask is here the very condition of subjectivity, of interacting with the world, of defining oneself in relation to others. It is also a mode of idealization and of a projected narcissism. It might be said that screen performances, particularly of stars, narrativize this tendency by foregrounding a repertoire of roles. The transition from one role to another across individual film texts is at once a sign of the actor's talents and evidence of the "emptiness" of the actor-as-sign. It is this emptiness that allows a star to become a popular cultural icon, a receptacle, like a wax mold, into which may be poured the social collectivity's needs and desires of the moment. Roland Barthes's classic reading of "the face of Garbo" speaks of a time in the history of cinema "when one literally lost oneself in a human image as one would in a philtre."[12] Likening Garbo's face to a mask in its mystical promise of transcendence, Barthes suggests a kind of interaction between the face and the mask that leaves this star's beauty suspended, so to speak, between two incompatible states. Although facial masks, even of the kind described here, are not common in the cinema, masquerading the body, "arranging" it in various ways so as to invite new combinations of meaning, so as to assert the body as acculturated, an absence known only through its significations, has remained a recurring feature in the cinema.

In the Bombay film, it has been the male star whose body has lent itself most, consistently to various forms of masquerade. In this chapter we shall explore how conceptions of the hero, coalesced around certain star personas, have rendered the discourse of nationhood as "creative geography," to appropriate Kuleshov's evocative phrase. The romantic hero as man of action can extend himself in myriad ways to transform and transcend his social conditions of existence and reconcile the irreconcilable. As his body at once orchestrates and absorbs difference, racial and cultural, dress, makeup, and behavior patterns serve to anchor recognition and invite misrecognition. Pastiche and parody are the hallmarks of identities which valorize fragmentation and yet seek wholeness.

The incorporation of several (transnational) identities by a single hero, expressed both visually and rhetorically (through song), was invested with an early and enduring appeal in Raj Kapoor's *Shri 420* (*The Gentleman Cheat*, 1955). The lyrics, roughly translated, mean:

> The shoes I'm wearing are made in Japan
> My trousers fashioned in England
> The red cap on my head is Russian
> In spite of it all my heart is Indian.[13]

This was the Nehru era and being national also meant, in some sense, to declare oneself to be international. The use of the body is as a particular nexus of culture and choice, a field of possibilities susceptible to infinite rearrangements. The irony, of course, is that the vagabond and rolling stone who is singing this song is laughing at himself because his assortment of clothing is also a signifier of his impoverished state and a reflection on the society of which he is a part. His nationalist message puts India at the center of a randomized global accumulation of accessories, seeking to put a distance between the core (heart, sentiment) and the periphery (limbs, outward appearance). India itself was simultaneously core and periphery: at once ancient and young, civilizationally advanced and "Third World." Suggesting transcendence, the body of the hero becomes a map on which nations can appear to coexist in harmonious yet distinctly separate spheres. Indian identity would have it both ways: to be a composite and yet claim a prior and more significant status. By transforming the social marginality of the filmic hero into the centrality of the Indian citizen, material needs are displaced onto a more intangible (emotional) level of experience.

The fifties hero also reveals another valorized feature of Indian culture which gradually disappears in films of the postsixties era: androgyny.[14] However, androgyny in a patriarchal society was only acceptable in evoking new and marginal states of being and consciousness. The desire to evolve or represent new forms of urban experience, particularly the fact of close proximity to different types and classes of people, found expression in the kind and gentle hero – Balraj Sahni in Amiya Chakravarty's *Seema* (1955), Dilip Kumar in Kidar Sharma's *Jogan* (*Ascetic*, 1950), Raj Kapoor in *Aag* (*Fire*, 1948) and *Barsaat* (*Rain*, 1949), Dev Anand in *Aandhian* (*Storms*, 1952), Sunil Dutt in *Ek Hi Raasta* (*One Path Alone*, 1956) are some examples – often dressed in the traditional *dhoti* and *kurta*, with the villain or buffoon adopting Western attire; for example, Johnny Walker in *Naya Daur* (*New Race*, 1957). Side by side, however, there was emerging the early noir hero with links to the Bombay underworld. Dev Anand in *Baazi* (*Wager*, 1951), *Kala Bazaar* (*Black Market*, 1960), and *Taxi Driver* (1954) epitomized this new type: cigarette dangling from the mouth, eyes slanted to look off-screen, a tone of daring, a posture of risk taking. This type was to reappear in the seventies and eighties.

A combination of factors is responsible for the emergence of the new film hero in the early sixties. The introduction of color, the perpetual search for new acting talent in the film industry, the death of acclaimed and popular filmmakers like Guru Dutt, Bimal Roy, and Mehboob Khan with their distinctive styles, perhaps even the passing of the Nehru era and the immediate concerns of nationhood all changed the film scene. *Junglee* (*Savage*, 1960) signaled the change from the deglamorized heroism of Raj Kapoor's Indianized Chaplin to the more cosmopolitan, rambunctious personality of the sixties hero. Psychoanalyst Sudhir Kakar creates a typology of screen heroes, distinguishing between the Majnun-lover of the fifties and earlier from the Krishna-lover of the sixties (his third type is the good-bad hero of the seventies and eighties). Dilip Kumar in *Devdas* (1955) and Guru Dutt in *Pyaasa* (*The Thirsty One*, 1957) are the ideal Majnun-lovers, passive, poetic, and childlike. In contrast, the romantic hero of the sixties is the Krishna-lover:

> He is phallus incarnate, with distinct elements of the "flasher" who needs constant reassurance by the woman of his power, intactness, and especially his magical qualities that can transform a cool Amazon into a hot, lusting female. The fantasy is of the phallus – Shammi Kapoor in his films used his whole body as one – humbling the pride of the unapproachable woman, melting her indifference and unconcern into submission and longing. The fantasy is of the spirited and androgynous virgin awakened to her sexuality and thereafter reduced to a groveling being, full of a moral masochism wherein she revels in her "stickiness" to the hero.[15]

It is now generally acknowledged that from the sixties to the late eighties, Indian popular cinema has been increasingly male-oriented. From Shammi Kapoor to Rajendra Kumar to Rajesh Khanna to Amitabh Bachchan, an escalating trend of male stardom seemed to evolve. (By a curious shift, the "new cinema" projected itself as a woman's cinema and provided the histrionic grounds for the emergence of the two foremost actresses of the postsixties era, Shabana Azmi and Smita Patil.) Recently, fifties star and highly regarded actress Waheeda Rehman explained her "semiretirement" from the Bombay film scene thus:

> I got fed up with the repetitive roles I was being offered. It was invariably the same story: that of the father being murdered and then the children growing up to avenge him and the widowed mother steering them through all kinds of hardships. It all seemed very stale and mechanical. Also, our films, male-oriented as they are, find little use for actresses; the story revolves around the men. Besides, after a certain age actresses are not readily accepted as heroines.[16]

These comments highlight both the entry into the big-budget or "multistarrer" era of Bombay filmmaking and the industry's perennial demand for new faces.

The heroics of natural identity

The first male star to break out of the mold of the fifties hero as champion and prototype of the underclass was Shammi Kapoor. As the younger brother of the very popular Raj Kapoor, Shammi sought to invest his screen image with a totally different appeal, one that was predicated on the lure of the all-powerful, all-enveloping presence of the romantic hero. Lacking Raj Kapoor's (and younger brother Shashi Kapoor's) more sensitive and chiseled features and smaller frame, Shammi could boast of a powerful physique, which he used to signal brute strength. Quite appropriately, his first film was entitled *Junglee* (*Savage*, 1960). This "retreat" into a more "natural" state is a distinct departure from the socially and culturally embroiled heroes of the films of earlier decades.

Their stance of commitment to progressive social change and to the values of film realism finds no place in this more vigorous narcissistic male persona. Social markers of class and region (urban or rural) are replaced by a more free-floating and individualized universe of rapid change and frantic movement. The boundaries between the external and the internal, so cherished by the fifties hero (and encapsulated by the song stanza quoted above), collapse in the new heroic image. All is surface; surface is all. The sixties hero is most comfortable straddling – and thereby eliminating – the distinctions between different social and national worlds. He moves effortlessly between the palace and the hut, not as an intermediary but as one to whom these distinctions are no longer significant or worth signifying. In *Junglee,* the polarities of wealth and poverty, endemic to the structure of the Bombay film, are mapped onto different forms of "naturalness": the Shammi Kapoor persona belongs to a very rich family but is basically an innocent with raw emotions and manners in need of taming; the heroine (Saira Banu) is outside (urban) civilization, symbolizing the beauty and playfulness of one used to the openness of natural surroundings. But it would be a mistake to read *Junglee* as merely one more Rousseauist parable, rather than as a deconstruction and reconstruction of a film hero. This is signaled by the parodic opening sequence, in which a voice-over presents an isolated protagonist-hero – a creature who does *not* invite identification because he is lacking in any semblance of human grace. Shammi Kapoor's exaggerated mock-serious acting (his eyes appearing cold and angry, his brow knitted, nostrils flaring, cheeks sucked into a pout) is a facade because generic expectations promise romance later on. Seated alone inside an airplane, a convenient phallic symbol, we are told that this symbol of masculinity gone awry is returning from England and America armed with the latest business training to take the Indian business world by storm. The association is deliberate, and yet the film, soon after, reveals the real reason for Shekhar's strangeness: a strict upbringing in accordance with rigid patriarchal-familial norms transferred through another parodied figure, his mother (Lalita Pawar). The scene is gradually set for the hero's transformation into an independent and likeable personality through the process of falling in love with a beautiful and fun-loving girl, Raj (Saira Banu).

Saira Banu is the quintessential new heroine (childish, unsophisticated, naïve) who complements the new film hero, and together they conquer the Bombay film's most exotic colony – Kashmir. The strategic importance of Kashmir as the eroticized landscape of the mind in the social imaginary of Indians (paralleling perhaps its political importance in configurations of the integrity and unity of the Indian nation-state) can hardly be overstated. Kashmir as the place for honey-moons and lovers, arising no doubt from its scenic beauty (it is known as the "Switzerland of India"), has been translated by the Bombay film into a symbol of purity and unspoiled nature and as visual therapy for audiences coping with life in overcrowded cities and towns. Kashmir, over which India has fought several wars with Pakistan, serves as the limit-text of what it means to be Indian: its geographical location at India's apex, its captured facial imprint of the Aryan inheritance, its demographic admixture of Hindus and Muslims, perhaps its ambivalent status as at once virgin ("no compromise on Kashmir," say the politicians) and coquette (eternally coveted by neighboring states) – all these serve to render Kashmir as both site of fantasy and national projection of overarching identity and connectedness.[17] Kashmir can therefore effect the transformation of the *junglee*-as-uncivilized, lacking social graces or emotions, to the *junglee*-as-naturally-exuberant.

The therapeutic nature of his experience of awakening love for an "unspoiled" girl-woman enables this new film hero not only to transcend the boundaries of social class (he is wealthy, she is not) but those between the human and animal worlds as well. In Indian culture, where ideals of manhood incorporate some attributes of femininity, the valorization of Shammi Kapoor's masculinity necessitates an association with the nonhuman or prior-human. He is the wild one, a visual anarchy, a body in frenetic movement: head jerking, arms flailing, shoulders and hips seemingly moving independently of each other. *Junglee* inaugurates the cinema of indulgence: spectacular shots of landscape, particularly of virgin snow and majestic mountain ranges, provide the playground for desire and fantasy where the possibility of physical union between the romantic couple is a palpable one. Rolling in the snow, the hero proclaims the joy of existence by inviting, rather than resisting, associations with an animallike state. The "Yahoo" song, which became as much Shammi Kapoor's insignia as "Awaara Hoon" (I am a vagabond) was Raj Kapoor's, is the animal mask which signifies a rite of passage. It also suggests the ambiguity of this transformational state.

For "real life" must be resumed in the big city. Shekhar returns home, a different man, eager to socialize with his employees where formerly he barked orders at them. The animal is humanized, and after a series of plot complications, he is able to convince his mother of the error of her "high-and-mighty" ways. As Raj and her father arrive, bringing with them a taste of the mountains, the pretensions of the rich crumble. All ends well, as youth and wealth are aligned in the obligatory happy ending.

An evening in Paris

The Bombay film hero of the sixties negotiates sociocultural and spatial mobility through creative uses of the masquerade. As the setting for romance shifts from national to international locations, the West is no longer an internalized presence/ absence in the hero's psyche but becomes the purely and wholly Other, the exotic backdrop against which the Indian hero and heroine can act out their fantasies of unhampered courtship and romance. Many big-budget films at this time seek the spectacle of Western sights and sounds, among them *Sangam* (*Confluence,* 1964), *Love in Tokyo* (1966), *An Evening in Paris* (1967), *Around the World* (1967), *Purab aur Paschim* (*East and West,* 1970), and *Hare Rāma Hare Krishna* (1971). Although occasionally, as in *Purab aur Paschim,* the West is stereotypically the scene of spiritual degradation or somnolescence, of violence and material craving, in most of the other films spectacle overwhelms moralism as the audience is sped along from one world capital to another (Paris-London-Vienna-Rome-Switzerland is the usual beat). The "domestication" of the West during this period coincides with India's brain drain and official concern over the loss of scientific and technically trained people who were emigrating to North America. The Bombay film feeds this longing of the average Indian to travel abroad by locating its narratives partially outside India.

An Evening in Paris presents a set of globe-trotting characters and a hero who is no longer anxious to proclaim his "Indianness." The film draws attention to itself as entertainment and spectacle in its opening sequence, when the protagonist, Shammi Kapoor, looks directly at the camera as he gyrates and sings, "Aji, aisa mauka phir kahan milega?" (Folks, when will you get such an opportunity again?). The hero promises to be a tour guide for the audience and to take them sight-seeing in Paris. The "evening" of the title refers to the evening at the movie theater, and the song exhorts, "Dekho, dekho, dekho, dekho, dekho!" (See, see, see, see, see!), an invitation to viewers to immerse themselves in visual and sensual enjoyment. This throwback to the promise of the earliest days of cinema, when the novelty of seeing distant lands and places was a major attraction, renews the process of "alienation" between the spectator and the cinematic apparatus, with the screen abolishing spatial distance and underscoring psychic distance simultaneously. Long-shots and tilted angles structure a sort of hierarchical arrangement between the world of the film and the world of the spectator, the first of which must forever be beyond the reach of the second. Yet the glamor of the West and of the rich (if not famous, on-screen) can lure the viewers to an entrancing evening.

An Evening in Paris brings together the attractive and chic Sharmila Tagore and, by now, the reigning sixties star, Shammi Kapoor, in a romantic drama that seeks to give a new twist to the age-old Bombay film themes of wealth-poverty, insider-outsider, heroism-villainy. Here we have both the hero and the heroine subject to different kinds of doubling and masquerade. The initial setting is Paris, where arrives Deepa (Sharmila Tagore), the beautiful daughter of a wealthy businessman, in search of true love. She wants to be loved for herself and not for the money she will inherit from her father. Paris, she is led to believe, will effect this miracle. Settling down in an apartment, Deepa initially tries to masquerade as her maid and is soon pursued by two men: Shekhar (Pran), her Paris guardian's son, and Sam (Shammi Kapoor), who passes himself off as a Frenchman who can speak Hindi. Both men frantically court her, trying to outwit each other in gaining her attention and affections. The lovers move from one foreign location to another, with Shekhar in tow, frolicking and romancing in extravagant and lavish settings.[18]

Then plot complications set in, and the romance turns into action drama. The villains are introduced so that the heroic side to the male protagonist's personality can be presented. Since nothing happens singly in the popular film and identities harbor subidentities, characters and events now reveal their sinister underside. It is soon clear to the audience that Shekhar, son of the honest caretaker/guardian of the heroine, is associated with a crime gang headed by Jaggu, whose name and iconicity evoke villainy through the accumulated force of repetition in countless previous films. The heroine, too, is metonymically associated with evil: Jaggu employs Suzie, a cabaret dancer who is the spitting image of Deepa and actually her long-lost twin sister. And the worlds of big business (represented by Deepa's father) and big crime (represented by Jaggu and his cohorts) come together when it is revealed that the disgruntled servant who had kidnapped Suzie-Rupa as a child is an associate of Jaggu. The centrifugal tendencies in the first half of the film are balanced by the plot's centripetal movement in the latter half as past and present, vendetta and retribution, lost innocence and sacrifice meet and do battle. Ironically, the hero alone is unburdened by a past and hence able to traverse contradictory states at will. He easily slips from playful Casanova to shrewd private eye, able to upstage the villains and rescue Deepa. A prolonged chase-and-fight sequence at the end of the film includes ostensibly hair-raising stunts over the Niagara Falls in Canada. As the wet and tired hero and heroine are rescued from a tiny ledge by a helicopter, they burst into song, one of the hit songs of the film.

A notable feature of the male-dominated romantic drama of the post-sixties era is that while the identity of the villain is fixed and self-evident, the proof of the hero's heroism is that he can change identities at will, if only temporarily and often playfully. The villain has no access to the masquerade (or his efforts to pass himself off as a good person are patently false and obvious); the hero, on the other hand, can literally become "the hero with the thousand faces." However, changing personas is a sign of ingenuity and sportiveness (Shammi Kapoor in one sequence masquerades as an Arab in flowing robes), rather than the eraser of cultural boundaries. All extranational identities are ultimately collapsible into a hyposta-sized Indianness, left suitably vague and no longer expressly articulated either through iconography or patriotic dialogue. (This condition changes again in the eighties, when both elements become strong markers of "Indianness.") Released from its moorings in history, tradition, or space, the concept of "Indianness" is naturalized through the mobile hero, an entitlement to a passport with the assurance of a return ticket. Like the hero's adopted name, "Sam," which can always be converted back to its original version, "Shyam" (another name for Krishna), the sixties hero inhabits several worlds at once, his identity always already recuperable. [...]

Notes

1 Jean Franco, "Beyond Ethno-centrism: Gender, Power and the Third World Intelligentsia," in *Marxism and the Interpretation of Culture*, ed. Cary Nelson and Lawrence Grossberg, pp. 503–515.
2 Ashis Nandy, "The Popular Hindi Film: Ideology and First Principles," *India International Centre Quarterly* 8, no. 1 (1981): 93.
3 Vijay Mishra, Peter Jeffery, and Brian Shoesmith, "The Actor as Parallel Text in Bombay Cinema," *Quarterly Review of Film and Video* 11, no. 3 (1989): 52.
4 See, for instance, the essays in the volume *Formations of Fantasy*, ed. Victor Burgin, James Donald, and Cora Kaplan, in particular, Joan Riviere's "Womanliness as a Masquerade" and Stephen Heath's commentary on it. In Heath's words, "In the masquerade the woman mimics an authentic – genuine – womanliness but then authentic womanliness is such a mimicry, *is* the masquerade ('they are the same thing'); to be a woman is to dissimulate a fundamental masculinity, femininity is that dissimulation" (p. 49).
5 Marjorie Garber, *Vested Interests: Cross-Dressing and Cultural Anxiety*.
6 See Mary Ann Doane, "Film and the Masquerade: Theorising the Female Spectator," *Screen* 23 (September–October 1982): 74–87.
7 James Naremore, *Acting in the Cinema*, p. 2.
8 Charles Affron, "Generous Stars," in *Star Texts*, ed. Jeremy Butler, p. 92.
9 Joseph Campbell, *The Hero with a Thousand Faces*.
10 [A. D.] Napier, *Masks*.
11 Robert Ezra Park, quoted by Naremore, *Acting in the Cinema*, p. 22.
12 Roland Barthes, "The Face of Garbo," in *Mythologies*, p. 56.
13 I have used Farrukh Dhondy's translation of this stanza that appeared in his article, "Keeping Faith: Indian Film and Its World," *Daedalus* (Winter 1985): 130. Dhondy wrongly attributes the song to the film *Awaara*.
14 See Ashis Nandy, *The Intimate Enemy: Loss and Recovery of Self under Colonialism*, pp. 1–63.
15 Sudhir Kakar, *Intimate Relations: Exploring Indian Sexuality*, p. 37.
16 *Filmfare* 38, no. 4 (April 1989): 77.
17 Kashmir as limit text of the Indian national imaginary is replayed in David Lean's *A Passage to India* when Lean departs from Forster's text at the end of the novel and effects a reconciliation between Aziz and Fielding in Kashmir, where Aziz has retired after the trial.

18 Sharmila Tagore's "bikini ourfit" worn in the film provided grist for the fanzines. Here we have a transgression of female identity through a reversal of the state of modesty, which functions as a signifier of femininity in the Bombay film. [...]

PART 2
Recent trajectories

8

Avenging women in Indian cinema
by Lalitha Gopalan

[...] Discussions of violence have to consider how films replete with avenging women, gangsters, brutal police force and vigilante closures stage some of the most volatile struggles over representations that shape our public and private fantasies of national, communal, regional and sexual identities.

[...] Firoze Rangoonwala definitively names the decade between 1981 and 1992 'the age of violence'.[1] Assembling Hindi films with vigilante resolutions from both 'parallel' cinema – Govind Nihalani's *Ardh Satya/Half Truth* (1984) – and the commercial industry, he identifies a marked shift towards escalating violence in this period. Rangoonwala [...] directs his sharpest criticism towards popular cinema for having 'succumbed to a hackneyed formula'. Arguably, dismissing formula-ridden popular cinema, however hackneyed it may be, unwittingly grants it processes of standardization of cinematic codes and narratives and, in turn, exorcises a widely held view that Indian cinema randomly picks up story lines only to finally deliver a *masala* film.

M. Rahman offers a less disparaging report of the Indian film industry in the 1980s by spotting the workings and consolidation of a new 'formula' in Hindi cinema inaugurated by N. Chandra's film *Pratighat/Retribution* (1987) [...] The common theme of these films, according to Rahman, is their portrayal of women as 'hardened, cynical, vengeful creatures'.[2] Interviewing director Chandra and prominent actresses like Hema Malini, Dimple and Rekha, who have all played avenging women, Rahman provides alternative viewpoints from within the film industry. While Chandra suggests that these violent films are generated in response to the voracious viewing habits of an audience that wishes to see something different from the stock male 'action' film, the actresses argue that screenplays with dominant and powerful women are a welcome break from stereotypical roles as submissive and dutiful mothers and wives.

Maithili Rao too identifies an emerging trend in the industry, set off once again by Chandra's *Pratighat*, a trend that she calls the 'lady avengers'.[3] Arguing that they 'reflect the cultural schizophrenia in our society', Rao reproaches these films for being 'hostile to female sexuality' and for passing themselves off as nothing more than 'victimization masquerading as female power'. This feminist spectator's critique neither figures in Rahman's interviews with directors and actresses nor does it address the tremendous box-office success of these films, however perverse they may be.

This [article] assumes that these contradictory and diverse readings of 'aggressive woman' films are provocative enough to warrant another look at their visual and narrative goriness; another reading of the configurations of femininity and violence staged in these films, I argue, will uncover the contours of their appeal. My reading strategies employed in this [article] are indelibly shaped by feminist film theory that argues for formal textual analysis as a means to grasp the articulation of sexual difference in cinema. Although it tends to focus heavily on Hollywood productions, feminist film theory remains useful for at least two reasons: first, deploying it for an analysis of Indian cinema interrogates a monolithic conception of 'national cinema' and opens the possibility of exploring points of contact with international filmmaking practices; secondly, its nuanced theorization of scopophilia and spectatorship holds up extremely well for the films discussed here. Despite a general move to place Indian cinema within international filmmaking practices, I do want to argue provisionally at this point that any Indianness we attribute to these cinemas lies in the various ways censorship regulations of the Indian State shape and influence cinematic representations; we must acknowledge and theorize the presence of the State when discussing the relationship between films and spectators.

Tailing the critical reception of these films is the frequent use of the term 'formula', which is bandied about to belittle the structures of repetition between films and only tangentially accounts for the viewer's pleasure. This paper explores how it may be equally possible that we are not only drawn to the visceral images in these films, but also to the various circuits of intertextual relays between and among them. [...] The theoretically more viable concept of 'genre' which allows us to place industry's suggestion that these films are different from male action films alongside critical evaluation which may condemn these films for cunningly representing female victims as vigilantes. In other words, only genre simultaneously addresses the industry's investment in standardized narratives for commercial success on the one hand, and the spectator's pleasure in genre films with their stock narratives structured around repetition and difference on the other. While culling production details from the industry to verify the spawning of genres is a legitimate line of inquiry, I employ textual analysis of different films to unravel the structuring of repetition and difference and firmly demonstrate the workings of a genre.

[...] We can isolate a genre of films I will call, after Maithili Rao, 'avenging women.' [...] Films open with family settings which appear 'happy' and 'normal' according to Hindi film conventions, but with a difference: there is a marked absence of dominant paternal figures. The female protagonist is always a working woman with a strong presence on screen. These initial conditions are upset when the female protagonist is raped. The raped woman files charges against the perpetrator, who is easily identifiable. Court rooms play a significant role in these films, if only to demonstrate the State's inability to convict the rapist and to precipitate a narrative crisis. This miscarriage of justice constitutes a turning point in the film – allowing for the passage of the protagonist from a sexual and judicial victim to an avenging woman.

The general features or this narrative and the production of horror in rape scenes point to its close similarity to rape-revenge narratives of Hollywood B films, especially horror films.[4] Critical writing on Hollywood rape-revenge films, particularly Carol Clover's work, suggests that the marginal status of these films, in contrast to mainstream Hollywood, permits them to address some of the unresolved and knotty problems on gender and spectatorship that are carefully regulated and managed by the mainstream. Clover turns to the sadistic and masochistic pleasures evoked by these horror films to suggest that B films are the 'return of the repressed' in mainstream Hollywood. Focusing on B horror films, where low production values are coupled with sex and violence, Clover argues that these films displace the woman as the sole site of scopophilic pleasure and open possibilities of cross-gender identification through the sadomasochistic pleasures encouraged by these films. The most compelling aspect of her work is the classification of these rape-revenge films within the larger rubric of *horror* films, a move that retains the sadistic and masochistic pleasures – prerequisites for watching a standard horror film – staged in these rape-revenge narratives. [...]

Instead of privileging the revenge narrative or the rape scenes as Rao does, it is more useful to explore how the narrative nuances of this genre are predicated on a cinematic logic that draws these two parts together. Rape scenes are not unusual in Indian cinema. They are, however, frequently subject to censorship rulings on grounds both of their irrelevance to the main narrative and the unseemly pleasure they evoke.[5] Yet rape scenes in avenging women films are indispensable to their narrative, repeatedly evoked as evidence in a court room sequence or repeated as a traumatic event experienced by the victim. In other words, the centrality of the rape scenes in the narrative heightens their intimate relationship to the subsequent revenge plot where, once again, there is a replay of negotiations between sex and violence.

While *Pratighat* is frequently cited as an originary moment in the avenging women genre, the combination of rape and revenge was already secured in B.R. Chopra's *Insaaf Ka Tarazu/Scales of Justice* produced in 1980. [...] *The Encyclopaedia of Indian Cinema* describes the conditions of reception that shaped this film:

> This notorious rape movie followed in the wake of growing feminist activism in India in the 70s after the Mathura and Maya Tyagi rape cases, the amendment to the Rape Law and the impact of, e.g., the Forum Against Rape which offered legal assistance to rape victims.[6]

References to the feminist movement are obviously one of the determining features structuring the reception of this film, but its notoriety points towards a different route of analysis where we have to consider how this film relies on our knowledge of these rape cases as a point of entry into fantastical stagings of our anxieties about women, sexuality and law, anxieties that in turn are set into motion, but not resolved, by anti-rape campaigns.[7] [...]

Insaaf Ka Tarazu opens with a rape scene. [...] The silhouette of a man first chases and then disrobes this woman. Another male figure enters the scene and a fight begins between them. The film returns to full colour when the potential rapist is fatally stabbed. The following credit sequence is a montage of stills from various religious and tourist sites in India with the soundtrack playing the title song of the film. These two sequences juxtapose rape against representations of India and this association with India is further played out in the film by naming the female protagonist Bharati – the feminine name in Hindi for India. These first scenes suggest considering female rape as an allegory of a beleaguered nation-state, a suggestion that, however, is not developed further in the film.

The second rape sequence in the film is distinguished from the opening sequence by the [...] absence of a male saviour. Using a calendar art print of a woman in bondage in the victim's (Arti's) bedroom as a reference point, the sequence provides glimpses of a rape scene that includes both coercion and bondage. Furthermore, the scene offers us another point of identification through the victim's younger sister, Nita, who accidentally walks into Arti's bedroom during the rape. Arti files charges against the rapist, Gupta. A number of social encounters between Gupta and Arti preceding the rape, combined with Nita's confused testimony, are employed in the court room to suggest that Arti was not raped but consented to have sex with Gupta. The court finds Gupta not guilty of rape.

The court's verdict in Arti's rape case comes as no surprise to the spectators, for the film mobilizes this doubt throughout the scene. For instance, Nita's testimony is crucial to this case but the defence lawyer convincingly argues her inability to tell the difference between coerced and consenting sexual relationships. The film frames Nita very much in the mould of a horrified voyeur witnessing a primal scene, thus infusing the scene with both fear of, and pleasure in, sexual knowledge, instead of recognizing it as sexual violation pure and simple. The sadistic-voyeuristic pleasure also surfaces here through the poster on the bedroom wall. The viewer might expect the poster's subject to be identified with the aggressor, a traditional strategy. Instead, the poster shores up a confusion between representations of rape and rape itself – thus eroticizing the scene of violation and escalating our masochistic identification with this scene. Privileging Nita's relationship to the scene, the film also exposes, and depends on, our inability as spectators to tell the cinematic difference between a scene of sexual consent and rape.

Notwithstanding the relationship between Nita's credibility as a witness and the court's verdict, Nita's ambivalence presses upon another aspect of the film's narrative – the unfolding of the revenge plot. Keeping pace with the ambivalence around the charge of rape in Arti's case, the film delays and reserves the revenge scenario until it can represent an unambiguous rape scene. It is only after Gupta proceeds to rape the virginal Nita in his office that Arti's revenge is allowed. In the film's climax Arti shoots Gupta, circumventing a judicial verdict on Nita's case. The film closes with another court scene where this time the judge abdicates his office for failing to deliver justice in earlier rape cases. Closing the rape-revenge narratives around a court scene or a figure of the State is now a standard feature of this genre and stands in sharp contrast to the male vigilante genre where the figure of the State is repeatedly undermined, for example in *Nayakan/Don* (1987). Although *Insaaf Ka Tarazu* did not have spin-offs for another seven years, the film established some of the basic conventions that squarely locate it as the inaugural moment in the avenging woman genre.

Pratighat is retroactively a classic of this genre because of the manner in which it consolidates some basic strains of the rape-revenge narrative. The film revolves around corrupt politicians and the ongoing crisis over law and order in a small town. The female protagonist, Lakshmi, is a college teacher who lives with her lawyer husband and his parents. The film opens with several scenes of hooliganism orchestrated by Kali – a *lumpen* youth leader – in Lakshmi's town. These scenes are also strung together to lead us through Lakshmi's conversion from an ordinary, disinterested citizen to an active intervenor in Kali's reign of terror. Her complete conversion to an avenging woman hinges on a crucial scene when she openly confronts Kali by filing a criminal suit against him and refuses to withdraw it even when he threatens to harm her. As the stakes continue to rise in their confrontation, Kali finally resorts to a gendered resolution: he disrobes Lakshmi on the street in front of her house, with all her neighbours and family watching in silence. This violation establishes the primary conditions for Lakshmi's revenge on Kali and his gang, and at the same time seals her estrangement from her husband. Lakshmi is rescued from this scene of public humiliation by Durga, whose own life has been scarred by Kali's violence – she was gang raped by Kali's men, and her husband tortured to death – and who nevertheless continues to galvanize opposition to Kali. Lakshmi moves into Durga's home, recovers, and receives support for her own revenge plan. [...]

[...] Clad in a red sari, Lakshmi garlands and anoints Kali at a public meeting and then repeatedly strikes him with an axe originally intended as a gift to him. The final killing scene is edited by juxtaposing shots of Kali's larger-than-life cardboard cut-out against the onstage altercation between Lakshmi and Kali, fight scenes between Kali's men and Lakshmi's students, and colour negative stills from the original disrobing scene. [...]

Two contradictions must be noted. Even as the film is critical of rape, rape scenes figure periodically in the narrative, signalling in each instance the consolidation of criminality and vigilantism with an increasing displacement of the State's law and order role. Similarly, criminalizing rape, the conceit employed in this film, appears to identify with a progressive legal position, but we find it cannot respond to the sadistic-voyeuristic pleasure prompted in the cinematic representations of rape. Kali's death may bear a formal resemblance to the disrobing scene, but is not subject to the same censorship regulations that underscore sexual representations in Indian cinema. *Pratighat*, nevertheless, irks us with the limits and possibilities of equating rape and revenge scenes and thus coaxes us to reconsider the masochistic underpinnings of the rape scenes in this genre. While the film relies on our masochistic identification in the rape scene to fully play out its horrifying potential, the sadistic dimensions of this very scene propel the revenge plot and remind us retroactively that the ensemble of elements in the rape scene is always a volatile marriage between sex *and* violence.

[...] *Pratighat* [...] opened the gates for other permutations and combinations of rape and revenge. [...] *Zakmi Aurat* picks a policewoman as its protagonist. With the rape scene occurring early in the narrative, the turning point emerges when the judicial system refuses to convict the rapists, in spite of policewoman Kiran Dutt's own testimony. Abandoning legal recourse, Kiran Dutt now joins forces with other rape victims in the city. Together the women come up with a fitting revenge plan: to snare the rapists and castrate them.

Kiran's gang rape is edited as a fight sequence that closes around a conventional representation of rape. The rape scene returns to the bedroom familiar from *Insaaf Ka Tarazu*, but with a twist. Refusing to linger on Inspector Kiran Dutt's body as the rapists strip her, the film instead focuses on the rapists as they tear down her jeans and fling them on the ceiling fan. The unrepresentativeness of the actual sexual act in this rape scene climaxes through a series of shot/reverse-shots of fetishized objects – the ceiling fan and a medium closeup shot of Kiran's screaming face.

The shot sequence employed in the gang rape of the female police officer creates the basic template for the castration revenge scenes. Again, details on the edge, like the doctor's operating gown, her mask and the overhead lamp, are excessively in focus and fetishized. The camera cuts off the entire abdominal region of the man, refusing to zoom in on a cloaked genital area. Rapid freeze shots of men's faces, and ninety-degree shots of the overhead lamp in the operating theatre signal the ongoing process of castration. This equivalence between the gang rape and castration scenes, spliced by repeating shot/reverse-shots of a face and an overhead object cinematically, attempts to balance rape and revenge.

Critics have lambasted this film for offering an improbable resolution to rape; however, such a reading assumes that films have an indexical signification to political reality instead of examining how their narratives repeatedly stage various fantastical possibilities of these very same realities for the spectator.[8] One of the crucial constitutive features of this genre is its vociferous stagings of 'reality' through familiar references: shots of real newspapers, photographs of Gandhi on courtroom walls, footage of the Indian flag, and so on. *Zakmi Aurat* relies more extensively on these elements than other films: the opening sequence shows us actual newspaper reports of various rape cases in India, and the film draws an obvious link between the Kiran Dutt character and Kiran Bedi – a well-known woman police officer in Delhi. Inhabiting the mise-en-scène, these authenticating details appear to be strategically placed to heighten our viewing pleasure of the unravelling horror plot, reeling the spectator into scenes of escalating horror that culminate precisely at the very juncture when the film plays on an uncanny resemblance to extra-cinematic icons and events. These narratives in general may not directly respond to, or satisfy demands of, justice in particular rape cases, but they do unleash scenes of resolution that both extend beyond the law of the State and expose the spectator's complicity in the terrifying rape sequences. [...]

[...] Films in this genre rely on convincingly meting out vigilante revenge that must equal, or even surpass, the horror of rape. While this equation produces ongoing narrative tensions, visual representations of rape in Indian cinema also remind us of the authority of censorship regulations, and suggest the possibility of sadomasochistic pleasures structuring these rape scenes. [...]

To mitigate and ward off such criticism, revenge scenes in these films have to be equally horrific in order to allow us to read the scenes of violent sex as rape *retroactively*. The narrative and visual machinations of this genre thus revolve around the problem of balancing rape and revenge: *Pratighat* settles rape by evoking figures of Hindu shakti goddesses and killing the rapist, whereas *Zakmi Aurat* resorts to an anatomical equation by suggesting castration as an act of revenge, and escalates the horror of rape by visually locating the castrated male body in an analogous position to the raped female body. Settling rape through castration resonates with a feminist utopia where, at least momentarily, the easy economic equation between the penis and phallus resolves the differences between gender and power that are constantly complicated by, and subjected to, the symbolic *difference* between the penis and phallus. The question is, while revenge narratives in this genre seek continuously to 'match' the horror of the rape, can they ever succeed?

Zakmi Aurat brings to a head the entire problem of visually and narratively matching rape with revenge through its absurd logic of five rapes to fifteen castrations, a logic that heralds a moratorium on this genre in its current configuration. [...] Even while revenge narratives, as Rahman informs us, provide female stars with more dominant roles, because women's access to avenging power in these films is intimately predicated on rape as a violent litmus test of gender identity, rape scenes are never neatly cordoned off from Indian cinema's extensive use of the woman's body as a stand-in for sex, as a crucial site of scopophilic pleasure. Faced with these contradictory demands, the avenging woman genre surfaces as a giddy masculine concoction: the rape scenes provide the narrative ruse for the revenge plan while also providing the spectator with a conventional regime of scopophilic pleasure. Revenge allows female stars to dominate the screen, but the genre demands that a violent assertion of masculine power in the form of rape is the price to exact for such power. Clearly, at the periphery of this genre where the interlocking narratives of rape and revenge are less than minimally finessed, gratuitously deploying rape does not sufficiently dislodge or displace conventional representations of women in Indian cinema or appease Rao's suspicions.

Located within the larger rubric of other violent action films produced in the same period, the more taunting feminist aspects of the rape-revenge films are most apparent in their narrative closures. Here the avenging woman's unhindered access to power is always limited by the arrival of the police; this finale differs markedly from the more assertive vigilante resolutions of the masculine genres like the gangster and bandit films. [...] If the social imaginary promotes a unity between symbolic law and the State, rape cases inject a dissonance between these sites of authority to remind us that 'issues' of honour and shame are only provisionally resolved through legal proceedings. For the victim, the State's betrayal in rape cases is equally accompanied by patriarchal abandonment and together they consolidate as the precipitating moment in the narrative that allows it to shift towards the revenge narrative. Faced with an orderless universe, the avenging woman narrative proceeds on a transgressive vigilante path, incites masculine anxiety about the phallic female, and opens the representational circuit for women on the Indian screen, but this unfettered power is undercut by finally reeling in the authority of the State and revealing the avenging woman's own overwhelming investment in the restoration of the social imaginary.

[...] Finding anything subversive about rape-revenge narratives, both at the register of the cinematic form and spectator's pleasure, leads us to some tangled issues plaguing feminist film theory. Laura Mulvey's classic essay 'Visual pleasure and narrative cinema' argues that 'Hollywood style at its best (and all the cinema which fell within its sphere of influence)' offers pleasure by enacting a conventional heterosexual division of labour in its narrative structure between active male and passive female for the masculine spectator. Challenges to Mulvey's essay, besides her own revision through melodrama, have been mounted by feminist film theorists as they move into other genres of Hollywood, particularly to B films that include horror, slasher and pornographic elements. Focusing on the less-than-best cinematic styles of B films that are directed at, and have, a loyal female audience and incorporate a heady combination of sex and violence, feminist film theory – Carol Clover's work on slasher films and Linda Williams's on pornographic films – has been forced to reconsider the dynamics between identification and pleasure, particularly sadomasochistic pleasure. [...]

It appears that the rape-revenge scenes in the avenging woman genre similarly rely on the generation of sadomasochistic pleasure, a pleasure that unwittingly challenges, however provisional it may be, the straightforward sadistic impulses of rape in Indian cinema. Because rape scenes are inextricably meshed with the revenge plot in this genre, the masochistic dimensions of the rape scene far outweigh its conventional sadistic associations, while at the same time the unfolding revenge plot leans on provoking the spectator's sadistic investments in revenge and punishment. Interweaving sadism and masochism through different filmic moments, this genre upsets the normalizing fetishistic economy with the fragmented woman's body as the central object, but complicating these generic pleasures is the ongoing tussle between every Indian filmmaker and the State over censorship. As a result, it is precisely through overt submission to censorship regulations that the commercial film industry parodies the authority of the State, a relationship that is not unlike the masochist's relationship to patriarchal law; therefore, we may have to consider the possibility of the rape-revenge device as yet another ruse to circumvent censorship, resorting once again to the woman's body. At the same time, tightening the rape-revenge equation unwittingly opens possibilities for cross-gender identifications. Not resolving the gender imbalance prevalent in social power relations, the contradictory forces of Indian commercial cinema beg for a reconsideration of the other identifications available in this heady combination of sex and violence. Responding in part to the debates on violence in Indian cinema which cast these representations solely in terms of their regressive effects on society, I suggest instead that violent scenes circumscribed by cross-cutting genre features and pressures can, in surprising ways, challenge patriarchy's normalizing overtones on the issue of gender, and constitute one of the crucial axes of spectator interests in these films. [...]

Before we commit ourselves to the idea that all roads to female aggression inevitably lead us to rape scenes in Indian cinema, it is worth remembering that this tight relationship between rape and revenge is a recurrent feature in Hindi cinema. Whatever peculiar production rationale helps to fortify this link, the yoking of rape with revenge cannot be disconnected from the modes of address structuring Hindi cinema: a national audience is always already its imagined addressee. In other words, its desire to command a national audience severely shrinks Hindi cinema's ability to stray from a successful, yet conventional paradigm.

However an appraisal of other regional cinemas, particularly Telegu films with the actress Vijayshanti in the lead, demonstrates that there are other contours to aggression, without the routine rape scene. [...]

Rumours and reports from the industry claim that Vijayshanti is one of India's highest paid female stars whose cachet at the box office is greater than most of her male counterparts. However, she too has had her share of rape-revenge narratives [...] Vijayshanti's own self-representation does not rest on emulating other heroines but, as she puts it: 'I always have to kick and pound the villains to pulp. That's why I'm called the Amitabh Bachchan of Andhra Pradesh.'[9]

When examining rape-revenge narrative, I steered away from considering the influence of the female star economy, choosing instead to focus on textual analysis. [...] Vijayshanti's films [...] despite their different directors, hold together as if to constitute a genre, and challenge my own marginalization of the female star economy in my previous readings of the avenging woman films. [...] Kodi Ramakrishnana's *Police Lock Up* (1992) [...] refuses any narrow casting of female aggressiveness and allows for an intriguing relationship between law and desire.

The narrative takes the following route: Vijaya – Vijayshanti – is an upright police officer who arrives in the town of Vishakpatnam to investigate a political assassination. She has to contend with corrupt policemen and a conniving and ambitious chief minister – Panjaraja – who we know is responsible for the assassination. Panjaraja accuses her of being a terrorist and Vijaya is thrown into jail. A second storyline now unravels: Shanti – Vijayashanti's double role – is the wife of a zealous police inspector – Ashok – who is frequently transferred because of his honesty. Shanti is obviously cast as Vijaya's alter ego: meek, clad in a sari, devoted to her husband and pining for a child. It is precisely this guilelessness that lands her in jail one curfew night. The police throw her into Vijaya's cell and the two see each other for the first time. Unlike stories of lost sisters and brothers that recur in Indian films, this scene does not drag in mothers and fathers to claim kinship between the two women. Instead, it moves quickly through the respective events that brought the two women to jail. The crucial detail that lends credibility to Vijaya's story of her capture is Shanti's encounter with a dying journalist who, mistaking Shanti for Vijaya, passes on details of yet another assassination scheme. Shanti suggests that they switch places so that Vijaya can complete her investigation and arrest the corrupt chief minister. Vijaya reluctantly agrees, and the following morning leaves with Ashok, now passing as his meek wife. The film now gallops along, plotting Vijaya's pursuit of the Chief Minister. We see her move effortlessly from sari to jeans, from submissive daughter-in-law to strong and masterful police official. Through various twists and turns that include the notorious international assassin John, the film ends in a temple courtyard where Vijaya and Ashok annihilate the villains. The wily politician is the last to go; Vijaya blows him up with his own bomb, strapped on with a belt, reminding viewers of the way Rajiv Gandhi was killed. The film closes with Vijaya and Shanti embracing.

Departing radically from both the rape-revenge narratives and male action films, *Police Lock Up* reconfigures the relationship between power, authority and gender, opening up a wide range of fantastical possibilities for feminist identifications. There are many obvious scenes of positive identification secured in the film. For instance, the film introduces Vijaya as a police officer driving her jeep through a series of slow-motion shots, thus breaking away from the routine logic of passage from victim to avenger in the rape-revenge genre. The film ungrudgingly celebrates her ability and success as a police officer by showing us elaborate details of her work. [...] What we do see in *Police Lock Up* is a woman's excessive investment in the law, a law that we often mistrust for the ways in which it gives feminism short shrift.

The cornerstone of this film's innovativeness, however, is its deployment of the double role. Indian cinema has long been fascinated with double roles and utilizes them both to recognize and bank on a star's popularity. [...] Demonstrating that the two women effectively and easily pass for each other – Vijaya as the submissive wife and Shanti as an aggressive officer – the film mobilizes change in each woman and closes around a less polarized distinction between the two. [...]

Rejecting a narrative closure around biological kinship, this film wrings out the full effects of masquerade. Vijaya's competency is asserted through her ability to masquerade not only as Shanti, but also a telephone line repair man and the killer John at various points in the film. Masquerade controls and mobilizes this film's narrative.

Joan Riviere's conceptualization of masquerade continues to abet theorizations of cross-gender identifications that attend the female spectator when viewing a masculine-ordered universe in Hollywood cinema.[10] [...]

It can be said that masquerade functions at different levels in *Police Lock Up*. The film is clearly located within the male action film genre where restoration of law and order dominate the narrative and always close on a conventional rearrangement of law and order. Usurping the standard male hero's role, that is, masquerading as a police officer, Vijayashanti plays this role to its full. The film supports this masculinization completely, for instance, by holding off song and dance sequences exclusively around her. Reeling Shanti into the narrative as an upright inspector's wife is a perfect foil for providing a feminine domestic space that both cushions and counterpoises Vijaya's aggressive public self, and together the two roles demonstrate Vijayashanti's ability to perform across different and competing terrains. Doubleness is further supported by naming the characters from parts of the star's full name thus 'assuring' the masculine subject, as proposed by Riviere, that behind the mask lies this powerful phallic figure that unites both halves of polar screen personalities.

The double role in this film also actuates a different fantastical staging of desire. The lack of parental origin as a reason for their resemblance unhinges the film from closing around a cosy sibling unity, while simultaneously unleashing a desire for the other. For instance, when Shanti suggests they switch places, the scope of this offer clearly extends to her spouse – we see Vijaya effortlessly passing for Shanti in her home, even masquerading her love for Ashok. It is only later in the film that Ashok reveals that he suspected Vijaya was not Shanti when she rejected his sexual demands. Of course, the film suspends all knowledge on the exact moment of his discovery, leaving open the possibility of a sexual interaction between Ashok and Vijaya. The switch thus opens the possibility of Ashok being exchanged as a sexual object between them.

We have seen the male version of this arrangement first proposed by Levi-Strauss and then ingeniously resurrected by Lacan and revised by feminists.[11] Eve Sedgwick's reformulation in *Between Men* shifts the exchange of women between men from a heterosexual matrix to homosexual.[12] Sedgwick proposes that women are exchanged between men to avert, ward off and occlude the articulation of homosexual desire for each other, while simultaneously oppressing women and producing homophobia. These terms seem uncannily reversed in *Police Lock Up*, raising the possibility that Vijaya and Shanti's full scale switching is driven by a desire for the other, however narcissistic it may appear. This reading is further endorsed by the final moment of the film where we see them embracing, a closure that displaces and postpones heterosexual resolutions. [...]

The film galvanizes one of the most common signs of love we can procure in Indian cinema to stage desire – a song and dance sequence spliced together as a dream sequence from Shanti's point of view. Triggered by Vijaya's visit and finding herself pregnant, Shanti longs to go home, but instead lulls herself to sleep by singing a song. This sequence is set around a pregnancy ritual, and she begins a duet with her husband, but soon substitutes him with Vijaya and the song closes around their embrace. Like the final embrace of the film, here too the heterosexual convention of these songs in Indian films is subverted. In the absence of any clear performative declaration of a lesbian identity in the film that may allow for a straightforward reading of a lesbian desire plot, I propose that *Police Lock Up* approximates a female buddy film genre that allows and encourages a staging of lesbian fantasies. As a police narrative, the film shadows and masquerades the male action genre to the hilt while surreptitiously displacing conventional expectations and resolutions attending its masculine counterpart.

In sharp contrast to the avenging woman genre, where the inept law and order system allows for the avenging plot to unfold with a closure that reintegrates the woman into the social and civic order, *Police Lock Up* and other Vijayashanti films harbour a less antagonistic relationship to the law. Located directly within the law, most prominently played out in *Police Lock Up*, the female protagonist is constantly settling law and order problems produced by corrupt politicians and policemen, a relationship with the State that is unabashedly accommodational. Nevertheless, Vijayashanti films raise some of the most knotty and unresolved problems attending representational struggles around femininity, violence and the State.

Notes

1 Firoze Rangoonwala, 'The age of violence', *The Illustrated Weekly of India*, 4–10 Sept. 1993, pp. 27–9.

2 M. Rahman, 'Women strike back', *India Today*, 15 July 1988, pp. 80–82.

3 Maithili Rao, 'Victims in vigilante clothing', *Cinema in India*, Oct.–Dec. 1988, pp. 24–6.

4 See Carol J. Clover, *Men, Women, and Chain Saws: Gender in the Modern Horror Film* (Princeton: Princeton University Press, 1992); Peter Lehman, "Don't blame this on a girl": female rape-revenge films', in Steven Cohan and Ina Rae Hark (eds) *Screening the Male: Exploring Masculinities in Hollywood Cinema* (New York: Routledge, 1993).

This explicit resemblance to Hollywood B movies throws up a set of new issues: it draws limits to 'national' styles of cinema, forcing us to consider the exchange and appropriation of cinematic styles across national boundaries. Every 'national' cinema has, of course, to contend with Hollywood hegemony, but if the points of contact between Indian and Hollywood film are the much maligned, yet often experimental, B films, it raises a host of fascinating questions relating to taste and the distribution networks of B films in the Third World.

5 See Aruna Vasudev, *Liberty and License in Indian Cinema* (New Delhi: Vikas, 1978) on censorship regulations.

6 Ashish Rajadhyaksha and Paul Willemen, *Encyclopaedia of Indian Cinema* (New Delhi: Oxford University Press, 1995), p. 416.

7 For a useful discussion on the public discussion of rape and the women's movement, see Ammu Joseph and Kalpana Sharma, 'Rape: a campaign is born', in Ammu Joseph and Kalpana Sharma (eds), *Whose News?: the Media and Women's Issues* (New Delhi: Sage Publications, 1994), pp. 43–50.

8 Farhad Malik, 'Fact and fiction', *Cinema in India*, Aug. 1981, pp. 5–8.

9 Interview with Vijayshanti, *Filmfare*, July 1993.

10 Joan Riviere, 'Womanliness as a masquerade', in Victor Burgin, James Donald and Cora Kaplan (eds), *Formations of Fantasy* (London: Methuen, 1986), p. 35. Mary Ann Doane's essays are good examples of this kind of appropriation. See Mary Ann Doane, 'Film and masquerade: theorizing the female spectetor', *Femmes Fatales* (New York: Routledge, 1991); 'Masquerade reconsidered: further thoughts on the female spectator'. *Femmes Fatales*. p. 33.

11 Claude Levi-Strauss, *The Elementary Structures of Kinship*, trans. James Harle Bell, John Richard von Sturner and Rodney Needham (Boston: Beacon Press, 1969). For a pithy elaboration of Levi-Strauss and Lacan see Jane Gallop, *The Daughter's Seduction: Feminism and Psychoanalysis* (London: Macmillan, 1982).

12 Eve Kosofsky Sedgwick, *Between Men: English Literature and Male Homosocial Desire* (New York: Columbia University Press, 1985).

9

Figuring Mother India: the case of Nargis
by Parama Roy

[handwritten: Nargis as a person / Nargis as a muslim woman, icon]

Prologue

In India, the 1970s, 1980s, and 1990s have witnessed an extraordinary increase in the (one-way) traffic between the domain of the popular cinema and the domain of national and state-level elective politics. The first celluloid star to translate his star quality into political capital was M. G. Ramachandran (MGR), the hero of more than two hundred and fifty films, mostly in Tamil, and the leader of his own party, the All-India Anna Dravida Munnetra Kazhagam (AIADMK), which he founded in 1972. [...] Stars in the Bombay cinema have nurtured and acted upon similar political desires and ambitions. The elections of 1984 saw three of them – Sunil Dutt, Vijayantimala Bali, and Amitabh Bachchan, the "angry young man" super-star of the 1970s and 1980s – elected to the Lok Sabha.[1] [...] [S]tars accumulate a kind of cultural capital in the cinema which seems eminently amenable to that other form of public life that is elective politics. What connects the publicness of the film star with the publicness of politics, elective or otherwise? And what happens to the rendezvous of national politics, broadly defined, and national cinema when its actors are gendered differently, and/or when their religious identities are differently produced?

This chapter can only multiply some of these questions, especially as it seeks to examine a more subterranean, fugitive, and speculative version of the filmic icon than the instances mentioned above. It examines the publicness of the actress Nargis, who was a highly regarded star of the 1940s and 1950s and who, though fascinated by politics and by political figures, never sought elective office herself. [...] It examines the transformation of Nargis into a national icon (signifying Indian womanhood), especially in the context of her highly acclaimed role in Mehboob Khan's *Mother India* (1957), and the way in which this fixes and monumentalizes a notoriously unstable star text.[2] [...] In taking up this question of the iconicity of the actress, [...] [the essay] also takes up perforce the question of Nargis's elusive but inescapable Muslimness; how does the Other become the icon that represents nationness? [...] [T]he story of Nargis, as I see it, is the story of a haunting, a story of the undead Muslimness that is neither present nor absent, not quite there but not quite convincingly buried, either. [...] In taking up the question of who or what bears the burden of Nargis's Muslimness, this story finds itself to be as much about the son of *Mother India* as it is about the mother herself. This chapter, then, functions as a brief, speculative analysis of the functions of iconicity and surrogacy in the registers of (Bombay) cinema and politics and of the discursive displacements from one to the other in the figures of Nargis and Sanjay Dutt. It is, if you will, a reading of the reciprocal and uneasy substitutability of two figures who carry considerable symbolic weight in ongoing struggles and anxieties regarding filmic and political representation, and "real" and "simulated" Indianness.

Any analysis of the parallel and sometimes intersecting production of the star biography and the filmic text must take into account the work of Rosie Thomas, who has brilliantly traced the contours of Nargis's star status, especially in relation to questions of her chastity in her personal life and in her filmic/mythical life as Radha in *Mother India*.[3] [...] My concern here is with the female star, who raises different questions and occupies a different place from the male star in the symbolic economy of the cinema, and with the star whose connection with politics is metaphorically and discontinuously established even as her enactment of Indian womanhood is literally and almost infallibly realized. Moreover, my concern is with the politics of the nation-state, to which the Bombay cinema bears a special and privileged relation. [...] Finally, and most importantly, I am interested in the ways the gendered star text might be interwoven with another form of identity – the religiopolitical one.

The instance of Nargis's variable success at being persuasively Indian underscores how persistently questions of religiopolitical identity in postcolonial India continue to be coded through the tropes of originality and impersonation, ownership and expropriation, depths and surfaces. This is particularly the case when questions of Muslim Indian identity are at stake. It is a commonplace that in the Hindu imaginary of the Indian nation, the Muslim carries a double and conflicting valence in relation to questions of indigeneity and authenticity. He (and this figure is usually though not invariably imagined as male) is the alien invader, destructive of properly Indian (read "Hindu") institutions, religious monuments, and ways of life; his loyalties are directed elsewhere, and he aggressively insists on his separateness from – but nonetheless within – an Indian and Hindu imagined community. [...] At the same time, though, that his religious Otherness is seen as essential, his profession of an authentic difference is spurious, since his Muslimness is the result of a (sometime) conversion. He is thus really a Hindu, albeit a lapsed, treacherous, or unwilling one, and he can be compelled by the Hinduness from which he has been forcibly wrenched. [...]

In their suturing of origin and legitimacy, both accounts – which reinforce rather than undo each other – stage Muslim Indian identity not only as a problem but also as a problem of (an always dubious) impersonation. It is upon this uncertain ground that one must locate the life and afterlife of the assimilated Muslim actress. What makes her the obvious choice for the ideologically freighted figure of (a Hindu) *Mother India*? In what ways is her filmic and personal exemplification of good Hinduness/good Indianness/good femininity both exceptional and counterfeit? How are we to read the process by which Sanjay Dutt becomes Nargis, and becomes Muslim, in the current moment? These are some of the questions to which this chapter on Muslim impersonation will address itself.

Nargis: the life

At the time of the release in 1957 of *Mother India*, which was the film with which she was conclusively associated from then on, Nargis was among the most prominent figures of the Indian cinema. [...] Nargis's mother, Jaddanbai, was by birth a *kothewali* (professional singer and performer/courtesan), well known in Allahabad and Calcutta [...]. [W]hen in 1928 a wealthy young medical student named Mohanbabu proposed to convert to Islam (thus becoming Abdul Rashid) to marry her, she consented. Nargis was born the following year [...] Jaddanbai moved to Bombay in the mid-1930s, having by this time established herself as a film producer, music director, and actress. [...] Though Nargis appeared as a child actress in *Talash-e-Haq* (1935), she was carefully educated, and her access to the world of films was strictly controlled. She was a student at St. Mary's, an elite girls' school in Bombay, and was to entertain hopes of training as a doctor, an ambition that her own father, Mohanbabu, had abandoned in order to marry Jaddanbai. She was with difficulty persuaded by her mother and her mother's friend, the director Mehboob Khan, to perform her first "adult" role at fourteen in the latter's *Taqdeer* (1943). All such scruples were set aside after the success of *Taqdeer*, though the young Nargis is said to have faced some degree of social ostracism from the families of her more respectable, non-*filmi* classmates.[4] [...] Certainly Nargis's feeling that the decision to be an actress was one from which there was no going back [...] is coded in terms analogous to those attendant upon a narrative of the loss of sexual innocence. [...] After a number of hits, which featured her opposite some of the best-known leading men of the day, especially Raj Kapoor and Dilip Kumar, she became one of the most important luminaries of the newly emerging star system in Bombay cinema; she was routinely billed above her male leads, and, for some years in the 1950s, she commanded higher fees than any of them did. The international success of some of the films (*Awaara*, 1951; *Shri* 420, 1954) that she had made with her lover, Raj Kapoor – which were runaway hits in the Soviet Union, West Asia, and North Africa – added another kind of nuance to her star image, as she became, in these post-Independence years, the ambassador of "Indian culture" on a world stage.

Nargis achieved a significant measure of star power in the years between the late 1940s and mid-1950s, not only because of her histrionic virtuosity [...] but also because of her very public romance with the rising male star Raj Kapoor. While it is true that Nargis was, as a review of a book on Raj Kapoor's films unequivocally states, central to the making of Raj Kapoor himself as an actor and a director and of RK Studios[5] (she worked at minimal wages for the studio and, in a partial throwback to the early days of the studio system, acted in non-RK films only at the pleasure of her lover), it was also true that her association with Raj helped invest her fully with star status. He had begun to pursue her very early in their association, and by the time they acted together in *Andaaz* and *Barsaat* (both

1949), they were already an item. Raj Kapoor was married and a father, in addition to being a Hindu. Their love affair was conducted without any particular subterfuge; and since they were young, glamorous, and successful, and from all accounts passionately in love with each other, they were envied as well as reproached. [...] The love scenes in *Barsaat* in particular were marked by an intensity hitherto unseen in the Bombay cinema. Critics have pointed to the unorthodox camera work and sound effects in the love scenes, with their lingering close-ups and a low-decibel pitch that intimates intimacy.[6]

The star biography took another significant turn in the mid-1950s, when Nargis realized that Raj Kapoor would not marry her, that is, he would not make her his second wife; he began instead to demonstrate a marked romantic interest in other actresses. Besides, it was becoming clear to her that her near-exclusive association with RK Studios was keeping her from important roles (such as that of Anarkali in K. Asif's *Mughal-e-Azam*, for which she had been chosen); some of her most highly regarded performances (though not necessarily the ones that brought her stardom) – in *Andaaz, Anhonee, Jogan,* and *Mother India* – were performed outside RK Studios, which had a fairly limited vision of the female lead's role in a film.[7] [...] Accordingly, she let Mehboob (who had "discovered" her and who had always begrudged Raj Kapoor his powerful claims on her) know that she was available for *Mother India*. A remake of Mehboob's 1940 classic, *Aurat* (Woman), *Mother India* was more self-consciously epic and nationalist. It was designed (among other things) to function as an implicit rebuttal of Katherine Mayo's notorious book of 1927 that had detailed the pathological sexual practices of Hindu males.[8]

The film was three years in the making, involving enormous resources and the paid and unpaid labor of thousands of people. When it was released in 1957, it was successful on a scale unprecedented in Bombay cinema. It ran for fifty weeks in Bombay, breaking all box-office records, and was granted tax-exempt status in the Bombay province; it was the first Indian film to be nominated for an Oscar (in the foreign-film category), and it won Nargis the Filmfare Award for 1957 as well as the Best Actress award at the Karlovy Vary film festival.[9] The role of Radha in *Mother India* was the one that irrevocably defined Nargis for the Indian cinema-going public as well as for the history of Indian film, not simply because of its epic scope and her own brilliance in it, but also because it effectively marked her departure – at the height of her career – from Bombay cinema. [...] [S]he bowed out of her acting career once Mehboob Khan's epic was completed. [...]

The fascination of the film was augmented by a behind-the-scenes story of its making, a story that was to constitute an epic narrative in itself. It is said that during the famous fire scene in the film, Nargis was trapped behind some burning haystacks and was rescued at considerable personal risk by the relatively unknown young actor Sunil Dutt, who played her wayward son Birjoo in the film. This is one of the stories most often repeated about Nargis, satisfying every expectation about life imitating art. [...] "Mother" and "son" fell in love and were married quietly in March 1958, at which point Nargis retired from her acting career. Marriage is said to have been her salvation. [...] She became an exemplary wife and the devoted mother of three children, especially of her son Sanjay. [...] She led an active life, working for her husband's film-production company, participating in government-sponsored delegations to foreign countries, and serving briefly as a member of the Rajya Sabha, to which she was nominated by her friend Indira Gandhi. During these years she was made unhappy by the delinquency and drug addiction of her much-pampered son and by her husband's criticism of her overindulgence of Sanjay. In 1980 a diagnosis of pancreatic cancer took her to New York for treatment; she died in Bombay in 1981, a month before her fifty-second birthday.

Before we read the intertextuality of the epic film and the epic life, we need to speak briefly of the film itself. *Mother India*, which is said to have played continually in one part or another of the country since its release, is one of the great classics of the Bombay cinema. It is the story of the trials of the peasant woman Radha, who spends her life battling the malign forces of nature and humanity and who assumes the mythic stature of the matriarch by the film's end. A devoted wife and the mother of four boys, she toils heroically at home and in the fields, enduring poverty and the rapacious extortions of the village moneylender, Sukhilala. Her husband loses his arms in an accident and forsakes his home, unable to bear the shame of his dependence on her. After floods have killed two of her sons and devastated her home and her harvest, the moneylender proposes to feed her children in exchange for making her his mistress. Sorely tempted though she is, she prizes her laaj (chastity) above all else and manages to rebuild her life. She raises her sons on her own and becomes "the mother of the whole village," keeping the villagers from fleeing their home after the floods. As she sings to them, in the name of Mother Earth, a map of pre-Partition India forms on the screen. In the second part of the film, Radha is older, her sons grown. Her older son, Ramu, is domestic and law abiding; her younger and rebellious son, Birjoo, is passionately devoted to her, a devotion that is intimately bound up in his keen sense of the wrongs done to her and to the village by Sukhilala. Becoming a bandit, he kills Sukhilala and attempts to abduct the moneylender's daughter in an attempt to counter the insult offered earlier to his mother's honor; but his mother, who regards the chastity of the village women as her own, kills him rather than letting him bring disgrace to the village. [...]

Part of the fascination of the film for Indian audiences is of course the iconicity of various constitutive moments: the trial by fire and the rescue, the prestige of motherhood, and the attainment of mythic status. This was to prove, for Nargis, literally the role to end all roles. [...] Only marriage and motherhood in "real life" could provide a script that matched the epic quality of the film. And while it is true that the female star's renunciation of films for marriage is the norm rather than the exception in the popular Hindi cinema and is routinely attended by the inflated rhetoric of the felicities of matrimony and motherhood, there is a way in which Nargis's preparation for that last, most exalted role had been distinctively, indeed uniquely heralded, by her own professional trajectory. [...]

Nargis: the star

Nargis was to remain a legend long after her exit from the screen, and any analysis of her enduring image must come to terms with the status of the star in Bombay cinema, which is, generally speaking, greater than anything that obtains in Hollywood. As Behroze Gandhy and Rosie Thomas point out in their essay on stardom in Hindi cinema, "The parallels between Indian stars and the gods of the Hindu pantheon are frequently remarked upon, both are colourfully larger than life, their lives and loves, including moral lapses, the subject of voyeuristic fascination and extraordinary tolerance, and stars accept, on the whole graciously, an adoration close to veneration."[10] Furthermore, "it [is] firmly believed that stars are a crucial ingredient in the success of any mainstream Indian film."[11] This is in large part, and in the current conjuncture, more true of male stars than of female ones, who have (since the 1960s) come to have increasingly subordinate roles in relation to the male lead.

The star system in Bombay cinema is not, of course, an indigenous phenomenon, and it cannot be understood outside the context of Hollywood cinema, which was immensely popular in the subcontinent for the first four decades of the century, until the "talkies" had effectively displaced the silent film. [...] The modern-day star system, which was the product of freelancing, began to emerge only in the 1940s, when independent producers, made wealthy by war profiteering and illegal arms trafficking, drew stars away from studios by bidding up their price. This was to lead eventually to the recasting of mainstream commercial cinema as "the cinema of the star rather than the cinema of the director, or the studio;"[12] stars were signed up even before decisions about script or direction were made.

The star system has been almost from the first overwhelmingly male dominated, female stars usually commanding (as in Hollywood) smaller fees and enjoying relatively brief careers as romantic leads. [...] Where male actors have (unlike Raj Kapoor) actually married actresses, it has almost invariably been with the stipulation that the wedding coincide with professional retirement. It speaks to the profoundly liminal status of the female star that she has so often occupied (or wished to occupy) the (distinctly secondary and officially illegal) position of the "second wife"; this includes some of the best-known actresses of the dominant and the parallel cinemas. It may speak to why these actresses are anxious to erect a cordon sanitaire between their status as lawfully wedded wives and their status as (mere) actresses. Nargis, for one, was anxious about the possibility of a respectable marriage, asking (in the context of a possible marriage with Sunil Dutt) only half-playfully, "Who will marry the daughter of a singing woman?" His offer of marriage may help in part to explain (what was commonly regarded as) her devotion and her gratitude to her relatively obscure and far less talented actor-husband.

Nargis: the sequel

The Bombay film industry has been, and continues to be, intertwined uneasily but closely with the gendered and religiously inflected discourse of nationalism and the nation-state; it is continually anxious to establish its legitimacy in the eyes of a state that looks upon it with suspicion as "both paltry and powerful."[13] Nargis was thus doubly liminal as an actress and as a Muslim subject; both identities involved complex negotiations not only within the postcolonial state but also within an industry whose inaugural moment was ineluctably tied to an emergent idiom of cultural nationalism. [...] In fact, the Bombay industry would claim on more than one occasion to have functioned as a de facto arm of state in generating through affect and consent a national unity in diversity that the postcolonial state had been markedly unsuccessful at achieving through its own institutions.

However, Congress nationalism of the 1930s and 1940s and, indeed, of the post-Independence decades could not but be haunted by the specter of its other, Muslim nationalism and, by sympathetic identification, the figure of the Muslim herself/himself as the sign of that intimate enemy. Faisal Devji's analysis of the Muslim in the symbolic economy of the Indian nation-state, while implicitly invoking a male subject, obviously has its resonances for pre-Independence Congress nationalism as well as for the Bombay cinema that is locked in an embrace with it: "In the history that the Indian state obsessively re-enacts, the Muslim separatist is nothing more than the original sign of its failure. The Muslim, in other words, represents a fundamental anxiety of nationalism itself: of the nation as something unachieved."[14] [...]

If this is what the films give us, what kinds of evidence might be adduced by what we will call the "life"? There, one looks almost in vain for those places where Nargis's Muslimness might be manifest. If there is one thing that characterizes such a figure, it is what might be deemed her "cosmopolitanism," a cosmopolitanism that overwrites the possibility of a Muslim difference and is aligned not only with that of the emerging Indian nation-state and its commitment to a secular modernity so-called but also with a specifically filmic variety of religious marking and unmarking. [...] Her background in fact marked her out as the interstitial figure representative of a new Indian modernity. Though her mother was a Muslim and her father had officially converted in order to marry her, his conversion is usually treated both as a matter of form and a sign of his magnanimity, as meaningless in one register but meaningful in another.

[...] As an actress, Nargis was noted for having moved away, after the commencement of her involvement with Raj Kapoor, from "the Muslim crowd" (including Mehboob), though she made several films with Raj Kapoor's rival, Dilip Kumar. When involved with Raj Kapoor (and hopeful of being his second wife), she routinely wore the *sindoor* of the Hindu wife, and it is possible that the relationship may have helped detach her from the signifiers of Muslim identity. When she married the Hindu Sunil Dutt, it was in an Arya Samaj (reformist/ revivalist Hindu) ceremony; their children were given Hindu names.

What is one to make of such unmarking, which while voluntary is rarely neutral? [...] I wish to speak of this identity (especially the identity of the "good Muslim Indian") as a persistent, insuperable, and continually negotiated problem. Paola Bacchetta has cogently described the varying place of the Muslim woman in Rashtriya Swayamsevak Sangh (RSS) fantasies about its own masculine hetero-sexuality; what is particularly fascinating is her account of the way the Muslim woman often figures as the subject of a (usually unreciprocated) desire for the Hindu nationalist male.[15] Nargis's devotion can fruitfully be read through such a lens, which may serve as a grid even for those who are not overtly Hindu nationalists, for Hindu nationalist thought, rather than necessarily contradicting the commonsense of the modern Hindu subject, represents it in radical form. Her legendary status is secured and her transcendence of her Muslimness confirmed through her desire for and devotion to a Hindu male savior. She can atone both for her Muslimness and for her enticement of a married Hindu male by living the *Mother India* allegory, which not only scripts her as heroically chaste but also – in the extraordinary scene showing an undivided continent reforming in response to her summons to the villagers to return – as a renouncer of Muslim separatism. Rosie Thomas has brilliantly described the appeal of *Mother India* to Indian audiences in terms of the gossip attaching to the sexual histories of its stars. [I wonder whether part of the appeal is not also due to the very fact of Nargis's Muslimness, this Muslimness functioning as an asset rather than a blot upon her status as ideal Indian woman, precisely because it can be shown to be erasing or overwriting itself in the assumption of the Radha role. If *Mother India* is, at least partially, an allegory of the repudiation of Muslim difference and of a becoming Hindu, then only a Muslim can assume the iconic position of that maternal figure.]

What interests me here is precisely this recessive, displaced quality of the Muslimness in the star persona and, indeed, in the filmography itself: Nargis – unlike her female Muslim compatriots Madhubala and Meena Kumari, for instance – did not appear in any major "Muslim" role. [...] How is Muslim woman represented in the (filmic) space of the nation? Where can one find it, if it is not only or most satisfactorily locatable in Muslim characters and stereotypes or in directors, songwriters, and producers? [...] I am, however, more interested in the traffic between star text and religious identity, in the repressions and displacements of Muslimness to the limits of the biography; I am interested, too, in the displacements that are necessitated by Bombay cinema's exhibition of its own "cosmopolitanism," a cosmopolitanism that is made deeply anxious by that sense of the abjected, the supplementary, that is Muslimness in Indian identity.

As we have seen, Nargis's Muslimness seems not to emerge in any obvious way from the legend of her life. [...] Her own publicly stated loyalties were powerfully, even hysterically, (Congress) nationalist and statist. [...] "In the new pattern of socialistic society laid down for our country, the emphasis will naturally be on rapid industrial progress, and India will need hundreds of thousands of working heroes and heroines to achieve the goal. The film artistes are duty-bound to portray them on the screen. Today, the film artistes are called upon to play more dynamic roles reflecting the spirit of 'new' India."[16] [...] If she sought an identification with any political figure, it was with Indira Gandhi (a personal friend, as her father Nehru had been, though to a less intense degree), whose representation as Durga or as Bharat Mata resonated powerfully with her most important role and her own sense of moral authority. (Several people – most notably Rajeswari Sunder Rajan – have in fact noted the parallels across the lives of Indira and Nargis and the reverberations of both in the script of *Mother India* – the mythic status, the imperiousness, and the devotion to an ungovernable son.)[17]

Where Nargis's Muslimness becomes most visible is in what persists as an afterlife and what refuses to stay buried. One important instance of this is the controversy that erupted immediately after her death, as if the mortality of the legend was what permitted a release of the disavowals that the fetishization of *Mother India* had reined in. Newspaper headlines marked her death as the passing of a legend: "Nargis: So Ends the Legend," "Last Journey of a Queen," "End of an Era." And yet there was something else, an appendage, an excess that seems always to haunt the figure of the "good Indian Muslim." According to Sunil Dutt, when she died he decided, for sentimental reasons (having to do with her remembrance of her parents in the last months of her life), to give her a Muslim burial rather than a Hindu cremation. There was free public speculation about this; given that Nargis had demonstrated her transcendence of her Muslimness through her films and the example of her life, her return to Islam, even in death, was deeply disturbing, raising questions about the genuineness of her (simulation of) non-Muslimness. If I may borrow a term from queer theory and queer activism, I would describe this as analogous to the outing of public figures at the time of their death; one is reminded inescapably of the trauma to heterosexual identity by the revelation of Rock Hudson's gayness when he was dying from AIDS.[18] In the case of Nargis, some reports claimed that she had left instructions to be buried as a Muslim, others that her brother (with the aid of aggressive Muslim mullahs) had insisted on Muslim rites in defiance of the widower's wishes.[19] As it was, the incident enhanced Sunil Dutt's stature as a renouncer (he had married an older woman, he had not insisted on his wife's renunciation of her religious identity, he had nursed her devotedly in her illness, and he had permitted a Muslim burial); but it also had the interesting effect of Islamicizing him, and of marking him out as the weak Hindu male, the most treacherous of the enemies within.

Sunil Dutt would come in time to be known, especially by the Hindu right, as a Muslim sympathizer. In 1993, when he was involved in providing relief to the victims of Bombay's vicious anti-Muslim riots (in which the police participated), he was accused by the Shiv Sena (a Hindu rightist group based in western India and powerful in Bombay) of undue partiality to Muslims. There were, according to Dilip Kumar, two attempts on his life, and the family received death threats. Later that year, in April 1993, and then again four months later, his son Sanjay, who was one of the highest-paid leading men in the industry, was arrested and jailed for possession of a smuggled AK–46 and ammunition in the aftermath of bombings in Bombay which are now widely believed to implicate Muslim underworld figures with ties to Pakistan and Dubai. He was believed to have obtained these from a Muslim film-production duo, Hanif-Samir, who were arrested for gun running in the Bombay blast case. He was imprisoned briefly, then released on temporary bail, allowing him to wrap up work on a film, *Khalnayak* (directed by Subhash Ghai, 1993), [in which] he played the role of a notorious terrorist and political assassin [...]. As in the case of his mother with *Mother India*, he began to be identified in fairly literal ways with (what was retrospectively recognized as) an important role; newspapers and magazines began to describe the new breed of violent Hindi films as inseparable from the violence of their (criminal, Muslim) backers. Hindu rightist groups campaigned against his films and those of his father. Sanjay was rearrested under the notorious Terrorist and Disruptive

Activities (Prevention) Act (TADA) and charged with conspiracy and sedition in the Bombay blast case, instead of being charged under the milder Arms Act. In October 1994 he was denied bail.[20] [...]

The Hindu right saw in Sanjay the lineaments of his Muslim mother (and his "Muslim-loving" father). Nargis's Muslimness, then, was never fully exorcised from the star legend; but the subtext that was more or less curbed in her lifetime was to take the form of an interesting displacement. She continues in some registers to be revered as a legend, with Doordarshan recently holding a retrospective of her films, but she also figures at the same time as a species of monstrous mother, as her husband and her son come to occupy the place of her Otherness. The fact that Sanjay was a spoiled and recklessly self-indulgent young man, who had been his mother's darling, has given for some people a certain credence to the substitution. The fact, moreover, of his visibility and popularity – he was the second only to Amitabh among male stars in Bombay – is fully congruous with the sense of the Muslim as the *familiar* enemy; thus the Muslim is not one of us, and the Muslim is, terrifyingly, one of us.

The scenario of the overfond mother whose indulgence (temporarily) spoils the son is a common one in the Bombay cinema, and in the eyes of many it seems to have been played out with uncanny literalism in the Nargis-Sanjay Dutt story. She is known to have been passionately fond of him, indulging him and lying for him in defiance of her husband's call for stricter discipline, and she is believed by many to have facilitated his addiction to a variety of drugs, including heroin. [...] His audiences, it is said, see him as carrying an aura of tragedy and vulnerability because of his mother's early death, an aura that belies the macho violence of his roles.[21] But the very prematurity of her death is also the sign of a refusal to die; she features as a contagion from beyond the grave, an unquiet specter inhabiting both the renegade Hindu husband and the violent, weak minded, and affectionate son. In this context, Sanjay's long and very public history of addiction makes him available as an easily pathologizable figure. The fact of his describing himself as always vulnerable to temptation ("It's a sickness that can't be cured") provides a rationalization for the stigmatization.[22] His addiction functions as an analog to, and perhaps the support for, the taint of his Muslimness.

It must be noted that, apart from the prosecutors and the Hindu right, he is believed to be innocent of the conspiracy charges, though he is believed to have had mob connections. An article in the respected fortnightly *India Today* also links the acquisition of the weapon to questions of religious identity. It conjectures that the frantic calls for help the Dutts received from besieged Muslims during the riots may have led Sanjay to this step, especially as the Hanif-Samir team began to frequent his home at this juncture.[23] He has become, unwittingly, a representative figure, not only of the enemy within but also of an entire industry's alleged subservience to Muslim mafiosi based in Dubai. The very word *Dubai* resonates powerfully in the Indian context, given the numbers of Muslim Indians who have gone there (and to other countries in the Persian Gulf) in recent decades as guest workers and returned to India comparatively wealthy and occasionally with a sharpened sense of religious affiliation. This is articulated in ways both subtle and obvious with the growing sense of Bollywood's thralldom to organized crime, especially Muslim organized crime; the trips made by famous major and minor stars to Dubai, and their reputed liaisons with alleged underworld figures, are seen as evidence of their subjection to these illicit, antinational influences.[24] Sanjay's apprehension led to considerable nervousness in the industry, nervousness that sometimes took the form of appeasing Bal Thackeray, the head of the Shiv Sena. It also became the occasion for the imposition of a number of demands by the Hindu rightist Bharatiya Janata Party in Bombay on the Film Makers' Combine: these included suspending producers and actors accused of antinational activities from trade bodies and new films and respecting "the Hindu way of life, culture and values."[25]

[...] [T]he very fact of his arrest and imprisonment without bail (along with hundreds of alleged coconspirators), despite his being the son of a Congress (I) member of Parliament, at a time when the party was in power at the state and at the federal level, is something of a testimony to the fact that suspicions of his Muslimness do not emanate solely from the Hindu right. TADA is in fact notorious for having been applied with extreme rigor to religious minorities, especially Muslims and Sikhs, and has been vociferously criticized by religious minorities and the Human Rights Commission. TADA does not clarify the nature of terrorist activity, encompassing acts violent and nonviolent, private and public, and places upon the accused the burden of proving their innocence;[26] in this regard it functions in ways that are already familiar to religious minorities, casting them as the abjected who must compulsively yet unsuccessfully keep enacting their good citizenship. At the moment Sanjay is out on bail and has resumed his acting career, thanks to the intervention of Thackeray. This is not testimony to the waning of Hindu fundamentalist zeal. Rather, it speaks to the power of the RSS chief, who can manifest his potency perhaps even more persuasively by withholding punishment than by inflicting it.

This is a sequel, not yet completed, to the life of Nargis. Even after death, she remains, as good Muslimness remains in the Indian polity and in Indian/Hindu public culture, as a phantasm, a ghost that lives and moves uncannily in our midst, not quite tangible and never fully exorcisable. Her career – in life and after it – illustrates in fascinating ways how disturbing and enigmatic a figure of (gendered) trouble the good Muslim is for Indianness. (The "bad Muslim," as a figure who insists on forms of religiously based separatism and retains the obvious signifiers of Muslim identity, is a far easier entity to respond to or manage.) As we have seen, the industry itself has showcased Muslim talent – in acting, direction, writing, and music – in a very substantial way; many Muslim actors and actresses have entered the imaginary of a movie-going public in the most spectacular ways. The good Muslim, then, is not simply a phobic object, to be responded to with punitive laws and pogroms and other forms of bigotry; s/he is also, and at the same time, the object of love and identification. Above all, s/he is a figure of unhappy intimacy who, despite manifold repressions and conversions, returns repeatedly and inauspiciously to haunt the wholeness of an Indian (Hindu) psyche/polity. [...]

Notes

1 Mira Reym Binford, "The Two Cinemas of India," in *Film and Politics in the Third World*, ed. John J. H. Downing (New York: Praeger, 1987), 147.

2 For an account of the negotiations between contradictory forces in the star texts of three "heroines," Fearless Nadia, Nargis, and Smita Patil, see Behroze Gandhy and Rosie Thomas, "Three Indian Film Stars," in *Stardom: Industry of Desire*, ed. Christine Gledhill (London and New York: Routledge, 1991).

3 Rosie Thomas, "Sanctity and Scandal: The Mythologization of *Mother India*," *Quarterly Review of Film and Video* 11, no. 3 (1989): 11–30.

4 Interview with Nargis, in *Indian Cinema Superbazaar*, ed. Aruna Vasudev and Philippe Lenglet (New Delhi: Vikas Publishing House, 1983), 252.

5 Gautam Kaul, "Review of Wimal Dissanayake and Malti Sahai's *Raj Kapoor: Harmony of Discourses* (New Delhi: Vikas, 1988)," *India Today*, 31 May 1988, 91.

6 Bikram Singh, "The Dream Merchant," *Filmfare*, 16–30 June 1988, 18.

7 T. J. S. George, *The Life and Times of Nargis* (New Delhi: Indus/HarperCollins, 1994), 127.

8 Mayo's *Mother India* was regarded in some circles as anti-Hindu and pro-Muslim (Sinha, "Reading *Mother India*").

9 B. D. Garga, "The Feel of the Good Earth," *Cinema in India* 3 (April–June 1989): 32.

10 Gandhy and Thomas, "Three Indian Film Stars," 107.

11 Ibid.

12 Vijay Mishra, Peter Jeffery, and Brian Shoesmith, "The Actor as Parallel Text in Bombay Cinema," *Quarterly Review of Film and Video* 11, no. 3 (1989): 53.

13 Kishore Valicha, "Why Are Popular Films Popular?" *Cinema in India* 3 (April–June 1989): 34. When I speak of nationalism(s) here, it is of Congress and Hindu nationalisms; despite the significant involvement of Muslims in the Bombay film industry, it has never supported implicitly or explicitly any form of Muslim nationalism.

14 Faisal Fatehali Devji, "Hindu/Muslim/Indian," *Public Culture* 5 (Fall 1992): 1.

15 See Paola Bacchetta, "Communal Property/Sexual Property: On Representations of Muslim Women in a Hindu Nationalist Discourse," in *Forging Identities: Gender, Communities and the State in India*, ed. Zoya Hasan (Boulder, Colo.: Westview Press, 1994), for a fascinating account of the Hindu nationalist male fantasy of the Muslim woman's desire for him. For a full account of the RSS, see Walter K. Anderson and Shridhar D. Damle, *The Brotherhood in Saffron: The Rashtriya Swayamsevak Sangh and Hindu Revivalism* (Boulder, Colo.: Westview Press, 1987).

16 R. M. Ray, *Sangeet Natak Akademi Film Seminar Report 1955*, 173–74.

17 See *Real and Imagined Women: Gender, Culture and Postcolonialism* (London: Routledge, 1993).

18 See Richard Meyer, "Rock Hudson's Body," in *Inside/Out: Lesbian Theories, Gay Theories*, ed. Diana Fuss (New York: Routledge, 1991) for an account of the heterosexual responses to the news of Hudson's gayness.

19 George, *Life and Times of Nargis*, 191.
20 Manoj Mitta, "TADA: Relentless Terror," *India Today*, 15 October 1994, 111.
21 M. Rahman and Lekha Rattanani, "Sanjay Dutt: A Fatal Attraction," *India Today*, 15 May 1993, 72.
22 Ibid.
23 Ibid.
24 M. Rahman and Arun Katiyar, "Bombay Film Industry: Underworld Connections," *India Today*, 15 May 1993; and Jeet Thayil, "From Reel to Real in 'Bollywood,'" *Asiaweek* [reprinted in *World Press Review*, October 1994, 45].
25 M. Rahman, "Sanjay Dutt: It's Not Over Yet," *India Today*, 31 May 1993, 67.
26 Harinder Baweja, "TADA: An Act of Terror," *India Today*, 15 September 1994.

10

What is behind film censorship? The *Khalnayak* debates
by Monika Mehta

Censorship, postcolonial state and sexuality

My research into the censorship debates reveals that the battles over Indian national identity are continuously waged on the terrain of sexuality; it is the female body which is overtly and overly marked as the sexual body. Both the proponents and opponents of censorship have argued whether the representation of sexuality was a part of Indian tradition; whether 'double-standards' for judging Indian vs. foreign films maintained Indian values, preserved colonial puritanism or reinforced a patriarchal status quo; and whether this national prudishness in any way affected the state's (and a portion of the public's) much desired goal – to be modern and democratic. [...] An important state mechanism for regulating the social organization of sexuality, censorship has been a key point of contact between the Indian state, the Bombay film industry and the Indian citizenry.

Re-framing censorship

Aruna Vasudev's *Liberty and License in the Indian Cinema* characterizes censorship as an act of prohibition that is dictated by the state.[1] This characterization of censorship suggests a limited understanding of power. It presumes that the exercise of power is uni-directional; that is to say, the state is the only actor who exercises power. In the theatre of censorship, power is exercised by the state, the film industry and citizenry in relation to one another. This play of power is not simply repressive. Rather, it (re)produces rules, practices parameters of debate, categories and subjects; in short, it produces the discourse of censorship. [...] [Through an analysis of a Hindi commercial film, *Khalnayak/The Villain* (1993),] I examine the play of power among the Indian state, film industries and citizenry [...] and in the process, re-theorize censorship as a productive activity.

The object of controversy: 'Choli ke peeche kya hai'

[...] The film song 'Choli ke peeche kya hai' (What is behind the blouse?) in Subhash Ghai's *Khalnayak* plunged the nation into a debate about morality. The lyrics of the song stood accused of transmitting improper sexual mores. [In the film], the villain Ballu (Sanjay Dutt) kills a politician and is captured by the hero, intelligence officer Ram Sinha (Jackie Shroff). While Ram[2] is visiting his girlfriend, sub-inspector Ganga (Madhuri Dixit), in Hindi cinema's version of an Indian village, Ballu escapes from prison and Ram is bombarded with accusations of incompetence. In fact, one reporter suggests that Ram failed to fulfill his duty as an intelligence officer because 'he was having a good time with Ganga'. Ganga, then, becomes the temptress who leads Ram astray from his duty to the police force and causes his failure. In order to redeem himself in the eyes of the police force, he must regulate his desire for her. Consequently, Ram vows to remain unmarried until he recaptures Ballu. In order to salvage her fiancé's reputation, and her own reputation since the townspeople have begun to wonder about Ganga's relations with Ram since he has not married her, Ganga disguises herself as a 'folk' dancer and sings the song 'Choli ke peeche kya hai' to seduce Ballu so that she can join his gang and eventually bring him to justice.

Ganga's guise as a dancer constructs the expression of her sexuality as a 'masquerade'. We as privileged spectators know that behind this guise is a 'pure' Ganga who loves Ram and who is enacting this role out of a sense of duty. At the beginning of the song sequence, which is composed of one hundred and fourteen shots, a veiled Ganga swaying to the sinuous rhythm of the flute enters the villain's den. Unlike the all-male audience who watch Ganga's entry, the spectators know that she is a representative of the police force and thus, of course, a danger to the criminal world. Interestingly, within the domain of criminals, Ganga is also constructed as the object of desire and as a lure which can destroy this world if she is not controlled. As Ganga, dressed in an itsy-bitsy, red-sequined blouse glides across the floor, the camera salaciously focuses on different parts of her anatomy. In this case, the technology of the camera and the editing processes construct Ganga as a desirable object. They also position the male audience within the diegetic space as voyeurs and extend the same position to the spectators in the theater. Although the technology of the camera and the editing processes construct Ganga as a sexual object, the privileged spectators, unlike the all-male audience in the diegetic space know that she is a sub-inspector and therefore, a subject of the Law.

After marking Ganga's entry, the camera cuts to another dancer, Neena Gupta as she demands 'Choli ke peeche kya hai? Chunari ke neeche kya hai?' (What is behind the blouse? What is under the veil?).[3] Employing a shot/reverse shot, the camera turns to Ganga, focusing on her blouse, as she slowly unveils and answers 'Choli mein dil hai mera, chunari mein dil hai mera, yeh dil mein doongi mere yaar ko, mere pyar ko' (My heart is in my blouse, my heart is under veil, I'll give this heart to my lover).[4] The camera lingers over Ganga's blouse and makes the *double entendre* visible. The reference is not only to Ganga's heart, but also to her breasts. After showing this interaction, the camera cuts and zooms on the smirking figure of Ballu, the villain who is simultaneously the desiring male subject and the criminal object under Ganga's surveillance. [...] What Ballu does not realize and the privileged spectator does is that behind the blouse and behind the veil is a representative of the police force masquerading as an object of desire.

Music industry and censorship

According to common market practice, TIPS, an established music company primarily involved in the film-music industry, released the audio cassette for *Khalnayak* featuring the tantalizing song 'Choli ke peeche kya hai' while the film was still in production. 'Choli ke peeche kya hai' could be heard on the radio and boom-boxes, and seen on the 'top-ten' shows in the form of music-videos created from publicity clips of *Khalnayak*. In India, the success of a popular film is often connected to the popularity of its music. The audio cassettes and music-videos not only serve as advertisements for the film, but also generate profits for the music companies; these profits are often passed along to the film producers. [Since 1980] the music industry has both expanded and flourished. As country-wide street sales of audio cassettes have drawn close to Rs. 5 billion annually, composers and music producers have been happily singing all the way to the bank. Approximately 150 Hindi music titles are released every year, with all India sales estimated at 1 million cassettes a day – inclusive of piracy.

In a letter written to the Ministry of Information and Broadcasting, Pandit Gautam Kaul, a concerned citizen, enumerated the adverse effects of the mushrooming music industry. In its new avatar as a major commercial film financier, the music industry had transformed the practice of commercial filmmaking, in particular, the production and distribution of songs. Kaul catalogued the detrimental effects resulting from this transformation:

> Recording of songs are completed even before the film goes into production and recording companies, without waiting for the release of the film, exploit the songs as investments. It is also noticed that there are some cases now where the songs of a movie announced for production proved immensely popular and the film remained unknown even after its release. There are possibilities that a full album of songs can be released, and the film may never be made. In such cases, the songs would be given nomenclature as 'private songs'.[5]

For Kaul, these *new* forms of production and distribution of film songs warranted immediate attention because they were circumventing state scrutiny. He suggested that the state tackle this issue by compelling producers to submit film songs to examining committees before their release and by creating offices for the certification of private and film music to regulate the burgeoning music industry.[6] [...] While state-censorship (in)forms filmmaking, practices of film production and distribution also have an impact on state censorship. In the process of drawing attention to the implications of a growing music industry for the practice of censorship, Kaul unwittingly demonstrated how technology, namely audio cassettes, revealed the limits of state authority. As a medium which was not subject to state censorship, audio cassettes could circulate and carry potentially subversive or, as Kaul feared, *vulgar* messages freely.

Legal petition against Khalnayak

As 'Choli ke peeche kya hai' circulated in the form of audio cassettes, R. P Chugh, an advocate and a Bhartiya Janata Party (BJP) supporter was among the many who heard the song. He filed a legal petition in Delhi alleging the song

> is obscene, defamatory to women community and is likely to incite the commission of offence. The song is grossly indecent and is being sung through cassettes at public places, annoying the people at large, the undersigned specially [*sic*].[7]

The veiled sexual reference made the song, in Chugh's eyes, not only obscene, but [also] derogatory to women. What increased his annoyance was the song's unhindered circulation in public. Chugh's cluster of complaints drew together three specific assumptions about sexuality – assumptions which are common to patriarchal discourse in India: first, that sexuality is obscene, second, that sexual references dishonor women and third, that sexuality's entry into public space disrupts social boundaries. Chugh's petition was a means for seeking redress against such affronts.

[...] Instead of voicing his dissent by other means such as a letter to a newspaper or magazine, Chugh filed a legal petition which produced a juridical relation among Chugh, the court and the addressees of the complaint. Such a relation constructed Chugh as a juridical subject and citizen who by calling upon the court to adjudicate, hailed the court as arbitrator in a dispute against other subjects, namely, 'the defendants' who included Tips Cassettes, the Central Board of Film Certification, Subhash Ghai & Mukta Arts, and the Ministry of Information and Broadcasting. In short, the legal petition both drew upon and reproduced a legal-juridical apparatus which is constitutive of the state.

As a juridical subject, Chugh [made several requests.] First, he called upon Subhash Ghai, the film's producer, and the censors to delete the song from the film. Second, he demanded that TIPS, the music company, be restrained from selling audio cassettes of the song. Third, he requested that the Board put a prior restraint on the exhibition of *Khalnayak* until the song was deleted. Fourth, he asked that the Ministry of Information and Broadcasting not allow the song to be aired on state-run television. Chugh's requests reveal that in the theater of censorship multiple entities are involved in the play of power.

[...] While the censors could excise 'Choli ke peeche kya hai' from the film *Khalnayak*, the Central Board of Film Certification had no authority to prohibit the sale of its audio cassettes; it could only exercise authority over *films* as stated in the Cinematograph Act of 1952. Technology, in this case the audio cassettes, revealed the limits of the Certification Board's authority. Another instance which demonstrated the limits of the Board's authority was Chugh's request to the Ministry of Information and Broadcasting. The regulation of state-television was a task allocated to the Ministry of Information and Broadcasting, not the Central Board of Film Certification which meant that Chugh had to contend with another technology, namely, television and the quirks of another authority, the Ministry of Information and Broadcasting.

The advent of liberalization in the nineties added a new twist to Chugh's request to prohibit the song from state-television. The rise of satellite television and innumerable private cable channels which were not regulated by the state meant that even if programs were prohibited on state-television, viewers could easily watch them on private channels. These new technologies revealed the fragility of national boundaries and state authority. [...]

Public debate on Khalnayak

Although the case was not successful in legal terms, it succeeded in stirring up a public debate on the representation of sex in cinema.[8] Shakti Samanta, the chairman of the Central Board of Film Certification in Bombay received approximately two hundred letters[9] for and against the deletion of the song from the film and from its trailer. Among those who wrote letters were members of the Bhartiya Janata Party, a Hindu nationalist party. In a letter supporting Chugh's petition, the President of the Women's Wing of the BJP in New Delhi wrote:

> 'Choli ke peeche kya hai' is an obscene song and as a result of which new anti-social elements have got the excuse of singing this song on seeing girls. Many incidents of Eve-teasing[10] have occurred. The film song singers only just to earn money are shamelessly singing such type of songs which are against the public interest [sic].[11]

According to her, 'Choli ke peeche kya hai' contributed to sexual harassment of women. [...] Vineet Kumar, who filed a case against *Khalnayak* at the Consumer Redressal Forum in Faridabad, cited an 'instance in Sambhal where a young man namely Raju, son of Shri Nazar resident of Miyan Sarai used to tease girls of respectable families by singing this un-parliamentry song [sic].' Kumar argued that the song should be deleted from the film on the grounds that it was 'against the culture, convention and moral of Indian society[sic].'[12]

Concurring with Kumar's sentiments, an affronted Ashok Kumar from the Integrity and Welfare Society wrote:

> One doesn't understand what the director Subhash Ghai wants to say to a cultured nation like India by showing songs with double meaning. When one's sisters and daughters are around and songs like these are played, one feels ashamed and embarrassed.[13]

Adding to the list of the song's detrimental effects, Mrs. Ram Gupta indignantly inquired what kind of culture and tradition would children learn from watching such a song.[14] Shweta Sanjay also expressed her concern about the song's effects on 'innocent minds':

> The audio playing of the said song has been disturbing parents and innocent minds throughout the nation. The said audio song should have been banned

immediately on its release ...I fail to understand as to how will parents feel while viewing the said film with their children and more so when they ask about the meaning of the said words.[15]

The letters suggest that the opponents of the song were morally offended by the lyrics and distressed about their effects upon children, women and Indian culture [by sexuality]. [...] [More specifically, at risk are] children whose 'innocent minds' are susceptible to corruption, women who require protection from sexual harassment, and Indian culture which needs to be shielded from vulgarity and immorality. [...] Furthermore, the letters align women, children and Indian culture, producing an opposing relation between sexuality and the vulnerable trio.

[...] Among the proponents of the song were exhibitors from Rajasthan. They sent out letters which clearly drew upon a common text. In the letters, they urged the Board to retain 'Choli ke peeche kya hai' in the trailer of *Khalnayak* on the following grounds:

> The above song is a very popular folk song of Rajasthan. It can be heard during Holi and other festivals in Rajasthan. We do not find anything vulgar in the above song. In fact we have seen many ladies singing the song. If the song was vulgar then the ladies would have never liked it.[16]

> I have seen the song on Zee TV and when I compared the words with the visuals I found nothing vulgar in it. The picturisation is also quite sober and we can enjoy with the family. We will request you to go through the song before giving us your decision and allow us to enjoy the beautiful song.[17]

If the opponents had argued that the song was against Indian tradition, its proponents cited its traditional pedigree, claiming it was a folk song which was sung at festivals. In fact, its supporters asserted the song could not be vulgar since women had been singing it. S. Nayyar, an interested citizen, supported their claim:

> If the reason for this is the so-called vulgarity and suggestiveness of the lyrics then it seems only right to point out that this is not the only song by far to have such lyrics. And this is a folk song – which means that it has been sung for decades and maybe centuries! While other songs which abound in double entendre and innuendo cannot even claim that distinction and have been written purely for the titillation of the masses. All these great moralists and puritans who have woken up so suddenly did not have much to say for the banning of other songs. My advice to them is to take the literal meaning of the song and forget about the so-called vulgarity. It's all minds anyway [*sic*].[18]

Arun Katiyar, in an article for *India Today*, confirmed that 'folk traditions, especially in Punjab, Gujarat, Rajasthan and Uttar Pradesh have spawned wicked lyrics.' However, he added that the songs are sung in *specific contexts* such as pre-wedding ceremonies. In these ceremonies, he explained that when 'women sing what is commonly called ladies' *sangeet* [songs] in Punjab, it is done more in fun than as a come-on.'[19] [...] The song's detractors claimed that it contributed to sexual harassment, constructing women as victims. Conversely, its proponents suggested that the song could not be vulgar since women had been seen singing it. Last, we have Arun Katiyar who confirmed the song's traditional pedigree, but contended that it had been dislodged from its context, in particular, pre-wedding ceremonies, which is to say the site of tradition. These positions seek to produce an 'Indian tradition,'[20] in which women are either sexual victims or guardians of morality and tradition. However, they shirk from representing women as sexually active beings.

Examining Committee's Report on Khalnayak

The 'nearly complete' *Khalnayak* and its trailer appeared before the Examining Committee in Bombay during the course of Chugh's petition and the public debate. The trailer for *Khalnayak* was submitted for certification a few days before the film. Initially, the Examining Committee ordered that the words 'Choli ke peeche kya hai' be deleted from the trailer as they violated the censorship guidelines, specifically 2(vii). However, after examining the entire film, the committee passed the trailer without cuts because it was satisfied that the line did not violate the guidelines in the context of the totality of the song. This happy ending did not take place immediately. [...]

After the committee members watched *Khalnayak*, they discussed their reactions to the film:

> The members felt the theme of the film, the song sequences, and fights would be better understood by children with parental guidance. The members therefore unanimously felt the film should be granted an 'UA' certificate with some cuts. The Examining Officer then informed the committee about the various letters received by CBFC [Central Board of Film Certification] for and against the film. The members after further discussion felt that the visuals in the song sequence were not vulgar, but the words 'Choli ke peeche kya hai' could be deleted.[21]

Public debate (in)formed the committee's decision to grant *Khalnayak* a 'UA' certificate subject to seven cuts, three of which pertained to the *first picturization of the song*. The song appeared in the film twice but the Examining Committee, Chugh's petition, and the public debate focused on the first picturization, one which Madhuri Dixit (the heroine of the film) and her entourage sing the song. The committee recommended the following cuts in the song sequence:

Cut No. 5 Reel No. 6:   Delete the words 'Choli Ke Peeche Kya Hai, Chunari ke Neeche Kya hai' [What is behind the blouse?, What is underneath the scarf ?] from the song sequence.

Cut No. 6 Reel No. 6:   Delete the visuals of Ganga pointing at her breast in the song where she sings the song 'Jogan bana na jay kya karu' [I can't bear being an ascetic so what should I do].

Cut No. 7 Reel no. 6:   Delete the close visuals of pelvic jerks of dancing girls in the beginning of the song 'Choli ke peeche' 2(vii).[22]

The committee informed the applicant, Subhash Ghai, of its decision. He accepted most of the committee's recommendations but appealed against cuts five and seven. The committee reconsidered its decision and unanimously waived cut five but retained cut seven. Ghai agreed to this compromise. Although the film had been examined, the final editing for *Khalnayak* was still in progress. After its completion, Ghai sent the committee a series of additions and deletions which were certified.

These events show that censorship is not simply the domain of the state; rather it is a site at which relations amongst the state, citizenry and film industry are negotiated. Furthermore, an analysis of the filmic narrative and these negotiations reveals that the censors are not the only ones who cut films. [...] [There are] two instances of cutting, namely editing and censoring. While the former is part of the 'creative' process, the latter is viewed as an imposition of state authority [and] [...] both instances contribute to the production of meaning, in short, to how the film is understood in its total social moment. In addition, the process of censorship is not limited to cutting. The film is classified 'UA' and given the appropriate certificate. What prompts this decision is the committee's uncertainty whether children will be able to acquire a *proper* understanding of the film, specifically sequences containing sex and violence, without parental guidance. The classification serves as signpost to parents, urging them to exert their authority and regulates how the film is understood.

In some part due to this controversy, 'Choli ke peeche kya hai' became a smash hit. In the eastern region alone, 'Choli ke peeche kya hai' sold over seven hundred thousand cassettes. According to market estimates, Tips, the music company which released the audio cassette, invested 12.5 million, including publicity, in the *Khalnayak* soundtrack, and sold over 5 million tapes, making the company a profit of Rs. 30 million. The lucrative profits made by Tips were most probably also shared with the producers of *Khalnayak*.[23] Considering the profits at stake, an editorial in *The Sunday Times of India* suggested that the 'Choli ke peeche kya hai' controversy was a marketing strategy engineered by the showman Subhash Ghai.[24] The legal petition to censor the song and the ensuing debate contributed to constructing it as an object of controversy.[25] When a controversial text enters the public domain, it becomes a marketable property due to its lure as a forbidden object. Its status as a forbidden object is constructed by the known act of censorship. Censorship in this case fueled desire. An effect of this desire was an increase in profits for the film producer and the music industry.

Intermission: interrupting female desire

While the first rendition of the 'Choli ke peeche' created much furore and discussion, the second rendition of the song did not attract the attention of the public or the Central Board of Film Certification. The song reappears in the film after intermission *a.k.a.* the food and bathroom break. In most cases, the intermission is a climatic point which takes place halfway through the film. This productive break, or cut if you please, is planned by directors and increases the profits of theaters which sell snacks and drinks at this time. The intermission is also a time when audiences discuss the film and form judgments. An outcome of these discussions may be a decision to leave or to 'cut-out'.[26]

In addition to linking, 'film audiences to adjacent economies,' the intermission is also an 'indispensable structuring device for the film.'[27] [...] In *Khalnayak*, the intermission partitions the film into two related segments. The first half of the film sets up problems/conflicts/enigmas and the second, offers resolutions.[28] [...] The first rendition of the song which appears in the first half of the film constructs female desire and sexuality as a 'problem'. The second half of the film, which features the second rendition of the song, resolves this 'problem' through the strategy of parody, amongst other mechanisms.

After the intermission, both Ganga and the audience find out that Ballu discovered Ganga's true identity at their first meeting, soon after she finished singing the song. This discovery not only unveils Ganga's identity as a sub-inspector, but, more importantly, reveals that her display of sexuality was a masquerade and that behind this masquerade is a pure Ganga. When Ganga realizes that she is actually being held hostage, she wants to leave and protests against her imprisonment by not eating. Ballu and his gang sing the song to coax her to eat. In a sequence composed of twenty-eight shots, Ballu and his gang don dancing attire – *ghaghras* (skirts) and *dupattas* (scarves) over their pants and shirts – and attempt to entertain Ganga. In ill-fitting costumes, Ballu and his gang clonk across the floor, parodying the earlier performance. The editing processes and camera angles do not sexualize the men's bodies as they imitate the earlier performance. Whereas the women's performance is spectacular and riveting, the men's performance is comical and ungainly. They fail miserably at being either sexy or alluring.

In contrast to the depiction of Ballu and his gang as voyeurs during the first picturization of the song, the technology of camera does not construct Ganga as a voyeur as she refuses to watch the men's performance. By the same token, the camera does not extend this position to the spectators in the audience. What is then behind the men's failure to perform as 'good' lures and Ganga's failure to act as a 'good' voyeur? [...] It is only women especially 'bad' women who can be 'good' lures; men are obviously the subjects of desire, not sexual objects. It is through humor that the second rendition defuses the threat of female desire and sexuality.

Although the song appeared twice in the film and on the audio cassettes, it was its first rendition which became the focus of public controversy. [...] [The] first rendition of the song was disruptive because the visual and verbal representation combined to produce female sexual desire. It was the articulation of this desire which was the problem: it posited that women were not only sexual objects, but also sexual subjects.

This problem is resolved in the filmic narrative by Ganga's reinscription as a pure woman. In a shoot-out, Ganga protects Ballu from the police by inserting herself in between the two. While Ballu escapes again, Ganga is arrested for aiding a criminal. She is accused of consorting with a criminal and is placed on trial for betraying the police service. While the police charges Ganga with treason, newspapers accuse her of a greater crime, namely, being unfaithful to her lover, and only Ballu can save Ganga's tarnished reputation. The film ends with Ballu's dramatic entry into the courtroom. He declares that Ganga is 'pure': she has betrayed neither her lover nor the police service. In fact, he announces that it was her purity which compelled him to return and surrender. While the film's conclusion upholds 'purity' as virtue, particularly for women, the abject figure of Ganga who sits in the trial box testifies to a silenced sexuality.

Reflections

In Chugh's petition, the public debate and the filmic narrative, the female body becomes the site and focus for the debate on the role of sex in Indian tradition. What complicates the debates on Indian tradition further is the specific function the film industry assumes in a growing capitalist market. Some members of the film and music industries claimed that 'Choli ke peeche kya hai' was a 'folk song' and hence, a part of Indian tradition. Within the capitalist market, such traditions are easily manufactured, packaged, publicized and sold. In *Khalnayak*, this film 'folk' song becomes a conduit for the commodified presentation of the female body. Bombay cinema's highly sexualized version of the 'village belle' is sold in theaters and video stores for huge profits. Thus, the film industry plays a crucial role in the commodification of female sexuality.

In this controversy, what needs to be problematized is both the repression of female sexuality and the commodification of female sexuality in the name of Indian tradition – and what needs to be explored further is the possibility of women's sexual agency. It is a possibility which is illuminated by revisiting the intermission and by attending to the film's reception. [...] [T]he intermission in *Khalnayak* does punctuate the filmic narrative, dividing it into two segments, namely, the 'problem' and the resolution. In doing so, it establishes a causal link between the two segments. However, the intermission also creates a temporal and spatial break as audiences leave the theater to buy snacks, go to the bathroom and/or converse with one another. In doing so, it can break the 'spell of the narrative'[29] and by extension, break the casual link between the two segments. It is by seizing upon this break that we can explore other strategies of reading, ones which are not dependent upon the ending or the resolution.

[...] During the period when this film was released, Madhuri Dixit, who plays Ganga became the highest paid film-actress to date in popular cinema. Among her many fans (including myself), Dixit was known for her stunning and sexy dance performances. It is not difficult to see why many middle class women in urban India would enjoy these performances. These women are often given gender training by families and the society at large on how to dress and how to speak. For the most part, they are warned that any public expression of sexuality on their part will lead to sexual violation. Whether women pay heed to these precautionary measures or not does not seem to matter since they are generally subjected to sexual harassment in any case. In an atmosphere where the consequences of any sexual expression are sexual violation or harassment, many of Dixit's middle class female fans find her performances pleasurable because they associate sexual agency with these performances.[30]

Janice Radway's insights help us in interpreting these responses. By attending to viewers' responses in a context, we can see that 'although ideology is extraordinarily pervasive and continually determines social life, it does not preclude the possibility ... of limited resistance.'[31] This resistance is carried out by viewers who 'appropriate otherwise ideologically conservative forms in order to better their lives, which have been controlled and dictated by their place in the social structure.'[32] I think by reading films such as *Khalnayak* against the grain, we will not only discover '"a code of prohibition and denial" – in the sense that cinema supplies what reality denies,' but we 'will also recognise the wounds that the "code of prohibition and denial" have inflicted on desire itself – wounds that are not external to but within the iconographic system ... that expresses rather than represses.'[33]

Notes

1 Aruna Vasudev, *Liberty and Licence in the Indian Cinema* (New Delhi: Vikas, 1978).
2 Hindi commercial cinema frequently uses names of religious and mythical figures as signposts for its audience. The names of the characters Ram, Ballu (an abbreviation of Balram) and Ganga refer to *Ramayana*'s dutiful Ram, to Balram who is easily angered, and to the goddess/river Ganga, respectively. The river Ganga is supposed to be pure and wash away sins of those who take a dip in it.
3 *Khalnayak*, 1993, dir. Subhash Ghai, videocassette. All translations are in the original essay.
4 Ibid.
5 Pandit Gautam Kaul, Letter to Shri Bhargava, 19 May 1993.
6 Shakti Samanta, Letter to Shri Brij Sethi, 25 June 1993.
7 R.P Chugh, Legal Notice sent to Subhash Ghai, Tips Cassettes & Records Company, Central Board of Film Certification, Minister of Information and Broadcasting and Director of Doordarshsan, 4 June 1993.
8 This controversy was subsequently taken up by politicians and lead to a stricter approach by the Central Board of Film Certification. See Usha Rai, 'Censor Board for ending denigration of ministers, officials in films,' *Indian Express*, 3 July 1994.

9 I have selected a few of the letters for the purpose of my analysis.

10 Eve-teasing refers to the sexual harassment of women.

11 President of the Women's Wing of BJP, Letter to female members of Parliament, 25 July 1993.

12 See the Legal Petition filed by Vineet Kumar.

13 Ashok Kumar, Letter to Shakti Samanta, 30 April 1993. The letter is in Hindi. My translation.

14 Mrs. Rama Gupta, Letter to Shakti Samanta, 27 April 1993.

15 Shweta Sanjay, Letter to Shakti Samanta, 4 April 1993.

16 Paras Cinema (Jaipur, Rajasthan), Letter to Shakti Samanta, 12 May 1993.

17 Rajesh Talkies (Ramganj District in Rajasthan), Letter to Shakti Samanta, 10 May 1993.

18 S. Nayyar, Letter to Shakti Samanta, 12 May 1993.

19 Arun Katiyar, 'Obscene Overtures,' *India Today*, 15 January 1994, 158.

20 Director of Nirman Theatre, Letter to Shakti Samanta, 7 May 1993. [T]he director of Nirman Theatre in Chandigarh ... inquired why the censors' and the public were agitated about 'Choli ke peeche kya hai', considering that songs such as 'Teri choli mein silwate kaise padhe' (What makes your blouse stretch/wrinkled?) and Raat bhar mua sone na de sooi lagawe ghari, ghari (All night a needle kept piercing me and didn't allow me to sleep) had been passed without evoking any censure or anxiety.

21 Bombay, Central Board Film Certification, Examining Committee Report on *Khalnayak*, 1993.

22 Examining Committee Report on *Khalnayak*.

23 Mannan, 'Hitting the Right Notes,' 51–53.

24 Saibal Chatterjee, 'Strange objects of desire' in *The Sunday Times of India*, 2 January 1994, 13.

25 See Kuhn, *Cinema, Censorship, and Sexuality 1909–1925*, 96.

26 See Lalitha Gopalan, *Cinema of Interruptions: Action Genres in Contemporary Indian Cinema* (London: BFI, 2002).

27 Ibid., p. 70.

28 [...] Prem Panicker 'The Second Coming.' www.rediff.com/entertai/2000/sep/07fiza.htm. Rediff Sept. 7, 2000.

29 Gopalan, p. 69.

30 [...] See Jyoti Puri, *Women, Body, Desire in Postcolonial India: Narratives of Gender and Sexuality* (New York: Routledge, 1999).

31 Janice Radway, *Reading the Romance: Women, Patriarchy and Popular Literature* (Chapel Hill: University of North Carolina Press, 1984), 17.

32 Ibid., 17–18.

33 Gertrud Koch, 'The Body's Shadow Realm,' in *Dirty Looks: Women, Pornography, Power*, eds. Pamela Church Gibson & Roma Gibson (London: British Film Institute, 1993), 36.

11

The home and the nation: consuming culture and politics in *Roja*
by Nicholas B. Dirks

There is one scene that is indelibly set in the memory of all those who have watched or read about Mani Ratnam's blockbuster film *Roja*, one of the most popular Indian films of 1992–3. Rishi Kumar, the hero who is held captive by Kashmiri separatist terrorists, leaps upon an Indian tricolour that has been set ablaze by the terrorists, angered by news that the Indian government will not negotiate a prisoner exchange. Rishi Kumar writhes in pain, but converts his pain into patriotism, moving his body in a valiant effort to contain and control the flames that threaten the ultimate modern symbol of the nation. He saves the flag, and rises, still on fire, to avenge the perpetrators of symbolic violence, with the soundtrack building in momentum to a song by Subramania Bharati that evokes the geographical unity and integrity of the Indian nation. The scene is framed, in a manner that seems clearly to set Islam against the principles of Indian nationalism, by shots of the main terrorist calmly praying to Allah. Various reports from viewers around India suggest that audiences are typically most demonstrative during this scene of patriotic self-sacrifice apotheosized into the visual pleasure of the nationalist spectator. But for a Tamil film made in 1992, the pleasures, and the associations, are in fact rather complicated. [...]

In short, the dramatic apotheosis of *Roja*, and the conspicuous jingoism of its most dramatic scene, was mediated by a great many other scenes from recent Indian political life, and the visual pleasure was as immediate as it was problematically aligned with the triumphs, as well as the contradictions and tragedies, of the national project signified by Rishi Kumar's sacrifice.

[...] *Roja* has called out for commentary and debate because, in a film that was both extraordinarily popular and well-made (and thus afforded pleasure even for viewers who were made particularly uncomfortable), the melodramatic love story becomes integrally intertwined with a larger story of nationalist struggle, against both Kashmiri separatists and Pakistani aggressors, and is told/enacted through the lives of ordinary (read new middle-class) citizens of the Indian nation. Tejaswini Niranjana set the tone for critical evaluation in her article in the *Economic and Political Weekly* (Niranjana 1994) in which she argues that *Roja* celebrates the new

Indian middle class, which is shown to be decent, secular, patriotic, and ultimately able to unite sacrifice and victory, nationalism and bourgeois desire. [...] The cultural nationalism of *Roja's* India [...] is predicated on middle-class consumption and managerial competence, Hindu forms of everyday life, and national opposition to the benighted forces of separatism/disruption within and their inevitable affiliation to the great threat from outside (always there, though not always named, as Pakistan). [...]

Niranjana reads the film as a symptom of (even as she sees it working through the magic of cinematic pleasure to naturalize) a new consensus about contemporary India [...] 'As the Hindutva forces reoccupy the discourses of liberal humanism in India, an anti-colonial bourgeois nationalist project is refigured and the secular subject is reconstituted' (Niranjana (1994: 79). [...] *Roja* has thus become a window onto the modern Indian predicament, discomforting precisely because the pleasure of its text is analogous to all the other pleasures promised (and in part delivered) by the contemporary spiral of liberalization and middle-class consumption. That cinema is all about pleasure, of course, is part of the problem, and in the case of the cinema of Mani Ratnam, definitely not part of the solution. Perhaps this is why the debate that follows the suggestions of Niranjana and the problems raised by *Roja* betrays a deep unease: what do we have at our disposal to counter the pleasures of the new apart from relentless critique and the implicit exhortation to the secular nationalism of an earlier age, when post-Independence exuberance, Marxist ideology, colonial memory, and middle-class subordination generated different rhetorics of political consensus, and different affects of national sentiment? Perhaps most paradoxical of all is the sense that the critical laments about *Roja* from left-wing intellectuals reveal a sense of loss that is as evocative, and as resonant with pathos, as the dominant message of the film itself, which vividly recalls, and mourns, the failure of both the Indian nation and the Indian state. But this too is fitting, for if the cinema is all about pleasure, cinematic pleasure is all about loss. [...]

Whoever is speaking (or making movies), there is a general recognition of the loss of something fundamental in India's birthright. When this loss maps itself onto an idea of the past that inscribes some nostalgic version of tradition onto the geography of subcontinental history, and then, often related, becomes the pretext for an embrace of certain opportunities in the new – whether around participation in the market or in a new politics of, say, Hindu assertiveness (the two frequently, though not always, seem to go together), the stage is set for what can only be a perilous attempt to re-enchant the nation and reconstitute the grounds of cultural (read national) identity. But despite all the trenchant criticisms of *Roja's* political framing, the film itself argues modestly for a personal politics of humanism, personal sacrifice and loyalty, love, and recognition. Despite the overarching nationalism, the film depicts 'security' (a word used, in English, throughout the film) as the only real reason of state; at the same time security is the basis for the state's immediate failure in the narrative drama of the film. The military is ennobled by the sacrifices of its members, but is ultimately the agent of a state that has lost its capacity to control the political agenda. In the end, *Roja's* bad politics may have less to do with its complicity in communalism and jingoistic nationalism than in the bankruptcy of old liberal ideals of individual will and goodness.

I. *Roja:* the movie

The film opens with the sound of warfare – regimental marching, armoured vehicles, automatic weapons fire – juxtaposed with gentle sounds of nature, the singing of birds – soon revealed as the soundtrack of the second beginning of the film. The titles come to a close when we hear the call to prayer, from an Islamic *mullah.* Under Mani Ratnam's careful control, the *muezzin* signifies place – Kashmir – but also evokes, particularly since his calls are blended so well with the sounds and sights of military action, danger. What follows in the opening scene of the film is a dramatic chase in the darkness of night, the scene signified by the opening martial noises, with the Indian army in pursuit of a band of terrorists; after serious combat and mortal losses, the army apprehends one of the terrorists, an especially menacing-looking man identified as Wasim Khan. The scene then shifts from the murky black and white combat of military night to the brilliant green and bucolic splendour of the south Indian countryside [...] The camera shows a young woman cavorting in ponds and fields, with scenes of agricultural labour and village life, mostly populated by women. [...] [A] young executive from Madras who is driving to the village to marry her older sister [...] Rishi Kumar enters the village, charms a number of sceptical older women who interrogate him about his intentions, and goes to meet his prospective in-laws. [...]

The plotted narrative is disrupted when Rishi Kumar is allowed (only because, we are told, he is a city boy) a private interview with the chosen bride in order to confirm his choice; she begs him to refuse the marriage because she has already pledged her heart to a village sweetheart, son of a man locked in a long-lived feud with her own father. Forced to defer her wishes to the agency of the bridegroom, she confounds Rishi Kumar, who hardly expected to come to a village and encounter female will in the form of refusal; to oblige her, he rejects her in public and chooses, in her place, the younger sister, Roja, who first planted her desiring gaze upon him. Now, however, Roja is terribly upset since her gaze had been vicarious on behalf of her sister, and she imagines that she has been forced to be complicit in ruining her sister's chances of happiness and her family's reputation. [...] All the differences between city and country are collapsed in love, once Roja realizes that her new husband has chosen her at her sister's request; 'modern' and 'traditional' narratives are so promiscuously intermixed that the viewer happily accepts the unlikely premise of the story, that the most modern of men chooses happiness through what seems a random choice made because he desires a village woman from a place he finds beautiful. The love story thus (barely) conceals its own allegorical character for, it seems, Rishi Kumar is in part the embodiment of urban middle-class nostalgia for the simple, rooted, unalienated, traditional life it has left behind. The city's desire for the village is here highly aestheticized, interchangeably impersonal, predicated on a romantic fantasy that combines the full cinematic firepower of the modern cinema with an impressive anthropological imaginary of folk village life and the rural feminine ideal. Significantly, the village is marked by class but not caste; the caste identities are hidden and either implicit or unimportant.[1] [...] But in the cosmopolitan fantasy of (male) urban (middle-class) romance with (female) village (peasant) India, marriage and love, legitimate sanction and sexual passion, free choice and fated accident, all comes out fine in the end.

[...] Just as the young lovers reconcile, the nuclear home is disrupted by the sound of the phone, informing, them that Rishi Kumar's boss, a senior cryptologist, has had a heart attack. [...] The boss now, from his hospital bed, asks his subordinate to go in his stead to Kashmir, where he must undertake a delicate assignment. He apologizes for sending him all the way to Kashmir, to which Rishi Kumar responds by saying: 'Kashmir is in India, isn't it? To go anywhere in India is part of my job.' This line [...] an explicit nationalist assertion [...] is made against the context of obvious contestation. [...] [T]he two set out for Kashmir, in a dramatic reversal of the usual conceit of a popular Indian film, where Kashmir was, until the recent political troubles, the ideal locale for romantic trysts and honeymoons. [...] For politics has intruded with its nastiness and its violence into the heart of the romantic narrative of Indian (cinematic) love.

[...] [T]he first episodes in Kashmir mimic the most romantic of Bollywood honeymoons; juxtaposed against occasional scenes of the cryptologist working at his computer, the two lovers traverse the landscapes of paradise – its high mountains, snowy fields, sylvan lakes – and finally consummate their marriage. The morning after, Roja wakes first, and goes unescorted to a nearby temple, to thank God for her wonderful married happiness and attempt to convey news to the village god she had earlier abused, due to what then seemed her grave misfortune, that all is forgiven. [...]

[W]hen Rishi Kumar panics at the disappearance of his wife (the empty bed after the night of bliss) and runs off to find her with only a limited escort, he sets himself up to be taken hostage by the terrorists who lie in wait. Although one might speculate that this momentary challenge to the secular rationality of the public domain was the cause for retribution, or at the very least realize the cost Rishi Kumar has now to pay for having allowed his wife to enter the space of his work, the scene is also one in which the sanctity of the temple, and the marital happiness that is being celebrated there, is violently disrupted by the forces of terror, which are of course Islamic. No matter how viewers decode the over-determined semiotics of this moment, the film suddenly changes register, and does so when, for the first time in the narrative space of Mani Ratnam's contrivance, the story of hero and heroine, male and female, collides.

Critical reviews of the film tend to focus, justifiably enough, on the way the secular message of the film is undermined by the coding of Hindu as secular and Islam as anti-secular. As Niranjana suggests, [...] the temple is for Roja what the state seems to be for Rishi Kumar, in what at first appears to be a symmetrical relationship. But [...] we should note that for Mani Ratnam's film the gender divide seems at some level much wider than that associated with religion. Mani Ratnam is careful to displace his sense of religious affiliation from a confessional to a national grid, with his final invocation of the betrayal of Pakistan, but he is much less concerned to complicate his depiction of gender relations. Roja may symbolize the nation for which Rishi Kumar is prepared to make the ultimate sacrifice, but Roja not only creates the opportunity for terrorist intervention, she refuses both the state's political logic and her own husband's calculus of sacrifice. Her body, which she throws in vain at the terrorists who capture her husband outside the temple, becomes the ground on which the contradictions of Mani Ratnam's narrative resist ultimate resolution.

No sooner is Rishi captured than Roja runs to the police station to demand his return. Frantic, she speaks hurriedly in Tamil to the uncomprehending officers, none of whom understand her southern tongue. Indeed, it is as if the gender division has been rendered linguistic, since even when the message of her husband's capture is translated, we now confront a fundamental incommensurability. [...]

[S]he declares that the state promised them security, and is thus obligated to do whatever is necessary to guarantee the safe return of her husband, who after all is a servant of the state. She refuses to enter into the discourse of state rationality, even after a heated, and poignant, exchange with Royappa, the chief army officer. [...] She finally manages to secure an audience with the Union Minister, who [...] promises that he will speak to the appropriate authorities and request action on her behalf. [...] Indeed, this capitulation, a major break in the narrative, sets up the possibility that Roja's personal romantic desire will altogether overtake the nationalist narrative (or, at least that put forward by the state).[2]

Meanwhile, Rishi Kumar is in the hands of Kashmiri terrorists. But his detention begins with art act of tenderness, performed by the sister of Liaqat Khan, the main terrorist. [...] Rishi [...] asks what they want. 'We want freedom.' 'Whose freedom?' 'Our freedom, for Kashmir, for all of us here, the flowers and the trees; we want freedom from your rule.' [...] He asks Liaqat Khan how many men he has killed (the number of men killed appears repeatedly as the index of barbarism), asks whether his leaders are in this country or in 'the neighbouring country', whether, if his leaders asked, he would kill his children? To the last question, Liaqat Khan responds by saying, 'Yes, this is a *jihad* with Hindustan.' After more discussion, Liaqat Khan says in frustration: 'These issues will not be solved by talk, but by partition.' And as a Subramania Bharati song celebrating the geographical unity of India begins to build momentum on the soundtrack, Rishi Kumar says, 'India will not be partitioned a second time.' When referring to the leaders from the neighbouring country, and when mourning the wound of partition, the film is unequivocal. But the terrorists are nevertheless firmly planted within India. Not only will partition be resisted, the terrorists must learn that their interests rest with India. And in the film, they learn this when fifteen of their number (in an even exchange with the Indian army), including Liaqat's younger brother, are massacred by the Pakistani army, an event announced on the television news, in the only filmic enunciation of the actual name of the territorial enemy.

For the first time, Liaqat is shown praying in a moment that contains no threat, but instead suggests the vulnerability and sorrow of a man who has just suffered a terrible loss. Rishi Kumar says to him softly, 'I am sorry. Your brother should not have been killed.' Liaqat confesses that 'they' have betrayed him, that now his group will have to carry on by itself. But Rishi does not let the issue rest, instead asking whether all the fighting and killing is in fact acceptable to his god: 'Is it in your religion that man should kill man? Is anyone pleased at the death of these children? Save people instead; wipe their tears, let go of your guns.' Through the death of a loved one, and through the common recognition of the betrayal/crime of Pakistan, the two individuals recognize each other. In this glowing humanistic moment, Rishi Kumar offers Islam a new 'secular' version of itself, splitting off the militant associations of jihad by associating it with another nation rather than another religion. Politics, even the discourse of freedom and oppression, vanishes in the overdeterminations of national rivalry, intention, and character.

But, as if to relieve the almost unbearable burden of conversion (and to return to the conventions of a political thriller), the moment of recognition is suspended by the arrival of news that the Indian government has reversed its stance agreeing to the exchange of Rishi Kumar and Wasim Khan. [...] The van [...] approaches the bridge at the other side of the river, but then disgorges cloth rather than a man, and drives off furiously. Roja, who runs across the bridge, gathers up what are revealed as Rishi's blood-covered clothes. She refuses to accept defeat, and announces [...] that she will find him: 'I will go to those rebel households; there must be a woman like me there.' She is right, for it turns out that Liaqat's sister has connived with Rishi to set him free, allowing him to escape the terms of the exchange that seem to Rishi, as they seemed to Royappa (and the state) at an earlier stage (before he was 'feminized'), as a national capitulation. Once again, the role of the woman has been to challenge the political terms of the state (or counter-state); but in this instance Liaqat's sister has acted not simply in the interest of saving Rishi's life, or of reuniting him with his wife, but rather to gratify his desire. [...] [W]hat might have constituted an alternative site of romantic possibility is suggested only by her inexplicable actions against the interests of her brother and his men, a mystery that is itself completely sublimated in Rishi's nationalist resolve. Can it be that she was seduced by Rishi, not for any love of his for her, but instead for his love for the nation? All these questions are left in abeyance as the camera shifts abruptly to the last action scene, an epic chase down glaciers and snow-covered slopes, as Rishi struggles to free himself from what he clearly sees as the logic of the state, the crime of exchange, all the while seeking to convert the sacrifice of one woman into the grounds on which the other, his beloved wife, would need neither make, nor occasion, any sacrifice at all, personal or national.

At the end of the chase, only Liaqat stands between Rishi and liberation. Rishi looks Liaqat in the eyes, and again their human connection prevails. Rishi says, 'You can't kill me; when your brother died I saw your pain.' And despite the possible implications of his actions for Wasim Khan and the movement, Liaqat tells Rishi to go indicating that in allowing his free passage he will expiate the death of his brother: 'I will wipe my tears now.' And so Rishi is finally free to join his beloved Roja, in a scene of final rejoicing and reunion.

II. *Roja:* the debate

The couple's embrace appears to signify the resolution of the myriad conflicts in the film. Husband and wife have been reunited, but without having to relinquish the dreaded terrorist, or to engage the terms of exchange that would have obviated the call for national sacrifice and contaminated the higher reason of the state. The state could have its cake and eat it too; moved by the personal tragedies of its ordinary subjects, it could respond humanely and yet find its higher purpose rescued by the sacrifices of its ordinary subjects. The Kashmiri terrorists created the terms of an exchange that had placed them firmly on the side of Pakistan and murder; by the end of the film they have returned Rishi Kumar in exchange for the sin of Pakistan, at the same time they have encountered, through the proximity and recognition of human tragedy and desire, the common humanity of all Indian subjects, whatever their particular politics. Thus both the state, in the first instance, and the nation, in the second, have been apparently triumphant. And the triumph has been accomplished by Rishi Kumar, a skilful middle-class technocrat who, even in the new age of liberalization, works for the state rather than a private corporation, but reveals himself also as a hero who refuses to accept the sullied political terms of compromise and exchange. Liaqat's sister demonstrates that even women, when acting out of natural instinct, compassion, and love for mankind (well, for Indian men), can convert their local desire into national service [...] And Roja herself gets her man back; the film seems to assume that her happiness will be even greater when she realizes that her husband returned of his own free will, outside the terms of exchange, inside a narrative of heroism.

Nevertheless, the triumphant though abrupt ending barely conceals the fissures and contradictions of the filmic story. First, neither the nation nor the state have remained unscathed. The nation itself is only invoked in the film through abstract symbols and slogans, personal sacrifice, and national rivalry. The nation has in fact failed to sustain the loyalties of many of its subjects, and can only hope to reclaim their loyalty once the betrayal of an opposing nation drives them back. The logic of opposition here works in part through jingoistic nationalism, in part through the memory of the primal wound, the historical tragedy of partition. But the problem with partition is that while it has produced the crisis that the state has constantly to confront and struggle to control, it also expresses the originary failure of the nation, the horrible fact that history, culture, and geography did not coalesce in the spirit of national unity. India's unity was fractured from the start.

The terms on which the nation can by hyphenated with the state have also been challenged on a number of fronts. The fact of partition has meant that the state has had to become, first and foremost, a security state; thus the loyal bureaucrat expends his dazzling cryptological skills in deadly combat with Pakistan, working for RAW rather than for India's industrial enrichment (as the real middle-class dream would have it), thus what should have been a honeymoon in India's romanticized theme park becomes a dangerous nightmare, thus the state must ask its ordinary citizens to sacrifice on a regular basis, to accept a state of constant warfare simply to maintain the quotidian borders of the polity. [...] The state is hardly pilloried in Mani Ratnam's account [...] But Roja's refusal to negotiate her emotional demands with the state is presented as more than simple female intransigence and familial isolationism. And in the story, the state does finally bend its resolve to special pleading. [...] The state's interests are not in the end protected by the state, but by a rogue individual acting on his own, and against the immediate plea, and particular interest, of Roja.

That the rogue individual (and exemplary citizen) is the beloved husband of Roja seems to ameliorate this subtextual aberration. But Roja's subject-position is shown to be highly contradictory, and deeply flawed: [...] she created the danger that led to the kidnapping in the first place. Even granting the validity of her critique of the state, she is presented as completely unmoved by nationalist sentiment and uninterested in the sacrifices of others. Despite her capacity to move into an urban household and marry a cosmopolitan technocrat, she is ultimately a village girl incapable of seeing the big picture. [...] [H]er only story is a simple love story. [...] In the end, Roja gets what she wants, though not how she chooses, and without any need for her to experience an epiphany of nationalist desire. Indeed, the conclusion of the movie patronizes Roja quite literally; she must be humoured, she must be satisfied, but ultimately either ignored or circumvented.

Why, then, is Roja the supposed centrepiece of the film? The simple answer to this question is of course that the film is a standard misogynist melodrama, in which Roja is the perfect object of desire; in so far as Roja becomes a subject of desire, she does nothing but cause trouble, which for the movie becomes the narrative mechanism that propels the drama and allows the conceit that her subjectivity – both in her actions and her emotional state – is at the centre of the story. But because of Mani Ratnam's cinematic ambition, the stakes are rather higher, and Roja becomes the site of allegorical desire: for a rural life and village self that have been lost by the urban middle-class technocrat; for a religious sensibility that can be recuperated without inflaming the communalist passions of Hindu fundamentalism or coming into competition with other forms of religious commitment that seem to be linked to nationalist violence, territorial ambition, and collectivist destruction of the humane individual; for a nationalist referent that pre-exists the terrible history of partition, that self-inflicted wound of national humiliation. *Roja* is, in the end, about loss, fantasy, and failure; and thus *Roja*'s ending is necessarily so incomplete, so unsatisfactory, so vague in its ultimate allegorical message. [...] [T]he pleasures of the film are purchased with extraordinary ambivalence.

[...] Tellingly, none of the film's reviewers have allowed the pleasures of the film to coexist with ideological critique; equally significantly, far too little is made of the genuinely pleasurable aspects of viewing the film, perhaps most importantly, the music, which is both catchy and, at times, sophisticated. At best, Rustom Bharucha, who is the most vigilant of *Roja*'s critics, notes that the deepest influence on Mani Ratnam is advertising, which provides him with the craft and the ideology of his filmmaking.

Bharucha's critique is situated in a larger interrogation of the rise of fascism and the associated complicities of the culture industry in contemporary India. [...] But Bharucha's [1994] larger critique, that the culture industry has only one totalizing ideological register and meaning, seems not only to make the enterprise of cultural criticism bankrupt and boring, it confers complete epistemological power to the forces of the right. [...]

Bharucha reads *Roja* as if its primary purpose was to naturalize India's undisputed claim to Kashmir, and to suggest that all the trouble and dissent concerning Kashmir is illegitimate, at best the manipulated result of Pakistani intervention. There is little doubt that the film presents a perniciously simple, one-sided account of the Kashmir crisis, avoiding all issues of history, sovereignty, not to mention the atrocious evidence of human rights abuses on the part of the Indian army. [...] He writes that it is a 'euphoric misreading to imagine that *Roja* is celebrating individualism above the power of the state. The fact is that Roja and Rishi Kumar are integrally a part of the state. If the fervent wife gets hysterical and places her husband above the state, that is only to be expected. Ultimately, it is the patriarchy of marriage and the benevolence of the state that protect her' (Bharucha 1994: 1394). [...] Although he elsewhere notes the complicities of market and state, he seems unwilling to accept any limitation on the modern legitimation and power of the state, in a manner that parallels his complete acceptance of totalizing discourses of state enunciatory power.

[...] Bharucha's concern is shared by Chakravarthy and Pandian (1994), who argue that the 'apparent inability of the state in the film actually masks its silent and powerful ability and in that sense the ultimate victors in the film are the state and the Hindu-patriarchal culture with which the desire of Rishi Kumar, the hero, coincides'. [...] *Roja* has become a vehicle for a particular set of political arguments about the state, communalism, gender relations, and the family, in the midst of which the film itself seems long forgotten.

If the *EPW* debate on *Roja* is ultimately disappointing, the point is not to return *Roja*, or film criticism generally, to the happy embrace of film studies, not something I could represent in any event. Academics and public intellectuals have an obligation to attend to the meanings and politics of popular cultural forms and forces, and to write against the positive reception accorded *Roja* in the mainstream Indian press that typically worked to justify the political, social, and cultural assumptions forefronted in political critique.[3] However, the metaleptic character of many political readings has the unfortunate effect of mistaking the symptom for the cause, of ascribing to culture the very power it would seek to possess in a world of post-modern mystification and symbolic overdetermination. It is necessary to attempt to understand the multiple registers through which cinematic pleasure works, why it is that cinema is so compelling, and why it might be that cinematic reception/interpretation/interpellation operates in such circuitous ways.[4] That *Roja* is retrograde seems virtually self-evident in the circles within which we write; but that it establishes its identities, elisions, and displacements through cinematic techniques that not only call upon the market-driven character of advertising but also open up a plenitude of affective and interpretive responses is something we must both recognize and engage. Mystification may work through screens that both displace and distract[5] while they also provide languages for testimony, and reflection, destabilization and slippage, catachresis and transcoding. [...] Rather, we should link political critique to the more sympathetic (though also analytical) project of engaging the power of the cultural form itself, as well as the spectatorial subjectivities that are shaped by these forms even as they occasionally refuse (or simply fail to absorb) the full implications and totalizations of fascist cultural projects. [...]

III. Desire and the nation

[...] [I]n my own reading of the film, I have sought to suggest the fractures, fissures, and ambivalences within the basic text that both problematize a simple political dismissal and convey the categorial weaknesses at the core of a seemingly triumphant state/market appropriation of the filmic text, though I grant the salience of all the political dangers (and then some) suggested by critics such as Bharucha. [...]

If the film does evoke, at least in its undercurrents, the failure of both the Indian nation and the state, it does so, [...] in the language of loss. Whatever may be blamed for the present impasse, the secularist self-representation of early Indian nationalism provided a post-colonial promise of progress and political utopia, amidst the pressing but practical problems of poverty and underdevelopment. The promise has now been declared empty, [...] The specific reason for this in the Indian case is partition, the historical fact that India no sooner shed its colonial skin than it experienced a nationalist nightmare, not just terrible violence and dislocation, but a fundamental challenge to the claims of universality and citizenship that nationalism had used to justify itself. [...] For India, [...], Pakistan represented its failure, its threat, and its new (post-colonial) self-justification. But increasingly the justificatory rhetoric has shifted in emphasis, from asserting the exemplary ideal of universal secularism and democratic representation *vis-à-vis* the other, to reacting to the security threat and the mystificatory cultural alterity of the other. And with this xenophobic reaction has come the increasingly visible tendency to see the other within, and to use the threat of the internal other to write a script of paranoid mimesis, eschewing secularism (now called pseudo-secularism) as a western/colonial imposition, embracing a refurbished Hindu religiosity as the authentic means to re-enchant cultural and national identity.

It is within this contemporary context that one can read *Roja* both as symptom of a larger crisis and as a text that articulates the fascist presuppositions of a new consensus. However, the film also works to expose some of the lies of that consensus. [...] The state has become increasingly paralysed by its double mandate, its security rationale necessarily endangering the actual security of its citizens. In *Roja* this tension is mediated by the heroic sacrifice of Rishi Kumar, but it leaves Roja herself unmoved, and almost widowed (no matter which choice the state might make). [...] Thus it is, perhaps, that Mani Ratnam simplifies the situation of Kashmir, eliding the political suppression of plebiscite and the military violation of rights, evoking the contemporary crisis as the inevitable outgrowth of partition, re-membering the nation as that dream forever fractured by history, and now finally recuperable only through melodrama. [...]

Perhaps melodrama has now become the unfortunate genre for narrating the post-colonial nation, a way to forget the tragic histories of colonialism in order to claim complete originality and to erase the eruptions of cultural difference that threaten to implode from within: to negotiate, in other words, the contradictory project of nationalism's universalizing primordialism. Homi Bhabha helps us understand the appeal of forgetting: [...] 'Being obliged to forget becomes the basis for remembering the nation, peopling it anew, imagining the possibility of other contending and liberating forms of cultural identification' (Bhabha 1991). But in the case of melodrama, remembering becomes the transposition of current anxiety onto historical memory, and the basis for imagining possibility becomes linked to empty narratives of desire and misleading calls for national enmity.[6] The love story that begins with misrecognition thus ends with misrecognition, the happy conclusion a cover for the dissatisfactions of home and world, love and politics.

If these ultimately unfulfilled and incommensurable narratives thus inhabit the ambivalence of *Roja* [...] they also line the empty shell of melodrama, providing vast and protected spaces for the writing of aggressive versions of cultural nationalism and religious fundamentalism. [...] [F]ilms like *Roja* both express and provide legitimations for a host of rewritings: of secularism as predicated in Hindu majoritarianism, of the protection of minority rights as the basis for constructing different grades of citizenship, of the national mission as the jingoistic maintenance of hostilities with Pakistan and other 'foreign hands', of the state as fundamentally about security on the one hand and the conversion of agendas of social justice to the subsidization of further inequalities in the name of the market on the other, of claims about national identity into recuperations of modern forms of tradition that mask communalism, retrograde gender politics, and greater state authoritarianism, to mention just the most obvious. And if the 'humanistic' sentiment of a film like *Roja* fails to satisfy, not only because it disinvests political responsibility but because it distracts individuals from the political character of their relationship to both state and nation, we must at least be prepared to point out the myriad ways in which this kind of liberal humanism fails to be sustained within the melodramatic narratives of contemporary popular culture as well as in the compelling account-abilities of modern political life, even as we must acknowledge, and seek to understand, the powerful (and pleasurable) effects these narratives can have.

Notes

1   Even in the Tamil version of the film, which usually marks caste position (certainly between Brahmins and non-Brahmins) rather conspicuously, the question of caste identity is confusing for those without a good sense of the local cultural cues. [...]
2   It is tempting to use this example to predicate some generalizations about the way desire always threatens to overtake the nationalist project, either by compromising its rationalizing rhetoric or by transforming it altogether. For an extraordinary analysis of the theoretical implications of the relation of self-recognition, desire, enjoyment, and the fascist proclivities of new democratic systems, see Zizek (1991). [...]

3 I take Bharucha's word for this, since I have not yet been able to locate most of the reviews to which he refers in his essay.

4 Preoccupations with pleasure have obviously been of central importance in film studies, which has used various theoretical discussions in psychoanalysis to formulate propositions about pleasure: about the relationships among identification, imagination, scopophilic mastery, phallic loss, transgression, disavowal, condensation, displacement, and bodily incorporation, to mention just a few terms, about which there are major disagreements and debates. If there is no consensus on how to treat pleasure, there is general agreement that pleasure is fundamental to understanding cinematic experience. Within feminist film studies, there is also general dissatisfaction with Laura Mulvey's early contention that cinematic pleasure requires the hegemony of the male gaze, and a lively sense of the appropriative possibilities of feminist perspectives. See Mulvey (1975/1981); Clover (1992); Penley (1989). But even in Marxist critical studies, for example in the work of Fredric Jameson, there is the acknowledgement that pleasure has to be taken seriously, if only in the commitment of the Marxist critic to politicize pleasure. See Jameson ([1988]: 73–4).

5 I use distraction here in a Benjaminian sense: he writes: 'Reception in a state of distraction, which is increasing noticeable in all fields of art and is symptomatic of profound changes in apperception, finds in the film its true means of exercise.' Benjamin (1982: 242).

6 Again, for a rather more pessimistic view of the relationship of desire and nationalism, see Zizek (1991).

References

Benjamin, Walter, 1982, *Illuminations*, London: Jonathan Cape.

Bhabha, Homi, 1991, *The Location of Culture*, New York: Roudedge.

Bharucha, Rustom, 1994, 'On the Border of Fascism: Manufacture of a Consent in *Roja*', *Economic and Political Weekly*, June.

Chakravarthy, Venkatesh and M.S.S. Pandian, 1994, 'More on *Roja*', *Economic and Political Weekly*, March.

Clover, Carol, 1992, *Men, Women, and Chain Saws: Gender in the Modern Horror Film*, Princeton: Princeton University Press.

Jameson, Frederik, [1988] *The Ideologies of Theory: Essays 1971–1986, Syntax of History*, vol. II, Minneapolis: University of Minnesota Press.

Mulvey, Laura, 1975, 1981, 'Visual Pleasure and Narrative Cinema', *Screen* 16: 6–18. Reprinted in her *Visual and Other Pleasures*, Bloomington, Indiana University Press.

Niranjana, Tejaswini, [1994] 'Integrating Whose Nation? Tourists and Terrorists in "Roja"', *Economic and Political Weekly*, 15 January: 79–82.

Penley, Constance, 1989, *The Future of an Illusion: Film Feminism, and Psychoanalysis*, Minneapolis: University of Minnesota Press.

Prasad, M., '*Roja:* Living the State', Unpublished Paper: 1994.

Zizek, Slavoj, 1991, *For They Know Not What They Do. Enjoyment as a Political Factor*, London: Verso.

12

Inside and out: song and dance in Bollywood cinema
by Sangita Gopal and Biswarup Sen

Of the various components that make up the standard Bollywood film, one feature in particular – the song-and-dance sequences which are present in every Bollywood film – draws special ire. Pointing to the blatant 'unrealism' of these musical interludes – the many changes of costumes within the frame of a single song, the sudden shift of locales from verse to verse, the depiction of armies of extras swaying and dancing along with the hero and the heroine – critics contend that song-dance sequences symbolize, in a condensed fashion, what is wrong with Bollywood films as a whole. The vulgar use of sexuality and the ostentatious displays of wealth which characterize most song-dance sequences point to a central truth about Bollywood: that it is a sensationalist and escapist art form which is driven solely by the dictates of the marketplace and is incapable of playing any progressive role whatsoever. This contribution argues that song-dance sequences, far from being exploitative segments of escapist fantasy, are in fact powerful acts of imagination which play a crucial role in the construction of Bollywood film as a unique and powerful popular art. Seemingly redundant to the text, the song-dance is actually an enabling device which has allowed Hindi film to posit versions and visions of modernity that would otherwise be unrepresentable. Song-dance is therefore both a measure of Bollywood's difference from western cinema, as well as an explanation of Bollywood's immense popularity all over the global South. It posits exterior and interior scenarios of modernity that the narrative is unable to depict, it envisions ways of acting and behaving not coded into the text, it registers the shock of the new not recordable by the prose of the film, and it affords the possibility of *jouissance* or joyous release that cannot be spoken by any character or voice. Overall, song-dance is a sign that helps us read the meaning of Bollywood films.

Music and the movies

It is agreed upon that if there is one feature that radically distinguishes Bollywood from other cinemas, it is the ubiquitous presence of the song-and-dance sequence.

This difference is most keenly felt by western observers used to the very different conventions of Hollywood filmmaking. Richard Corliss observes that 'in the midst of the starkest plot twists, everyone sings and dances. Virtually all Bollywood films are musicals'.[1] Even sympathetic foreign critics are forced to admit that 'For many Westerners, though, the songs are the real deal-breakers – which is why they are often the first element a Bollywood go-getter thinks about removing when plotting a crossover to the "mainstream" (read "white") audience in America and Europe'.[2] But songs are not a problem only for white audiences; many Indian commentators also believe that song-and-dance sequences detract a terrible toll from aesthetic value of Hindi films:

> The most irritating aspect of the song in the Hindi film is its sheer irrelevance. Many of them can be deleted entirely without in any way affecting the film's content, and many of them suppressed would do much to improve the general quality of the film. In an avowed musical of the *Baiju Bawra* type [1952 film about a musician], it is a different matter – for it is part of the film – but the interminable singing in films of a totally different nature is rarely justified. It merely slows up the action and confuses the major issues at stake. The mounting tension of a drama suddenly collapses it and it holds up the story. In the middle of what should be an exciting chase, it is an inanity. These sort of things account for the illogical and shapeless nature of an otherwise good Hindi film.[3]

Addressing the topic almost thirty years later, Ram Gopal Verma reiterates Sarkar's critique when he states:

> I believe ... that songs are principally responsible for 70 per cent of the bad films we make today. Songs will work ... when they are integral to a film ...but the problem arises when no matter what the nature of the subject, you *ghusao* some songs into it and start manipulating the screenplay ... I'm not going to have any songs in *Bhoot* either. My intention is to scare the hell out of people. Why should I subject them to locations in New Zealand?[4]

Some critics go even further than Verma, denying all validity to artworks that employ these devices. Questioned by an interviewer as to whether she would ever try her hand at a Hindi film extravaganza, the noted director Aparna Sen announced: 'No, I am not into song-and-dance movies. That's not my kind of cinema so I can't do it very well. I usually opt for meaningful cinema.'[5]

Some scholars explain the existence of the song-and-dance sequence by arguing that it evolves both from the classical traditions of Indian civilization as well as from the tenor of daily life. Thus, Barnouw and Krishnaswamy point out that in the Golden Age of Sanskrit theatre, the idea of drama was inseparably linked with song, dance and music. Though drama in India went into decline under Muslim rule, it was revived in the nineteenth century. Even though this new drama sought to imitate and adapt European models, it simultaneously reverted back to ancient usage by including song and dance. This practice was then imported into cinema with the advent of sound, 'the Indian sound film of 1931 was not only the heir of the silent film; it also inherited something more powerful and broad-based. Into the new medium came a river of music, that had flowed through unbroken millennia of dramatic tradition'.[6] This argument from tradition is not very convincing, for it begs a number of important questions. First, since so little of contemporary culture has any links to the age of Kalidasa, why was song-dance the one element which has survived till today? 'Continuity' by itself is not sufficient to account for this persistence; we need to demonstrate why this one facet from classical Sanksrit culture continues to be of such importance in the modern world. Second, this thesis cannot explain why song-dance sequences are so popular in cultures (like Russia, the Middle East and East Asia) which have no Sanskritic antecedents. Are we then required to posit similar underlying features for the classical traditions of all these cultures? Third, this argument makes no attempt to account for the entertainment value of the song-dance sequence. If the song-dance is detrimental to the work as a whole, why do so many people continue to be fascinated by this device?

The traditionalist explanation for the song-dance is complemented by a culturalist or anthropological account, like the one below from film director Vinay Shukla, which argues that the song-dance is a reflection of what happens at the level of the day-to-day:

> Why don't we just look at our own society? Every occupation – fisherman or postman, farmer or warrior, rajah or jogi – has a song attached to it. Every occasion – birth, death, marriage or separation – is accompanied by a song. Every festival, every season has a song about it. Songs are a way of life for us. If an important occasion is a meal, songs are its spices – leaving the meal incomplete without them.[7]

Shukla's point may be empirically true, but it lacks force. A culturalist account of this sort is true not only for India but also for all primitive and traditional societies. In fact, the only societies in human history where songs are *not* a way of life are the modern, industrial societies which we now inhabit and where music and all arts in general are detached from daily life practices and placed in a sector labelled 'entertainment'. The weakness of the culturalist approach is that it takes the relation between music and ritual or practice found in traditional societies (the link between music and religion or sowing and reaping for example) and illicitly transposes it onto that between two spheres of culture (music and narrative film). Nor does such an argument offer any evidence that we are more musical than other cultures. In fact, one could point to instances where we are *less* musical. Thus, while it is common for sports fans in Britain or the United States to start singing in unison, sports audiences in India are noisy but never burst into song the way they do in the terraces or stadiums in the west. Moreover, what such an argument forgets is that Bollywood is also a factory which produces art in a commodity form, it is pure artifice which need pay no fealty to the real conditions of life. Even if song-dance is integral to our daily lives – and this assumption is questionable – there is little reason for Bollywood to pay such an extraordinary degree of importance to it. Neither the traditionalist nor the culturalist accounts, then, provide adequate explanations of a phenomenon which not only is important in its own right, but also has had a huge impact on other cultural forms.

Given the extraordinary significance of the song-dance, it is quite astonishing that Indian academics writing on film have largely chosen to ignore the topic. Song-dance, then, remains crucial to Hindi film. Any film theory which aspires to completeness must therefore engage with the phenomenon and seek to explain it. The film scholar Lalitha Gopalan challenges the commonly held view that song and dance sequences are inserted into films only as spectacles tangentially linked to the narrative.[8] Rather, she argues, we need to differentiate their relationship to the storytelling and examine how they delay the development of the plot, distract us from other scenes of the narrative, yet also bear an integral link to the plot. Moreover, song and dance sequences call our attention to other interests: 'For instance, the abrupt cut to exotic locations sparks the tourist interests of the viewer, and similarly the object-laden *mise en scène* endorses consumerism'.[9] Importantly, Gopalan brings to the foreground a notion that many others have only implicitly alluded to – that the alliteration is misleading, that Bollywood cannot be read as a kitschy version of Hollywood, and that in fact its utilization of song-dance constitutes a radically different way of filmmaking.

The specific role played by song-dance in Bollywood films can be understood only by analysing its relation to the rest of the filmic text. Most commentators have held that the song-dance does no work for the text, and is a mere distraction or diversion. The argument here is that song-dance in Bollywood films is in fact a crucial component of the filmic text because it performs a function that the rest of the text – the story or the narrative – cannot perform.

Bollywood films may involve a lot of singing and dancing but there can be no justification for equating them to Hollywood musicals. In fact, as many commentators have pointed out, most Hindi films contain elements of all the genres: comedy, slapstick, musicals, action adventure, thrillers and drama. The proliferation of styles within the same text has led some to claim that all Bollywood films fall under the rubric of one super-genre – the 'social'. That may well be true, but we also ought to acknowledge the possibility that a categorization based on western notions of genre may not be very productive in the case of Indian cinema. The use of indigenous genres – like BACHCHAN films or NRI (non-resident Indian) films – is more likely to give us a better grasp of the similarities and differences that make up the body of Bollywood films. Such an inquiry must still of course account for universality of the song-dance. Since an analysis based on genre is unlikely to provide us with an answer to this question, here, the strategy is to try to elucidate the meaning of the song-dance by looking at its functionalities, that is, by analysing the work that it does within the film itself. More specifically, we suggest that the song-dance performs two crucial sets of tasks on behalf of the filmic text: first, it creates an 'outside' for the filmic text providing both a context for the film as well as linking it to other cultural practices, and second, it acts as an instrument for building interiority and subjectivity, for projecting models of the individual self. In the enactment of these tasks the song-dance enables the film to articulate a stance which it could not otherwise. In other words, without song-dance the Hindi film would be less, not more.

As an agent of exteriority, ever since the introduction of sound, film songs have enjoyed an existence outside of the films they were written for. As others have argued, film music became practically synonymous with popular music, being regularly featured on state-run media like All-India Radio and Doordarshan. Though songs and song-dances were tied by nomenclature to their textual origins – thus a song like 'Gaata Rahe Mera Dil' would always be identified as being a number from the film *Guide* – their circulation on Vividh Bharati and television shows like *Chitrahaar* ensured that they ultimately became autonomous objects. This detachment is best illustrated in the case of remixes: when Bally Sagoo remixes 'Roop Tera Mastana' for club audiences in London and Toronto, it is the song which is the object of reference and fetishization and its filmic origins lose all significance. Thus the notes in Sagoo's *Best of Bally Sagoo* CD attribute the song to Anand Bakshi and R.D. Burman but make no mention of *Aradhana*.[10] Songs, played on radio, cassettes and CDs, and song-dance sequences played on television and on DVDs as well as in clubs and parties constitute a vast extra-textual world which extends far beyond the films where they were originally located. In other words, song-dance establishes a cultural space which is external to film and autonomous from it.

The externality of the song-dance is not just material for it also diverges from the text at the level of semantics. It has been observed by many that song-dance serves the touristic gaze as well as tying in with an ideology of consumerism. Through the frenetic display of landscape and monuments the song-dance makes the viewer mobile, while the equally flashy montage of bodies fashioned by commodities enforces an appetite for consumption. If song-dance is a sort of advertising tool for capitalism, it is also an instrument for reportage that inserts bits of reality into the filmic text. Song-dance in Hindi film has foregrounded city streets (most notably in Raj Kapoor films) and rural landscapes, public spaces like schools, railway stations, military displays and parades, factories and bazaars. Over the years, song-dance can be said to constitute a vast documentary giving us glimpses of modern India: the machinery of its progress, snapshots of its leaders, and the various constituents that added up to make its social whole. In fact song-dance has often come closest to being a social realist art form. It is quite ironical therefore that song-dance has been repeatedly castigated as 'escapist' or 'fantastic' or simply 'unreal'. Those critics who have focused exclusively on the 'singing round the tree' (which itself contains the realism of advertising) have misrecognized the strongly realistic components of the format. In conclusion then, song-dance creates a fertile outside for the text which is articulated through a variety of media and energized by the flow of commodities that has very little relationship to the film itself. Song-dance can, therefore, be described as participating in the construction of a public or national culture, where the latter terms are to be understood in a spatial and territorial way. The more the spread of a cultural form the more public or national it is. Song-dance therefore *publicizes* film by spilling beyond its boundaries. Yet song-dance is more than just a conduit between film and the outside, it is an autonomous art form that establishes a secondary zone of culture within the public sphere.

Song-dance produces exteriority, but at the same time it also contributes to the creation of interiority and private space. Song-dance provides a space inside which the characters of the text can be more deeply individualized than what the narrative would allow. In other words, singing, rather than dialogue, expresses the innermost aspects of heroes, heroines and even sidekicks. This individualizing function explains the song-dance's overwhelming focus on romance. If by romance we understand that desire which belongs uniquely to one individual, then the song-dance facilitates the process of individuation and the creation of a private self through the mechanism of romantic love and yearning. Song-dance privatizes at the level of the body by depicting lovers alone in vast public spaces. In Raj Kapoor's classic film *Sangam* (1964), the song-dance 'Ye Mera Prem Patra Parkhar' shows Gopal (played by Rajendra Kumar) and Radha (played by Vyjanthimala) confessing their love for each other via the instrument of a letter (which is later discovered by Radha's future husband Sundar, played by Raj Kapoor). The song is sung while the lovers run around in a large garden which is absolutely empty. This desolation is not realistic, for the song-dance knows fully well that public gardens in India are always teeming with people. Indeed, in its exteriorizing mode the song-dance overpopulates space, with ensembles of dancers or just plain crowds. The garden in *Sangam* is empty not by accident but due to a theoretical necessity: because it signifies the asocial terrain where the desire of one reciprocates the desire of the other. The evacuation of the social, the emptying out of history occurs because the philosophy of romantic love demands that the self that loves can only come into being in a shared solitude with the other. Love is private, as is well known, but more importantly only the private can love.

Most Hindi film stories involve a struggle about love, because it is the burden of almost every filmic text to carve out some sort of independent individuality for its protagonists. Insofar that the text promotes this philosophy of individualism in conjunction with older notions of self and society (feudal, religious etc.), it is forced to make compromises in its depiction of individualized love. Thus parental approval always casts its shadow upon romantic love: lovers often meet each other as little children pushed into friendship by their parents; or they fall in love with exactly the person their parents wanted in the first place, or the nobility of the loved one convinces a reluctant parent that this love ought to be blessed. Whatever the strategy, the narrative always flows towards parental consent, because the text is always bisected into a half that projects freedom, desire and individuality and another which brings into play societal forces structured around family and convention. By masquerading as just 'song and dance', the song-dance can get away with more. It is not required to pay fealty to tradition and can represent individuality in a far more radical manner than the narrative. The song-dance therefore posits a strong version of the privacy and the private self. This is evident even in those sequences which are peopled. It is customary for lovers to speak to each other (and only to each other) while in the midst of the social through the device of the song. Song lyrics very often become a secret code utilized by lovers to speak desire in the midst of many. Though this device is hackneyed it continues to have strategic value because of the text and the audience's joint assumption that privacy and the interior is not quite private and is always encroached upon by the public and the outside.

To recapitulate, the song-dance has a double function, it over-produces the text in two directions: outside and inside. The song-dance inhabits an external territory of other media through the circulation of songs and videos, more crucially it becomes a site for the representation of several orders of externalities: of landscape and sightseeing, of fashion and sexuality, of history and politics, of industry and agriculture, in short of the ever-changing face of the social. Concurrently the song-dance functions as an agent that institutes many registers of interiority: private thoughts, private gestures, private languages, romantic love with all its sorrows and joys, in short psychic desire. Song-dance is a coin stamped with the measure of the social on one side, and the likeness of a self driven by longing and desire on the other, and it allows the filmic text to purchase a version of modernity which the narrative cannot afford. Whereas the 'story' in a Bollywood film always labours as a mediator between tradition and modernity, the song-dance is at liberty to perceive and to jubilantly announce the modern in all its contemporary glory.

The suggestion that modernity is encoded in 'fantastic' song-dances may seem preposterous to those who hold that only 'realistic' cinema can lay claim to representing the truth about the present. From this perspective it is not Bollywood but alternative cinema – known variously as new cinema, parallel cinema or art cinema – which can justifiably be described as providing a window to the modern. The distinction between art cinema and popular or commercial cinema is usually framed simply as the difference between good serious cinema and bad degenerate entertainment.

For most writers on the subject, it is the new cinematic tradition rather than Bollywood escapism, which is capable of comprehending and adequately representing Indian modernity. This dominant view needs to be supplemented by looking at how Bollywood alongside the new and parallel cinema has played the crucial role in articulating the contours of Indian modernity. In saying this we do not mean in any way to detract from the significant achievements of new cinema: its focus on material problems, its advocacy on behalf of the oppressed, its refreshing departure from the star system in its casting, its use of a realist mode of storytelling, and its laudable mission of exposing our societal ills. What we are contesting is the view that this list of attributes adds up to the only and the most adequate representation of modernity. Stylistically, new cinema was modelled on neo-realism and it inherited all the limitations of that form. By being excessively committed to the quotidian and the ordinary, new cinema ended up as somewhat dreary and outdated even at the moment of release. Its syntax and imagistic was that of the documentary, its semantics were that of progressivist social engineering. In its determined and dour manner new cinema was at one with the rest of statist production: governmental architecture, dams, factories and other industrial sites that bore the mark of planning. It is hardly surprising that like all State goods, new cinema had little appeal for either a global cosmopolitan market or for the public at home. Satyajit Ray's reputation notwithstanding, most new cinema met with a polite reception abroad, for it offered nothing to viewers in the first world. More importantly it failed to capture the imagination of Indians at large.

Those who hold new cinema to be inherently superior to Bollywood face the burden of answering two crucial questions. First, why did new cinema fail to tantalize a foreign audience in the way Bollywood is doing today? Second, why does new cinema gather dust in the archives, while films like *Awara*, *Mother India*, *Sangam* or *Sholay* continue to resonate in the collective memory of the film public? The fact that new cinema petered out at the very moment when India opened up to global media via television suggests that new cinema belonged to a protectionist moment. Bred by state patronage and overly committed to a mission of earnest reformism, new cinema collapsed under the pressure of the global real. This failure of new cinema to survive the advent of globalization ought to lead us to also question its most vaunted attribute: realism. It could be argued that the adoption of realism by new cinema was a function of its role in nation-building. As Madhav Prasad has observed, 'Under the FCC aegis, realism became a national political project ... It was a realism devoted to the mapping of the land, producing the nation for the state, capturing the substance of the state's boundaries'.[11] As the work of the western film theorists on mainstream Hollywood cinema has demonstrated realism can be an ideological tool serving to legitimize the given state of things and block out the possibility of radical thought. Such a mode of representation is incapable of productive fantasy and of imagining the new. Modernity is not simply the transposition and application of a set of ideals and practices that are already in place (and it is this limited sense of modernity that motivates new cinema), it is equally concerned with the articulation of what has yet come to be. Thus only those forms which re-present reality, and not just represent it, through a manufacturing of the new, can truly be called modern.

Unburdened by new cinema's doctrines, Bollywood too can produce moments of transcendence where what is truly new can emerge. Hindi film's ability to generate utterly new conceptions of the present is very well brought out in Sudipto Kaviraj's essay on the song 'Ay dil hai mushkil' (Oh my heart, it is difficult) from the Dev Anand film *C.I.D.* Kaviraj contrasts the image of the city produced by this hit song with more literary representations of urban spaces found in the work of several modernist Bengali litterateurs. The latter can only pessimistically portray the cityscape as one of decline and death, the song, on the other hand, while cataloguing the many hardships that attend city life, can simultaneously affirm 'yeh hai Bombay meri jaan [This is Bombay, my life]'. As Kaviraj points out

> Both poetry and popular films gave rise to specific aesthetic structures with very different readings for the meaning of city life. For the high poetic discourse the image of the city is a dark one where lives are unfulfilled and people go through the subtle defilement of their everyday existence ... By contrast, the cinematic image of the city is more complex, it contains the dark image, but this is constantly relieved by an opposite image of hope and optimism ... The filmic representation might be less self-consciously artistic [but] its image of the city was of a space of contradictions – where different

types of things took place. It was not just a scene of constant, unremitting despair. The Bombay of the films was in this respect in subtle and important ways, unlike the high artistic depiction of Calcutta, *a city of joy*.[12]

The joy that Kaviraj points to is the joy of urban life; it is the *jouissance*, or ecstasy, that arises from being in the city, from city-being. This being is *new* in the sense that it is not derivable from history, from cause and effect, from tradition and convention, or from previous expectation and anticipation. Nor is the new of modernity oriented towards the future, it is most definitely not a blueprint or a precursor. It stands resolutely in the present; its duration is only of the moment. The new is never realized, it never fully comes to be. We only glimpse the new but never grasp it.

Modernity is encoded in texts not only by historicist representations of its encounter with tradition (which involves a fixed notion of what modernity is) but also by the irruption of the new and the joyous. While narrative in Bollywood is preoccupied with a working out the implications of the historical binary, song-dance is the device which presents modernity in its autonomous version, unmediated by history, as that which is radically novel. The presentation is a mere glimpse, for both the new and the joyous are ephemeral and transitory. Song-dances are quanta, packets of bound energy, that tantalize us with the notion of possibility. Consider two examples, one from the 1960s, one contemporary. The song-dance sequence 'Main Kya Karun Raam Mujhe Buddha Mil Gaya' performed by Radha (Vyjanthimala) is a production of female sexuality which is radically new for its time: it suggests that the heroine, normally represented as pure, can perform a 'cabaret' and yet remain within the space of conjugality. Moreover, the song-dance grants Radha an agency and authority that is denied her in the narrative itself. The story marginalizes Radha's desire in favour of the homoerotic dynamic between Gopal and Sundar. Thus even though Radha loves Gopal, and he secretly loves her in return, he is unable to announce his love because Sundar has already laid claim to her. Gopal's friendship for Sundar becomes the hegemonic principle which governs the action in *Sangam* leading in the end to Gopal's sacrificial suicide at the end of the film. While this negation of female desire is in keeping with the patriarchal practices of Indian society of the 1960s, the song-dance produces a set of new possibilities for female sexuality. It may be argued that such an empowered sexuality has not yet come to be and that desire is still under patriarchal control. Such a critique is misplaced because it assumes that the new, to be valid, must be predictive. We ought to countenance the possibility that the new may never be realized, and that the aesthetic and ontological force of the new may lie in precisely the fact that is never instantiated in history.

To take a more contemporary example, consider the song-dance 'Pretty Woman' in *Kal Ho Na Ho*. During this sequence Aman Mathur (played by Shah Rukh Khan) stands outside the house where Naina Catherinen Kapoor (played by Preity Zeinta) lives, and proceeds to woo her through song. The gesture is common enough in the tradition of song-dance; what makes the difference here is the locale. By situating the song-dance sequence on a Manhattan street the film is able, through a number of innovative artistic moves, to transform a simple love song into a stunning tableau of global India. First, there is the audacious transformation of the classic Roy Orbison song into a 'Hinglish' number that melds Hindi lyrics, English phrases and electric guitar into a contemporary love song. What is different here from previous borrowings from the west is that the 'theft' is openly announced, indicating India's growing global stature and increasing sense of equality with the first world: if the Beatles could put classical sitar into English pop, we can as easily place rockabilly into Hindi *gana*. Globalization at the level of music is replicated at the level of visuals. As Aman sings his romantic message, he is joined not only by New York desis, but also by an entire rainbow coalition – black, white, yellow, brown. Suddenly, the entire world is singing along in Hindi, the new global lingua franca! The moment is fecund one for it amounts to a revelation of two intertwined but independent truths: first, Indians are now fully global, they are here, there and everywhere, at ease and assured of their place; and second, our sensibility, our way of singing and dancing, which we may call Bollywood is now the world's mode of being as well. The 'Pretty Woman' sequence in *KHNH* is extraordinary: what we witness is Bollywood using its own techniques to announce its arrival on the world stage. Song-and-dance, judged by common sense to be a peculiarity or aberration, paradoxically becomes, in this context, a passage to universality.

Song-dance functions as a sign for Bollywood and for Indian popular culture as a whole and is a device of *excess*, one that allows the filmic text to posit ecstatic visions of the new. It is this very excessiveness that allows Hindi film to find international fans and thus become transformed into the cultural form known as Bollywood. The song-dance, known and loved all over the world, is Bollywood's essence. Bollywood, more than any other cultural form, has taken on the task of presenting the emerging shapes of modernity to our eyes. It has done so with song and with dance, and has in the process, enabled our popular culture to become truly global.

Notes

1   Richard Corliss, 'That Old Feeling', *Time Online Edition*, 30 July, 2003.
2   David Chute, 'Planet Bollywood?' *LA Weekly*, 7–13 March, 2003.
3   Kobita Sarkar, *Indian Cinema Today* (New Delhi: Sterling, 1975), 1.
4   Ram Gopal Verma, *Filmfare* interview, March 2003, 64–65.
5   Aparna Sen, *Filmfare* interview, March 2003, 104.
6   Erik Barnouw and S. Krishnsawamy, *Indian Film*, 2nd edition (New York: Oxford University Press), 72.
7   Shukla, Vinay. 'Exploring the Popular Narrative'. www.graftii.com/ezine27.aspx (accessed. 17 February 2008).
8   Lalitha Gopalan, *Cinema Interruptions: Action Genres in Contemporary Indian Cinema* (London: British Film Institute, 2002).
9   Ibid 15.
10 Sagoo, Bally. *On Screen: The Best of Bally Sagoo*. Desi Thug Release Group, 2005.

11 Madhava Prasad, *Ideology of the Hindi Film: A Historical Construction* (New Delhi: Oxford University Press, 1998), 190.
12 Sudipta Kaviraj, 'Reading a Song of a City – Images of the City in Literature and Films', in *City Flicks: Cinema, Urban Worlds and Modernities in India and Beyond.* Occasional paper no. 22 (Preben Kaarsholm, Roskilde University, 2002), 70, italics mine.

13

Invisible representation: the oral contours of a national popular cinema
by Sheila J. Nayar

[N]ation-states are incomplete regions for the purposes of analyzing cinema. Neither from a production nor a consumption standpoint do political boundaries sufficiently divide, group, or structure world cinema. If global cinema is more than the sum of all the national cinemas, then the task confronting us is to develop a set of regions more meaningful and more powerful in explaining the phenomenon as a communications medium.

– Gerald M. McDonald, in *Place, Power, Situation, and Spectacle*

Orality invisible

The theme of social inclusion as it relates to media readily anticipates consideration of race, gender, class, and other such visible markers of identity. But what about *invisible* modes of identification and representation that link outwardly divergent cultures and groups? In other words, though film may be a visual medium, not everything that determines one's representation on screen is necessarily related to sight. Too often we limit our assessment of how viewers are being socially excluded from the media experience on the basis of physical *presence*, neglecting other seminal ways in which groups or, indeed, entire subcultures, such as that of the subaltern,[1] may be finding representation – and not always in a manner wedded to national or linguistic boundaries.

Take, for example, the case of a Nigerian villager who has never left the confines of his or her community, yet finds an Indian popular film – seen without the benefit of sub-titles or dubbing – completely comprehensible, even culturally *familiar*.[2] Indeed, a film as "indigenous" and "nationalistic" as *Mother India* (1957) continues to be embraced by audiences of other nations and races and languages and histories, as if it were in fact recounting the story of Mother Nigeria, or Mother Egypt, or of Romany Gypsies in Eastern Europe or Swahili-speaking girls in Zanzibar.[3]

To be sure, scholars have speculated (albeit, often only in passing) as to why such disparate nations identify so intensely with these Hindi-language popular films – films which are, incidentally, frequently ridiculed by critics for their *masala* ("spice-mix") blend of tawdry escapism, formulaic storytelling, and narratively irrelevant song-and-dance numbers. Some analysts have (also in passing) attributed this peculiar trans-cultural identification to a parallel experience of modernization encroaching on traditional society (one of the films' common themes). Others maintain it derives from a mutual privation that privileges escapist melodrama and the presentation of a material utopia, while still others contend that it is born of shared family values, or of poorer nations' inability to afford better, more substantive entertainment. (These Bollywood films are, after all, comparatively cheap entertainment imports.) These are of course reasonable theories and under no circumstances invalid.[4] But is it not possible that in our commitment to that which we can readily measure with pens and computers, or support through an intellectual reasoning carefully organized and modified on paper, a much broader infrastructure of identification has been missed?

My mention of these instruments of writing and the processes that accompany them is not solely rhetorical. It relates significantly to the theory I want here to suggest. Indeed, I think one of the reasons we may have neglected this other possibility is that – by virtue of the technologies we possess – we are, in actual fact, more *same* than different. That is, one thing binds us (for, if you are reading this, you are one of "us" – irrespective of your race, your culture, your gender, or your class). This one thing separates and distinguishes us from millions of others (from 300 million such people in India alone), and thus makes this invisible transcultural identity that much harder to conceptualize, let alone to identify. I am speaking here of literacy – of our literacy, and hence of the non-literacy of others – and of the cognitive consequences of this as they apply to an individual's comprehension, organization, and experience of the world.

Why might a Nigerian villager who has never left his or her village call a film like *Mother India* culturally familiar and completely comprehensible? Perhaps it is because such movies do not take the form of a literacy-driven object. Instead, the conventional Indian popular film possesses clear characteristics of oral performance and orally transmitted narratives, conspicuously sharing traits with, for example, Homeric epic and the Indian *Mahabharata*. It is a cultural product that has been historically circumscribed by the psychodynamics of orality – that is, by the thought processes and personality structures that distinguish a non-writing mindset; and, as such, it is a product that employs specific devices and motifs that are traditionally part of orally based storytelling.[5]

Though English and humanities scholar Walter Ong contends in his seminal book *Orality & Literacy: The Technologizing of the Word*[6] that the characteristics that distinguish oral narrative are somehow of the past, receding (though perhaps residually still apparent in modern times), this may not be the case. It may simply be that, up till now, there has been no comprehensive application of the orality-literacy paradigm to visual media. Studies have been limited more or less exclusively to the anthropological study of oral peoples and to the investigation of the oral presence as it appears (or is disappearing) in *written* texts. In recent years, for example, there has been a noticeable shift from the study of orality as reflected in print to an interest in and focus on its consequences for computer and Internet communication.[7] A legitimate transition, to be sure, but one that is still grounded in the *written* word.

But visual narrative is like written narrative, in the sense that it too is a text and hence requires a kind of "reading." And perhaps, in order to be comprehended or appreciated, some cinematic narrative forms require of their spectators what Roland Barthes has referred to as a "writerly" mindset.[8] But what if an individual does not possess such a mindset? What if, due to his or her functioning in a non-literate or low-literate or oral-privileging environment, s/he does not have the cognitive skills required? Of course, those of us who are readers, who are citizens of print, "are so literate that it is very difficult for us to conceive of an oral universe of communication or thought except as a variant of a literate universe."[9] But an oral person absorbs and organizes, and retains and recalls information differently. For instance, s/he cannot organize thoughts with syntactical sophistication (for, it is literacy that turns one's thought processes into more complicated shapes). In such a universe, the knower is incapable of being separated from the known,[10] and as such, his or her relationship to the world, to the group, and to the self is radically different from that of the person who can search a computer for data, or read about a character's psychological struggle, or even look up a street name on a city map.

So, where does one "reside" when life is inhabited without the benefit of text? What is history when it exists bereft of documented and verifiable facts? What can one remember – indeed, how *must* one remember – in order not to forget?

I am not trying to recommend that there is some distinct and definitive split between "oral" and "literate" films, nor some great fixed opposition between "oral" and "literate" films – or, worse yet, between literate and illiterate. But certainly the number of years that the average student in the United States must devote to honing a "higher order of thinking"[11] – some 15 to 20, if one counts college – attests to the length, breadth, and complexity of acquiring a literate mindset.

Imagine, then, a film industry such as Bombay's, whose primary mission these past 50 years has been profit; to be sure, it is in such an industry's interest to reach the largest audience possible. Now, imagine that this is an audience with a historically significant percentage of non- and low-literate viewers, and also one not bound by a serviceable lingua franca. (Significantly, only one-third of Indians are native Hindi speakers.) What does an industry of this type do? If it's savvy, it shapes its product into one that satisfies the greatest numbers. And orally-based characteristics of thought and storytelling would not only make a visual product accessible to the oral mindset; given that they are more elemental, more universal, perhaps even more natural, they would also render a visual product more "readable" to those unschooled in the spoken language of the film. No wonder, then, that such films have been popular in nations with significant numbers of non- or low-literate viewers. True, India's recently expanded upper-middle class, in conjunction with a wealthier audience of Indians abroad, is starting to make subtle inroads into the Bollywood film formula landscape. But the films that succeed with *non*-elite audiences (i.e., rural, uneducated) rarely depart from this oral lattice-work.

So, let us examine some of these oral particulars. Their presence can be seen in some of the industry's biggest hits of the past five decades, including *Mother India* (1957), *Sholay* (*Flames*, 1975), *Khal Nayak* (*The Villain*, 1993), *Baazigar* (*Trickster*, 1993), and *Hum Aapke Hain Kaun* (*Who Am I to You*, 1994).

The oral contours of the conventional Hindi film

Pastiche and preservation

One of the most broad psychodynamic characteristics of orally based thought is the tendency toward the additive rather than the subordinative. Without the ability to write, to store, and to organize information elsewhere than the brain, the possibility of developing structural cohesiveness, of manipulating a story for tight shape and flow – especially as regards lengthy narrative – is impossible. Indeed, the "analytic, reasoned subordination that characterizes writing"[12] arises *with writing itself*. Without writing, meticulously sculpting a sentence – let alone an entire plot – is quite impossible. Oral narratives are hence, by noetic necessity, episodic, sequential, and additive in nature. Works such as the *Mahabharata* and African oral epic are not built upward into some kind of pyramidal form, but are rather constructed around techniques like the use of flashbacks, thematic recurrences, and chronological breaks. This is because these are the only ways to handle extended narrative, to keep it manageable, memorable, and uncomplicated. For this reason, orally inscribed narrative – and this includes Bombay cinema – often has the feeling of being piecemeal and disaggregative, of being coarsely stitched together. It is pastiche – but quite without the post-modern self-consciousness.

One of these oral structural devices in particular, the flashback, deserves consideration. Its prevalence in oral epic is due in large part to its facilitating a movement between data more easily transmittable in separate containers. To be sure, the oft described "boxes within boxes"[13] feel of oral epic arises to a large degree from the repeated use of the flashback. In the Hindi film, we are constantly being transported back and forth and back again in time – between various storage spaces, so to speak – to watch the playing out of this romance or that crisis. In *Sholay*, for instance, there is a police chief's story-within-story recall of his meeting two thieves whom he plans now to hire to execute his vengeance; this is followed by a protracted flashback to the chief's once idyllic family life and also its tragic ruination at the hand of the film's nemesis, Gabbar Singh; and finally by a third portraying the once exuberant, spirited life-force of the police chief's daughter-in-law, who is now reduced to forlorn widowhood.

In the more recent *Khal Nayak*, we straggle in and out of a rough, crude underworld tale, a Ram and Sita-type love story, not to mention a mother-son melodrama, stalling on several occasions to voyage back in time and witness the childhood experiences that led to the protagonist's transformation into a heinous villain, as well as the traumatic aftermath of that particular metamorphosis on the boy's upright family.

As with lengthy oral narrative, in the typical Hindi film there are also numerous sidetracks or "parallel skits" that, unlike subplots, have little to no bearing on the major story line. These digressions may be fun, funny, maudlin, titillating, even gruesome, but they are neither particularly revealing of character, nor narratively instrumental. Much like the African oral epic, where episodes of, say, horror or comedy are developed for their independent appeal,[14] Hindi film is rife with stand-alone sketches and anticipated deviations, often of a humorous or violent nature and similarly amplified for full effect. In *Sholay*, one finds a solid 15 minutes of the first half dedicated to the two goodhearted anti-heroes' extraneous gambol through a prison sentence. In *Hum Aapke Hain Kaun*, the servants' vaudevillian mishaps take the spectator down a narrative blind alley for the sheer sake of enjoyment. And certainly this collective willingness to digress is reflected in the obligatory song-and-dance numbers that punctuate, sometimes puncture, virtually every conventional Hindi film.

To be sure, the Hindi film is oft derided by film scholars and critics for its stringy and episodic nature, for its lack of an "organic consistency."[15] Sometimes this lack of any organizing principle, this constant detouring and often lengthy meandering, is kindly attributed to its imitating indigenous precursors like the *Mahabharata*. But, rather than paying tribute to or being modeled on ancient tales, the Hindi film and the earlier oral epics are, I believe, cognate with respect to form. (Certainly many of the characteristics of the Hindi film that have been dubbed "indigenously Indian" by critics are also common to oral performance and orally based narrative irrespective of national or cultural boundaries.) Other similarities seem to bolster this point – like a second broad psychodynamic characteristic common to orality: the commitment to a conservative-traditionalist rather than experimental mindset.

Whereas the literate mindset looks toward experimentation in storytelling, that is, toward the achievement of something different, original and unique, the oral mindset inhibits such thought experimentation. As Ong points out, this is because a mind that must be the holder of all things is naturally inclined toward pragmatism and conservatism, not toward speculation and discovery.[16] Originality (as the literate mind understands that term) necessitates an ability to move away from the original via notes, or books, or a computer screen – to leave a work, or a body of work, in order to change it. But if one *cannot* leave the original for fear of losing it altogether (and hence of losing the self that is carried forward through time), then such movements are resisted, are in fact self-annihilating. So any contemporary shifts in social relations, any tensions *du jour*, even the jazzy emergence of fads and technologies, are less "touted for their novelty" than synchronically "presented as fitting the traditions of the ancestors."[17] In other words, the new is invariably incorporated into the old (and in some manner, the "forever"), resulting in a kind of mythic "telescoping" of temporalities, as social psychologist Ashis Nandy has perceptively identified with reference to Hindi film.[18] In *Khal Nayak*, for instance, we find that the modern pursuit of a terrorist via cell phones, helicopters and fast cars ends with a simple, coherent (and some might say, regressive) return to mythic patterns and human relations – not to mention clear-cut allusions to the epic *Ramayana*. And in *Baazigar*, the contemporary city setting naturally segues by the film's end to ancient ruins and deep-rooted principles regarding family obligation and honor.

Relatedly, because the fabric of oneself in oral cultures is transmitted by word of mouth, from one person to another, from the previous generation to the next, what this also implies is that self-preservation is an inherently *collective* affair, a group endeavor. As a result, communal structures of personality are fostered, with things being "we"-inflected rather than "I"-inflected.[19] (Indeed, the assertion of *individual* rights, as Marshall McLuhan has noted, appears only with the rise of print.[20]) Certainly this is applicable to the Bombay film industry, which specializes in "we"-inflected dramas that consistently and continuously conserve the traditional order. The movies, like the oral epics before them, ensure that the way things *are* is, in the end, restored – and triumphantly so. The emphasis is similarly on the preservation of the ordered society, which is considered in oral narrative the "highest good and goal toward which the hero's physical and intellectual development is bent."[21] This is not to say that there cannot be all measure of disruption, disorder, and discord during the course of a story – through displays of intergenerational aggression, say, or the transgressing of civilly sanctioned boundaries. But, by the end, the existing social order must be preserved. Those who have gone amiss must be punished, banished, or destroyed, or prove themselves certifiably penitent, for only such actions can ensure that the "communal self" is not atomized.[22]

So, in *Mother India*, we have Nargis shooting her wayward son rather than allowing him to run roughshod over the ethics of their community. In *Sholay*, it is Gabbar Singh who is eliminated, with the village returned to the good management of the police chief. In *Khal Nayak*, the villain, awash in sudden moral conviction, surrenders before the city. And in *Hum Aapke Hain Kaun* where no villains exist, two families – united by a marriage that has since terminated due to a death – are wedded together again by another marriage within the same family. All ends happily because in effect all ends *just as it started*.

Though it is true that these resolutions are to some degree shaped by censorship codes – and are therefore taken by some analysts to be a metaphoric if not blatantly pro-state product of government intervention – the fact that such endings are firmly anticipated by audiences implies a deeper *raison d'être*. After all, audiences *reject* films that do not uphold the status quo; and in light of the findings in orality studies, it seems quite feasible that such patriotic (sometimes even jingoistic) overtones is in actual fact a modern extension of the oral mindset's conservatism as regards the communal self. What else could explain the unwavering embrace by audiences in Ghana and Turkey of *Mother India* despite its blatantly nationalistic ardor?

But what then is there if originality and uniqueness are eschewed? Certainly Homer was inventive and artful in his poetic enterprises. Still, his was a different kind of artfulness – not to mention a kind similarly attributable to the Bombay cinema. For Hindi films, like the oral epics that preceded them, [23] manipulate *public* stories. They too creatively re-fashion a flotilla of formulae and themes that an audience has come to know and expect. Additions and alterations are of course made, but to material that is already part of a collective storehouse of experience and knowledge.

This then explains the Hindi film spectators' acceptance of, if not preference for, formula films that the slightly contemptuous critic might term inflexibly redundant and endlessly repetitive of themes and story lines, and the more sympathetic critic might characterize as possessing a kind of *déja-vu*-ness.[24] And it is true: when one sinks into a Bollywood theater seat, one can predict with a fair amount of accuracy some of the elements or motifs of story about to be encountered: there will be the flowering of a romantic love, followed by a romantic crisis most likely spurred by a villain (perhaps a parent or really malicious felon); there will be the distress of a mother, the sacrifice of a son; an oath; vengeance; malefactors punished and social injustices put right by the hero; and the romantic couple re-united and the community victoriously returned to its harmonious state.

Perhaps you are here reminded of Vladimir Propp's analysis of the narrative structure of fairy tales. Indeed, analysts have often labeled Hindi films "fairy tales," or "myths,"[25] and this is largely because this kind of storytelling is, to literate minds, profoundly ahistorical, exhibiting a tendency to fly in the face of "realism," to revert to fantasy endings. But if we take into account how the oral mindset must synthesize all experience into a present story – that is, that each tale in the telling must be a repository of the past, and "a resource for renewing awareness of present existence"[26] – then Hindi film's sameness, its repetition, its aforementioned telescoping of temporalities, makes complete sense. The storyteller's art lies in being able to entwine the old formulas and themes with the new, in being able to "read" the audience's desire for the novel from *within* "a deep sense of tradition, which preserves the essential meaning of stories."[27]

If we are willing to concede that the films' formulaic nature, their grand-scale redundancy, is born of their orally inscribed communal nature – of their being a public, as opposed to private, property – then another peculiar characteristic of the Hindi film is explained: their proclivity for quoting each other. That is to say, there are incessant references in Hindi films to prior Hindi films, an endless borrowing cum stealing of previous movies' tunes, lyrics, dialogue, iconic props, whole characters, and sometimes even entire plots.[28] In *Hum Aapke Hain Kaun*, for example, the characters assemble one evening to play an extended (in terms of screen time, at least) game in which characters recite passages, sing songs, and dialogically act out complete scenes from other movies (including *Sholay*). *Hum Aapke Hain Kaun* has itself been referenced, used, and abused in at least half a dozen movies since that film's 1994 release, by way of reprised melodies, quoted lines, borrowed costumes, embezzled props heavy with sentimental weight, and even one farcical send-up of a musical number. In Hollywood, some of these strategies would indubitably result in hefty legal suits. But the concept of plagiarism, of idea-ownership, is a consequence of literacy, more specifically of print.[29] In the oral universe, there is no such thing. One cannot steal what belongs to the collective consciousness of the group. Of course, such pilfering is not only for the purpose of repeating knowledge in order that it live on and maintain its relevancy; repetition is also "a token of the joy of recollection."[30] The viewer, in other words, joins in a highly *participatory* event, an overtly shared memory-event that is pleasurable precisely because it is continuous with other films, not separate from them.

The good, the bad, and the wordy

There are other characteristics of orally inscribed narrative that may be less broad, but that unequivocally play out with equal significance in the Hindi film. Their reasons for being may perhaps be evoked best in the form of a question: If one must store information exclusively in the mind, how must a story – with its transitory oral utterances – be executed so that it can be thus stored? In the Hindi film, the answers are manifested in two ways: verbally (as one might expect), and also visually.

One of the traits of oral performance, of oral cultures even, is agonistic delivery. That is, there exists the tendency to perform verbally in a manner that is, by literate turns of phrases, dynamic, thick, excessive, or flatulent. This is because knowledge in the oral world, incapable as it is of being disengaged from the act, is situated within the "context of struggle."[31] Knowledge exists *in* the speaking – as outward display, as event; and as such, it necessarily "engage[s] others in verbal and intellectual combat."[32]

This is certainly not hard to discern in the conventional Bollywood film, where actors do not so much talk as spout, orate, and hyperbolically perorate, and where success is wholly in the *doing* of things. Heroes and heroines have no problem talking out loud to themselves; but their discussions are neither about nor demand from an audience anything that is analytical, self-reflective, or categorizationally abstract. Talking and existing is fully tied to the operational world.[33] As Nandy has averred, though without being cognizant of its connection to orality, Hindi films are "anti-psychological"; there is no "interior" story. Nothing exists within a character that is not said. And so, when the police chief in *Sholay* wants vengeance, he expresses himself in the form of a highly dramatized oath, full of bravura and overstated spite. And when in *Hum Aapke Hain Kaun* there is discussion of familial ethics, it is housed not in personal admittances or intimate confessions, but in publicly shared truths or memories – that is, in clichés, in proverbs, in forms of utterances that are guarded against change because they render knowledge easily transportable.

It is rare, in fact, to find a Hindi film that has not, by its denouement, skidded into language that is noticeably aphoristic. For example, in *Baazigar*, just prior to that film's violent showdown, the protagonist declares imperiously to his fiancée about her diabolical father: "You have only seen the crown on his head. Look under the thief's sleeve and you will find blood." We then witness in flashback the pitiful aftermath of her father's depravity (i.e., his father and sister are dead, his mother stricken with dementia). When we return to the present, it is to the protagonist informing his betrothed with axiomatic import: "You have only been pricked with a thorn. I have been wounded with a trident." Some literate minds may find such dialogue platitudinous, even embarrassing, but that is only because long-term exposure to print has engendered an anxious need to be original, to shun clichés.

Agonistic display in oral narrative (and cultures) manifests itself in other ways, too. Because of the give-and-take nature of oral communications – the fact that all knowledge must pass through word of mouth – inter-personal relationships are generally kept high.[34] In order to render interaction in a story memorable, then, physical behavior is presented in a fashion that is celebrated, exaggerated, even extreme. In Homer, for instance, one finds enthusiastic portrayals of gross physical violence: of "slaughtered corpses" and "bloody filth," of "jaws glistening, dripping red," as "brazen spearhead[s] smash [their] way clean through below the brain in an upward stroke."[35] As for the *Mahabharata*, who doesn't shudder at Bhima's placing his foot upon the throat of his enemy, so that he might rip open his breast and drink his warm lifeblood? The same applies to Hindi film, where, stagy as they may be, fight scenes are grisly and blood-soaked, with lurid sound effects enhancing the kung-fu kicks, snapped limbs, gruesome impalings, and glass panes literally shattering and plunging "clean through below the brain in an upward stroke." In the protracted 12-minute showdown of the aforementioned *Baazigar*, for instance, an already embattled, blood-soaked Shah Rukh Khan downs seven savage thugs twice his size, is choked once, thrown against a wall twice, finally is skewered (in slo-mo) – and still he lives long enough to crawl into the lap of his mother, where he can die in maudlin, regressed, and oratorical splendor.

But this is the case not only for antagonistic interchanges; it is equally so for approbatory ones. One will find equal cinematic energy invested in extravagant praise and an unabashed – and to literate minds, overripe – glorification of others: of stoic mothers and sacrificing sons, of virtuous daughters and pals-for-life. For instance, in *Sholay*, we find the two male leads racing down a rural road on motorcycle, declaring boisterously in song, "This friendship will never be destroyed; we'd sooner die than let that occur"; and in *Khal Nayak*, the villain's "Ma," cast here as the receptacle of all goodness and the mute bearer of all ills, is exalted on several occasions, including during an argument, within a sentimental song, and even between the punches of a fistfight.

Amplification and polarization – and their inevitable by-product, melodrama – are also part and parcel of the characters who inhabit orally inscribed narrative. Colorless personalities – characters who are quiet, still, delicately nuanced – cannot survive in such a world. They must, like the mnemonic phrases of an oral epic, be organized into some kind of form that will render them permanently memorable. Hence Bollywood is populated by one-dimensional, oversized, and inflated personalities who can be classified (almost mnemonically) into stereotypes like "wicked dacoits" and "beautiful village girls," or "victimized mothers" and "millionaire's sons." They are big, they are brash, they are epic. They stand out from the background; they cannot belong to it. (In fact, the Indian movie stars – who, for many spectators, have a status akin to that of gods – themselves tend to stand out from the roles they are inhabiting, with most stars playing the same "mnemonic personality" over and over and over again.)

Of course, one might also say that the background itself stands out, in the sense that these stories are always enacted upon sets that are optically excessive, visually voluble. The Hindi film universe is, after all, one of sprawling mansions and evildoer hideaways that smack of Disneyland, of idyllic villages inhabited by folk who sport spangled costumes of crisp, clean silk. The real is discarded in preference for the grand, which is certainly more memorable. Fantasy – or, rather, the fanciful, the cinematically resplendent and utopian – though indubitably speaking to an audience's desire for escape from a much less fanciful existence, also fortifies sights and sounds, rendering them less forgettable. The same could be said for the Hindi film's propensity for amplified camerawork, such as its heavy, but never ironic, use of multiple zooms-in on a heroine's horrified look, or its rapid encirclings of the leading man in trouble. Though perhaps excessive and over-wrought to the literate mind, such emphatic cinematography provides cues to the spectator that are easy to read, and so to remember – a modern day extension, perhaps, of the oral epic's reliance on clichés.

Finally, we must mention the Hindi film's commitment to a Manichean world, one where a highly polarized good and evil are pitted against each other, and where good (that is, the collectively agreed-upon moral order of the world) beats out – virtually *without fail* – all dark, destructive forces.[36] This should not be surprising, given the reliance on outsized characters who are themselves heavily polarized, the focus on exterior exploits rather than interior consciousness, and the inclination toward the preservation of the existent social structure. This aspect too can be explained when one looks to the structures and performative aspects of orality. For, in an oral universe, the memory cannot retain information that is not sufficiently amplified; nor can the individual afford trajectories that do not pragmatically bolster collective survival. Thus, for very good reason, the ambiguities of existence, the nuances of the psychological self, the grayness of the moral universe, the ordinariness of human life – all those characteristics to which texts circumscribed by literacy are so rigorously devoted – are here rarely to be found.

Oral cinema beyond India

If characteristics of oral performance and orally-transmitted narratives were reflected more subtly or less numerously in the Hindi film, it would not be possible to argue that the industry has been largely contoured by the particular cognitive needs of its spectators. But the fact that so many appear so prominently, so resiliently, suggests theoretical legitimacy. Of course, this does not imply that there are not other historical, cultural, or aesthetic influences on the form and content of India's popular cinema and on its success outside national borders. But, certainly it seems that, up to this point, orality's contouring of the Hindi film has been fairly substantial. Further, many of the Bollywood movie's perceived inconsistencies and oft-cited contradictions as a text and practice actually make sense when examined through the prism of orality.

But what about beyond the borders of India? There are other nations that cater to audiences with large non-literate, or low-literate, or linguistically diverse populations; and wouldn't one expect to find national cinemas elsewhere that pay inadvertent heed to the noetic requirements and expectations of their audiences? Certainly. However, there is as yet no similar work on other national cinemas whose roots may have been, or whose existence continues to be, inspired or constrained by an invisibly represented body of spectators. Still, some important evidence from secondary sources seems to confirm the theoretical claim being made here. For instance, in *Planet Hong Kong*, David Bordwell commences his study of Chinese popular cinema with a detailed description of its "distinct aesthetic."[37] Though apparently unacquainted with the movies' oral underpinnings, he describes the form and energies of that mass entertainment as being: (i) non-contemplative, (ii) non-realist, (iii) "Manichean," (iv) loosely plotted (and of "kaleidoscopic variety"), (v) kinesthetically arousing, (vi) flashback-using, (vii) tradition-refining (as opposed to originality-seeking), (viii) favoring formulas and clichés, (ix) brutal in their violence, (x) plagiaristic, and (xi) possessing a tendency to "swerve into a happy ending."[38] I can think of no better support from an un-invested outside source than this, and would propose that the common "aesthetic" shared by these two cinematic forms suggests that orality might prove a worthy departure point from which to analyze the cultural, aesthetic and sociopolitical vicissitudes of various visual media worldwide.

In fact, witnessing orality's vivid circumscription of one nation's cinema assists in exposing its more subtle and sometimes splintered forms elswhere: in Egyptian cinema, and the Italian peplums (mythic "sword and sandal" movies) of the 1940s and '50s, and Hollywood blockbusters, like *Titanic*, *Rambo* and *Lara Croft: Tomb Raider*; in the *Amar Chitra Katha* comic books and Japanese *manga*; in Doordarshan's *Ramayana* mini-series, Mexican *telenovelas*, and American serials like *Xena: Warrior Princess*; even in MTV and the current spate of popular video games. In other words, narrative heavily inscribed by orality still persists, even within societies that are ostensibly highly literate. It is not a disappearing phenomenon, only a migratory one.

But with regard to the primary audience with which I have been dealing, that is, those of a subaltern status, certainly the new discovery of this transcultural identity has repercussions as regards social inclusion. For programs or movies that the literate-minded tout as superior, meaningful, or original, as being about something *real*, about something that *matters*, may speak more to an individual's literate biases, of his or her literate construction of the world, than to what constitutes an authentic or valid – or even real – representation.

Once, not too long ago, a rhetorical question that has now grown quite famous was forwarded in print: "Who speaks for the subaltern?"[39] We might modify that question somewhat in relation to the *media* and this invisible marker of identity, and ask: Who speaks in the *language* of the subaltern, so that his representation can be self-accessed and her identification assured? After all, can we rightly say that a media image is "representing," if the spectator it is representing is from the outset noetically excluded from comprehending it?

Of course, with respect to Hindi popular film, one might contend that the subaltern has been speaking all along, and that perhaps it is the built-in limitation of the intellectual community, with its critical imprimatur derived exclusively from *literate* thought and perception, which has caused it to miss this fact – or, at the least, to read only with ideological curiosity and stringent concern what is in fact a form of subaltern self-constitution.

Notes

1 See Gayatri Chakravorty Spivak, "Can the Subaltern Speak?" in *Marxism and the Interpretation of Culture*, ed. Cary Nelson and Lawrence Grossberg (Urbana, IL: University of Illinois Press, 1983).

2 See Brian Larkin, "Indian Films and Nigerian Lovers: Media and the Creation of Parallel Modernities," *Africa*, vol. 67, no. 3 (1997), pp. 406–440; and "Bollywood Comes to Nigeria," in *Samar 8*, Winter/Spring (1997).

3 See Carla Power and Sudip Mazumdar, "Bollywood Goes Global." *Newsweek*. February 28, 2000. Online. July 26, 2002. http://discuss.washingtonpost.com/ nw-srv/printed/int/socu/a16653–2000feb21.htm. 6 pp.

4 For those interested in other perspectives on the Hindi popular film and its *raisons d'être*, see, amongst others, Sumita Chakravarty, *National Identity in Indian Popular Cinema, 1947–1987* (Delhi: Oxford University Press, 1998); Rachel Dwyer and Divia Patel, *Cinema India: The Visual Culture of Hindi Film* (New Brunswick, NJ: Rutgers University Press, 2002); Fareed Kazmi, *The Politics of India's Conventional Cinema: Imagining a Universe, Subverting a Multiverse* (New Delhi: Sage Publications, 1999); Vijay Mishra, *Bollywood Cinema: Temples of Desire* (New York: Routledge, 2002); and Ravi Vasudevan, ed., *Making Meaning in Indian Cinema* (Delhi: Oxford University Press, 2000). Also of value is the 1981 edition of *India International Centre Quarterly*, vol. 8, no. 1 (New Delhi: India International Centre, 1981) and the various film-related writings of Sara Dickey, Wimal Dissanayake, Ashis Nandy, and Rosie Thomas.

5 Some of these characteristics of orally-based narrative as reflected in Hindi film were first presented in Sheila J. Nayar, "The Impact of Orality on Indian Popular Cinema," *Visual Anthropology*, vol. 14, no. 2 (2001), pp. 121–154.

6 Walter Ong, *Orality and Literacy: The Technologizing of the Word* (London: Methuen, 1982). It should be noted that Ong's book consolidates and systematizes the orality-related theories and ideas of many scholars, including his own. Other significant (sometimes inadvertent) contributors to the field upon whose work his own book is based include Jack Goody, Eric Havelock, A.R. Luria, Marshall McLuhan, and Milman Parry. As pertains to this project, see especially Goody and Watt's (eds.) groundbreaking and indispensable *Literacy in Traditional Societies* (Cambridge: Cambridge University Press, 1968) – especially their introductory essay, "The Consequences of Literacy"; McLuhan's *The Gutenberg Galaxy: The Making of Typographic Man* (Toronto: University of Toronto Press, 1962); and the many (oft anthologized) essays by Eric Havelock, including "Some Elements of the Homeric Fantasy," in *Homer's Iliad*, Harold Bloom, ed. (New York: Chelsea House Publishers, 1987). Also of great value and influence have been Isidore Okpewho's *The Epic in Africa:*

Toward a Poetics of the Oral Performance (New York: Columbia University Press, 1979) and David Olson and Nancy Torrance's (eds.) *Literacy and Orality* (Cambridge: Cambridge University Press, 1991), in which appears, amongst other valuables, another Havelock essay, "The Oral-Literate Equation: A Formula for the Modern Mind."

7 The best means of confirming this claim is simply to surf the Internet. Sites exploring orality and literacy's interface with the new language of cyberspace abound – especially as they reify, substantiate or intersect with Ong's claim of a new age of *secondary orality*: a programmatic kind of orality induced by electronic technology, and one more "deliberate and self-conscious," given its being "based permanently on the use of writing and print." Ong, 136.

8 See Roland Barthes, *The Pleasure of the Text* (New York: Farrar, Strauss & Giroux, 1975).

9 Ong, 2.

10 Ibid., 105.

11 Scholar in the cognitive science of learning and instruction Laura Resnick describes this "higher order of thinking" as a cluster of interrelated activities that permits one the ability to yield *multiple solutions* and to make *nuanced judgments* (the emphases are hers); to apply *multiple criteria* and to deal with *uncertainty* – all in a manner that is *nonalgorithmic* and *complex*, in that the process can neither be specified nor always rendered "visible." Further, such thinking is defined by an *effortful* ability to *self-regulate* the thinking process and to *impose meaning* (3). As Resnick acknowledges, such "higher order goals are nothing new. They represent what might be called the 'high literacy' strand in the education of history" (3). This is of course not to suggest that there cannot be complexity or subtlety to oral people's thinking, but rather that theirs is architecturally fashioned out of different needs and circumstances. For more, see Resnick, *Education and Learning to Think*. Washington D.C.: National Academy Press, 1987. Online. August 17, 2002. <www.nap.edu>.

12 Ibid., 37.

13 Cedric Whitman made this observation vis-à-vis the *Iliad*, noting – as Ong summarizes – that the epic was "built like a Chinese puzzle." Ong, 27.

14 Isidore Okpewho, *The Epic in Africa: Toward a Poetics of the Oral Performance* (New York: Columbia University Press, 1979), 209.

15 Vijay Mishra, "Decentering History: Some Versions of Bombay Cinema," *East-West Film Journal*, vol. 6, no. 1, January (1992): 112.

16 Ong, 41–42.

17 Ibid., 42.

18 Ashis Nandy, "The Popular Hindi Film: Ideology and First Principles," *India International Centre Quarterly*, vol. 8, no. 1 (1981): 91.

19 Ibid., 69.

20 Marshall McLuhan, *The Gutenberg Galaxy: The Making of Typographic Man.* (Toronto: University of Toronto Press, 1962), 220.

21 Robert Scholes and Robert Kellogg, *The Nature of Narrative* (New York: Oxford University Press, 1966), 36.

22 According to Manthia Diawara, the tales of African *griots* also consistently conclude with a "restoration of traditional order." See his "Oral Literature and African Film: Narratology in Wend Kuuni," *Questions of Third Cinema*, Jim Pines and Paul Willemen, eds. (London: British Film Institute, 1989), 201.

23 Ong, 36, 60.

24 It is Nandy, 90, who contends that Hindi film audiences are expected to know a film's major elements by heart and, in this way, experience *déjà vu*.

25 See especially Sudhir Kakar, "The Ties that Bind: Family Relationships in the Mythology of Hindi Cinema," *India International Centre Quarterly*, vol. 8, no. 1 (1981), 11–22.

26 Ong, 98.

27 Walter Ong, "Oral Residue in Tudor Prose Style," *PMLA*, vol. 80, no. 3 (1965): 149.

28 Certainly, one might say that these films are intertextual. But they are intertextual only in the manner that *all* language is intertextual. The term, as it is utilized in current critical parlance, permits us no real latitude here, as it applies too stringently to written texts – to literature and "modern poetic language," as Julia Kristeva terms it in *Revolution in Poetic Language*.

29 Ong, *Orality*, 130–133.

30 Okpewho, 154.

31 Ong, *Orality*, 44.

32 Ibid., 44.

33 The psychologist A.R. Luria noted the absence and/or non-privileging of these cognitive qualities and features in the illiterate Russian peasants he interviewed in the Soviet Union, from 1931–32. See Ong, *Orality*, 49–57.

34 Ibid., 45.

35 Homer, in Okpewho, 209.

36 Of course, there are exceptions to every rule – see the classic *Pyaasa* (The Thirsty One, 1957), or the more recent *Satya* (Truth, 1998), for instance. However, of the 100 or so films of the past two decades that qualify as *hits* or *superhits*, not a single one that I have seen actually "transgresses" this moral-order-imperative.

37 David Bordwell, *Planet Hong Kong: Popular Cinema and the Art of Entertainment* (Cambridge: Harvard University Press, 2000), 2.

38 Ibid., 2–20.

39 Gayatri Chakravorty Spivak, "Can the Subaltern Speak?," *Marxism and the Interpretation of Culture*, eds. Cary Nelson and Lawrence Grossberg (Urbana: University of Illinois Press, 1983): 271. [...]

14

Imagining the family:
an ethnography of viewing *Hum Aapke Hain Koun ...!*[1]
by Patricia Uberoi

'I'm for the joint family system, because the joint family represents Indian culture; nowhere else in the world have they got this system still' (Miss India contestant, 1995).[2]

In a year of numerous box-office 'flops', the romantic family drama, *Hum Aapke Hain Koun ...!* (*HAHK* [...]), was a phenomenal commercial success, reportedly grossing more than any other film in the history of Indian cinema.[3] After more than six months, the film is still showing to packed houses in Delhi and elsewhere;[4] tickets for matinees are still sold 'in black'; and many viewers – [...] – are returning for their third, fourth, and fifth viewings, clapping, cheering and weeping at appropriate moments, anticipating the dialogue, and strumming to the beat of its very popular songs. Delighted distributors compare the film to some of the great blockbusters of yesteryear – *Sholay* and *Mughal-É-Azam*, for instance. With opulent sets, no fewer than fourteen melodious songs, a star-studded cast with Madhuri Dixit and Salman Khan in the lead roles,[5] and a canny marketing and distribution strategy,[6] this movie has enticed cinema audiences back to the theatres in unprecedented numbers, allaying industry fears that Indian commercial cinema had entered a phase of irreversible decline. In a single stroke, *HAHK* appears to have neutralized the subversive effects of the contemporary alien 'cultural invasion' and the debased cultural values of the front-benchers, bringing back nostalgic memories of a bygone golden era of Indian cinema.

This is nothing short of remarkable, for *HAHK* completely lacks the *masala* (spicy) ingredients of sex, sadism, and violence that are believed to be *de rigueur* for a successful 'Bollywood' production. [...]

It is now conceded, with a mixture of wonder and relief, that the unprecedented commercial success of *HAHK* may actually lie in the fact that it is *not* a *masala* movie. [...]

[T]he singular feature of *HAHK* [...] which I seek to address here, is that it is quintessentially what is classed in popular parlance as a 'family' film – 'family' understood in the double sense of (i) *for* a family audience; and (ii) *about* family relationships, inclusive of, but much broader than, the true romance that provides its basic story-line. As one viewer is reported to have said:

The family in this film is very important. It's not a Madhuri or a Salman film [the romantic leads] but the story of a family (Mishra, 1995).

[...] The film is not about the family *as it is*, but about the family as people would *like it to be*: [...] Said Asha:[7]

> What I liked is that everyone has good relations with each other, which is not generally found in families ... This is how it *should* be. It's an ideal family.

[...] [C]lean family movies are just as demanding of critical and political interpretation as the 'blood and gore' films that have attracted so much public and media attention: and that not merely because they have proved exceedingly profitable! Thus I look here at some of the responses to *HAHK* of film industry personnel (directors, stars, producers, distributors), film critics, and north Indian viewers, privileging the voice of the latter and seeking to understand what is meant by the universal classification of this film as a clean and morally uplifting 'family' film. I then look, as a sociologist of the family, at the ideal image of the family that the film narrative of *HAHK* seeks to construct and project, and the deliberately incomplete erasures that this process entails. Finally, I reflect on the wider social functions that such a fantasy of ideal family life might perform in the light of the sort of social science critiques I have referred to above. [...]

[In *HAHK*] Kailash Nath (Alok Nath) is a bachelor industrialist, and guardian of his two orphaned nephews: Rajesh (Mohnish Bahl) and Prem (Salman Khan). Through the mediation of the boys' maternal uncle (Ajit Vacchani), a marriage is arranged between Rajesh and Puja (Renuka Shahane), the elder daughter of Prof. S. S. Chowdhury (Anupam Kher) and his lovely wife (Reema Lagoo), both of them, as it happens, old college friends of Kailash Nath's.

Side by side, through a series of life-cycle rituals of engagement, marriage, pregnancy and childbirth, Rajesh's younger brother, Prem, is attracted to Puja's younger sister, Nisha (Madhuri Dixit), and determines to marry her as soon as he can set up independently in business. He confides in his sister-in-law, who has incidentally been charged with the responsibility of finding a wife for him.

Puja has Prem tie a necklace on Nisha as a token of his love and commitment, but immediately afterwards she falls to her death without communicating this development to the rest of the family. Both families are grief-stricken over Puja's tragic death, and Rajesh is quite distraught worrying over the upbringing of his motherless son.

Unaware of the troth between Prem and Nisha, the elders in the family decide that the best solution to Rajesh's dilemma and sorrow would be for him to marry Nisha, who is already giving her sister's child a mother's love. Nisha agrees to the match, mistakenly believing she is to be married to Prem, while Prem conceals his personal anguish out of love and concern for the well-being of his elder brother and infant nephew, and obedience to the will of senior family members.

As the marriage of Rajesh and Nisha is about to take place, Lallu, the loyal family servant and Prem's confidante and friend, appeals to Lord Krishna to intercede. With the help of Tuffy the dog, the true situation is revealed in the nick of time. Prem and Nisha are united with family blessings.

I. What makes a 'clean' movie?

[...]

The lack of vulgarity

For the last several years, the Indian media and the general public have been obsessed with the sexual content – what is euphemistically called 'vulgarity' – in popular cinema, particularly in the song-dance items. [...]

Cinematic vulgarity is popularly believed to stem from two distinct sources, operating in baleful combination: from the culturally alien and morally corrupting influence of Hollywood movies; and from the debased cultural values of the lower classes – the 'front-benchers' – on whose patronage the success of any movie ultimately depends (Kakar, 1981: 12–13). [...]

In all interviews, my informants were at pains to stress that *HAHK* contained no 'vulgarity'. This is clearly one aspect of its classification as a 'family' film, that is, that the whole family (grandparents, parents, and children) can watch it together without embarrassment. This is a criterion that apparently carries great weight in the popular mind (Mishra, 1995; Zaveri, 1994a). The songs and dances are deemed clean – *saaf-suthra* – and 'tasteful' (Zaveri, 1994a). Thus, while Salman gets a drenching on two occasions, Madhuri correctly (in the opinion of some viewers) passes up the opportunity to get soaking wet too and 'burst into an obscene number' (Mishra, 1995). (Indeed, a sceptical onlooker, presumably a distributor-financier, witnessing the filming of the movie's most spectacular song, *Didi, tera dewar diwana*, had declared that such a song would never catch on with the general public unless it had at least a dash of 'rain' to jazz it up [Zaveri, 1994a]!) Moreover, as Asha pointed out to me, 'there is no bedroom scene': the 'first night scene' and the 'honeymoon scene', those staple ingredients that she insisted were often 'deliberately created' in commercial Hindi cinema – and, given the stress on pre-marital virginity, the focus of much sexual fantasy and anxiety – are carefully 'avoided'.

Curiously, Asha's comment discounts the chase after the groom's shoes that fortuitously lands Prem and Nisha together on a bridal-type double bed, to the whistles and applause of the audience. Curiously, too, neither she nor anyone else took offence at, or even bothered to remark on, the blatant suggestiveness of Prem's symbolic seduction of Nisha on the billiard table: Prem acknowledges her as the woman he's been waiting for; their eyes meet across the table; and with calculated precision and understated exhilaration, he shoots the billiard ball into the waiting hole. [...]

[...] From a carefree, mischievous, chocolate-licking lass on roller-skates, Nisha becomes increasingly demure, soon expressing her growing affection for Prem in rather 'wifely' ways. [...] Simultaneously, she outgrows her adolescent boldness and becomes so bashfully tongue-tied that she finds herself, at the critical moment, unable to confess to her love for Prem and to reject the proposal of marriage to Rajesh (even when she is given a good opening by Rajesh himself). Similarly, Prem matures from a teasing kid brother to a young man in love – 'Shit! I love her', is his exclamation of delighted self-recognition – to an established man-of-the-world with a business of his own, prepared to sacrifice his personal happiness for the higher good of his brother and family. In other words, the blossoming of romantic love and mature sexuality is not scripted as increasing licence, but as increasing inhibition – the end of playfulness and an induction into the discipline of conjugality, within the larger discipline of joint family living.

[...] As filmmaker Shohini Ghosh has pointed out (n.d.), *all* the man–woman relationships that are explored in the course of the film in fact disclose a greater or lesser degree of 'erotic tension'. Particularly suggestive, however, are the customary cross-sex 'joking relations' of the north Indian kinship system,[8] which can plausibly be read as playful surrogates for the sexual relation of husband and wife (cf. Kolenda, 1990: 144) and which are typically the subject of bawdy songs in exclusively women's rituals at the time of marriage (Kolenda, 1990; also Fruzzetti, 1990; Hershman, 1981: 163–8, 175, 185; Jamous, 1991: 197ff.): the relations of *jija–sali* (sister's husband/wife's younger sister); of *dewar–bhabhi* (husband's younger brother/elder brother's wife); and, very often, of *samdhi–samdhan* (cross-sex co-parents-in-law). Each of these relations is explicitly foregrounded in one or another of *HAHK*'s spectacular songs.

The *jija–sali* relationship is foremost in the shoe-stealing incident and the song through which it is articulated. While the choreography pits the boys of the groom's party against the 'sisters' of the bride (a group marriage fantasy?), the libretto makes clear that the relations are of the 'groom's *salis*' and the 'bride's *dewars*'. And, as already noted, the song ends with the bride's sister, blushing, on a bridal-type bed along with the groom's younger brother. As Pauline Kolenda has remarked in reference to the set of cross-sex joking relations between affines in north Indian kinship, this song 'reiterate[s] the purpose of the contact between the two groups – to establish a sexual relationship between a male member of one group and a female member of the other' (1990: 144).[...]

Of the many viewers I spoke with who insisted that *HAHK* represents 'traditional' Indian culture (see below), not one thought to point out that the content of such women's marriage songs is typically irreverent and bawdy to the point – very often – of obscenity (see e.g. Hara, 1991: 103; S. Singh, 1972; Werbner, 1990: 260). (In fact, the Arya Samaj and other social organizations have worked hard over the last century to reform or eliminate these undesirable genres – genres which are, incidentally, a specifically *female* form of expression and protest [Chowdhry, 1994: 392–7; cf. also Banerjee, 1989].) So, while the teasing songs of *HAHK* are themselves innocuous enough, judging by cinema hall reactions, there is every likelihood that, for many in the audience, they conjure up recall or anticipation of the sexually explicit content of the traditional marriage songs, and of the wider popular culture of affinity in north India (S. Singh, 1972; Srinivasan, 1976). [...]

[...] *HAHK*'s supposed elimination of 'vulgarity' seems to carry a double meaning: one, explicitly foregrounded, is the avoidance of the *masala* ingredients found in so many contemporary Hindi movies; the second, unacknowledged, the sanitization of a bawdy folk tradition of women's songs, making them fit – or *almost* fit – for mixed viewing, and for 'representing' Indian culture and tradition. Perhaps this is what has made this film so recognizably one *of* and *for* the Indian middle classes, rather than for the class of 'rickshaw wallahs', that is, the front-benchers, who are usually regarded as the arbiters of popular cinematic style and taste.

The display of affluence

Judging by several viewers' comments, another notable aspect of *HAHK*'s overall impression of decency is its unembarrassed endorsement of upper-class, indeed affluent, lifestyles – no poverty or 'simplicity' here. [...] The two homes on display, including that of the less prosperous professor, were much admired by my companions (my attention was called to the beautiful kitchen, the 'tasteful' marriage decorations, and the like); costumes are gorgeous, and now much copied in the subsidiary fashion industry this film has spawned (Zaveri, 1994a: 6–7); lavish gift-giving is a conspicuous feature of all ceremonial occasions; and the food is utterly mouth-watering (cf. Bharucha, 1995: 802), and frequently deployed to index the quality and intimacy of social relationships. [...]

[...] [O]n the whole, the display of opulence was accepted without guilt, and with no indication – in the film narrative or in audience reactions – that affluence might be corrupting or ill-gained, as was so often the case in the Hindi movies of an earlier era, where poverty signalled virtue and wealth, spiritual depravity (cf. Jayamanne, 1992: 150; also Bharucha, 1995: esp. 802). [...]

[...] [I]t is clear that *HAHK*'s supposed lack of 'vulgarity' implied a distancing from the carnal desires of the working classes and was metonymically linked in some subtle way to the film's consistent display of the fetishized symbols of middle-class consumerist desire. [...]

The family as 'tradition'

Any number of viewers stressed – [...] that *HAHK* is not only a film about the Indian 'joint family' and the sacrifices individual members have to make on its behalf; it is simultaneously a film about Indian 'culture, society and tradition'. Said Asha, summarizing the opinion of her friends:

> Everyone likes and enjoys it. It shows Indian culture and society and tradition ... What we see in our families, we see it on the screen.

She then went on to give examples of what she meant, for instance, the play of hiding the groom's shoes by the bride's sisters and friends, a practice of which she had earlier said, during a viewing of the film: 'It *was* common; not now.'

The element of nostalgia was even more prominent in the testimony of Daljit Kaur. In her rambling reflections on *HAHK,* she repeatedly emphasized that the film shows domestic rituals and family relationships as they once *were* and as they *should be,* but not as they currently are in a degenerate world. In praise of the film, she noted: 'It shows all the *rasmas* (ceremonials), and in a most enjoyable way.'

Now this (like Asha's comment) is a rather unexpected perspective on the Indian cultural tradition, for it clearly identifies *folkways,* rather than *sanskritic rituals,* with the essence of 'tradition'. [...] Though this evocation of the folk tradition goes rather against the grain of Indian modernism which [...], has mostly sought to purge the Indian tradition of the excrescences of the folk tradition and restore it to its pristine and uncontaminated form (Chakravarti, 1989; Chowdhry, 1994; Mani, 1989; Nandy, 1995), it is consistent with an alternative modernist strategy whereby the folk tradition in its manifold forms is appropriated for nationalist and developmental ends (e.g. Rege, 1995: 30–2, 35–6; K. Singh, 1996). [...]

Altogether, judging by the comments of viewers, it seems that the classification of *HAHK* as a 'clean' movie involves a complex of features: the avoidance of the routine Bollywood *masala* ingredients of sex, sadism, and violence; the display of affluent lifestyles, effortlessly achieved and maintained; the exploration of the ennobling theme of individual sacrifice on behalf of the family (rather than, for instance, the celebration of violent revenge); and the evocation of ideals of Indian culture and tradition, subtly Hinduized,[9] embourgeois-ized (to coin a horrible neologism) through the naturalization of affluence and, for that matter, Aryanized, for the tradition of Indian kinship that is celebrated is a generalized north Indian one ([...] Uberoi, 2003). How these disparate features hang together to constitute a contemporary sense of self and society, and the politics of this construction, are questions to which we will shortly turn, but meanwhile it is important to address the central theme of the film: *the Indian family.* What are the features of *HAHK's* construction of the ideal of Indian family life? Is there a 'politics' to this construction, too? And what is the relationship between this ideal and the common assessment of the film as a good, clean movie?

II. The constitution of the ideal Indian family

[...] [W]here the psychoanalytic perspective focuses on the elementary relation-ships of the *nuclear* family, *HAHK* posits the naturalness or

The ideal of the joint family

[...] For the last century-and-a half, if not longer, public opinion in India has been obsessed with the spectre of the imminent break-up of the Indian joint family system through processes of urbanization, industrialization, westernization, individualization and the liberation of women. Many professional sociologists of the family are sceptical on this score (e.g. Goode, 1963; Shah, 1974; 1996; Vatuk, 1972), but even the most sceptical of them concede that the joint family is, if not a *fact* of traditional Indian society, at least a deeply held traditional *value* that continues to provide the underlying principles of household-building strategies in South Asia, though differently for different regions, castes, and communities. A.M. Shah, in typical 'sociologese', has termed this the principle of 'the residential unity of patrikin and their wives' (1974: 48ff.).

It is notable that *HAHK*'s cinematic affirmation of joint family ideals has been achieved through the consistent *erasure* of the set of factors that characteristically puts the joint family structure under strain. Thus, there is no antagonism between the father (or father-figure, Kailash Nath) and the sons, for Kailash Nath simply does not act like a despotic patriarch (cf. Mukherjee, 1995); he is also not in competition with the sons for their mother's love, for their mother is long since dead. There is no tension between the two brothers – the younger one willingly sacrifices for the elder when the moment comes. There is no tension between mother-in-law and daughter-in-law: for good measure, the mother-in-law role has been eliminated from the story-line[10] and Puja comes into a home where she is the unchallenged, and very welcome, 'house-lady'. And there is no tension between sisters-in-law: had Puja not died, her *devrani* would have been her own, much-loved sister, a prospect with which she was obviously quite delighted.

All this is almost too good to be true, as my informants remarked with candour, no doubt reflecting on the complexities of their own family situations. The sort of individual sacrifice required to keep the joint family harmoniously functioning 'is not generally found in families', I was told. Nonetheless, my informants remained convinced that the ideal was possible and worthy of attainment, if not in their own families, due to various contingent reasons, at least in *other* people's families, or in the Indian family as it had once been.[11] [...]

III. The pleasures of viewing: voyeurism, narcissism, and a happy ending

[...] [A]s Bharucha convincingly argues (1995), [*HAHK*] is very much a product of the Indian liberalized capitalist economy of the 1990s. The old antimonies of South Asian melodrama (Jayamanne, 1992: 150; F. Kazmi, 1999: 144–5):

	rural	:	urban
::	poor	:	rich
::	East	:	West
::	good	:	bad

– antimonies which, it has been suggested (Kakar, 1989; Nandy, 1981: 81, 95–6; 1995) are reflective of the psychic conflicts and existential circumstances of popular cinema audiences – no longer hold good. In *HAHK*, bucolic pastoral scenes are merely romantic interludes between one urban setting and another.[12] The heroines are modern, educated young women (Nisha studies 'computers'), and the heroes successful young businessmen (cf. Mayaram, n.d.: 7–9).[13] Wealth is effortlessly acquired, and accepted without guilt, an effect achieved both through the display of the fetishized objects of the capitalist economy, promised in unlimited abundance, and through the consistent erasure of the signs of labour and poverty. Plenitude is convincingly naturalized. The tragic death of Puja, as Bharucha points out, is only a brief interruption in the heady flow of fun and frolic in this 'non-stop roller-coaster of laughter, food, songs and games' (1995: 801). Moreover, the pleasures of consumption are subtly (or not-so-subtly) linked with the valorization of the family, reinforcing the opinion held by many of my informants that affluence is an important enabling factor in harmonious family life. Similarly, wealth is no longer opposed to, but is metonymically linked in the film with, Indian culture and tradition: indeed, some informants took voyeuristic pleasure in observing life-cycle rituals being celebrated on a scale that their own limited means would never allow:

> It is impossible for a middle class father to celebrate his daughter's wedding on such a scale, so my daughter and I would rather watch it in a film (Mishra, 1995).

Needless to say – and the focus on life-crisis rituals naturalizes this elision – the national tradition is assumed to be Hindu, 'otherness' being either excluded, or co-opted through caricature.[14] As Bharucha sarcastically sums it up, *HAHK* exemplifies

> the ease with which the market has been embraced within a matrix of upper-class, 'traditional', Hindu cultural values, with an appropriate dose of religiosity to keep the 'family' happy, and very discreetly ... to keep the others out. Of course, if they wish to enter this matrix, they will always be welcomed with a cup of tea and absorbed (1995: 804).

In this interpretation, the pleasure of viewing is effectively the pleasure of voyeurism, that is, of being witness to a spectacle of unlimited consumption. This assessment is confirmed by several viewers' comments, and by the participatory reaction of the cinema hall audiences: when, for instance, the new icon of Indian femininity,[15] Madhuri Dixit, comes down the stairs in her gorgeous purple and gold costume for the '*Didi, tera dewar diwana*' sequence, she is greeted by sighs and wolf-whistles of appreciation.[16] But the comments of viewers also suggest a strong, and very narcissistic, identification with the happy family ideal, no matter what their personal family circumstances.

In the defining of 'taste' in Indian cinema, two interrelated criteria are characteristically employed to differentiate the high-brow or parallel cinema from the low-brow commercial cinema: (i) the absence/presence of music, song, and dance (see Beeman, 1981); and (ii) 'realism' (e.g. Chakravarty, 1996: Ch. 3; Nandy, 1981: 92, 95–6; 1995; Rajadhyaksha, 1993) [...] [in *HAHK*] the presence of these songs does not apparently detract from the appearance of realism as far as the viewers are concerned. One might argue that this is because the film focuses on a segment of Indian social life – marriage and other life-crisis rituals in their non-sanskritic aspects – where music, song, and dance are always much in evidence, but this of course does not explain why courtship and the declaration of love, or a lovers' phone conversation, should also be rendered in song, as indeed they are.

The deployment of the criterion of 'realism' to discriminate the good from the bad in Indian cinema may appear to imply the rather patronizing assumption that the masses of viewers, like primitives or children, are unable or unwilling (given their individual or collective psychological compulsions) to distinguish fantasy from reality, myth from truth. It comes as something of a surprise, then, to find a wide spectrum of viewers self-consciously complimenting *HAHK* on what they see to be its true-to-life, mimetic projection of the realities of Indian family life. (Of course, one should not discount the possibility that ordinary Indian viewers have internalized the critique of Indian popular cinema *vis-à-vis* high and middle cinema, or Hollywood productions.) Mr Sharma's[17] comment was typical: 'This is a very good film. Seeing it is like being in one's own living room, with all the family around.' [...]

And a middle-aged woman interviewed on television declared: 'It's as though you're watching a video cassette of a marriage in your own home.'[18] [...]

Conversely, criticism of the film often focused on details that, in the eyes of viewers, impaired the verisimilitude of the representation: [...] the unbelievable cleanliness of the temple; the maid Chameli's outrageously 'ethnic chic' costume; the careless feasting of the *barat*; the *filmi* 'misunderstanding' that makes Nisha think that she is to be married to Prem until she actually holds the wedding invitation in her hands [...] The intervention of Lord Krishna, though miraculous, was not adversely commented on. Perhaps viewers did not consider the idea of the participation of the deity in their domestic dramas unrealistic; and in any case this intervention is neatly naturalized through the agency of the wonder-dog, Tuffy.

The appearance of verisimilitude in *HAHK* is artfully enhanced by a number of fantasy scenes, well marked out as such. Nisha's cousin Bhola, smitten by Rita, sees her transformed into the legendary Shakuntala on every encounter. As Prem watches a video of the wedding revelries, Nisha suddenly materializes in the room with him. The '*Didi, tera dewar diwana*' sequence (the pregnancy ritual) has two surprising fantasies – discounting, that is, Prem's swinging from the chandeliers and flipping backwards up onto the balustrade: Prem finds himself suddenly surrounded by half-a-dozen or so infants, and then, inexplicably, appears pregnant in a clinging white shift: a terrible and misplaced excess of fecundity!

But these little flights of fancy, much relished by the audience, serve only to reinforce the overall impression of the verisimilitude of representation. This was the case even for those, like Daljit Kaur, who insisted that the film portrayed a bygone era more than a contemporary reality of family relations; or like Asha, who felt that it portrayed an ideal of harmonious family life that was, as she frankly put it, 'not usually found in families'.

Such is the magical illusion created by *HAHK*, that its picture of ideal family life carries the stamp of authenticity and provokes narcissistic enjoyment *even when* contradicted by the personal experience of viewers. In other words, it has succeeded in creating what Govind Nihalani has so aptly termed 'believable fantasies', fantasies just within – or just outside – reach (cf. Kazmi, 1995; also Gupta, 1996): If not one's *own* family life, which is contingently imperfect, viewers see *HAHK* as a truthful rendition of the family life of *others* in the imagined community that is modern India. This 'utopian' effect, as I have argued above, is in no small measure achieved by the erasure – or near-erasure – from consciousness of the harsher realities of Indian family and social life, leaving only the faintest traces in Mamiji's several mean-mouthed comments. This is actually a rather unusual strategy in Indian popular cinema which characteristically (or at least until heroes began to act like thugs, and heroines like vamps) had white and black, good and evil, well differentiated, with little space for shades of grey (Nandy, 1981: 89). *HAHK* is almost all white: 'saccharine-sweet', said Sunita dismissively.

Besides the pleasures of voyeurism and narcissistic identification, *HAHK* also affords the pleasure of following a stereotypical romantic story through to its happy ending, though it does so almost at the expense of the sense of realism that it had so carefully built up. This perhaps explains both the cathartic effect of the last-minute resolution of the narrative crisis (and release of 'erotic tension') for many in the audience, for whom such, strategies are familiar, and the disappointment of some viewers, [...] who felt that the dramatic twists of the love story [...] made the film, ultimately, too much like other Bombay commercial movies. [...]

Despite its highly simplifed structure, this is a universal love story (Radway, 1987), but it is inflected by the mythic conflicts that typically structure the constitution of a romantic narrative in the cultural context of South Asian popular cinema: the conflicts between *dharma* (social duty) and desire, and between freedom and destiny [...] These conflicts have to be reconciled before a love story can be brought to a satisfactory happy ending. Prem and Nisha nobly renounce their desire for each other, out of love for their elder siblings and concern for their infant nephew; in effect, in deference to the wider interests of the joint family as a moral institution. Yet ultimately, thanks to the intervention of Lord Krishna and Tuffy, they are enabled both to do their duty by the family as well as by themselves. [...]

The second conflict is that between the freedom to choose one's own partner, and the need to conform to social expectations or to the force of a higher destiny. When asked by his sister-in-law what sort of marriage he wants – an arranged or a 'love' marriage – Prem replies without hesitation: 'an arranged love marriage'. And this is what he finally gets, though for a while it seems he will have to forego his own choice of partner in deference to family elders and in the context of an unexpected and tragic turn of fate (cf. Nandy, 1981: 95). Judging by audience reactions, the resolution of this mythic conflict at the very last minute is a source of enormous emotional satisfaction, albeit somewhat undermining the impression of mimetic realism that the film had earlier conveyed.

IV. The emblematic family

[...] Prem, our hero of *HAHK,* drives a white Jeep scrawled all over with graffiti after the style affected by Delhi 'yuppies'. Prominent among these inscriptions is the phrase: 'I love my family', signed, for good measure, 'Prem'. Presumably, this unusual graffito is an instruction on how to read the film – as the story of a young man, serendipitously named 'Prem' ('love'), who is prepared to sacrifice his individual love for the sake of his family. This gesture, as we have noted, was interpreted by viewers as an act of great nobility on behalf of an institution which is believed to epitomize at once the singularity, and the excellence, of the Indian tradition.

For quite understandable reasons, a number of recent critiques of the mass media in India have addressed themselves to the ideological implications of the iconicization of women, or of the Hindu tradition, or of both together, as representing the modern Indian nation, and linked these motivated representations in turn to the caste, class, and communal orientations of the governing and non-governing elites of Indian society. In this context, it is interesting to note that the promotion of the joint family ideal as an emblem of Indian culture and tradition – not only in *HAHK*, which is an outstanding contemporary example, but in a large number of movies in the century-long history of Indian cinema – is a question that has hardly been acknowledged, except insofar as it overlaps (as of course it must) with the question of feminine roles and imagery. Nor have continuities or changes in the cinematic representation of family relations been the object of the same degree of scrutiny as, for instance, the changing roles of heroes and heroines, linked to the character of the wider social, cultural, and political order of contemporary India. [...]

[...] [T]he family is certainly a very important agency for the reproduction of social inequality in contemporary Indian society. This occurs not only through the process of child socialization, but also through the system of arranged marriage and through the deployment of 'social capital' to ensure that, insofar as is possible, children inherit or surpass their parents' social class position (Béteille, 1991). [...]

For most, as India globalizes, and as the 'imagined economy' can no longer convincingly iconicize the nation (see Deshpande, 1993), the family remains, and not merely by default, the sole institution which can signify the unity, uniqueness, and moral superiority of Indian culture in a time of change, uncertainty and crisis.

Notes

1 [...] For this project, I conducted informal interviews with a variety of persons, for the most part of middle- and lower-middle class status, at the theatres before and after shows, and in other settings. For various contingent reasons, my informants were mostly female, though I did consciously try to remedy this bias as my study progressed. I was not able to correct the middle-class and urban bias of my sample of interviewees, but viewing the film in cinema halls, rather than on video, gave some indication of the responses of the 'front stalls'. However, the reactions of rural viewers remain opaque, as do those of viewers in other regions of the country (see also [note 8]).

2 Contestant at the *Femina* Miss India International contest, when asked: 'Are you for or against the joint family system?' (Metro TV, 13 February 1995). Her answer was enthusiastically applauded by the audience.

3 Over Rs 200 crore (est. 2002), a figure subsequently equalled by another romantic family drama, Aditya Chopra's *Dilwale Dulhania Le Jayenge* [...] *HAHK* was similarly said to have broken all records for the sale of Hindi film music (Zaveri, 1994b), the plagiarization of the music cassette generating a notable court case.

4 *HAHK* went on to celebrate its 'jubilee' – i.e. a 100 week run – at Mumbai's Liberty cinema in August 1996.

5 Others in the cast include: Renuka Shahane; Mohnish Bahl; Reema Lagoo; Anupam Kher; Alok Nath; Ajit Vacchani; erstwhile 'vamp', Bindu; Sahila Chadha; and Laxmikant Berde.

6 For the first time in Indian cinema, the Barjatyas made imaginative use of local cable television to promote the film and to publicize the 'family' feeling that went into its making and that purportedly existed between the stars on the sets (Doraiswamy, 1996: 127). Rajshri productions had imposed a moratorium on release of video rights, releasing the film in a select number of cinema halls: initially at only one cinema in Bombay, followed by the release of twenty-nine prints for India and six overseas, to a total eventually of just 450 prints (*Filmfare* 4 [1995], interview with Kamalkumar, Rajkumar and Ajitkumar Barjatya of Rajshri Productions, following the *Filmfare* Best Film Award (1994); see also Doraiswamy, 1996; Kazmi, 1995; Majumdar, 1995; Sangwan, 1996). This strategy of keeping control over the distribution process against the widespread practice of video piracy has meant much greater returns for both producers and cinema hall owners, some of whom were able to improve the facilities in the theatres on the strength of the profits from *HAHK* alone (interview with cinema hall owners and a representative of Rajshri Productions in the TV programme, 'Show Biz Masala', DD Metro Channel, 4 April 1995). A number of my companions viewing *HAHK* remarked on how many years it was since they had last watched a movie in a suburban cinema hall – and how very shabby the theatres had meanwhile become.

7 Educated working woman, aged 35. All names of interviewees are pseudonyms.

8 As some critical south Indian informants pointed out, *HAHK* presents a typically *north* Indian perspective on the kinship system (see also Bharucha, 1995: 802). Understandably, north Indian viewers see it as simply a film about *the* Indian family. This naturalization of the values of north Indian kinship may be seen as consistent with a larger historical process of cultural hegemonization of the northern over the southern culture of kinship, a process that has probably intensified in recent times (see Uberoi, 1993: 33–4, 45–9; 2003; Trautmann, 1979).

9 A point made by several critics, notably Bharucha (1995), F. Kazmi (1999: 150ff); and Mukherjee (1995), alluding in particular to the agitation over the Ram Janmabhoomi temple issue that had resulted in the demolition of the Babri Masjid in December 1992 and widespread riots thereafter (cf. Rajagopal, 1999, 2001).

10 The same narrative strategy is followed in a subsequent family film, Subhash Ghai's *Pardes* (1997) [...] Note that the nearest role to a villainness in *Pardes*,

the spiteful Neeta, is a senior kinswoman in the affinal home (i.e. the groom's *caci*). Her role is not unlike that of Mamiji in *HAHK*.

11 Ethnographers have often noted the 'continued faith' in traditional family values and ideals of joint family living even when their informants themselves live in supposedly modern, 'urbanized', nuclear family set-ups. See e.g. Sinha (1993: 32, 273).

12 Indeed, as Shohini Ghosh perceptively remarks (n.d.: 2), most scenes are set in the private space of the two homes of the intermarrying families, and there is quite minimal engagement with the outside world.

13 Interestingly, the original film on which *HAHK* was based, Rajshri Productions' moderately successful *Nadya Ke Paar* (1982), had the heroine as a village girl, not a city girl (interview with Sooraj Barjatya, *Filmfare* 4 [1995]).

14 For instance, the role of the poetry-spouting Muslim doctor (played by Satish Shah) in the film.

15 The reference is to publicity around M.F. Husain's series of paintings of Madhuri Dixit (the *Times of India*, *Delhi Times*, 5 May 1995).

16 It is relevant that in this song Prem is first a voyeur on a desirable spectacle ('gentlemen not allowed'), then witness to a parody of himself within the spectacle, and finally himself a participant in the action, taking the lead and vanquishing the false *dewar*.

17 A 55-year-old administrative officer.

18 'Show Biz Masala', DD Metro Channel, 2 May 1995. Videotaping the marriage ceremony is almost *de rigueur* in urban areas now, even for the working classes (see Sengupta, 1999).

References

Banerjee, Sumanta, 1989. 'Marginalisation of Women's Popular Culture in Nineteenth Century Bengal'. *In* Kumkum Sangari and Sudesh Vaid, eds, *Recasting Women: Essays in Colonial History*, pp. 127–79. New Delhi: Kali for Women.

Beeman, W.O., 1981. 'The Use of Music in Popular Film: East and West'. *India International Centre Quarterly*, Special Issue on *Indian Popular Cinema: Myth, Meaning and Metaphor* 8, 1: 77–87.

Béteille, A., 1991. 'The Reproduction of Inequality: Occupation, Caste and Family'. *Contributions to Indian Sociology*, n.s. 25, 1: 3–28.

Bharucha, R., 1995. 'Utopia in Bollywood: "Hum Aapke Hain Koun ...!".' *Economic and Political Weekly* 30, 15: 801–4.

Chakravarti, Uma, 1989. 'Whatever Happened to the Vedic *Dasi*: Orientalism, Nationalism and a Script for the Past'. *In* Kumkum Sangari and Sudesh Vaid, eds, *Recasting Women: Essays in Colonial History*, pp. 27–87. New Delhi: Kali for Women.

Chakravarty, Sumita S., 1996 [1993]. *National Identity in Indian Popular Cinema, 1947–1987*. Delhi: Oxford University Press.

Chowdhry, Prem, 1994. *The Veiled Women: Shifting Gender Equations in Rural Haryana, 1880–1990*. Delhi: Oxford University Press.

Deshpande, Satish, 1993. 'Imagined Economies: Styles of Nation Building in Twentieth Century India'. *Journal of Arts and Ideas* 25–6: 5–35.

Doraiswamy, Rashmi, 1996. 'The Home and the World: Images of Self-perception'. *India International Centre Quarterly: Signs of Our Times*. Summer: 123–29.

Fruzzetti, L.M., 1990. *The Gift of a Virgin: Women, Marriage and Ritual in a Bengali Society*. Delhi: Oxford University Press.

Ghosh, Shohini (n.d.). 'Hum Apke Hain Kaun? Pluralizing Pleasures of Viewership'. Unpublished manuscript.

Goode, W.J., 1963. *World Revolution and Family Patterns*. New York: The Free Press.

Gupta, D., 1996. Ritualism and Fantasy in Hindi Cinema. *Times of India*, 28 August 1996.

Hara, Tadahiko, 1991. Paribar *and Kinship in a Moslem Rural Village in East Pakistan*. Tokyo: Institute for the Study of Languages and Cultures of Asia and Africa.

Hershman, P., 1981. *Punjabi Kinship and Marriage*. Delhi: Hindustan.

Jamous, Raymond, 1991. *La Rélation Frère-soeur: Parenté et Rites Chez les Meo de l'Inde du Nord*. Paris: Editions de l'Ecole des Hautes Etudes en Sciences Sociales.

Jayamanne, L., 1992. 'Sri Lankan Family Melodrama: A Cinema of Primitive Attractions'. *Screen* 33, 2: 145–53.

Kakar, Sudhir, 1981. 'The Ties that Bind: Family Relationships in the Mythology of Hindi Cinema'. *India International Centre Quarterly*, Special Issue on *Indian Popular Cinema: Myth, Meaning and Metaphor* 8, 1: 11–21,

———, 1989. *Intimate Relations: Exploring Indian Sexuality*. New York: Penguin. (Republished in *The Indian Psyche*. New Delhi: Viking Books.)

Kazmi, Fareed, 1999. *The Politics of India's Conventional Cinema: Imaging a Universe, Subverting a Multiverse*. New Delhi: Sage Publications.

Kazmi, Nikhat, 1995. 'The Film as Hero: Bollywood's Big Comeback'. *Sunday Times* (24 December 1995): 17.

Kolenda, P., 1990. 'Untouchable Chuhras through their Humour: "Equalizing" Marital Ties through Teasing, Pretence and Farce'. *In* Owen Lynch, ed., *Divine Passions: The Social Construction of Emotion in India*, pp. 116–53. Delhi: Oxford University Press.

Majumdar, V., 1995. 'Reel Rights'. *Hindustan Times*, Sunday edition, 2 April 1995.

Mani, Lata, 1989. 'Contentious Traditions: The Debate on *Sati* in Colonial India'. *In* Kumkum Sangari and Sudesh Vaid, eds, *Recasting Women: Essays in Colonial History*, pp. 86–126. New Delhi: Kali for Women.

Mayaram, S., n.d. 'Love, Marriage and Sexuality in Hindi-Urdu Popular Cinema and Literary Writing'. Unpublished MS.

Mishra, P., 1995. 'A Film for the Family'. *Pioneer* (Delhi), 19 April 1995.

Mukherjee, M., 1995. 'The HAHK Phenomenon: Appeal of Permanence and Stability'. *Times of India*, 22 May 1995.

Nandy, Ashis, 1981. 'The Popular Hindi Film: Ideology and First Principles'. *India International Centre Quarterly*, Special Issue on *Indian Popular Cinema: Myth, Meaning and Metaphor* 8, 1: 89–96.

———, 1995. 'An Intelligent Critic's Guide to Indian Cinema'. *In* Ashis Nandy, *The Savage Freud, and other Essays on Possible and Retrievable Selves*, pp. 196–236. Delhi: Oxford University Press.

Radway, Janice A., 1987. *Reading the Romance: Women, Patriarchy and Popular Literature*. London: Verso.

Rajadhyaksha, A., 1993a. 'The Epic Melodrama: Themes of Nationality in Indian Cinema'. *Journal of Arts and Ideas* 25–6: 55–70.

Rajagopal, Arvind, 1999. 'Thinking About the New Middle Class: Gender, Advertising and Politics in an Age of Globalisation'. *In* Rajeswari Sunder Rajan, ed., *Signposts: Gender Issues in Post-Independence India*, pp. 57–100. New Delhi: Kali for Women.

———, 2001. *Politics after Television: Hindu Nationalism and the Reshaping of the Public in India*. Cambridge: Cambridge University Press.

Rege, S., 1995. 'The Hegemonic Appropriation of Sexuality: The Case of the *Lavani* Performers of Maharashtra'. *Contributions to Indian Sociology*, n.s. 29, 1 and 2: 23–38.

Sangwan, S., 1996. 'Selling Celluloid'. *Pioneer*, 3 February 1996.

Sengupta, Shuddhabrata, 1999. 'Vision Mixing: Marriage-video-film and the Video-*walla*'s Images of Life'. *In* Christiane Brosius and Melissa Butcher, eds, *Image Journeys: Audio-visual Media and Cultural Change in India*, pp. 279–307. New Delhi: Sage Publications.

Shah, A. M. 1974. *The Household Dimension of the Family in India*. Delhi: Orient Longman,

———, 1996. 'Is the Joint Household Disintigrating'? *Economic and Political Weekly* 31, 9: 537–42.

Singh, Kavita, 1996. 'Changing the Tune: Bengali *Pata* Painting's Encounter with the Modern'. *India International Centre Quarterly*, Summer: 60–78.

Singh, S., 1972. 'An Introduction to the Structural Analysis of *Sithnian*'. *In* S.S. Noor, ed., *Structuralism and Literature*, pp. 14–20. Patiala: Vidwan Press.

Sinha, Raghuvir, 1993. *Dynamics of Change in the Modern Hindu Family*. New Delhi: Concept.

Srinivasan, Amrit, 1976. 'Obscenity, Address and the Vocabulary of Kinship'. *Journal of the School of Languages*, JNU: 71–7.

Trautmann, T.R., 1979. 'The Study of Dravidian Kinship'. *In* Madhav M. Deshpande and Peter Edwin Hook, eds, *Aryan and Non-Aryan in India*, pp. 153–73. Ann Arbor: University of Michigan Press.

Uberoi, Patricia, ed., 1993. *Family, Kinship and Marriage in India*. New Delhi: Oxford University Press.

———, 2003. 'Kinship Varieties and Political Expedience: Legislating the Family in Post-Independence India'. *In* Emiko Ochiai, ed., *The Logic of Female Succession: Rethinking Patriarchy and Patrilineality in Global and Historical Perspective*, pp. 147–76. Kyoto: International Research Center for Japanese Studies.

Vatuk, S., 1972. *Kinship and Urbanization: White Collar Workers in North India.* London: University of California Press.

Werbner, P., 1990. *The Migration Process: Capital, Gifts and Offerings among Muslim Pakistanis.* New York: Berg.

Zaveri, S. 1994a. *Madhuri Ka Hai Zamana. E-times,* 25 November–1 December: 4–7.

———, 1994b. 'Heart Busters'. *E-times,* 30 December–5 January 4–7.

PART 3
Bollywood abroad and beyond

15

The 'Bollywoodization' of the Indian cinema: cultural nationalism in a global arena
by Ashish Rajadhyaksha

Rajnikant in Japan

The West may have the biggest stalls in the world's media bazaar, but it's not the only player. Globalization isn't merely another word for Americanization – and the recent expansion of the Indian entertainment industry proves it. For hundreds of millions of fans around the world, it is Bollywood, India's film industry, not Hollywood, that spins their screen fantasies. Bollywood, based in Mumbai, has become a global industry. India's entertainment moguls don't merely target the billion South Asians, or desis, at home: they make slick movies, songs and TV shows for export. Attracted by a growing middle class and a more welcoming investment environment, foreign companies are flocking to Bollywood, funding films and musicians. The foreign money is already helping India's pop culture to reach even greater audiences. And it may have a benign side-effect in cleaning up an Indian movie industry business long haunted by links to the underworld ('Bollywood Goes International', *Newsweek International,* 28 February 2000).

Let us keep aside for a moment the gross misrepresentations in *Newsweek* – the Indian film industry is not solely based in Mumbai, 'foreign money' is still hardly available for film *productions* even though it would like to cream off non-local *distribution* profits; such money is not necessarily distinguishable from the 'underworld' and is, therefore, not exactly what you would describe as 'benign'. *Newsweek*'s assumptions about good and bad money are unsustainable and pernicious.

Let us concentrate instead on just what this literature claims is happening. For something like the past decade, leading up to *Newsweek*'s final consecration, a range of print and television media have been claiming some rather dramatic developments in the Indian cinema. Practically every newspaper has commented, usually in the same breathless prose as *Newsweek,* on the phenomenon: there is a craze for 'Bollywood' *masala* that quite exceeds anything we have ever seen before; from Tokyo to Timbuctoo people are dancing to Indipop, names like Shah Rukh

Khan are circulating in places where people may never have heard of Indira Gandhi, and there is apparently money to be made. Everyone, it seems, is scrambling – new Bollywood websites continue to emerge, new distributors and intermediaries rise with new ideas of how to exploit this development, new television channels are seen, satellite technology is projected with unprecedented ability to overcome distribution inefficiencies – every one of these powered by entrepreneurs and their venture-capitalist backers, and their unique idea about what will earn money.

On what is this hype based? Interestingly, in the past year, the box office of an Indian cinema made indigenously was itself less central to the phenomenon than a range of ancillary industries, mostly based in London, including theatre (the much-hyped London stage musical *Bombay Dreams,* a collaboration between Indian composer A. R. Rahman and Andrew Lloyd Webber), the music industry, advertising[1] and even fashion (the extraordinary month-long 'Bollywood' festival of food, furniture and fashion marketing in Selfridges, London), all of which culminated in the extraordinary marketing exercise known as *Indian Summer* in July 2002 (see BBCI, 2002).

All of this began, it is usually said, with the four films which *Newsweek* too mentions as having made distribution history, three of them directly or indirectly Yash Chopra productions: *Dilwale Dulhaniya Le Jayenge (DDLJ,* 1995), the film which in some ways started it all, *Dil To Pagal Hai (DTPH,* 1997), Karan Johar's *Kuch Kuch Hota Hai (KKHH,* 1998), and Subhash Ghai's *Taal* (1998). Before all these, there is of course the original box-office hit *Hum Aapke Hain Kaun?* (1994). Of *Taal,* for example, producer and noted 'showman' of Hindi cinema Ghai said,

> There'll be 125 prints of *Taal* only for the foreign market. This is almost a three-fold increase since *Pardes,* for which I'd made 45 prints, and five times that of *Khalnayak.* Hindi films now have a significant market in the US, Canada, UK and the Middle East. It is making inroads into South Africa and Australia. And it is also popular in Japan, Hong Kong, South East Asia and, of course, Mauritius. In most if not all these countries, Hindi films are no longer weekend events, they are showing three shows everyday wherever they're released. Now, beginning with *Taal,* there will be vinyl banner hoardings advertising the films on the roads of the Western cities. Everybody, including the Westerners, will now see what films are on! The whole world will take note, because we will also be on the net (Sengupta, 1999).

How much did these films collectively earn? That is difficult to say, but *The Economic Times* reported that

> The first big success of the new Bollywood is *Who Am I to You? (Hum Aapke Hain Kaun?* dubbed), a musical that focuses on two weddings. Thanks to its untraditional (sic) plot and effective marketing, it's India's biggest hit ever. Playing for nearly a year, the film grossed more than $30 million, a phenomenal amount in a country where the average moviegoer pays 65% admission and the average movie makes about $3 million – barely what an art-house film makes in the U.S. (Moshavi, 1995).

Of *Taal*, the same paper reports that it was

> released around the world on August 13 (and) grossed' the highest average collection per cinema hall (per screen average) for movies released in north America on the August 13–15 weekend. According to Weekend Box-Office figures, the first three-day collections were $591,280. Released simultaneously in 44 theatres in North America, *Taal* has set a record for Bollywood releases abroad by notching the highest first three-day collections with $13,438 per screen. Though there is no independent verification, a press release by Eros Entertainment Inc, the distributor of the film abroad, claimed that *Taal*'s initial collections have even surpassed that of Hollywood blockbusters like *Haunting*, *The Blair Witch Project* and *Eyes Wide Shut* (*The Economic Times*, 21 August 1999).

All these are undoubted marketing successes, and the releases in particular of *Kuch Kuch* in South Africa, *Dil to Pagal Hai* in Israel and the brief weekend when *Taal* made it to the top 10 in the US domestic market are now the stuff of marketing legend. On the other hand, here is a salutary fact: *Newsweek* claims that 'India's movie exports jumped from $10 million a decade ago to $100 million last year, and may top $250 million in 2000.'

Contrast these figures with the brief dot.com boom when every Indian Internet portal such as satyam online, rediff-on-the-net and planetasia marketed itself with Bollywood paraphernalia. Following the unprecedented sale of just one portal, indiainfo.com, for Rs 500 crore (or over $100 million), it would have been a safe argument that just 10 of the top websites of the time (as computed by a *Businessworld* issue, 'Hot New Dot.coms', 24 January 2000) were in that period collectively worth more than the total box-office earnings of the Indian film industry.

There was and continues to be a real discrepancy involved. Contrary to *Newsweek*'s statement that Bollywood is 'India's film industry ... based in Mumbai', perhaps we could argue instead precisely that at least in one sense this is not so: that Bollywood is *not* the Indian film industry, or at least not the film industry alone. Bollywood admittedly occupies a space analogous to the film industry, but might best be seen as a more diffuse cultural conglomeration involving a range of distribution and consumption activities from websites to music cassettes, from cable to radio. If so, the film industry itself – determined here solely in terms of its box office turnover and sales of print and music rights, all that actually comes back to the producer – can by definition constitute only a part, and perhaps even an *alarmingly* small part, of the overall culture industry that is currently being created and marketed.

If *this* is so, then behind it all is a real difficulty, one that for all its being unprecedented has a disarmingly familiar tone. The fact is that nobody responsible for the production of the film narrative, if we include in this the producers, directors and stars responsible for the nuts-and-bolts assembly of the cinematic product that goes into these markets, actually knows what's going on. How do they make sense of these developments? Why is *Dil To Pagal Hai* popular in Tel Aviv, why now? How would they convert all this hoopla into a stable market that would guarantee their next product an audience? Nobody quite knows the overall picture, and it's worth exploring some of the literature that's emerged on these developments to speculate on just why that is so.

Amitabh Bachchan, for example, was one of the iconic stars of the 1970s and early 80s, before his career nose-dived following the 'first-ever' effort to corporatize the film industry with the lame-duck ABCL which most critics say was 'an idea before its time'. Despite not having had a substantial hit for over a decade, Bachchan is India's most famous 'film personality' mainly through a Bollywoodized makeover that owes itself to television (he hosted the Hindi version of *Who Wants to be a Millionaire* for Star TV), and he has this to say:

> Evidently, our film personalities have begun to matter in world fora. Hindi cinema is gaining worldwide recognition and I don't mean only those films which make it to Berlin or Cannes. Once, I was walking down London's Piccadilly Circus and I saw this group of Kurds running towards me. (*Laughs*) I thought they wanted to assassinate me. But they stopped right there and started singing songs from *Amar Akbar Anthony* and *Muqaddar Ka Sikandar*. Rajnikant is tremendously popular in Japan. And I'm told that our stars are known even in Fiji, Bali and Chile. Amazing! But we're not marketing ourselves properly. Someone out there is making pots of money at our expense (interview, 'Netvamsham!', *The Times of India*, 18 July, 1999).

Who is this mysterious 'someone' making money and how come Bachchan does not know? Let us explore this further with the instance that Bachchan himself provides, perhaps the most bizarre instance in this whole new development: the sudden, inexplicable, popularity of Rajnikant in Japan.

Rajnikant is, of course, well known as perhaps the biggest Tamil film star ever, after the legendary M. G. Ramachandran, but it is also important to say that his career has largely been restricted to that language, despite several efforts to get into Hindi film where he has often played subsidiary parts in Bachchan films (*Andha Kanoon*, 1983; *Giraftaar*, 1985; *Hum*, 1991) and one marginal effort in a Hollywood production (*Bloodstone*, 1989). Within Tamil Nadu where he reigns supreme, on the other hand, he has demonstrated all the hallmarks of a major star who knows his audience and his market: he has carefully constructed his screen persona, built a team around him that understands how to work it, has even tested out his popularity politically when he campaigned on behalf of the DMK and was at least partially responsible for its victory in the 1996 elections.

And then came his Japanese success. Here is the *New Indian Express* on this phenomenon:

> An entire generation of recession-hit Japanese have discovered a new hero: Rajnikant. Jayalalitha's bete noire and the man with that unflagging swagger and oh-so-cool wrist flicks has emerged there as the hippest craze after Leonardo Di Caprio and *Muthu*, his 150th film, is the biggest grosser in Japan after *Titanic*. So far the film has been seen by over 1,27,000 Japanese in a

23-week run at Tokyo's Cinema Rise alone, netting as much as $ 1.7 million and premieres on satellite television in June ('Rajnikant Bowls over Japanese Youth', *The New Indian Express,* 10 June, 1999).

So how does one explain this success? B. Kandaswamy Bharathan, executive producer at Kavithalaya, credited with having masterminded the Japanese marketing of this film, offers a typically 'Bollywoodist-culturalist' explanation:

> The movie carries an important message – that money is not everything in life. Instead, it propagates human values, highlighted in the first song itself – and this philosophy appealed to the Japanese audience. This is especially significant for a youth that's been talked down about for not being as hardworking as the post-war generation (ibid).

Indeed. Keeping aside the distortions by which the producer of *Muthu* represents his own production, in fact a violent feudal drama addressing caste differences, I am reasonably sure that if one were to ask Bharathan why this film proved a hit and no other, and how he suggests that Rajnikant capitalize on this sudden popularity to stabilize a Japanese market for his next film and his future career, we may perhaps get an honest answer, that he has no idea why *Muthu* did well in Tokyo.

Cinema versus the Bollywood culture industry

> 'Says Ft. Lauderdale housewife Sameera Biswas, "We go to the movies to keep our culture alive"' (*Newsweek International* 28 February, 2000).

> 'Kids in Bombay go to night clubs to become Western. Here (i.e. in Brisbane) we go to assert our Eastern identity. The basic difference lies there' (Fiji Indian enthusiast of Indipop, quoted in Ray, 2000).

The main contention of this paper seeks to separate out the Bollywood industry from the Indian cinema. It suggests that while the cinema has been in existence as a national industry of sorts for the past fifty years (the Indian cinema of course has celebrated its centenary, but the industry, in the current sense of the term, might be most usefully traced to the post-World War II boom in production), *Bollywood* has been around for only about a decade now. The term today refers to a reasonably specific narrative and a mode of presentation – the *Newsweek* essay, for example, quotes Plus Channel's Amit Khanna as saying that 'Indian movies are feel-good, all-happy-in-the-end, tender love stories with lots of songs and dances ... That's what attracts non-Indian audiences across the world' and to this we could add 'family values' and their palpable, if not entirely self-evident, investment in 'our culture'. To such content we would need to also add a distinctive mode of presentation, couched in the post-Information Technology claims that Indian enterprise has been making in the past few years of global competitiveness, and by language such as:

> Spurred by competition from dubbed versions of such flashy Western hits such as *Jurassic Park* and *Speed*, Bollywood is rushing to enter the era of high tech films. Producers are founding new companies, boosting their marketing, and seeking new sources of financing ... [C]ameras are rolling for the first Bollywood high-tech films. CMM Ltd., an 18-month-old special-effects company backed by such stalwarts as State Bank of India, has bought more than $1 million worth of software and hardware from Silicon Graphics Inc., the Mountain View (California) computer company whose special-effects equipment is used by nearly every Hollywood studio. The technology is key to a still untitled film featuring Indian megastar Shah Rukh Khan in a double role, allowing him to appear with himself in the same scene. Silicon Graphics is lining up other clients in India as well (Moshavi, 1995). [...]

Today, as Tharoor shows (or rather unwittingly demonstrates) the term comes with its own narrative, one that we could perhaps call techno-nostalgia, and is clearly not restricted any more to solely the cinema but informs a range of products and practices. It would certainly have informed the displays around the Swaminarayan Sanstha's Cultural Festival of India in Edison, New Jersey, in 1991, when you apparently entered through large gates signifying traditional temple entrances and named Mayur Dwar (Peacock Gate) and Gaja Dwar (Elephant Gate), and saw traditional artisans sharing their space with entrepreneurs from Jackson Heights selling electronic products, with sponsorship from AT&T. Of this form, most directly demonstrated in recent cinematic memory by the foreign-returned Rani Mukherjee in *KKHH* suddenly bursting into the bhajan *Om jai jagdish hare*, Sandhya Shukla has this to say:

> Emerging as it did out of a constellation of interests – Indian, Indian-American and otherwise American – the Cultural Festival generated questions about common ground: where was it and how did it function? [T]he Cultural Festival deliberately intertwined culture, nation and identity in its production of metaphors and myths. *With the synchronous developments of international capital and diasporic nationalism, we see infinitely complex realms of cultural production* (*Cultural Studies*, 11:2, emphasis added).

The 'our culture' argument, of which Bollywood forms an admittedly prime exemplar, clearly then also informs a range of productions, all combining the insatiable taste for nostalgia with the felt need to keep 'our (national) culture alive': from websites to chat shows, from Ismail Merchant and Madhur Jaffrey cookery programmes to advertising, soap operas to music video, niche marketing of various products, satellite channels, journalism, the Indipop 'remix' audio cassette and CD industry.

If, then, we see Bollywood as a culture industry and see the Indian cinema as only a part of it, even if a culturally significant part, then it is also likely that we are speaking of an industry whose financial turnover could be many times larger than what the cinema itself can claim. This would be true of the export market, but, if we include the extraordinary 'dotcom' boom being witnessed in India right now, it may even be already true within India itself.

The transition, or crossover in marketing terms, from a domestic film product which has comparatively few options for merchandising its products to one that more successfully gears itself for exploiting the new marketing opportunities that Bollywood now presents, are today palpably evident, certainly to any clued-in filmgoer. The difference between the 'Bollywood' movie and the rest of the Hindi and other language films being made would be, say, the difference between Karan Johar and David Dhawan, between Shah Rukh Khan and Govinda, between *Phir Bhi Dil Hai Hindustani* and *Anari Number 1*.[2] While *Hum Aapke Hain Kaun?* was perhaps the first Indian film to recognize and then systematically exploit a marketing opportunity here, it has since been most visibly Shah Rukh Khan who has been committed to the Bollywood mode, earlier mainly as an actor (*DDLJ, Pardes, DTPH, KKHH*) but this year with *Phir Bhi Dil Hai Hindustani*, having personally taken charge of its global marketing.

I want to drive a further wedge into the difference, by pointing to two crucial consequences of making this a distinction between the cinema and the more generalized Bollywood culture industry. In one obvious sense, Bollywood is of course identical to the Hindi (if not Indian) cinema: film continues to remain the most prominent presence, the figurehead of the global 'Indian' culture industry. However, in ironic contrast, whereas practically every other ancillary industry seems to have by now defined an audience, a market, and a means of sustained production for that market, the cinema continues to suffer from its old difficulties of defining a generic production line and thus of defining a stable channel of capital inflow.

Let us see the problem as one of *defining culture economically*. If one were to extrapolate a larger theoretical question from all this, it would be: what are the circumstances under which cultural self-definitions *resist* economic or (we could now add) political resolution? And why does the cinema suffer from this problem in India, when other forms from television to radio to the music industry and, of course these days, the Internet, seem to have no problem here?

To ask the question in these terms is, I suggest, to get to the very basis of why the Indian cinema exists at all. It is the further contention of this paper that since the second World War, when the Indian cinema first defined itself as a mass-culture industry, the very reason for why it occupied so crucial and prominent a space in the emerging post-war and – more crucially post-partition – public sphere has actively forced it to resist capitalist organization. The globalization of this duality in the past decade under the aegis of Bollywood, I finally suggest, leads us to important insights into the phenomenon that I shall argue is also, and among other things, the globalization of a crucial set of conflicts bred into Indian *nationalism*. [...]

Exporting the spectator: new sites for modernism

There is a near unanimity that the right kind of recognition would eventually lower the cost of an industry, where expenses and price of funds are mindboggling. Thanks to the well accepted practice of tapping undisclosed money, particularly the mega-budget ones, the string of financiers (mostly operating through fronts) extract a rate of return which is three to four times the interest a commercial bank would possibly charge ... This unpredictability has become inseparable from films. Immediately, I can't think of an evaluation procedure by which I can call a production viable,' said a senior PSU bank official. Bringing the activity within the banking parlance of 'productive purpose' appears to be the crux of the matter. 'Is it an income generating asset? This is neither manufacturing nor trading nor agriculture nor self-employment,' said a private bank official ... 'We may consider the track record of a producer, personal investments and net worth and ability to repay if the production flops and then take a short-term loan backed by sound collaterals. But will this attract the filmwallas? They might get a better deal from sources they have been tapping so far,' said an official of one of the older private banks (Ghosh, 1998).

Sushma Swaraj, then, offering 'industry status' to the cinema, was clearly making an intervention more complex than what the Film Federation of India necessarily saw as the issues. The problem was old, even tediously familiar; the circumstances however were brand new.

There is one crucially important sense, perhaps, in which the new international market opening up for Indian film could be continuing its old symbolic-political adherences. It is possible that the Indian cinema's modes of address have opened up a new category for spectatorial address that appears not to be accounted for by, say, the American cinema after it discovered the story-telling mode for itself and after numerous critics and theorists went on to assume that this mode was globally relevant, that 'we all internalize at an early age as a *reading competence* thanks to an exposure of films ... which is universal among the young in industrial societies' (Burch, 1990). If this is so, then in several places, like Nigeria, whose distinctive reception of Indian cinema has been analysed so remarkably by Brian Larkin (1997) or among the Fijian Indians in Australia who even make their own Hindi films on video, as examined by Manas Ray (2000), or for that matter among audiences who still flock to Indian films in Trinidad and South Africa, there could be people still going to these films precisely for what Hollywood cannot be seen to offer. It is possible that the cinema's addressees are entering complex realms of identification in these places which would definitely further argument around the nature of the cultural-political mediation that the Indian, or possibly the Hong Kong, cinemas continue to allow.

Evidently, *this* was not the market that was pressuring Swaraj to define a law offering industrial status to film. Nor was this the market that has film distributors and producers in Bombay in a tizzy, wondering how they can rake in their megabucks or go corporate. In fact, a recent news item about Burma and how popular Hindi films are there, speaks of print rights of *Taal* being sold for $10,000, a 'relatively high amount by Burmese standards' (Jha, 2000).

In the Bollywood sense of the export of the Indian spectator to distant lands, I want to suggest another kind of export: the export of Indian nationalism itself, now commodified and globalized into a 'feel good' version of 'our culture'. If so, then what we are also seeing is a globalization of the conflict, the divide, central to nationalism itself: the divide of *democracy* versus *modernity*, now playing itself out on a wider, more surreal, canvas than ever before.[3]

We don't know too much about this right now, but in conclusion, I would like to state the following issues that could be of relevance.

First, the question of *modernism*. If the civil and political society divide means anything at all, it shows how prevalent, foundational, and indeed how virtually unbridgeable the divides in India have been across the chasm of modernity. It is true that *something* has happened recently which seemingly wipes them away as though they have never existed, and different people have tried to explain this erasure differently. Arjun Appadurai's famous formulation of 'modernity at large', modernity cleansed of the mechanics of geographical belonging by the diaspora and the cyber-neighbourhood, certainly offers the *terrain* on which this insiderism is acted out (Appadurai, 1997). There do nevertheless seem to be larger, and still unanswered questions, which might be asked of the theorist but even more directly of the practitioner of Bollywood culture. For example, why now? The transition of cultural insiderism away from its heartland, away then from its historic political function of creating a certain category of citizen, and into something that informs the feelings of the visitor to the Brisbane night club, quoted earlier, who wants to go there to 'assert her Eastern identity' – this transition would clearly have something basic to offer in its rewriting of the *very trajectories of modernism* that have historically linked places such as India to the 'West'. Why does it seem so simple to pull off today when the Indian cinema has sought this transition to national legitimacy since at least the 1960s, without success?

A second question deals with the area of cultures resisting economic and political resolution. Bollywood clearly is reconfiguring the field of the cinema in important ways. What does it pick as translatable into the new corporate economy, what is it that this economy leaves behind? This would be as important a cultural question as an economic one.

For example, I believe it is demonstrable that practically all the new money flowing into the cinema right now is concentrating on the ancillary sector of film production. On one side, software giants such as Pentafour and Silicon Graphics use film in order to demonstrate their products, so that it is unclear as to whether, say Shankar's *Jeans* (1998), noted for all its digitalized camerawork and produced by Hollywood's Ashok Amritraj was more an independent feature film surviving on a pay-per-view basis or a three-hour demo take for Pentafour's special effects. On the other, the range of consumables increasingly visible on film screens – Stroh's beer in *DDLJ*, Coca Cola in *Taal*, Swatch watches in *Phir Bhi Dil Hai Hindustani* – are symptomatic of the nature of funding that the cinema increasingly depends on.

If so, it would be the final irony of the Bollywoodization of the Indian cinema that the very demand that the industry has sought from the government for so many decades could be the reason for its demise. The arrival of corporate-industrial-finance capital could reasonably lead to the final triumph of Bollywood, even as the cinema itself gets reduced only to a memory, a part of the nostalgia industry.

Notes

All references in this essay have been drawn from the Media and Culture Archive of the Centre for the Study of Culture and Society, Bangalore. I am grateful to Tejaswini Niranjana and to S. V. Srinivas for their comments, as well as to the participants in the 'Bollywood Unlimited' conference at the University of Iowa 1998, and to Philip Lutgendorf, Corey Creekmur and Rick Altman, for their responses to an earlier version of this paper.

1 So *The New Indian Express* (29 October 1999) reports that 'The opening titles of Sooraj Barjatya's forthcoming film *Hum Saath Saath Hain,* billed as the most cracking release this Diwali, will feature an important new player in Bollywood: Coca-Cola. The cola giant, in its bid to scramble to the very top of the Rs 3500 crore soft drinks market, has spent a comparatively smaller amount, Rs 1.5 crore, on branding Barjatya's family film and ensuring its release as *Coca-Cola Hum Saath Saath Hain'.*
2 While difficult to define precisely, the difference is roughly that between a low-end local production with little ambition to new global markets, and a glossy internationalized production.
3 Chatterjee elaborates his 'civil' versus 'political' society argument by suggesting that while modernity was the main agenda for the former, democracy could be seen as the main issue addressing the latter. So, in effect, the entire debate around modernism, around high and low art, around areligious secularism versus theories of caste and religion could be mapped around this often unbridgeable divide between modernity and democracy (Chatterjee, 1997).

References

Appadurai, Arjun (1997), *Modernity At Large: Cultural Dimensions of Globalization,* Oxford University Press, New Delhi.
BBCI (2002), www.bbc.co.uk/asianlife/film/indiansummer/index/shtml
Burch, Noel (1990), *Life to those Shadows,* University of California Press, Berkeley.
Chakravarty, Sumita (1993), *National Identity in Indian Popular Cinema 1947–87,* University of Texas Press, Austin.
Chatterjee, Partha (1997), 'Beyond the Nation? Or Within?', *Economic & Political Weekly,* 23:1–2, 4 and 11 January.
Cormack, Mike (1994), *Ideology and Cinematography in Hollywood, 1930–39,* St. Martin's Press, New York.
Ghosh, Sugata (1998), 'Industry status: Cinema may find itself going round trees'. *The Economic Times,* 12 May.

Jha, Lalit K. (2000), 'Mania for Hindi movies sweeps Myanmar', *The Hindu,* 29 February.

Larkin, Brian (1997), 'Indian Films, Nigerian Lovers: Media and the Creation of Parallel Modernities', *Africa,* 67:3.

Moshavi, Sharon (1995), 'Bollywood breaks into the big time', *The Economic Times,* 3 October.

Patil, S. K. (ed.) (1951), *Report of the Film Enquiry Committee,* Government of India Press, New Delhi.

Prasad, M. Madhava (1998), *Ideology of the Hindi Film: A Historical Construction,* Oxford University Press, New Delhi.

Ray, Manas (2000), 'Bollywood Down Under: Fiji Indian Cultural History and Popular Assertion', in Stuart Cunningham and John Sinclair (eds.), *Floating Lives: The Media and Asian Diaspora,* University of Queensland Press, St. Lucia.

Sengupta, Ratnottama (1999), 'Taalis for the Showman', *The Times of India,* 8 July.

16

Bollywood and the frictions of global mobility
by Nitin Govil

Look at *Titanic* – it's a Hindi film. *Gladiator* is a Hindi film. *Woody Allen's Everybody Says I Love You* is beautiful, just like a Hindi film. James Bond always does well in India – that's a Hindi film. Man, I want to be James Bond. Please make me the first Indian James Bond

(Shah Rukh Khan, Bollywood superstar, quoted in Dalton, 2002)

Towards a standard of convertibility

'Bollywood dancing,' Honey Kalaria explains in her 2003 home fitness video *Bollywood Workout*, 'can transform you into quite a versatile dancer.' Promising the first program to employ 'ancient-modernized dancing techniques,' Kalaria expresses a cheery conviction in Bollywood's capacity for dynamic recombination. This juxtaposition of histories, places and vernacular forms is one of the many reasons that Bollywood has functioned as a general principle of syncretism – or at least a 'byword for cool' – in the field of cultural production (Aftab, 2002). Yet in the frenetic pace of contemporary global information exchange, where the old economies of scale are outflanked by the new 'economies of variety' (Moulier Boutang, 2000), Bollywood seems to be dancing to a beat that is louder than ever.

As the founder of the first dance academy in Britain to offer classes in 'film-inspired' modern Indian dance, Kalaria has a material stake in advertising Bollywood's transformative powers. Her enthusiasm is also part of a broader international interest in Bollywood that took off in the mid-1990s with the release of Hindi films like *Dilwale Dulhaniya Le Jayenge* (1995), *Pardes* (1997), *Dil to Pagal Hai* (1997), and *Kuch Kuch Hota Hai* (1998). Targeting South Asian expatriate audiences with fantasies of middle-class mobility driven by the loss and recovery of 'traditional Indian values,' the international success of these films helped launch *Dil Se* to the box-office top ten in Britain in 1998 and *Taal* into the US top twenty a few years later. In 2000, six screens of a 30 screen multiplex built just outside Birmingham were dedicated to Hindi films, part of a growing trend throughout the UK. For decades, Hindi cinema had traveled to Britain, Fiji, Trinidad, Dubai,

Tanzania, South Africa, Mauritius – in fact, any country home to a significant South Asian diaspora – across legal distribution networks, non- and quasi-legal, large-scale, pirate reproduction industries, and more mobile forms of tactical media exchange such as smuggled prints, dubbed videocassettes and multi-generation audiotapes. This interoperability of legal and non-legal distribution networks has long enabled the distribution of Hindi cinema among broader audiences in the Soviet Union, Nigeria, Malaysia, Afghanistan, Egypt, Singapore, Japan and the US. However, when Hindi film icon Amitabh Bachchan's Madame Tussaud's wax effigy was unveiled in 2000, the year after he had been voted 'Star of the Millennium' in a BBC News Online poll and the same year that the Film Federation of India announced that Indian film exports had topped $100 million for the first time (with Hindi films making up 95 per cent of the haul), it was taken as a sign that Bollywood had officially arrived as a global cultural force.

Bollywood feted a celebration of its own at the first International Indian Film Awards ceremony in 2000 at London's Millennium Dome, with the show broadcast live to over 120 countries. The same year, Sony acquired overseas rights for *Mission Kashmir*, which became the first Hindi film to open in New York's Times Square after Sony had bought the overseas rights for 120 million rupees, covering 60 per cent of the film's production costs (Joseph, 2000: 44). It turns out that all this was just a preview of coming Bollywood attractions. The international success of *Kabhi Kushi Kabhi Gham* in 2001 was part of a public confirmation of Bollywood's 'ascent' to the mainstream Western media consciousness (Iordanova, 2002). Launched at the Venice Film Festival, *Lagaan* was nominated in the Best Non-English Language category for the 2002 Academy Awards in the United States; the same year Andrew Lloyd Webber premiered *Bombay Dreams* on stage.

Alongside these spectacular forms of global visibility, a more mundane but nonetheless crucial tribute came in the shape of Bollywood's inclusion in the hallowed lexicon of the English language. On 13 June 2001, the *Oxford English Dictionary* (OED) online edition listed an entry for 'Bollywood' for the first time. When the new OED illustrated print edition was published two years later, Bollywood joined 'Botox' and 'Viagra' as new terms of English language general circulation, with a list of 112 citations testifying to the proliferation of Bollywood as a shorthand for the 'Indian film industry, based in Bombay.' While it had served popular wisdom to suggest that Bollywood had been coined by a *Cineblitz* journalist in the 1980s, the *OED* claimed the origins of the term in H. R. F. Keating's 1976 novel, *Filmi, Filmi, Inspector Ghote*. In the novel, detective Ganesh Ghote investigates a murder on the Bombay set of *Khoon ka Gaddi* and muses:

It must have been the title of the film they were making. But the Production Manager had spoken the words with such awe, as if they were bound to be rich with meaning for whoever heard them, that he felt abruptly lost again. *Khoon ka Gaddi*. It meant *Cushion of Blood*. No, surely not. Ah yes, *gaddi* in the sense of a rajah's seat of honor. A throne. Yes, *Throne of Blood*, that sounded more likely.

(Keating, 1985: 14)

Even at the original scene of the crime, *Filmi Filmi* suggests a re-enactment: the novel that purportedly mentions Bollywood for the first time concerns a Hindi film production of *Macbeth* that references another cinematic transposition of the Shakespeare play, Akira Kurosawa's 1957 film *Kumonosu-jô* ['spider Web Castle'], released in the US as *Throne of Blood*. The *OED*'s reference to Bollywood's 'origin' in Keating's novel therefore suggests a term implicated in a palimpsest of translations, copies and remakes. Bollywood's messy, originary mimeticism is borne out by Prasad's (2003) etymology of the term. In 1932, Wilford Deming, an American engineer who briefly worked with Ardeshir M. Irani on the production of the first Indian sound film, sent greetings to *American Cinematographer* magazine from 'Tollywood' – a reference to Tollygunge, the Calcutta suburb that housed a number of film studios. Thus, notes Prasad, 'it was Hollywood itself, in a manner of speaking, that, with the confidence that comes from global supremacy, renamed a concentration of production facilities' in its own image (Prasad, 2003: 17). From Tollywood, it was just a matter of time before the clever alliteration of Bollywood struck the Hindi film industry centered in Bombay. Many critics, for example Virdi, have inveighed against the term, suggesting that Bollywood is 'weighed with misnomers about Hindi film as a mere Hollywood mimic' (Virdi, 2003: 21).

Bollywood's primary claim towards the multiple histories and directions of cultural flow, however, is contained within 'Bollywood' itself, a heteroglossic term that connotes a complex set of material and discursive links between Bombay and Hollywood. At the same time, in its equivocation to a global yet distinctively Indian – if not alternative – modernity, Bollywood is a *frictional* term that testifies to what Tsing calls the 'awkward, unequal, unstable, and creative qualities of interconnection across difference' (Tsing, 2005: 4). To follow Larkin's investigation of Hausa video re-significations of Hindi cinema iconography in Nigeria, Bollywood resonates globally precisely because of this 'interwoven process where Western media, Indian media, and local cultural production interact, at times coalescing and at other moments diverging' (Larkin, 2003: 178). Here, Bollywood is aligned with the broader social impact of Indian popular cinema. Through the heterogeneous deployment of folk forms, Indian cinema offered a way to indigenize global mass culture through the matrix of the popular; at the same time, cinema repackaged the vernacular into mass cultural forms that allowed entry into the global modern (Nandy, 1998).

Yet it is a mistake to conflate Bollywood with Indian popular cinema, even though there are partial alignments. As Rajadhyaksha (2003) notes, Bollywood can be understood as a relatively new culture industry designed to integrate the packaging of big-budget Hindi films across an array of international promotional sites from shopping malls and multiplexes, TV game shows, fashion runways and dance extravaganzas, to soft-drink and fast-food advertising, sports marketing, music videos and cell phone ring tones. Bollywood is now part of an apparatus that facilitates the transnational mobility of Indian media more generally. In this chapter I would like to retain Rajadhyaksha's (2003: 30) idea of the *recent* emergence of Bollywood, not 'to drive a wedge' between Bollywood and the Hindi and other regional cinemas' (the point that Bollywood tries but cannot speak for the diversity of Indian cinema is beyond question) but to understand how

Bollywood cuts across flow and contra-flow in the globalization of the culture industries. Through a set of commodity logics that inscribe Indian popular cinema within a broader set of global medias, Bollywood articulates certain contemporary processes shaping transformation and interconnectivity in the field of cultural production. This chapter touches on four overlapping commodity logics: the formalization of informality; the portability of the national; the production of singularity; and the permanency of crisis. These four overlapping logics help explain how Bollywood practices – across texts, institutions, industries and spaces – intersect and diverge with the global networks of exchange in media culture today.

The formalization of informality

Beginning in the mid-1980s, a series of fiscal and political crisis forced the Indian government to reexamine, and in some cases overturn, the assumptions that had structured the national economy after Independence. The ensuing push towards 'market liberalization' in the late 1980s and 1990s was designed to 'reform' the infamously complex state regulatory apparatus, lift import and export restrictions, smooth the flow of commodity products for the Indian consumer, and bolster international confidence in India through the solicitation of non-resident Indian investment. Urged on by the powerful international lending agencies like the World Bank, India began to shift from postcolonial developmentalism towards market-oriented neoliberalism. After Independence in 1947, the Indian state's commitment to rapid modernization focused on the nationalization of capitalist production in the communications areas of banking, transportation, postal, telecommunication and electronic systems (McDowell, 1997).

Deprived of state infrastructural support granted to these 'legitimate' communication industries, cinema was not considered among these iconic projects of Indian developmental modernity. However, cinema did serve as the vehicle for social reformers and other groups that understood it more as 'a vice, like gambling and prostitution, that must be curbed through taxation and strict censorship' (Prasad, 1998: 126). This alignment between the regulation of screen consumption and the management of civic virtue underscored the proliferation of a quasi-national network of import/export councils, development corporations, and enquiry committees that cleared a space for the state to function as both 'patron and disciplinarian' for the Indian film industries beginning in the 1950s (Pendakur, 2003: 59). However, in the wake of 'economic liberalization' in the late 1980s and 1990s, the Indian film industry became more central to the re-imagination of the Indian state.

In 1998, the Indian government finally granted 'industry status' to its domestic film trade. Easing restrictions on foreign collaboration under the new regime, the Indian government encouraged the Indian film industry to look outward and recruit international capital via foreign media investment. Film and television industries were relieved of export-related income tax – an exemption which was extended to individuals and partnerships in the media trade in 2000. In early 1999, the Indian government allowed foreign equity of up to 100 per cent in film production and distribution, legislating automatic approval to foreign investment in film companies provided that local partners contributed 25 per cent of the equity capital. Wholly owned subsidiaries of the foreign majors were given preference based on an established track record in the Indian market, consolidating the existing interrelationship of Indian producers and Hollywood distribution networks (Lall, 1999).

The state's 'official' interest in the capitalization of film production through the enabling of foreign investment seems incongruous given the usual practices of the Indian film sector. Since the collapse of the studio system in the 1950s, the Indian film industry has functioned as a speculative economy that subsists by articulating the interests of short-term entrepreneurial investors with longstanding patronage networks, using 'black' market and cash economies designed to avoid taxation regimes, and verbal contracts for above- and below-the-line labor. While Indian banks were trusted with creating new corporate funding for cinema production, for all the post-liberalization rhetoric of 'legitimate' institutional financing, the Industrial Development Bank of India sanctioned just over $13 million for film financing in 2001; this for a film industry with an annual turnover of over $800 million (Indo-Italian Chamber of Commerce and Industry, 2003).

As Naregal (2001: 39) notes, commercial Indian cinema has 'survived mainly through exploiting surplus merchant capital available through parallel money markets'. Furthermore, the Indian film industries depend on historical interrelationships between networks of informal/occasional labor and craft/trade unions that form intricate itineraries of work linked through custom, patronage, and transitory affiliation. How are these material informalities of the Indian film industry compatible with the new corporate language of organization, transparency, and accountability that has marked the entry of Indian cinema into international capital markets even as it has suffered spectacular failures domestically?

Contemporary Bollywood provides a language with which to think through the incongruity between informality and corporatization, and a site for a partial redress. This redress is partial because as the high-profile scandals of underworld influence on Bombay film production have destabilized the terrain of film financing, they have also popularized the gangster film and catapulted the figure of the cinematic don to a new level of popularity. In fact, the underworld don serves as a kind of mirror to the cult of the Indian management guru, who prioritizes the acquisition of those knowledge forms designed to network Indian entrepreneurial cultures into the global mainstream. Like the underworld don and his 'Company,' the business school graduate and the management consultancy engender a certain reflexivity within capitalism (Thrift, 1998). This reflexivity is one price of entry into global capital markets, particularly as exchanges like the US Nasdaq require more stringent transparency from non-American firms than they do from domestic ones. At the same time, the rationalization of reflexive knowledge has assumed a growing priority within the industry to reform the Bollywood mode of production, 'which has essentially come to mean high cost and waste' (Pendakur, 2003: 34).

The porosity (Liang, 2005) of formal and informal practices is further illustrated by the features of Bombay film production, which, despite its high-profile support of copyright and anti-piracy reform, actually operates in a field where *illegality is not exterior to the proper domain of the film industry but constitutive of it*. In a moribund domestic exhibition space where the heterogeneous audiences of the single-screen theater are neglected in favor of the middle-class patrons of the multiplex, Bollywood's cultures of anticipation are still mobilized through pirated media, neighborhood cablewallahs and bootleg DVD parlors. In addition, through the everyday practice of scripting 'unauthorized' remakes not only of itself, but also of Hollywood, 'world,' and regional Indian films, Bollywood's improvisational mode of production assembles idioms, genres, and translations that dynamize a form vacillating between innovation and cliché (see Ganti, 2002). In order to support this rapacious capacity for re-signification, Bollywood engages the practical politics of cultural production in India, where 'nonlegality was never a performative or political stance, but a functional one' (Sundaram, 2002: 128).

While Rajadhyaksha (2003) is right to note that corporatization has not been fully implemented in the Indian film industry's drive for transparency and foreign investment, the impossibility of its realization of full legal compliance was acknowledged at the very conference that announced industry status for Indian cinema, where Amit Khanna, current chairman of Reliance Entertainment, noted that 'corporatization is an attitude' (Khanna, 1998). Here 'attitude' functions through a performance of deferral, locating Indian film corporatization within the 'not-yet' of capital, a rhetoric familiar to the well-worn narratives of underdevelopment (Chakrabarty, 2000). At the same time, the presence of deferral in enunciation of corporatization means that Bollywood can speak the language of formalization – primarily through the forms of reflexivity enumerable to the global market – even as its practices engage histories of informal cultural production and the possibilities of response to changing media ecologies. In other words, even as it has moved towards corporatization, Bollywood operates only within the recognition of it as a kind of *limit*.

The portability of the national

On a visit to the US in 1964, Dilip Kumar remarked that Indian cinema could achieve greater international success by focusing on 'universal' themes while becoming 'more specifically Indian' (quoted in Canby, 1964). Here one of Hindi cinema's icons captures the contradiction of national cinema, where 'internalism is necessarily tempered by an awareness of exteriority as a shaping force' (Schlesinger, 2000: 24). Of course, the umbrella category 'Indian films' covers diverse local and regional practices that are far too heterogeneous in language, theme, and narrative to be collected under the sign of the national. However, Bollywood's enactment of India as a kind of 'multimedia spectacle' might give us some sense of the ways in which 'ethnic, regional and national identities are being reconstructed in relation to globalized processes of intercultural segmentation and hybridization' (García Canclini, 2001: 136; see also Govil, 2005).

'National cinema' first emerged as a concept within the field of cultural policy as Hollywood consolidated its European exports after the World War I decimation of local screen infrastructure (Thompson, 1996). Since this initial formulation, national cinema has been defined through two antinomies. First, national cinema refers to a set of representational practices produced under a centripetal logic of 'local' coherence – in terms of authorship, location, audience, narrative, genre and style – and a set of institutional practices through which the state exercises a mandate of preservation against the tide of the foreign – in terms of subsidies for film production, quotas, and other import restrictions. Second, national cinema refers to a set of relationships produced through a centrifugal logic that prioritizes dispersion over cohesion, whereby movements like Mexican national cinema and New German Cinema are validated as national expressions not because of their exclusivity but through their international circulation and relations with other industries (O'Regan, 1996). The longevity and global reach of national cinemas rests on their address of these centripetal and centrifugal dynamics.

The claim that all Third World texts are condemned to speak in the register of national allegory (Jameson, 1986) is supposed to have been relegated to an unfortunate stumble in an early engagement with postcolonial theory from the outside. Yet we are forced to re-confront the question of the national in the common mischaracterization of Bollywood as Indian national cinema. This misconception reveals a deeply entrenched majoritarianism at a time when the violent epistemology of cohesion in the national project has been so effectively coordinated by right-wing movements like the Shiv Sena. Evoking national cinema in the Indian context creates a monstrous alignment between the cultural politics of nationalist primordialism and Bollywood's export-oriented narratives. Here the politics of authenticity are reproduced through the expatriate Indian's attempted reintegration in a culture s/he left behind to pursue material wealth in the West.

The conflation of the particularity of Bollywood and the generality of 'the' Indian film industry is ironic given that Bollywood's primary language (Hindi) is implicated in the colonial rationalization of Indian language diversity, the fomentation of divisions amongst stakeholders in Hindustani literary culture, and the dissemination of an elite Indian nationalism (see Orsini, 2002). Hindi's complex role in both colonial and counter-colonial governmentality demonstrates the complexity of its emergence as the Indian collective voice. This complexity is flattened out by Das Gupta's (1968) infamous vilification of the Hindi film industry as a producer of *All-India* films that presents to its 'family audience' the technologized spectacles of modernity only to resort to the comforts of traditional life, thereby generalizing the postcolonial everyday to the extent that it is emptied of meaning. As Mazumdar (2001) demonstrates, the location of the Hindi cinema industry in non-Hindi-speaking Bombay, its early adoption of Parsi theatrical culture, and its employment of film practitioners displaced by the India–Pakistan partition actually helped to preserve the cultural presence of Urdu even in the national climate of Hindi's gradual Sanskritization.

As sound technology was developed in the 1930s, Indian geo-linguistic diversity forced the early regional film industries 'to fashion products that could move among a series of markets through dubbing, multiple versions,' and the exchange of cultural labor (Vasudevan, 2000: 120). Bollywood's strength as a global cultural form is indebted to this history of the Indian film industries' obligation toward flexibility in addressing the politics of cultural difference. Nevertheless, the misconceived idea of Bollywood as Indian national cinema produces identity narratives that articulate both the exclusive condition of an everyday lived within a particular bounded realm and an *inclusive* category that can support the portability of national identity (Sassen, 1998). If, as Hardt and Negri put it (2000: 105), 'national particularity is a potent universality,' then the resolution of what appears to be a fundamental antinomy is realized in the project of modern Hindu nationalism. As Blom Hansen notes in his discussion of the globalization of *Hindutva* in the late twentieth century, the Hindu nationalist claim of an

> alternative universalism is no longer a critique of the West, but rather a strategy to invigorate and stabilize a modernizing national project through a disciplined and corporatist cultural nationalism that can earn India recognition and equality (with the West and other nations) through the assertion of difference.
>
> (Blom Hansen, 1999: 231)

In this way, the fatal misrecognition of Bollywood as Indian national cinema recasts Dilip Kumar's fantasy of Hindi cinema's global relevance as the nightmare that lies just below the surface of a dream.

The production of singularity

Global cities function as command and control centers for the circulation and distribution of transnational economic, financial and technological flows. As sites for the concretization of the global economy, these cities internalize the inequalities associated with the classic modern duality of center and periphery (Sassen, 1994). Implicated in the space-based logics of acceleration, decentralization, and dispersion, these global cities are organized around the place-based logics of agglomeration, concentration, and accretion. The idea of Bombay as co-terminal with Bollywood helps dampen – not obliterate – the techtonic grindings of space and place in the globalization of the culture industries. 'Hollywood' attempts to do the same through the promotional industries designed to produce a fictional locus of American media production even as its labor economy is dispersed throughout the world (see Miller *et al.* 2005; Goldsmith and O'Regan, 2005). The globalization of the culture industries operates through the deployment of a singularity that produces the global and the local as mutually imbricated spatial forms. Sometimes, as with Bollywood and Hollywood, these spaces can refer to real places; but the 'Bombay' referenced by Hollywood is experiencing a period of intense transition as it disappears from bureaucratic and cinematic representation.

The Bombay referenced by Bollywood is no longer recognized by the Indian bureaucracy. In November 1995, in a maneuver that looked like a purging of the city's colonial past; through the Hindu right-wing's evocation of a powerful local nativism, the city's name was officially changed to 'Mumbai.' However, the politics of Hindu exception that motivated the name change actually inscribed Mumbai as a vernacular marker of an indigenous urban modernity in support of Indian distinction in the global commodity space (Blom Hansen, 2001). Mumbai is deployed through a provincialism designed to exorcise Bombay of its Western past – what Salman Rushdie famously derided as its 'culture of remakes' – in order to realize its 'original' Indian identity in the global present (Varma, 2004). The recent launch of *Time Out Mumbai* magazine, designed to showcase 'the changing mindset of people wanting to live well' (Borod, 2004), attests to the speed with which Mumbai has been branded and packaged in Indian consumer culture. Of course, this packaging is more than cosmetic, as it has been accomplished through the violent practices of slum clearance and forcible eviction that engender forms of cleansing and disappearance in the global city. While 'Bombay' may have disappeared from the government rolls, the emergence of Mumbai evokes the recovery of a primordial Indian identity that is, like other traditions of the national, both activated by and protected from the global present.

Furthermore, the rich tradition of referencing the city in Hindi popular cinema is also undergoing rapid transformation. Bombay has always resonated in the popular imaginary as a study in contrasts: between wealth and poverty; the skyline and the slum. Yet as Hindi cinema was a site for the vernacularization of Bombay, Bollywood creates a space for its dispersal through the narratives of global consumer mobility. As Mazumdar (2006) argues, Hindi cinema invoked the city through the representation of the street, the city crowd and the footpath. In many of Bollywood's globally marketed films beginning in the 1990s, these classic representations of Bombay's everyday life at the street level have been anesthetized and supplanted by the symbolic spaces of commodity consumption like the shopping mall and the multiplex, as well as the modern interior designs of the upper-middle-class Indian home. These spaces represent the projection of India into the global commodity fantasy.

The globalization of Bollywood is clearly situated within a Bombay defined by these institutional and aesthetic 'strategies of disappearance' (Abbas, 1997). This alignment is defined by the preservation of a locality and its transliteration into the global entertainment space. Following the economic 'liberalization' initiatives of the late 1980s, the new objective of Indian audiovisual policy has been, as Mukherjee (2003: 17) notes, 'to strike a balance between the preservation of the rich cultural heritage of the nation and increased efficiency and global competitiveness of that sector through privatization and foreign investment'. Bombay provides a nodal point for Bollywood's articulation of popular cinema to Indian transnationalism. What better place to represent Bollywood's global linkages than the reimagination of Bombay as real and imagined space?

The permanency of crisis

The cover of a recent issue of *Outlook* magazine is emblazoned with a dramatic statement of crisis: '132 Films, 124 Flops – This is Bollywood's WORST year ever.' Inside we read about the sorry state of affairs: director Karan Johar has sworn off making yet another 'crying, singing, dancing, happy movie.' In a year marked by the extravagance of *Devdas,* producers and critics openly indict a hit-driven industry run amok with bloated star salaries, marketing, and publicity budgets; distributors refuse advance bookings in favor of commissions; social scientists claim that 'Bollywood's mythmaking is collapsing'; there are calls for the rationalization of budgets, a greater degree of professionalization, and attention to scripting as process; 'everyone's in the panic room,' says writer/director Anurag Kashyap (Joshi, 2002).

As with most Bollywood narratives, there is something familiar about this story. At the 1998 conference that announced the formalization of the film industry, the president of the Federation of Indian Chambers of Commerce and Industry (FICCI) – an organization founded in 1927 to consolidate countercolonial calls for greater indigenous management, participation, and ownership in Indian industry – implored attending Ministry of Information and Broadcasting officials to recognize Bollywood's patriotism: 'whenever there has been a crisis ... be it war with Pakistan, or in times of great national tragedy, we have seen that people from this sector have come forward and given all help to the nation' (Modi, 1998). What the FICCI president failed to mention – mere hours before the onset of India's nuclear tests at Pokhran – was that Bollywood not only responds to national crisis, but actually functions in *a state of permanent crisis.* The permanence of crisis is partly due to the fact that commercial Hindi cinema operates in an economy of risk management that is different from that of the other global culture industries. Contemporary Hollywood, for example, balances cost and predictability through a cybernetic system of budgetary rationalization enabled by market research and the feedback between audience preference and box-office returns. Faced with the severity of state disciplinarity in the shape of entertainment and income tax, however, the Indian film industries have never invested in Hollywood-style administrative competency via auditing and other technologies of corporate enumeration. In fact, the Indian state creates a disincentive to the collection of institutional statistics or systematic data. This lack of systematic or verifiable data is a constituent feature of Bollywood's improvisational mode of production.

Crisis is therefore part of the melodrama of Bollywood as a culture industry – but like one of its classic heroes, Bollywood reemerges in the face of predation and dire odds. Even the crisis of 2002 has been supplanted by the success of new 'crossover' films that boosted the fortunes of the Indian box-office in 2005. The historiography of crisis is punctuated by a before-and-after tipping point that often takes the shape of single, 'industry-altering' films such as *Lagaan* or *Devdas.* While crisis is both the engine of Bollywood's innovation and the explanation for cliché, it also presents a way for Bollywood to extend its own boundaries. As Marx famously observed, crisis structures the global mobility of capital through a process of internalization: 'the tendency to create the world market is indirectly given in the concept of capital itself. Every limit appears as a barrier to overcome' (Marx, 1973: 408).

Posing Bollywood as a perennial problem in constant need of a solution systematizes a set of demands and the mobilization of disparate connections:

between the business and industrial community (give us more stable forms of investment!); the state and the film sector (recognize our industry as legitimate!); management and cultural labor (give us a more disciplined star and script system!); enforcement authorities and distributors (curtail media piracy!); and producers and foreign investors (come and help us!). In this way, the issues presented as critical in the industry create strategic opportunities for Bollywood to present itself in perennial threat of irrelevance at home in order to justify its growing relevance in the world. The speech genre of crisis is motivational, it inspires a proliferation of connections in the exhortation of transformation. Bollywood's crisis is what allows its biggest movie star to claim in our opening epigraph that so many Hollywood films are Hindi films too.

Bollywood, inside and out

In the mid-1970s, the Indian film industries repeatedly failed to meet annual export targets of $15 million, often falling as much as 50 per cent short. While some traditionally strong film-importing nations, like Singapore, Syria, Lebanon and Jordan had begun to view Indian cinema imports as a threat to the development of their own industries, blame for soft export figures was also cast on a complex regulatory apparatus, the length of Indian films, and a difficulty in translating 'local' forms into 'universal' themes that could travel well. Throughout the 1970s and the 1980s, the government attempted to rationalize the export of Indian cinema under a single regulatory agency, but individual Indian film exporters found a more piecemeal, country-by-country approach that could generate the greatest possible revenue (especially with video and television rights).

By the early 1990s, bolstered by export markets in the Middle East and other places hostile to US film distribution, Indian film exports were up to $20 million, but it was not until the turn of the century that the export market topped $100 million dollars. While these numbers are clearly speculative, they nonetheless indicate, a considerable exponential progression. Aamir Khan, the star and producer of *Lagaan*, a stirring tale of counter-colonial agitation nominated for the foreign language Academy Award 45 years after another Oscar-nominated story of national integration (*Mother India*), gets at the heart of the rising fortunes of Indian film exports when he notes, 'I don't see the problem in addressing an international audience even from a business point of view' (personal interview, Bombay, 21 November 2002).

This business point-of-view is an amalgam of textual, spatial, industrial, and institutional strategies designed to maximize the potential of inter-connectivity within the constitution of Bollywood and its drive for global relevance. Bollywood is serviced by a morphology that internalizes the movement between flow and counter-flow, while managing the universal and the particular in the projection of India into the global commodity space. The four commodity logics detailed in this chapter are not simply manifestations of Bollywood, but indicative of fundamental tensions at a time when the complexity and risk of cultures of circulation have elevated 'connectivity itself [as] the significant sociostructuring value' (LiPuma and Lee, 2004: 19). These tensions are part of the aftershocks of the displacement of the Keynesian state by the neoliberal market and the forms of transparency and accountability that have emerged as a new ethic of corporate governance. Flow and counter-flow are critical to a Bollywood vernacular that is produced through complex strategies of appropriation, derivation, and difference. Yet in its engagement of informality, portability, singularity, and crisis, Bollywood's prioritization of linkage, transversality and assemblage pursues the flexibility that is 'both the product and condition of late capitalism' (Ong, 1999: 240).

This flexibility has its rewards, of course, but also its price. If Bollywood remains committed to achieving global relevance through the nostalgic project of recovering primordial national sentiment, then it will be drowned out by the plodding, martial strains of majoritarian triumphalism. On the other hand, if Bollywood can move along the frictional trajectories inscribed in its name, well, that's a beat more of us might dance to.

Acknowledgments

Many thanks to Denise McKenna, John McMurria, Ranjani Mazumdar, and Bhaskar Sarkar for their comments and suggestions. Also, thanks to the South Asia Center at the University of Pennsylvania for their support in presenting part of this material at the *Cinema South Asia* conference in early 2006.

References

Abbas, A. (1997) *Hong Kong: Culture and the Politics of Disappearance*. Minneapolis: University of Minnesota Press.

Aftab, K. (2002) 'Brown: the new black! Bollywood in Britain', *Critical Quarterly*, 44(3): 88–98.

Blom Hansen, T. (1999) *The Saffron Wave: Democracy and Hindu Nationalism in Modern India*. New Delhi: Oxford University Press.

Blom Hansen, T. (2001) 'The proper name', *Violence in Urban India: Identity Politics, 'Mumbai', and the Postcolonial City*. New Delhi: Permanent Black, pp. 1–19.

Borod, L. (2004) 'A passage to India', *Folio*, 1 August: 8.

Canby, V. (1964) 'Indian film industry here; many vexations, lack of theatres; difficulties in breaking even', *Variety*, 21 October.

Chakrabarty, D. (2000) 'The two histories of capital', *Provincializing Europe: Post-colonial Thought and Historical Difference*. New Delhi: Oxford University Press, pp. 47–71.

Dalton, S. (2002) 'Meet the Khan-do guy', *The Scotsman*, 14 August, p. 5.

Das Gupta, G. (1968) 'The cultural bias of Indian cinema', in C. Das Gupta, *Talking About Films*. New Delhi: Orient Longman, pp. 3–18.

Ganti, T. (2002) ' "And yet my heart is still Indian": the Bombay film industry and the H(Indianization) of Hollywood', in F. Ginsburg, L. Abu-Lughod and B. Larkin (eds) *Media Worlds: Anthropology on a New Terrain*. Berkeley: University of California Press, pp. 281–300.

García Canclini, N. (2001) *Consumers and Citizens: Globalization and Multicultural Conflicts*, trans. G. Yúdice. Minneapolis: University of Minnesota Press.

Goldsmith, B. and T. O'Regan (2005) 'Still at the center: studios and the United States', in B. Goldsmith and T. O'Regan *The Film Studio: Film Production in the Global Economy*. Lanham, MD: Rowman & Littlefield, pp. 177–203.

Govil, N. (2005) 'Hollywood's effects, Bollywood FX', in Mike Gasher and Greg Elmer (eds) *Contracting Out Hollywood: Runaway Productions and Foreign Location Shooting*. Lanham, MD: Rowman & Littlefield, pp. 92–114.

Hardt, M. and A. Negri (2000) *Empire*. Cambridge, MA: Harvard University Press.

Indo-Italian Chamber of Commerce and Industry (2003) *Internationalisation of the Indian Film Industry*. Mumbai: IICCI/Bhalchandra Printing.

Iordanova, D. (2002) 'Bollywood calling: marketing in the global diaspora as exemplified by Bollywood cinema', trans. T. Jones, *Springerin*, 7(1).

Jameson, F. (1986) 'Third-World literature in the era of multinational capitalism', *Social Text*, 15: 65–88.

Joseph, M. (2000) 'Riverdale sonata', *Outlook*, 6 November: 42–51.

Joshi, N. (2002) 'Flop show: Bollywood's ship faces unfriendly trade winds at box office, prompting serious introspection', *Outlook*, 25 November: 48–56.

Keating, H. R. F. [1976] (1985) *Filmi Filmi, Inspector Ghote*. Chicago: Academy Chicago Publishers.

Khanna, A. (1998) 'Industry status for the film industry', remarks presented at the National Conference on 'Challenges before Indian Cinema'. Bombay, 10 May.

Lall, B. (1999) 'India opens up film to foreign firms', *Screen International*, 11 June.

Larkin, B. (2001) 'Degraded images, distorted sounds: Nigerian video and the infrastructure of piracy', *Public Culture*, 16(2): 289–314.

Larkin, B. (2003) 'Itineraries of Indian cinema: African videos, Bollywood, and global media', in E. Shohat and R. Stam (eds) *Multiculturalism, Postcoloniality, and Transnational Media*. New Brunswick: Rutgers University Press, pp. 170–92.

Liang, L. (2005) 'Porous legalities and avenues of participation', in M. Narula, S. Sengupta, J. Bagchi and G. Lovink (eds) *Sarai Reader 05: Bare Acts*. Delhi: Sarai/CSDS, pp. 6–17.

LiPuma, E. and B. Lee (2004) *Financial Derivatives and the Globalization of Risk*. Durham. NC: Duke University Press.

McDowell, S. (1997) *Globalization, Liberalization and Policy Change*. London: Macmillan.

Marx, K. (1973) *Grundrisse: Foundations of the Critique of Political Economy*, trans. Martin Nicolaus. New York: Penguin.

Mazumdar, R. (2001) 'Figure of the "Tapori": language, gesture and cinematic city', *Economic and Political Weekly*, 29 December: 4872–80.

Mazumdar, R. (2006: forthcoming) *Urban Allegories: The City in Bombay Cinema*. Minneapolis: Minnesota University Press.

Miller, T., N. Govil, R. Maxwell, J. McMurria and T. Wang (2005) *Global Hollywood 2*. London: British Film Institute.

Modi, K. K. (1998) 'Introduction to Sushma Swaraj valedictory session', remarks presented at the National Conference on 'Challenges before Indian Cinema'. Bombay, 10 May.

Moulier Boutang, Y. (2000) 'A mutation of political economy as a whole,' *Mutations,* Harvard Project on the City and Multiplicity. Barcelona: ACTAR, pp. 70–83.

Mukherjee, A. (2003) *Audio-visual Policies and International Trade: the Case of India.* Hamburg: Hamburg Institute of International Economics.

Nandy, A. (1998) 'Indian popular cinema as a slum's eye view of polities', in A. Nandy (ed.) *The Secret Politics of Our Desires: Innocence, Culpability and Indian Popular Cinema.* New Delhi: Oxford University Press, pp. 1–18.

Naregal, V. (2001) 'The Mafia and the media get along: notes on contemporary media distribution and the public sphere in India', *Sagar: South Asia Research Journal,* 7: 37–18.

Ong, A. (1999) *Flexible Citizenship: The Cultural Logics of Transnationality.* Durham, NC: Duke University Press.

O'Regan, T. (1996) *Australian National Cinema.* New York: Routledge.

Orsini, F. (2002) *The Hindi Public Sphere, 1920–1940: Language and Literature in the Age of Nationalism.* New Delhi: Oxford University Press.

Pendakur, M. (2003) *Indian Popular Cinema: Industry, Ideology, and Consciousness.* Cresskill: Hampton Press.

Prasad, M. M. (1998) 'The State in/of cinema', in P. Chatterjee (ed.) *Wages of Freedom: Fifty Years of the Indian Nation-State.* New Delhi: Oxford University Press, pp. 123–46.

Prasad, M. M. (2003) 'This thing called Bollywood', *Seminar,* 525 (May): 17–20.

Rajadhyaksha, A. (2003) 'The "Bollywoodization" of the Indian cinema: cultural nationalism in a global era', *Inter-Asia Cultural Studies,* 4(4): 25–39.

Sassen, S. (1994) *Cities in a World Economy.* New York: Pine Forge Press.

Sassen, S. (1998) 'The de facto transnationalizing of immigration policy', in C. Joppke (ed.) *Challenge to the Nation-State: Immigration in Western Europe and the United States.* Oxford: Oxford University Press, pp. 49–85.

Schlesinger, P. (2000) 'The sociological scope of "National Cinema"', in M. Hjort and S. MacKenzic (eds) *Cinema and Nation.* New York: Routledge, pp. 19–31.

Sundaram, R. (2002) 'About the Brazilianization of India', in Geert Lovink (ed.) *Uncanny Networks: Dialogues with the Virtual Intelligensia.* Cambridge, MA: MIT Press, pp. 122–31.

Thompson, K. (1996) 'Nation, national identity and the international cinema', *Film History,* 8(3): 357–69.

Thrift, N. (1998) 'Virtual capitalism: the globalization of reflexive business knowledge', in J. G. Carrier and D. Miller (eds) *Virtualism: A New Political Economy.* New York: Berg, pp. 161–86.

Tsing, A. L. (2005) *Friction: An Ethnography of Global Connection.* Princeton: Princeton University Press.

Varma, R. (2004) 'Provincializing the global city', *Social Text,* 22(4): 65–89.

Vasudevan, R. (2000) 'National pasts and futures: Indian cinema', *Screen,* 41(1): 119–25.

Virdi, J. (2003) *The Cinematic Imagination: Indian Popular Films as Social History.* New Delhi: Permanent Black.

17

Itineraries of Indian cinema: African videos, Bollywood, and global media
by Brian Larkin

The tape recorder, the device that conveys love between the two main characters in the Nigerian (Hausa) video film *In Da So Da K'auna* (The Soul of My Heart, [1994, dir. Ado Ahmad]), is a mediating device, filtering, on several levels, the physical and symbolic boundaries among characters, societies, and technologies. Sumayya sits in her bedroom as a boy brings in a tape from her lover, Mohammed. The camera zooms in to a medium close-up as she turns on the tape recorder and hears her lover announce he will sing to her "Lambun Soyayya" (The Garden of Love). She sits still, for a full three minutes, as the camera moves to an extreme close-up on an immovable face. There is no reaction, no expression, and the viewer is forced to contemplate the unspectacular practice of listening. In this sensual, physical scene, a visceral declaration and acceptance of love occurs and in the intimacy of a bedroom lovers share the same space but only by virtue of the mediating capacity of the tape recorder. The tape recorder mediates sensual relations between lovers by making Mohammed, the lover, present by prosthesis. And in doing so it also mediates between Indian films and Nigerian Hausa videos, enabling the declaration of love through song, so central to Indian films and their popularity in Nigeria, while preserving the sexual segregation necessary to Hausa Islamic values.

Indian film has been a global media form for more than half a century and strikingly successful in competing with, and sometimes dislodging, the suzerainty of Hollywood in the global arena. Yet compared to the substantial literature on global Hollywood, Hindi film is only beginning to be theorized as a form of global media, rather than national cinema. To conceive of Indian film in this way we need to examine the specific reasons why Indian film travels; how its appeal shifts across differing societies and sometimes in the same society over time. For some societies Hindi cinema represents tradition, a space outside of, and alter to, the cultural spread of Western modernity; for others, the cultural address of Indian film is future-oriented, modern, and cosmopolitan. For Indians outside of India it is a way of enacting and representing a diaspora, whose songs, plots and fashions generate the affectual ties and emotional memories that tie a collectivity together.

For non-Indian audiences the films present a cultural other, religiously, racially and culturally removed from everyday life in Africa or the Middle East and whose sympathies with the films take place through a complex process of identification and alienation. To understand the varying reasons why Indian film provides amenable spaces for global cultural imagining means taking seriously a decentered media theory and refiguring our categories of what counts as global media and why.

The popularity of Indian films with Arabs, Malaysians, Senegalese, or Nigerians, as well as with diasporic Indians reveals the mobilization of desire and fantasy that animates global cultural flows. These moments of borrowing are the choices individuals and cultures (in the case of extended, elaborated genres of music or film) make out of the range of mass-mediated cultural goods available to them in order to make those cultural goods do symbolic work locally. Until recently, discussions of global media were dominated by the dichotomy of the dominance or resistance to foreign (Western) media. For media theory in particular, cultural imperialism and its more recent avatar, globalization, offered not just a description of the world but a way of theorizing how media operate typing economy, politics and symbolic form together in a materialist theory of culture. The hegemony of Western media forms, particularly from America, emerges from their ties to modes of international financing, marketing agreements, intellectual property regimes and distribution and exhibition networks that provide the infrastructural underpinning that facilitate the movement and penetration of these media forms. It is this reason, as much as their production values, star systems, and plots that designates them as "global media" and it creates a structural underpinning that alternative media forms cannot compete with. One of the reason that Hindi cinema, like Egyptian film and other non-Western cinemas, were not conceived of in terms of global media was precisely because they lacked this infrastructural economic underpinning, rather than any lack of popularity across national borders. But the globality of Indian cinema took place in the margins of the realms of distribution controlled by US media corporations relying on different infrastructures of distribution and exhibition. They traveled to areas where Hollywood remained hugely popular but so, often, were still other film forms from Egyptian to Hong Kong cinema. If, in a place such as Cairo, Hollywood films compete with Egyptian, Hong Kong and Indian films it suggests we need to shift our critical questions to ask what pleasures do Indian films offer that Hollywood films do not? What cultural work do Hollywood films accomplish that is different from Hong Kong films? The presence of one media flow does not mean the obliteration of others, as people take diverse meanings and different pleasures from various types of media available to them.

In this article I examine the migration of Indian film outside of India and raise questions about what is entailed in conceiving of Indian film as a global cinema. I am particularly interested in how, over more than half a century, Indian films have spawned a range of cultural phenomena – Greek "Indoprepi" songs from the 1950s, contemporary Hausa video films in Nigeria, Tanzanaian taarab music – in societies outside of India and its diaspora and will discuss examples of this below. This longevity and geographical spread points to the diversity of reasons that

Indian films travel. These are complex cultural texts that are not stagnant but continually changing and their polysemy creates a range of openings through which global politics of identity can be contested. The circulation of cultural forms across boundaries always involves practices of translation and filtration as elements that might prove incommensurable to a society (their Hinduness in Muslim Hausa society for instance) must be downplayed or sloughed off while others are heightened. A young South Asian in 1980s Britain watching the films for a connection to an imagined homeland, or as an ethnographic pedagogical text for the reproduction of "correct" cultural values is watching these films in a very different way from urban Russians in the 1950s or Muslim Malaysians today. In the context of northern Nigeria, the setting I know best, I argue Indian film offers a "third space" for Hausa audiences that mediates between the reified poles of Hausa Islamic tradition and Western modernity (a false dichotomy to be sure, but one that remains deeply meaningful to people's political consciousness. For a more detailed discussion see Larkin, 1997). Indian film offers Hausa viewers a way of being modern that does not necessarily mean being Western. This multifacetedness is key to their success and to their popularity. For instance, Indian film also offers Hausa a cultural foil against other dominant ethnic groups in Nigeria such as Igbo and Yoruba so that the popularity of Indian film with Hausa audiences is so great that, in the north of Nigeria at least where Hausa are based, they are used by both Hausa and their others as means of defining identity and locating the temporal and political nature of that identity. When Hausa videomakers incorporate elements of Indian films into their videos they are thus engaging a complicated series of cultural hierarchies external and internal to the nation, setting our understanding of the operation of transnational media within a more complicated terrain. [...]

In Nigeria, Indian films offer ways of being modern and traditional that create a template for exploring the tensions of postcoloniality. In the Indian diaspora, Bollywood can be both a conduit into an essentialized, traditional past and the site for the production of a hip, hybrid present. Indian films betray a love/hate relation with both the West and a mythic India and in doing so open up interstices in which heterogeneity and ambivalence flourish, allowing the films to be both Westernized and traditional; corruptor of local values and a defender of them. Vasudevan (2000) analyzes the ways Indian films create a politics of cultural difference by reinventing themselves to establish dialogue with and assert difference from universal models of narration and subjectivity. He analyzes these workings internally to India, but the same process operates on a global stage. Indian films travel because they become a foil against which postcolonial identity can be fashioned, critiqued, and debated. They allow an alterity to Hollywood domination but offer their own aggressive commercialism in its stead that is at the same time traditional and modern. The reasons for the global popularity of Indian films crucial to the ability to map and understand the phenomenon of global popular media lie in this interwoven process where Western media, Indian media, and local cultural production interact, at times coalescing and at other moments diverging.

Before I turn to the relation between Indian film and Nigerian Hausa videos, I first wish to make a brief detour in order to contextualize the rise of Nigerian videos [since 1993] and what this means for our understanding of that discursive construct "African cinema."

Nigerian video films and the end of African cinema?

By cinema in this heading I refer not just to a body of films but to the critical cultural project that is inherent to the idea of African cinema (see Cham and Bakari, 1996; Diawara, 1992; Pines and Willemen, 1989; Ukadike, 1994). This is clear in the overt political and aesthetic project of "third cinema" (Pines and Willemen, 1989) but more important has informed state media policy and practice in many postcolonial nations. The concept of "national cinemas" derives from a legacy where the nation-state is posited as the definer and defender of cultural values (cf. Meyer, 1999). The Nigerian state sponsored "Nigerian" cinema to preserve "Nigerian" values, and so on. The video industry, by contrast, emerged outside of state participation, frequently in opposition to it and driven largely by commercial rather than political motives.

In what is truly a remarkable cultural renaissance in Africa, [since 1995] a mass media genre Nigerian video film has come to dominate local media production and to become regionally hegemonic in exporting media to other nations in West and East Africa. Over 3,500 of these video films have been released in the general market. These "films," shot and released on video but known locally as films, can be broadly broken down into three main categories according to language (and culture): Yoruba, English, and Hausa (for an introduction, see Haynes, 2000). The appearance of these films is remarkable in that the industry developed outside of state or foreign support, in a time of intense economic deprivation and based wholly on a mass viewing audience.

These films nearly all exhibit the qualities that Vasudevan (2000) associates with the cinema of "transitional" societies negotiating the rapid effect of modernity: the cinematic address is to a world governed by kinship relations; the plot is driven by family conflict; melodrama predominates, relying on excess, Manicheanism, and privileging the moral over the psychological. In "Nigerian" videos, the term used to refer to English-language videos (as opposed to Hausa or Yoruba videos), this melodrama is intensified by the use of horror and the supernatural. Here magic mixes with the world economy, and capitalist accumulation is only possible through occult means. Husbands sacrifice their wives to become rich, mothers bewitch their children, and the devil, through his intermediaries, is ever present in Nigerian life. In dramatizing the work of witches and the prevalence of human sacrifice, video films move from the world of melodrama into the suspense and gore associated with horror. Nigerian films, in particular, are known for their special effects, as humans transform into animals, witches fly through the night, and money is magically produced (for similar issues in Ghanaian film, see Meyer, 2003). It is the mixing of melodrama with horror and magic and the linkage of financial with sexual and spiritual corruption that makes the melodrama of

Nigerian and Ghanaian video film distinctively African. In contemporary postcolonial West Africa, where the everyday suffering of the vast majority stands in stark
contrast to the fantastic accumulation of the small elite, the tropes of sorcery,
witchcraft, and supernatural evil have provided a powerful way to express the
inequalities of wealth.

African cultural heritage here is rarely represented as the valued cultural
patrimony we are familiar with from the debates around African cinema. Rather it
is frequently represented as evil, a place where the forces of darkness operate
unchecked, a representation that is the outgrowth of the emergence of what Meyer
has termed (in another context) a Pentecostalist public culture (Meyer, 2003;
Marshall-Fratani, 1998; Ukah, 2000) in which styles of Pentecostalist discourse
have proliferated in a variety of popular cultural forms. Nigerian videos address a
cosmopolitan public in which the modern and the Pentecostalist, consumption and
Christianity, are intertwined. The realist verities of modernist development and
cultural authenticity are rejected, as is any attempt toward a progressive political
project. These videos represent the working out of a specific form of Nigerian
melodrama in a society that is both modern and sacred. Peter Brooks's argument
that melodrama rises when the traditional hierarchies of a sacred society are
dissolved captures the sense of spiritual insecurity and permanent transition that
marks Nigerian melodrama, but God, the devil, and the supernatural are the
everyday forms through which modernity emerges (on melodrama as a postcolonial project, see Abu–Lughod, 2002).

The rise of these videos highlights several ironies inherent in the concept of
African cinema. African cinema, for instance, has tended to refer to the films
Africans produce rather than those they watch. Films that travel under the sign of
African cinema are still much more readily available in festivals in London, Paris,
and New York, than they are in Abidjan, Lagos, or Mombasa. The calls by African
filmmakers for a "popular" film practice glossed over the fact that this cinema
referred first and foremost to an auteur artistic practice that rarely had to rely upon
the marketplace or a mass audience for its funding and survival. This now stands
in stark contrast to the rise of local video film industries in countries such as
Ghana and Nigeria that, while accused of being much more "Westernized," are
successful in an African marketplace. Video filmmakers have been much less
concerned with ideas of cultural authenticity and cultural value. Most clearly,
Nigerian videos have indeed fashioned aesthetic forms and modes of cultural
address based on the experiences of the societies they address rather than those of
the West, a prime concern of third cinema, but this fashioning has emerged not so
much in opposition to Hollywood and Western cultural values, but through and
out of the history of that engagement.

So far I have used the term Nigerian videos or Nigerian film without
unpacking the regional hegemony that is built into this concept. As Jonathan
Haynes (2000) has pointed out, the scholarly and film festival circuits that have
deployed the concept of "African cinema" have found it extremely difficult to deal
with the issue of ethnicity and of subnational difference. This is in part the legacy
of the struggle against colonialism and, later, against a cultural imperialism that
downplayed ethnic allegiance in favor of identification with the nation-state. In

part, it also has to do with the history of cinema studies, which has tended to concentrate on the dynamics of national rather than ethnic cinemas. Nigerian videos, however, are divided into Yoruba-, English-, and Hausa-language films. The term Nigerian films in fact often refers to English-language films primarily made by Igbo and minority group producers who address their productions to a pan-Nigerian, English-speaking urban subject. This means the claim to "Nigerian-ness" has been constructed through exclusions, as a specific form of urban culture and experience serves as the sole basis of a pan-Nigerian address. This is an urbanism marked by fast-growing capitalism, consumption, Pentecostalist Christianity, the occult, temptation, and corruption, the central themes around which the abstraction of "national" cinema and national subject is constructed. If these videos address a cosmopolitan "modern," urban subject, then Muslim Hausa are the internal other against which that modernity is imagined. Hausa cosmopolitanism, focused as it is on dynamics in the Muslim world more than in the West, is readily stigmatized as "backward," "traditional," and "ignorant," in southern Nigerian stereotypes. For Hausa viewers and Hausa filmmakers, the melodramatic form of southern Nigerian videos with their focus on sexual and magical excess, their unrelenting materialism, the frequent stereotyping of Pentecostalist pastors as culture heroes makes these videos an ambivalent space for cultural imagining. As one Hausa video storeowner said to me, while he sold southern videos, he wouldn't allow his family to watch them. This is not to say that southern Nigerian videos are not popular in the north, where they do sell well, but the form, content, and even distribution of Hausa videos have developed along strikingly different lines. And it is here that Indian films have proved to be a powerful intertexual presence.

Hausa video films

While magic, materialism, and corruption are all present to a certain extent in Hausa video films, perhaps the primary narrative difference is the focus on love and romance and the spectacular development of this through song-and-dance routines (waka da rawa in Hausa) a generic convention rarely seen in English-language videos. The focus on love comes about for a number of reasons. Most obviously, the first Hausa videos evolved from a literary genre of local Hausa-language love stories, soyayya books (see Furniss, 1996; Larkin, 1997). These became hugely popular among youth just at the time that the first Nigerian videos were being produced in the south of Nigeria. The first Hausa videos tended to be adaptations of these "best-selling" books and maintained their preoccupation with love. This tendency was intensified, however, by several producers who sought to make films that were explicitly not like southern Nigerian videos and were closer to Hausa culture. In this search for alterity producers fell back on familiar cultural forms that were separate from southern Nigeria: soyayya books and Indian films.

Indian films and Hausa viewers

First imported by Lebanese cinema owners in the 1950s, by the early 1960s Indian films were, perhaps, the dominant film form in the north. Since that time Indian films have remained an integral part of the Nigerian media landscape and form the everyday media environment through which people move. Stickers of Indian stars emblazon trucks, cars, and bikes of the north. Popular stars are given Hausa nicknames, such as Sarkin Rawa (King of Dancing) for Govinda, or Dan daba mai lasin (licensed hooligan in the same way that James Bond is licensed to kill). Indian jewelry and clothing have influenced Hausa fashions and Indian film songs and stories have penetrated everyday Hausa popular culture (see Larkin, 1997).

In northern Nigeria there is a familiar refrain that Indian culture is "just like" Hausa culture. While indeed, there are many similarities between Hausa and "Indian culture" (at least how it is represented in Indian films) there are many differences, most obviously the fact that Indians are predominantly Hindu and Hausa are Muslim. The popularity of Indian films rests, in part, on this dialectic between difference and sameness that Indian culture is both like and quite unlike Hausa culture. It is the gap between difference and sameness, the ability to move between the two, that allows Indian films to function as a space for imaginative play in Hausa society. The intra Third World circulation of Indian film offers Hausa viewers a way of imaginatively engaging with forms of tradition different from their own at the same time as conceiving of a modernity that comes without the political and ideological significance of that of the West. Moreover, when Hausa youth rework Indian films within their own culture by adopting Indian fashions, by copying the music styles for religious purposes, or by using the filmic world of Indian sexual relations to probe the limitations within their own cultural world, they can do this without engaging with the heavy ideological load of "becoming Western."

The sense of similarity and difference is produced by the iconography and mode of address of the films themselves as well as by the ways in which Bollywood deploys a reified "culture" that acts as a foil against which Westernization in its myriad forms can be defined. Bollywood films place family and kinship at the center of narrative tension. Traditional dress is remarkably similar to that of Hausa: men dress in long kaftans similar to the Hausa dogon riga over which they wear long waistcoats much like the Hausa palmaran. Women dress in long sarees and scarves that veil their heads in accordance with Hausa moral ideas about feminine decorum. Indian films, particularly older films, express strict division between the sexes and between generations. Hausa audiences are not familiar with the main tropes of Indian religion, but they realize that the visual portrayal of Hindu religion and Indian tradition provides a cultural field that is frequently opposed to the spread of "Westernization" or modernity. It is this reified sense of tradition that Hausa refer to when they say that they "have culture" in a way that American films seem to lack. Britain and America are the structuring absences here and form the Other(s) against which Hausa can define their relation to Indian culture as similar. Hausa recognize the similarity in traditional dress; more, they realize the relational value of how one wears traditional dress. When characters code-switch from English to Hindi, when they elect to wear Western instead of Indian clothes, when they refuse to obey parents and follow their own desires, Indian films create a narrative in which action is based on moral choice. Ashis Nandy recognizes a communal mode of address in this moral choice in Indian film, arguing that commercial Indian cinema tends to "reaffirm the values that are being increasingly marginalized in public life by the language of the modernizing middle classes, values such as community ties, consensual non-contractual human relations, primacy of maternity over conjugality, priority of the mythic over the historical" (1995, p. 202). In short, the battle is against the values associated with Westernization.

It is the discourse around love, especially the tensions between arranged and love marriages, that has most influenced Hausa viewers. Indian films provide Hausa youth with an alternative style of sexual interaction, a different pattern of speech and bodily affect between the sexes. As these patterns of behavior have migrated to Hausa videos, the effect has been exhilarating. This migration is, of course, a matter of translation and accommodation and not merely copying. Like Indian films themselves, the act of borrowing plots, dance style, or visual effects entails detailed processes of rejection and addition, a stripping of superfluous detail and insertion of culturally relevant matter. Jeremy Tunstall's (1977) argument that Indian films were a dream factory locally assembling dreams manufactured 10,000 miles away (in America) has recently been decisively countered by the work of Tejaswini Ganti, who traces the transformations of narrative and form that go into the "copying" of an American film by an Indian one (Ganti, 2002). In the next section, I turn to this work of translation in the Hausa context, tracing the global flow of Indian film to Nigeria through the adoption of themes of love and song and dance sequences in Hausa video, concentrating on a transitional video, *In da So Da K'auna* (The Soul of My Heart, 1994) by the author/producer/director Ado Ahmad.

The introduction of new media forms always brings with it moments of ambivalence as the potential possibilities of the medium have to be reconciled within existing social and cultural norms. *In da* is a fascinating example of this ambivalence, especially when compared to the subsequent evolution of Hausa films. When *In da* was released in 1994, it was one of about four or five Hausa videos (there are less then ten Hausa feature films). In contrast, in 1999 alone, 125 Hausa videos were released in the market. *In da* inaugurates a new cultural form in a society where previously none existed, and introduces visual and narrative themes that have strong overlaps with Indian films. But because it is an innovation it foregrounds an uncertainty about how these themes should be handled and what the reception of this new form will be. *In da* treads delicately over themes that later videos represent unproblematically and is interesting because it is a transitional video that reveals the cultural work that goes into the process of cultural translation.

In da So Da K'auna

In da is set among the world of the urban elite in Kano, Nigeria. It follows the relationship between a rich girl, Sumayya (Ruk'ayya Mohammed), and a poor man, Mohammed. The theme of love and the sexual precociousness of the heroine signify the intertextual presence of Indian film. Sumayya initiates contact and pursues Mohammed, against his admonitions that their difference in status can never be overcome. In reality, as director Ahmad told me in an interview, Hausa women are expected to be sexually modest, and such an open pursuit would be socially unacceptable. His dilemma as a director was how to invoke the desire and romance of Hindi cinema, while at the same time preserving a Hausa moral universe. The film treads delicately through the rituals of courtship in ways that seem unimaginable when compared to contemporary videos.

In one of the central scenes of the film, Mohammed declares his love for Sumayya. Until this point he had resisted her advances, wary of the gulf between them in terms of wealth and status. The scene consists of a series of parallel edits between the two. It opens with the lovers separated in space and time. Mohammed is in his dormitory at school; Sumayya is in her bedroom writing a letter to Mohammed. Music plays in the background as Sumayya writes. As the film cuts to Mohammed reading her letter, the same music continues to play, linking the lovers across the rupture of space and time. As the scene continues, Mohammed writes back. Their experience of each other is mediated by writing. The scene heightens when, as Sumayya receives her letter from Mohammed, his face is superimposed over the letter. As his voice-over reads the contents, the camera zooms in on Sumayya and his face appears again, superimposed over an extreme close-up of Sumayya.

Ahmad here preserves sexual segregation in the diagetic space of the film. While Mohammed's body is absent from Sumayya's room, his physical presence is made manifest through his voice and his superimposed face, permitting the lovers to share the same cinematic frame. This is a careful game that allows Ahmad to allude to the intimacy and sexual interaction familiar to Hausa viewers from Indian films while keeping its sexual excess safely separate. Ahmad repeats this narrative device frequently in the film, separating lovers in space and establishing that separation through a series of parallel edits and the mediating device a letter, a tape, or even dreams to create a space for the lovers to unite through sound and montage.

The bedroom is a key space here. Sumayya first spies Mohammed as she passes him sitting outside with a group of friends. This is a male activity forbidden to Hausa women, especially wealthy ones, who are expected to remain inside the domestic space. Sumayya is narratively identified with her bedroom: this is where she writes her letter to Mohammed telling him she loves him; it is where she plays his tapes and where she returns to and listens to them after (later in the film) he tells her they should separate. Spatially and visually, then, Sumayya stays where a proper Hausa woman should be, restricted to the interior space of the house where men rarely are allowed to visit. It is only the fantasy of the film that allows her to move out of that space.

Visually these scenes are marked by restriction and immobility. In the song sequence I described in the introduction and in the scene where Sumayya first reads Mohammed's letter Sumayya is confined by both her bedroom and by the extreme close-up on her unmoving face. This restricted consummation of love is in stark contrast to the kinetic freedom of the dancing in Indian films. Here, the Hausa film stays within the bounds of cultural realism, adopting moral and bodily codes of Hausa expression, yet it always threatens to transgress that boundary with its constant mimetic reference to a fantasy world outside of local Hausa norms. This transgression was noted frequently by a group of young Hausa friends I watched the films with. The muted, minimalist nature of the love scenes seemed, to me, to bear little relation to the excess of Indian films, but for them the song scene was hilarious and immediately seemed culturally false. "Indian song!" one friend shouted as the scene began, "How can someone sing songs to a woman?" he asked in amused disgust. Hausa viewers know that a sequence such as this, or scenes in which couples openly declare their love for each other or even spending unchaperoned time together, go against the conventions of Hausa sexual interaction. For them, such scenes are obviously derived from the style of courtship in Indian films.

In da, in its emphasis on love and relationships, and on the spectacular use of song-and-dance sequences, represents an early attempt at what is rapidly becoming an elaborate genre in Hausa cultural life. In contemporary films, song–and-dance sequences are common and few betray the cultural and religious delicacy of this transitional film. To take one example, the film *Daskin da Ridi* (dir. Aminu Mohd. Sabo) includes a love song sequence between Indo (Hauwa Ali Dodo) and her lover Yarima (Nasir Ismail). The song sequence opens with a medium shot of the couple splashing each other at a lakeside. It then cuts to them holding hands and running toward the camera and then, cutting again, to the two of them, still holding hands, running up a small hill. Still in medium shot, they begin to dance and sing to each other. As the sequence progresses, Indo dances away from Yarima. He follows, chasing her playfully, and they splash each other again. Here the use of Indian film style is blatant and unashamed: the lovers change clothes frequently during the song sequence; Indo sings in a high-pitched voice more reminiscent of the famous Indian playback singer Lata Mangeshkar than of a Hausa singer, and the teasing, playful chasing is associated strongly with Hindi film. The difference from Ahmad's delicate balancing act seems immense. When Ahmad adapted *In Da* from his book he changed one of the scenes so that Sumayya dropped a ring into Mohammed's hand rather than putting it on his finger as she did in the book. Unsure if Hausa audiences would tolerate physical contact of any kind, he developed a style that allowed sharing of filmic space while preserving strict physical separation. In contrast, instead of being separated in space and time, nearly the entire Daskin sequence is filmed as a two-shot with both lovers constantly present in the frame.

In da and *Daskin* are revelatory of the deep intertextual influence that Indian films have had on the evolution of Hausa video film form. As I suggested elsewhere (Larkin, 1997), this influence has emerged because Indian films are useful repositories for Hausa audiences to engage with deeply felt tensions over the nature of individual freedom and familial responsibility, providing a safe imaginative space outside of the politicized contexts of western and southern Nigerian media. Indian films work for Hausa because they rest on a dialectic of presence and absence culturally similar to Hausa society but at the same time reassuringly distant. These films have allowed Hausa filmmakers to develop a genre of video films that are strikingly different from those of their southern Nigerian compatriots. This is not to say that the success of Hausa videos does not generate its own controversy. The engagement of Hausa with Indian films involves a sort of mimicry that carries with it the ambivalence of border crossing. As Hausa videos have boomed so has criticism of their cultural borrowing, leading in 2001 to a state ban on mixed-gender song sequences. Interestingly the intense criticism has not focused on Indian films (which are unaffected by any censorship) but on the Hausa written and visual forms that are accused of translating their themes into Hausa social life.

Conclusion

Contemporary Indian film theorists have insisted on the "Indianness" of Hindi film. Chakravarty (1993) has elaborated on structuralist film theory to argue that Hindi film has developed a "communal" mode of address that interpellates an individual spectator as part of a wider national or religious community rather than as an isolated viewer. Vasudevan (1993, 2000) and others have examined the concept of the "darsanic" mode of vision enacted in Indian film. They argue that the formal construction of filmic meaning depends upon mobilizing extra-filmic cultural and ritual modes of knowledge in the (Indian) audience at least in certain genres. These arguments emerge from the long-standing struggle against cultural imperialism and a desire to establish the cultural logics of a film form not totally subsumed by the Hollywood narrative and form. Studies of non-Western film therefore derived from the need to explicate the alterity and particularity of national cinemas partly, as Willemen has argued, to resist the "projective, universalizing, appropriation" that situates the Western experience of media as the model for the rest of the world (Willemen, 1991, p. 56; see also Shohat and Stam, 1994).

Similarly, in this essay, I have sought to decenter the Western experience of media, not by insisting on the alterity of Nigerian video but on its thoroughgoing intertextuality. At the same time, I have tried to place the historical and geographic spread of Hindi films at the center of an analysis of global media, rather than on the margins of a theory centered around Hollywood and the West (for a similar argument, see Ginsburg et al., 2002). Timothy Mitchell has recently argued that modernization continues to be commonly understood as a process begun and finished in Europe, that to be modern is to take part in a history defined by the West and against which "all other histories must establish their significance" (2000, p. 6). The privileging of Western media as the only "global" media has had a similar effect, downplaying the social significance of other long-standing global flows. By highlighting the global flow of Indian films, I do not mean to downplay the cultural and financial hegemony of Western media, especially since Indian films travel, in part, precisely because they counter Western media. I do want to suggest, however, that we must shift our focus to analyze the cultural flows of goods that do not necessarily have the West at their center.

The reasons Indian films travel and have traveled are diverse, evolving, and culturally specific. While southern Nigerians cite the popularity of Indian films among Hausa audiences as evidence of the northerners' "backwardness," for young British Asians sampling dance beats with Hindi film tunes, Indian films can be the source of a hip hybrid modernity (Sharma et al., 1997). Analyzing Indian films as global media entails revising the ways in which media scholars have tended to conceptualize national and transnational media. It necessitates revising our concept of African cinema to understand Indian films as part of African media. Similarly, the excellent work on the cultural particularity of Indian cinema, specifying the Indianness of Indian cinema, only goes partway in helping us to understand the phenomenal popularity of Hindi films in cultures, religions, and nations whose grasp of Indian and Hindu realities is weak. Central to this project should be the acceptance of diverse media environments in which audiences engage with heterogeneous cultural forms. Hausa youth, who listen to fundamentalist Islamic preaching, admire Steven Seagal, are captivated by the love tribulations of Salman Khan, and are voraciously consuming emerging Nigerian videos are part of a postcolonial media environment in which the Western domination is only a partial and contingent facet of global media flow.

Acknowledgements

This chapter benefited from critical comments by Meg McLagan and Birgit Meyer. Many of my ideas and knowledge about Indian films came from innumerable conversations with Teja Ganti. Likewise my work on Nigerian video has emerged in dialogic relation with Jon Haynes and Birgit Meyer. All three will recognize their presence here. I thank Ado Ahmad for his generosity and help in this research and I thank Ibrahim Sheme, Abdullah Uba Adamu, and Yusuf Adamu for their insights on Hausa video and for their untiring efforts to stimulate a critical cultural debate about Hausa media and culture. I also thank the editors for the careful work they put into this [chapter].

References

Abu-Lughod, Lila (2002) "Egyptian Melodrama, Technology of the Modern Subject?" In *Media Worlds: Anthropology on New Terrain*, ed. Faye Ginsburg, Lila Abu-Lughod, and Brian Larkin. Berkeley: University of California Press.

Chakravarty, Sumita (1993) *National Ideology in Indian Popular Cinema 1947–1987*. Austin: University of Texas Press.

Cham, Mbye, and Imruh Bakari (1996) *African Experiences of Cinema*. London: British Film Institute.

Diawara, Manthia (1992) *African Cinema: Politics and Culture*. Bloomington: Indiana University Press.

Furniss, Graham (1996) *Poetry, Prose and Popular Culture in Hausa*. Edinburgh: Edinburgh University Press.

Ganti, Tejaswini (2002) "The (H)Indianization of Hollywood by the Bombay Film Industry." In *Media Worlds: Anthropology on New Terrain*, ed. Faye Ginsburg, Lila Abu–Lughod, and Brian Larkin. Berkeley: University of California Press.

Ginsburg, Faye, Lila Abu-Lughod, and Brian Larkin, eds (2002) *Media Worlds: Anthropology on New Terrain*. Berkeley: University of California Press.

Haynes, Jonathan (2000) *Nigerian Video Films*. Athens: Ohio University Press.

Larkin, Brian (1997) "Indian Films and Nigerian Lovers: Love Stories, Electronic Media and the Creation of Parallel Modernities." *Africa* 67, no. 3: 406–440.

Marshall-Fratani, Ruth (1998) "Mediating the Global and the Local in Nigerian Pentecostalism." *Journal of Religion in Africa* 28, no. 3: 278–315.

Meyer, Birgit (1999) "Popular Ghanaian Cinema and 'African Heritage.'" *Africa Today* 46, no. 2: 93–114.

Meyer, Birgit (2003) "Ghanaian Popular Cinema and the Magic in and of Film." In *Magic and Modernity: Dialectics of Revelation and Concealment*, ed. B. Meyer and P. Pels. Stanford: Stanford University Press.

Mitchell, Timothy (2000) "The Stage of Modernity." In *Questions of Modernity*, ed. Timothy Mitchell. Minneapolis: University of Minnesota Press.

Nandy, Ashis (1995) *The Savage Freud: And Other Essays on Possible and Retrievable Selves*. Princeton: Princeton University Press.

Pines, Jim, and Paul Willemen, eds (1989) *Questions of Third Cinema*. London: British Film Institute.

Sharma, S. A. and J. Hutnyk (1997). *Disorienting Rhythms: The Politics of the New Asian Dance Music*. London: Zed Books.

Shohat, Ella, and Robert Stam (1994) *Unthinking Eurocentrism: Multiculturalism and the Media*. London: Routledge.

Tunstall, Jeremy (1977). *The Media Are American: Anglo-American Media in the World*. London: Constable.

Ukadike, Nwachukwu Frank (1994) *Black African Cinema*. Berkeley: University of California Press.

Ukah, Asonzeh F–K. (2000) "Advertising God: Nigerian (Christian) Video Films and the Power of Consumer Culture." Paper delivered to the Consultation on Religion and Media in Africa, Ghana Institute of Management and Public Administration (GIMPA), Greenhill, Accra, Ghana, May 20–27, 2000.

Vasudevan, Ravi (1993). "Shifting Codes, Dissolving Identities: The Hindi Social Film of the 1950s as Popular Culture." *Journal of Arts and Ideas*. 23/24 (January): 51–85.

Vasudevan, Ravi (2000) "The Political Culture of Address in a Transitional Cinema." In *Reinventing Film Studies*, ed. Christine Gledhill and Linda Williams. pp. 130–162. Oxford: Oxford University Press.

Willemen, Paul (1991) "Negotiating the Transition to Capitalism: The Case of *Andaz*." *East-West Film Journal* 5, no 1: 56–66.

18

'Ever since you've discovered the video, I've had no peace': diasporic spectators talk back to Bollywood *Masala*
by Jigna Desai

Bollywood is often seen as a manufacturer of desire and fantasy. For diasporic viewers, these fantasies are presumed to be nostalgia-tinged paeans to family, tradition, and a Hindu-nationalist nation. Simple conceptions of nostalgic viewing have been offered but cannot and do not provide adequate explanations for diasporic and global Bollywood. Beatrix Pfliderer and Lothar Lutze reductively posit that

> the broad-based appeal of Indian films is a cohesive force in a community, otherwise split by linguistic and cultural differences. For the first-generation immigrants who remain nostalgic for the home country these films, with their familiar sights and sounds, provide an emotional satisfaction, irrespective of the quality of the picture, which few other things can rival.
>
> [Pfliderer and Lutze 1985: 6]

Assessing the impact and function of Indian cinema raises questions of viewership and consumption in much more complicated ways than suggested here. However, while most analyses of the consumption of Indian cinema assume simple nostalgia as the primary impetus for viewing films, this essay suggests that this narrow and essentialist explanation has too long been used to describe heterogeneous, contra-dictory, and complex viewing practices. If we take Bollywood in relation to or inclusive of diasporic cinema, then the relationship between diasporas and the South Asian nation-state is brought into question. Diasporic Bollywood can be understood as interrogating nationalisms, regimes of the state, as well as practices associated with nostalgia, rather than simply reproducing a reterritorialized nation-alism.

In examining the South Asian Canadian film *Masala* [1991] by Srinivas Krishna, this chapter interrogates the relationship between diaspora and home-land, and specifically the most common paradigm assuming that diasporas and diasporic cultures [passively and nostalgically consume and then] duplicate homelands and their authentic cultures. [...] The film complicates not only the simple nostalgia often associated with diasporic belonging, but also the idea of the production of diaspora as constituted simply by displacement [rather than through active process of imagination and re-production]. [...] *Masala* foregrounds a diasporic spectatorship that challenges the idea of nostalgic and passive consumption of homeland cultural products and forwards the diasporic imaginary as the site performing and defining the relationship between the diaspora and the homeland. Furthermore, the film overturns the idea that diasporic cultures are constituted simply by the language, religions, or culture (cultural productions) of the homelands; *Masala* contests framing diasporic culture as a replication of an authentic original homeland, and instead suggests that they are mutually constituted. [...]

Opening with the explosion of an airplane (the unnamed fictionalized depiction of Air India flight 182), *Masala* interweaves the stories of several families in a Toronto Hindu community during the late eighties. In this diasporic hybrid film, interspersed are fantastical dream sequences or musical numbers from the perspective of various characters, as well as dialogues with the god Krishna via the VCR. The film balances its tragic plot lines with a comic tone and farcical characters. One of the storylines centers around the upper middle class couple Lallu (Saeed Jaffrey in one of three comic roles) and Bibi Solanki as they search for a wife for their medical student son Anil. The Solankis' lives are turned upside down by the appearance of Bibi's leather jacket clad, ex-junkie nephew Krishna whose nuclear family died on the plane. The Solankis also court the Canadian minister of multiculturalism in an attempt to gain power as political representatives of the Indian community. They, in turn, are courted by Bahuda Singh, a Sikh taxi driver and radical, who wants to store contraband in their shop basement. In exchange for hiding what they assume to be arms for the separatist Sikh struggle (but turn out to be cases of toilet paper), the Solankis accept a bribe of $500,000 and conspire to monopolize the Canadian and Sikh sari trade. But carefully laid plans go awry when the incompetent Mounties interfere.

Interwoven with this story is that of Lallubhai's poorer cousin Harry Tikkoo (also played by Jaffrey), a stamp-collecting postal carrier who has lost his wife in the bombing of the flight and lives with his two daughters Sashi and Rita, son Babu, and mother Shanti (played by Hindi film and theater actress Zohra Sehgal). When their house is at risk of foreclosure, the family responds in different ways: Harry resigns himself to fate and his stamp collection, Babu absorbs get-rich quick info-mercials and scrutinizes over the details of no money down real estate; and Shanti asks the deity Krishna (Jaffrey again), who appears on her VCR, to intervene and save her family from foreclosure. The deity Krishna obliges by placing in Tikkoo's possession a valuable and historical Canadian stamp later valued at $5 million. Predictably, the government attempts to procure the stamp in the name of "Canadian cultural heritage," a claim which avid philatelist Harry Tikkoo meets head-on with litigation. The situation is resolved only by wheeling and dealing compromises between his politically savvy daughter Sashi and the minister of multiculturalism. The protagonist Krishna further ties together the two families – he is Bibi Solanki's nephew and the lover of Tikkoo's daughter Rita. This mortal Krishna searches for meaning and location within the community and his identity, as he alternatively accepts and rejects Lallubhai's offers of a home, job, and money. Although he finally aligns himself with the Tikkoo family and larger South Asian community through his relationship with Rita, he is killed in a racist hate crime while protecting Tikkoo's son.

Camp as disidentification strategy

This next section evaluates cultural critiques and strategies, such as camp and resistant spectatorship, employed in diasporic cultural productions that seek to challenge dominant narratives. More specifically, it examines how diasporic texts and spectators articulate identification and disidentification processes from contested and contradictory spaces, and in doing so produce diasporic cultural politics. José Esteban Muñoz [1999], describing a similar form of cultural production and reception as disidentification, writes,

> Disidentification is about recycling and rethinking encoded meaning. The process of disidentification scrambles and reconstructs the encoded message of a cultural text in a fashion that exposes the encoded message's universalizing and exclusionary machinations and recircuits its workings to account for, include, and empower minority identities and identifications.
>
> [Muñoz 1999: 31]

Hence disidentification processes exhibited through camp mimic and parody, reconstructing dominant culture into hybrid productions in the interest of non-dominant politics.

In discussions of camp, the tendency is to discuss it either as style encoded in the cultural products or as the mode of reception by the viewer. This discussion, however, attempts to encompass both production and reception as a strategy of disidentification in *Masala*. [...] [As a] space of alternative order, plausibility, and belonging, theatrical camp allows the possibility of cultural critique within a circumscribed arena; and more importantly, it signifies the ability to disidentify with the dominant as a community.

Ethnic humor and kitsch have been employed as camp's corollaries to describe oppositional or negotiated engagements and re-presentations of dominant cultural discourses within ethnic and racial minority, as well as nonbourgeois, communities. Camp, ethnic humor, and kitsch have been primarily linked together because they share humor as the strategic mechanism of critique to disarm dominant discourses. Comedy provides a critique of dominant ideologies at the same time, as it remains intimate with the cultural discourses it interrogates. [...] Scholars such as Pamela Robertson [1999a, 1999b] and Muñoz [1999] have tried to rescue camp from charges of depoliticization and ahistoricity by attempting to build on its queer politics.

Similarly, in my employment of it as a cultural critique forged in South Asian diasporas, I posit camp as a historically and geopolitically located cultural strategy that evokes not only queer, but also racial and feminist politics in regard to transnational cultural production. Moreover, I emphasize camp's politics as deriving from poststructural challenges and deconstructions of fixed essential categories. Camp in its postmodern reincarnation is associated with a critique of authenticity: "If you can't be authentic (and you can't), if this doesn't feel like real life (and it doesn't), then you can be camp" (Bartlett [1999:] 182). In Bartlett's conceptualization of camp [...] reiteration functions as citation of an original that does not exist. Offering drag as an example, [Judith] Butler [1999] finds that while the performance cites that which is authorized as the original and therefore gains authority from the reference, it also rewrites and dismantles the originality of the original. [...] It is this aggrandized gap between original and copy that I suggest is probed and exploited by camp, especially in critiques of the authentic and the original.

[...] [C]amp can possibly be harnessed to analyze ironic performances of gendered national and racial identities that are connected to a diasporic politics of home and identity. [...] Thus, Robertson [1999a: 267] suggests that camp redefines and "historicizes these cultural products not just nostalgically but with a critical recognition of the temptation to nostalgia, rendering both the object and the nostalgia outmoded through an ironic, laughing distanciation". In *Masala*, camp can be seen as parodying the dominant construction of the relationship between the homeland and the diaspora, and questioning the authenticity and authority of the "original." Therefore the relationship between diaspora and homeland is not one of *a* copy to *the* original, but of copy to copy. Camp becomes a mode of recycling and remaking what is continually seen as an original into copies. In *Masala*, it creates repetition with difference, not in some apolitical postmodernism, but in the specificity of its material, political, and historical conditions.

While *Masala* plays on many political aspects of camp, such as gender, race, sexuality, and class, it is the combination of these associated with diasporic politics that I examine here. Following these revamped discourses of camp, I read *Masala* as producing a mode of camp that subverts dominant Indian cinema and Canadian cultural apparatus as originals [through an homage to and subversion of Bollywood.] This mode of camp works through rather than rejects these cultural forms. [In other words, the] film is intimately familiar with, engaged with, and invested in the subject of its critique. Krishna utilizes two popular genres of diasporic consumption – the masala film and the mythological serial epic (which I discuss shortly). Masala films are the intertextual films of Bollywood often with familiar structure, plot, sequences, and stock characters. While masalas develop and shift, the films are recognizable by their combination of romance, family drama, melodrama, and musical numbers. Viewers also recognize the actors who play certain character types, and follow the actors' lives very much like ongoing productions themselves. In fact, *Masala* makes several intertextual references to Bollywood cinema. The film features not only romance, social and family drama, but also fantastical musical sequences. In order to satirize and remobilize dominant

Indian cultural production, the film camps the masala films of Indian cinema, utilizing recognizable characters and plot (i.e. estranged hero reunited with community by heroine) and structural elements (e.g. music and dance sequences separate from the realist plot structure).

While I do not have the space to discuss fully the history, significance, and function of musical sequences in Hindi cinema, I want to briefly discuss their nondiegetic role in *Masala*. In masala films, the musical numbers, though often external to the plot, are integral to the exegesis of the film and expound on fantasies and desires. Additionally, musical numbers make visible the material production of the film against the conventions of the social realist melodramatic plot; therefore, these extravagant and expensively costumed scenes are often shot in settings that are removed from the location of the plot, in places such as Switzerland, Britain, and the United States. Yet, while Bollywood musical numbers are often set in the West, until recently they have seldom depicted desires identified as diasporic. *Masala*'s musical numbers function in the mode of Hindi cinema, as sites of fantasy and desire, but reiterated with difference. In *Masala*, Krishna mimics and reformulates the form of the musical numbers from Bollywood cinema (in addition to Western musicals and music videos) – Hindi and English lyrics, dance sequences with elaborate costume changes and backup dancers, lip-synched performances by the characters, and explicit expressions of desire. Three nondiegetic musical inserts occur in the film, the first focused on Rita, the second on Lallu Solanki singing his own version of "My Way," and the third on Anil Solanki.

The first dance number features Rita with Anil dancing in cowboy-western garb, in a courtesan outfit, and then in aviation gear flying a plane. The daydream sequence, an homage, satire, and remake of the musical sequences in masalas complete with costume and location changes, focuses around the idea of flying in three different segments. The first segment, set in a Western carnival, reflects American country and western culture and music sung in English; the second segment features an interior scene in which Rita sings in Hindi dressed in courtesan or nightclub dancer garb; and the third part, also sung in English, is a hybrid (third) space of a plane. The musical sequence evokes the masala and the Western musical, à la *Seven Brides for Seven Brothers* in ways that do not allow non-Bollywood viewers to immediately dismiss the film for its musical numbers. The film, though primarily evoking a Bollywood convention, slyly comments on the presence of musicals in Hollywood and Western cinemas. Thus, when the number switches to Hindi and the more ambiguous interior scene, the film firmly identifies Bollywood as a site of familiarity and intimacy. The final section of the song most strongly articulates the hybrid desire of diasporic subjects and the hybrid space of diasporic cinema. Rita finds the mobility she seeks flying among the clouds in her own plane as Anil floats by, persuaded by her English and Hindi beckonings to fly with her. She sings to Anil (and the audience) "to listen to your body, take charge of your life, and fly with the sky as our own." While the first two sections (via Hollywood and Bollywood) feature Anil as the object of her desire, the third section shifts the focus of Rita's desire. In the final segment, her desire is more complicated as she seeks escape and (upward) mobility through flying lessons and romance.

In *Masala*, the musical sequences reflect the various desires of characters: romantic escape and physical mobility through flying for Rita Tikkoo, financial and political power as well as fame through monopoly capitalism for Lallubhai Solanki, and the simultaneous fulfillment of patriarchal and bourgeois privilege in the form of a hypersexualized arranged marriage for Anil Solanki. More generally, the musical numbers indicate the ways in which the diasporic characters form the grammar of their desires from homeland, particularly Bollywood narratives. Rita's fantasy, for example, is triggered by a television announcement on the upcoming broadcast of a Hindi movie starring Amitabh Bachchan and Rekha. However, *Masala* presents diasporic subjects in the process of negotiating and rewriting these narratives, simultaneously critical of and complicit with these productions. The musical numbers, therefore, repeat with a difference these desires, but not as the copy of some original desire, but rather the recycled and remobilized dreams located in particular historical and cultural contexts.

The film's narrative challenges the desires presented in the musical numbers. In this sense, the film campily and ambiguously undermines identification processes and desires. Though the performances mimic the performances of Bollywood cinema, they are also undermined and ultimately fail for several characters. For Rita, her desire to escape the consequences of her intersectional positionality as a woman of color (experienced through the family, economic hardship, marginalized employment) and find happiness remains unfulfilled within the film, especially as her lover Krishna is killed in a racial hate crime. [...] Rita, neither mother nor wife, neither pilot nor leader of the youth wing of Asian multiculturalism, is poignantly displaced at the end of the film. *Masala* refuses to resolve diasporic displacement by redefining home through the heterosexual romance or upward mobility [...] [that has become the hallmark of the Bollywood genre known as the non-resident Indian (NRI) film]. All romances are terminated as possible conclusions to the film. [...] The film rejects these postcolonial, nationalist, and gendered resolutions to diaspora wherein women and their bodies become the sites of negotiating home [and homeland].

Instead, the critical diasporic viewer is left critiquing the heterosexual, nostalgic, and individualized subjectivities forwarded by dominant narratives to fill the absence of representation in the racist nation-state. *Masala* not only provides a feminist critique of diasporic patriarchy [...] [unlike Bollywood films such as *Dilwale Dulhania Le Jayenge*, it also forecloses the possibility of reproducing Indianness within the diaspora via normative gender roles and marriage]. [...] Through its queer-affiliated politics of camp, the film challenges the normative romantic narrative.

[...] The film itself provides the means for its own dissection and critique of camp and disidentification as cultural strategies. While the film balances the excesses of camp with the tragedy of death, it more importantly leaves Rita without desire or identification. At the end of the film, as Krishna lies bleeding to death as a victim of a racial hate crime, he ironically utters "this was not supposed to happen." Yet, throughout the film, Krishna's position has been as the "bad" subject rejecting the South Asian community and resisting Canadian assimilation in opposition to Anil's "good" subject who identifies with almost all aspects of dominant Canadian and Indian cultures. Reflexively undermining the character's masculine bravado and incredulity, Krishna the director wisecracks about the ending of the tragicomic film. But the film does not conclude there with the death of the hero, it continues beyond tragedy and comedy to the dilemma of the heroine. In this sense, *Masala* monitors and marks the limitations of camp and its dependence on mimicry, reiteration, and performance to resolve, exploring the possibilities and limitations of disidentification most clearly at the end through Rita. Furthermore, it reaches beyond the limitations of a white-normative camp through a repeated revealing of the violence of racial ideologies and practices. Alive, but without desires, she is neither the good nor bad subject. She is disidentified. [...]

Diasporic spectatorship

[...] *Masala* compels an analysis of the global trade and flow of (cultural) commodities, exploring the economics that enable these technological innovations to change the nature of diasporic relationship to the homeland. The film, therefore, additionally investigates the ways in which diasporas receive, consume, and make meaning of [Bollywood]. [...]

The film and culture industry participates in (re)presenting the homeland to the diaspora in a supposedly one-way relationship in which dominant cultural narratives are produced in the homeland and passively consumed by the diaspora. Thus, diasporic audiences are constructed as quiescent and nostalgic consumers of Bollywood cinema and televised serials. The films are seen as providing comfort or familiarity as emblems of national homeland culture. (In the opening scene of *Masala*, the viewers doze and sleepily watch the videos.) However, audiences do make "meaning" of the films in contradictory, negotiated, and sometimes oppositional ways. Diasporic viewers, for example, may position Bollywood or Indian vernacular cinema in opposition to dominant Hollywood and Western national cinemas or may subvert representations of India or diaspora to their own purposes. Most importantly, cinema significantly contributes to processes of diasporic identity formation, and thus is central to thinking through pleasure and power and how they impact subjectivity.

Film scholars have highlighted the necessity of understanding spectatorship in relation to subjectivity. Christian Metz [1975] relates the response of the spectator and the "look" produced through the film apparatus to processes of identification. Influenced by Metz, as well as Lacan and Althusser, feminist film scholar Laura Mulvey reconceives these discussions through gender, postulating female spectatorship within film theory, and asserting concepts such as the male gaze. Her formulation places the female spectator in the masochistic position of identifying with the female victim or in a crossidentified position with the male protagonist observed through a male gaze. Thus, Mulvey's [1975] essay "Visual Pleasure and Narrative Cinema" denies agency or desire to the subject, constructing the female spectator with the "choice" of identifying with the dominant male gaze or with the victimized and passive female, suggesting that only rejection of cinematic pleasure would forestall (heterosexual and patriarchal) complicity. Later, Mulvey [1981] redefines this proposition to assign the spectator a sense of agency in the process of viewing, but still operating within the Lacanian framework of dominant gender relations. Subsequently, feminist and queer studies scholars such as Chris Straayer [1996], Kaja Silverman [1992] and Teresea de Lauretis [1989] argue for appreci- ating and delineating the multiple ways (including cross-gender or bisexual identification and oscillating mobile identification) in which women and queer spectators can subvert, negotiate, undermine, as well as be interpellated by the spectatorial positioning and gaze of the film. [...]

Stuart Hall's [1980] theory for encoding and decoding dominant cultural texts from a nondominant position suggests that texts are encoded with denotative and connotative meanings which can be read in a variety of ways in relation to the dominant systems of representation. He offers three modes of decoding: (1) the dominant mode that reads dominant products following the dominant logic with which they are encoded, (2) the negotiated mode that operates by recognizing the constructedness of cultural products without necessarily challenging their authorial power, and (3) the resistant or oppositional mode that demystifies, deconstructs, and/or critiques dominant cultural production. The viewer, not bound to any one fixed position, therefore may slip and shift from one mode to another. Conse- quently, Hall's schema provides a paradigm for discussing the multiple and contradictory practices of engagement. Importantly, in Hall's work this paradigm is not established in order to suggest that each viewer has infinite agency and constantly displays resistance. I, in turn, do not employ this model to suggest simply that spectatorship is always negotiated and conflicted, but rather to examine how and when those shifts and negotiations occur.

Bollywood [...] can be seen to encode a national gaze, one in which the (deterritorialized) spectator aligns himself as part of the national narrative. The dominant mode in this case encodes and decodes national belonging in a form of citizen spectatorship along such lines as religion, gender, class, caste, and sexuality. This dominant mode is the only mode in which diasporic spectatorship is currently imagined and discussed. However, audience members, building on Hall's proposi- tions, may construct differing relationships with these national narratives, adopting dominant, negotiated, or resistant modes of decoding in relation to dis- identification processes. The diasporic spectator decoding dominant national narratives of Indian culture industries may acquiesce to the dominant mode, performing the role of displaced culturally different citizen (as non-resident Indian for example). In contrast, [...] diasporic spectatorship may also present noncoop- erative modes of decoding. Thus negotiated or resistant diasporic spectatorships may challenge the narratives of longing and belonging, opposing, resisting, and in *Masala*, literally talking back to the films. In this case, the film parodies the nostalgia that is associated with dominant diasporic spectatorship, marking di- asporic spectatorship as sometimes ironic, oppositional, and active. Krishna interjects the possibility of an active and adaptive diasporic spectator who does not disrupt the steady unidirectional transnational flow of Indian film distribution but complicates consumption. Therefore, in the film, the diaspora is not imagined as a passive audience eager to consume neatly packaged commodities exported from Bollywood industry, but as active translators and producers of meanings who accept, negotiate, and adapt ideologies.

Masala probes, prods, and transforms the position of the diasporic spectator of dominant national narratives in negotiated and resistant modes of decoding. *Masala* obviously refers to Indian cinema and in particular masala films through its title; additionally, the text also evokes the religious mythological film or serial through a fond satirical portrayal of the god Krishna as a campy and ineffectual deity. The live performance of religious drama has an extensive and diverse history throughout the subcontinent and consequently has led to development of the religious genre in cinema and television that owes many of its characteristics to these various dramatic traditions. (See Philip Lutgendorf [1990] on the development of the televised serial *Ramayan* in India and its relation to traditions of dramatic performance.) Hindu religious epics, especially the *Mahabharata* and the *Ramayana*, are incredibly popular televised serials in India and, as Marie Gillespie [1995] and Purnima Mankekar [1999] discuss, often watched as a mode of worshipping. In the film, the video deity Krishna from the opening scene reappears later when the grandmother Shanti Tikkoo prays and then worships by watching a video. The scene opens with Shanti praying to an idol of Krishna at a homemade altar. She pops in the video *Krishna* as part of her religious observations. His appearance through the VCR parodies Hindu émigrés' nostalgic attempts to recapture their national ties and to reproduce their cultural roots, as well as portray worshipping, through repeated viewings of the video epics.

It is significant that *Masala* references Krishna (and therefore more loosely the *Mahabharat*) rather than Rama (and the *Ramayan*). The latter serial was critiqued as communalist by many scholars, activists, and critics who saw it as furthering Hindu nationalism, while the former was seen as more inclusive and less hegemonically Hindu. The *Ramayan* (a variation of *Ramayana*), first telecast in 1987 on the state-run television channel Doordarshan and directed by well known Ramanand Sagar, received unprecedented ratings – an estimated astounding 80–100 million viewers (Lutgendorf [1990:] 136). (Non-Hindu religious minorities such as Sikhs and Muslims also watched the serials, though Purnima Mankekar [1999] in her ethnography on television watching argues they made different meanings of them.) The *Ramayan*, supposedly constructed out of multiple versions of the epic, nonetheless produced a Hindutva nationalist narrative of Lord Rama as noble king and Sita as dutiful wife. The serial's evocation of Ram Rajya (the rule of Rama) encodes the Hindu nationalist discourse of a contemporary Ram Rajya through the achievement of a pure Hindu national culture and a Hindu nation united by its devotion to Rama. Directed by the famous Bombay film director B. R. Chopra and also appearing on Doordarshan, the epic serial of the *Mahabharat* (the televised version of the *Mahabharata*) was seen by over 200 million viewers. In contrast to the *Ramayan*, however, *Mahabharat* questions the corruption of state power and its protection of its citizens along with praising devotion to Krishna. The story of two warring branches of a family, the *Mahabharat* ponders actions and their motivations through dialogues between the Pandavas and the Lord Krishna. In general, emphasizing politics, from state politics to family politics, the serial addresses national narratives of the "private" and "public" within a liberal framework. Instead of either a Hindu nationalist Rama or a politically Machiavellian Krishna, *Masala* features a playful and flirty deity who demands devotion but whose national identification is disruptive.

Krishna appears on the VCR as Shanti begins to watch and worship with the *Krishna* videotape. Watching the videotape constitutes both acts of prayer and pleasure in narrative. Gillespie [1995: 363] comments that for some faithful Asian British, in addition to providing entertainment, "viewing is thought to bring the gods into you and if, after watching, you can bring the gods into your dreams then it is considered to be like a divine visitation where blessings are bestowed and requests can be favored." Mankekar concurs that many viewers in India watched the religious serialized epics, especially the *Ramayan*, as if participating in a religious ritual; she gives the example of one family that bathed before the serial and watched with folded hands as if at a religious ceremony ([Mankekar 1999: 226). (Ironically, one might note that while *Masala* circulated in India to a limited but receptive audience, some fundamentalist and conservative Indians in Canada saw it as a sacrilegious portrayal of Krishna. Responding quite in the dominant mode, these diasporans condemned the movie on charges of religious blasphemy for its portrayals of the hybrid deity.)

In *Masala*, Shanti's viewing of the video thus represents not only a diasporic spectatorship, but also a different relationship between the devoted spectator and the deity. As the scene continues in the film, the camera cuts to the VCR and video and zooms to the TV, in which Krishna the god chants "Shanti Shanti." She (and the audience) soon realizes that he is addressing her in order to grant her a boon for her devotion. Though the dialogue that follows is satirically inflected by diasporic hybridity, the request and transaction are familiar tropes. Krishna, who deems himself "master of the airwaves," is a media-savvy diasporic hybrid sighing "oy vey" who later dons hockey gear, but nonetheless faithfully appears to reward devotees. Not to be outdone in hybridity, Shanti replies to his grant of a boon: "My son is a dreamer. He has lost his ambition and collects stamps. We are outsiders here. Make it like it was before we came to this country of no money down and supply side economics." Krishna apologizes that he cannot as he is outside of his jurisdiction, but promises to intervene to eliminate the risk of foreclosure. Krishna's appearance does not seem shocking or unnatural to viewers who are familiar with Hindu narratives in which gods materialize to grant rewards for devotion or *bhakti*. Mankekar ([1999: 199]) suggests that bhakti, "the personal relationship of surrender and absolute devotion between a devotee and the subject of her worship," is a prevalent mode of engagement with the television productions. Mankekar and Lutgendorf both comment on the actual act of *darsan* carried out in relation to the televised serials. Darsan, most simply defined, is the "visual perception of the sacred" (Eck quoted in Mankekar [1999:] 200).

In the case of *Masala*, the relationship between the viewer and the deity begins in the dominant mode of the devotee and the deity in the Hindu process of darsan; moreover, the darsanic gaze operates in the film in multiple ways. Furthermore, the viewing of religious serials raises questions about spectatorship and processes of identification as well. Thus, at another level, we may want to consider the darsanic gaze as a prevalent component of spectatorial looking in Hindi cinema. Finally, the darsanic relationship can also be considered metaphorically to describe the relationship between the diasporic spectator and the homeland culture.

Considering political, cultural, and material specificities, dominant Hindi cinema and television may well construct different spectatorships [within different geopolitical locations and different from] those of Hollywood cinema. [M. Madhava] Prasad ([2000: 74]) argues that the spectator of Hollywood cinema, an individualized position of voyeurism and identified with a figure in the narrative, is not typical of Hindi cinema. Instead, he sees the darsanic gaze as a model for spectatorship of Indian cinema in general. This scopic relationship is different than Western ones theorized in feminist film scholarship, for example, which assumes a spectator constituted by identification processes that desire to be and identify with the object of the gaze. In this scopic relationship between the deity and devotee, the deity bestows darsan upon the devotee who receives it. Prasad writes that the "practice signifies a mediated bringing to (god's) presence of the subject, who, by being seen by the divine image, comes to be included in the order instituted and supported by that divinity" ([2000:]75). Therefore, desire and identification in darsanic positioning are not based on the wanting or wanting to be like the object of the gaze. Prasad characterizes darsan as one in which

> the devotee's muteness is a requirement of the entire process. The devotee's look, moreover, is not one that seeks to locate the divinity. [...] It is not a look of verification but one that demonstrates its faith by seeing the divinity where only its image exists and by asking to be seen in turn.
>
> [Prasad 2000: 75]

While I am hesitant to characterize the Hindu darsanic gaze as a predominant and primary structure of spectating in Hindi cinema as does Prasad, I nonetheless recognize its potency in describing the scopic positions of the diasporic and religious spectator.

The darsanic relationship metaphorically describes (and differs from) the dominant mode of diasporic spectatorship. It seems possible to employ the darsanic relationship as an analogy for the diasporic spectator who gazes in devotion at the purity and splendor of the authentic national culture of the homeland that is mutely revered and worshipped as pure and sacred. The spectator's darsan therefore enacts the performative aspect of national and/or nostalgic diasporic identification processes. However, unlike the darsanic relationship that does not center on identification processes (i.e. symbolic identification), the diasporic relationship is an imaginary one in which the diasporic spectator desires and aspires to be like and imitate the original upon which it gazes. The spectator not only desires to be recognized by the authentic, but also to resemble and perform it.

Thus far, I have for the most part discussed the representations that depict what Hall might characterize as the dominant and negotiated modes of decoding texts. I want to turn now to the more resistant and oppositional modes. Attesting to the resistant modes of diasporic spectatorship, the director Krishna transforms the VCR from an instrument of passive viewing to an interactive hybrid apparatus that positions the diaspora as more than peripheral and passive. Shanti is at first surprised that Krishna begins to address and converse with her as she sits down to pray. But her interactions with Krishna quickly move from those of a mute, devout, and obedient devotee to those of a quick, confident, and technologically savvy spectator. Shanti freezes the deity in a pause when the doorbell rings and she is displeased with his handling of the situation. Diasporic Shanti is able to manipulate and control the representations produced by the homeland, her ability affirming the dialogic rather than unidirectional relationship between the diaspora and the homeland. While she is framed by the cinematic apparatus as the devoted subject within the framework of dominant narratives, as diasporic spectator Shanti literally interrupts the constructed gaze reformulating the intersubjective relationship. In contrast to the silence associated with darsan and the mute devotee looking only to be seen, this diasporic devotee calls forth and talks back to the god, challenging his power and authority. Later, when Shanti has mastered control of the darsan, beckoning Krishna when she pleases, Krishna complains "Ever since you discovered the video, I've had no peace." Shanti, an articulate diasporan, retorts that she's "had no justice." Here is diasporic spectatorship of dominant texts at its most resistant and oppositional. The film evokes the power of diasporic consumption and spectatorship in its ability not only to negotiate, resist, and oppose narratives, but also to rewrite them.

Of course, not all diasporic viewers resist or rewrite narratives in the same way. Shanti is a Hindu spectator and her negotiations and resistances differ from that of a resistant Sikh spectator position that challenges the Hindu-normative narration of the secular postcolonial Indian nation-state. When Krishna appears in all his adorned and armed glory in front of Bahuda Singh and Rita Solanki, who are trapped in the sari shop by the Mounties, he is dismissed by Singh. Singh deflates Krishna's bravado as out of place and time in diaspora and modernity. This second diasporic oppositional spectatorship allows us a different view of Shanti's spectatorship, which can now be critically reevaluated in light of its Hindu normativity and bourgeois cultural nationalist associations. The darsanic relationship between diaspora and homeland is reformulated by Singh who does more than talk back to homeland narratives; he writes them [albeit on toilet paper], therefore not only challenging the construction of diasporic spectatorship and consumption, but also of diasporic cultural production and circulation, thus further probing the *a priori* relationship between diaspora and homeland.

Conclusion

In this chapter, I have considered models of diaspora in which diasporas are understood as merely duplicating the culture of the homeland point of origin. I have reformulated paradigms in which the diaspora is taken to be merely an impure copy of the authentic original through a discussion of camp and resistant diasporic spectatorship as strategic critiques of dominant culture in diasporic cultural production. The film *Masala* poses possibilities of disidentification from and with dominant cultures (in this case Indian and Canadian) for diasporic subjects. [...]

Masala [...] question[s] the very formation of the question of displacement, challenging the normative narratives of diaspora that assume that they are formed from the act of displacement from a given homeland. It questions the anterior time of that construction and formulates diasporas and homelands as mutually and dialectically constituted. In doing so, the film, of course, undermines the logic of multiculturalism which assumes that identities and peoples are associated with the fixed sites of the homeland nation-state with "natural, primordial, and organic" connections between identity and place. The implications lead us to begin to reformulate diasporic and transnational studies, concentrating not on how diasporas replicate but produce and consume homelands and cultures. Finally and most importantly, *Masala* examines the relationship between nostalgia and cinema, suggesting how the [Bollywood] cinematic apparatus may function in diasporic processes of (dis)identification and in non/nostalgic viewing that imagine community.

References

Bartlett, Neil (1999) "Forgery." *Camp: Queer Aesthetics and the Performing Subject.* Ed. Fabio Cleto. Ann Arbor: University of Michigan Press, pp. 179–84.

Butler, Judith (1999) "Gender is Burning: Questions of Appropriation and Subversion." *Feminist Film Theory: A Reader.* Ed. Sue Thornham. New York: New York University Press, pp. 336–49.

de Lauretis, Teresa (1989) *Technologies of Gender: Essays on Theory, Film, and Fiction.* Bloomington: Indiana University Press.

Gillespie, Marie (1995) "Sacred Serials, Devotional Viewing, and Domestic Worship: A Case-Study in the Interpretation of Two TV Versions of the *Mahabharata* in a Hindu Family in West London." *To Be Continued ... Soap Operas Around the World.* Ed. Robert C. Allen. New York: Routledge, pp. 354–80.

Hall, Stuart (1980) "Encoding/Decoding." *Culture, Media, Language.* Ed. Stuart Hall, Dorothy Hobson, Andrew Lowe, and Paul Willis. London: Unwin Hyman, pp. 128–38.

Lutgendorf, Philip (1990) "Ramayan: The Video." *The Drama Review* 34(2): 127–76.

Mankekar, Purnima (1999) *Screening Culture, Viewing Politics: An Ethnography of Television, Womanhood, and Nation in Postcolonial India.* Durham: Duke University Press.

Metz, Christian (1975) "The Imaginary Signifier." Trans. Ben Brewster. *Screen* (Summer): 14–76.

Mulvey, Laura (1975) "Visual Pleasure and Narrative Cinema." *Screen* 16(1): 6–18.

Mulvey, Laura (1981) "Afterthoughts on 'Visual Pleasure and Narrative Cinema,' Inspired by *Duel in the Sun.*" *Framework* 15(17): 29–38.

Muñoz, José Esteban (1999) *Disidentifications: Queers of Color and the Performance of Politics*. Minneapolis: University of Minnesota Press.

Pfleiderer, Beatrix and Luther Lutze, eds (1985) *The Hindi Film: Agent and Re-agent of Cultural Change*. Delhi: Manohar.

Prasad, M. Madhava (2000) *Ideology of the Hindi Film: A Historical Construction*. Oxford: Oxford University Press.

Robertson, Pamela (1999a) "What Makes the Feminist Camp?" *Camp: Queer Aesthetics and the Performing Subject*. Ed. Fabio Cleto. Ann Arbor: University of Michigan Press, pp. 266–82.

Robertson, Pamela (1999b) "Mae West's Maids: Race, 'Authenticity,' and the Discourse of Camp." *Camp: Queer Aesthetics and the Performing Subject*. Ed. Fabio Cleto. Ann Arbor: University of Michigan Press, pp. 393–408.

Silverman, Kaja (1992) *Male Subjectivity at the Margins*. New York: Routledge.

Straayer, Chris (1996) *Deviant Eyes, Deviant Bodies: Sexual Re-Orientations in Film and Video*. New York: Columbia University Press.

19

Queer as *Desis*: secret politics of gender and sexuality in Bollywood films in diasporic urban ethnoscapes
by Rajinder Dudrah

The international mass media talked about the summer of Bollywood in Britain in 2002. In particular, the month of May saw the celebration of Bollywood-inspired fashion and lifestyle accessories at Selfridges stores in the cities of London and Manchester over 23 days. There was mainstream coverage leading up to and of this event on the television, on radio, in the press, the glossy style magazines, and the Sunday newspaper supplements.[1] The following month Andrew Lloyd Webber's musical *Bombay Dreams* opened at London's Apollo Victoria Theatre in June. Around this time also, pop stars were using the aesthetics of Bollywood cinema to add an extra zest to their music, videos, style and popular iconography: Basement Jaxx's song "Romeo" and Holly Valance's track "Kiss-Kiss" are just two cases in point.

Numerous other examples could be listed from British popular culture as taking up the Bollywood interest, which carried on over into 2003: the British television series *Footballers Wives*, and the British soap opera *Emmerdale Farm*, both aired on the ITV channel, consisted of Bollywood-inspired sets or sub-plots in which white characters were playing out their fantasies of the "other". High street fashion outlets such as Top Man, Top Shop and H&M were selling Bollywood-inspired clothes and accessories. Interestingly, the same style glossies (*Marie Clare*, *Cosmopolitan* and *Vanity Fair*) that were celebrating Bollywood in 2002 were claiming by 2003 that the Bollywood fashion-fad had now passed and that its readers should move on. In this context, "brown" was "the new black" but Bollywood in Britain was being celebrated amidst orientalist and exotic sensibilities in the British mainstream rather than for its emergence as a serious addition to popular culture (Aftab 2002).[2]

On the one hand, then, Bollywood received widespread publicity and was noticed in 2002, certainly in the UK and more widely in the international arena. On the other hand, however, what needs to be noted is that it was the camp, kitsch and fun aspects of Bollywood as safe commodification that was overplayed in a lot of the images and written text that accompanied the celebration and appropriation of Hindi cinema in Britain over the last few years. Camp, kitsch and fun have always been part of Bollywood cinema but these were used in simplistic ways in these aforementioned examples that the mainstream cultural and entertainment industries focused on. The colourful and larger than life references from Bollywood cinema were used as commodified kitsch and were therefore trivialised in the mainstream appropriation of Bollywood, rather than also acknowledging the cultural politics that Bollywood's camp and kitsch might enable.

Related to this celebration, and interestingly only until a few years ago, Bollywood cinema was being ridiculed or marginalised in serious western film scholarship. Bollywood has often been termed as a cinema of the masses, as trivial and everyday, something that the lower classes enjoy for basic pleasures.[3] This view of Bollywood was somewhat at odds in the actual commodification of Bollywood as a consumer experience, especially in the Selfridges store where loud and glittery aesthetic arrangements were used simply to sell goods and make a profit. For example, Bollywood film stars' designer bathrooms and bedrooms could be replicated in British homes for up to £15,000. Cushions and pillows were on sale from £40 up to £500 each. These are just two examples of the many high-priced items that were on sale. Clearly, this was a different kind of Bollywood mass audience (Asian and non-Asian) with a considerable amount of spending power that Selfridges was appealing to. The glitter, the colour, the music, the talks, the fashion all relating to popular Hindi cinema was well intentioned but what is being suggested here is that there was something not quite right about this particular celebration of Bollywood. The festivity espoused here was one where consumption was heralded as a privileged economic activity and the use of Bollywood as a cultural resource was underplayed, at best, if not missing altogether.

The point being made is that the camp and kitsch festivities around Bollywood in the summer months of 2002 was not just a construction of the Western cultural and entertainment industries but that they were drawing on, although in implicit ways, the aesthetics and conventions of Bollywood cinema and its popular culture without wanting to be overwhelmed by the cultural politics of Bollywood's camp and kitsch. What is being alluded to here is the difference that exists between the mainstream mass culture/corporate use of Bollywood as style to sell goods versus the use of the same aesthetic features by queer *desis* in the diaspora to read themselves back into Bollywood.[4] Thus, I am drawing attention to the difference between camp as commodity and camp as a mode to cultural and political identity.[5] In order to develop and differentiate between this comparison it is important to begin to think about the recent visibility of Bollywood as a cosmopolitan style that is linked to the queer use of Bollywood by its urban South Asian and diasporic audiences; and the queer use of Bollywood that facilitates it as the new site of the hip and the cool which then gets appropriated by the mainstream cultural and entertainment industries, albeit in simple ways. This chapter, then, is a call for the need to think about supplementing the apolitical uses of Bollywood style by exploring some of its hitherto unremarked political uses; and in this case as its political uses are made sense of and recreated by queer *desis*. This is a point of departure, a line of flight that takes us away from simple understandings of Bollywood cinema and its popular culture towards considering how queer *desis* appropriate Bollywood, and how this can be understood as different to white mainstream queering strategies that also draw on and recreate popular cultural references from Hollywood cinema, albeit in nuanced ways [...].

And it is really this idea of some of Bollywood's promiscuous features around the queer and camp pleasures of gender and sexuality that I want to explore in this chapter and particularly in the diasporic British Asian context as a site in the transnational circulation of Bollywood cinema and popular culture where transformations in meaning are contested and proclaimed. The aesthetics of Bollywood films, not least their songs and dances that are inscribed with culturally specific mores as well as slippages around gender and sexuality, warrant a consideration of them as promiscuously moving in and out and in between heteronormative and queer desires and sensibilities. As a way of moving towards that, I will consider how it is now possible to theoretically begin to conceptualise Bollywood in more complex and useful ways, as of late, a number of serious academic studies have appeared, giving the popular Hindi cinema of India its due attention (e.g. Appadurai 1996; Chakravarty 1996; Nandy 1998; Prasad 1998; Rajadhyaksha 1998; Kazmi 1999; Dwyer 2000; Vasudevan 2000; Mishra 2002; Virdi 2003). Whilst these authors deal with Bollywood cinema and its possible translations both in India and in the South Asian diasporas, they do not deal explicitly, if at all, with issues of gender and sexuality as also articulated in interpretations of popular Hindi cinema. I aim to suggest, therefore, how it might be possible to dialogue this recent scholarship with queer readings of Bollywood.

I want to use three authors here as starting points for my argument. The first is Ashis Nandy (1998) and the [second] is Madhava Prasad (1998). Both are based in India and have written about the popular Hindi cinema experience in the Indian sub-continent. I then want to move on to the work of Arjun Appadurai (1996) as a way to think about the translation of the Bollywood cinematic and popular cultural experience as amalgamated into the lives of its British Asian audiences, or for at least those audiences that partake in Bollywood-related activities. The chapter also engages with and brings into dialogue these three aforementioned studies with the small and important body of work that has appeared in recent years attempting to address queer readings of Bollywood cinema and delineates this research in terms of my own project (Gopinath 2000; Kavi 2000; Rao 2000; and Waugh 2001). Using a threefold theoretical excursion into Bollywood (developed via Nandy, Prasad and Appadurai), I will then offer a reading of the pleasures of gender and sexuality at a British Asian gay and lesbian club night as a way of arguing for the need to think more about the Bollywood experience in the South Asian diasporas, focusing in particular on song and dance sequences from the films that are translated and re-created.

Bollywood's secret politics of the everyman/woman

Let us begin with Ashis Nandy (1998). Nandy argues that popular Hindi cinema in India gives emphasis to the everyman/woman perspective by stressing the concerns of the people of the slums and the lower-middle classes, deploying their informal and tacit theories of politics and society. Using the example of cinema, Nandy is primarily concerned about the social tensions and cultural antagonisms between the bourgeoisie and the upper-middle classes on the one hand, and between the lower-middle classes and people living in the slums on the other. For Nandy, and rightly so, popular Hindi cinema comprises the ability to shock the bourgeoisie with the directness, vigour and crudeness of its language and representation, whilst also including them at the same time. As he goes on to say:

> An average, 'normal', Bombay film has to be, to the extent possible, everything to everyone. It has to cut across the myriad ethnicities and lifestyles of India and even of the world that impinges on India. The popular film is low-brow, modernizing India in all its complexity, sophistry, naivete and vulgarity. Studying popular film is studying Indian modernity at its rawest, its crudities laid bare by the fate of traditions in contemporary life and arts. Above all, it is studying caricatures of ourselves.
>
> (Nandy 1998: 7)

Nandy's idea about a caricature of selfhood can be usefully extended to think about a notion of self-identity, and in this case self-identity as formed through the consumption of Bollywood films, as implicated in a modernity of nation building in India. This includes ideas about looking to the future, i.e. the promise of post-independence India. And the disappointment when that promise is constantly broken as for example in communal riots, bride burning, corruption in public life and so forth. In short, Nandy invites us to think about how popular cinema not merely shapes and is shaped by politics, he invites us to think more about how it also *constitutes the language for a new form of politics* (my emphasis), one that includes historical and contemporary analysis, and elements of futurism. It is useful to develop and extend Nandy's idea of how we might start thinking about Bollywood as a resource for cultural politics in the South Asian diasporic context – to begin to think about the ways in which Bollywood cinema provides queer *desis* with semantic and visual cues through which they can engage in a cultural politics; but before we get to that via Appadurai, it is also important to heed the words of Madhava Prasad.

Ideology and Bollywood cinema

Prasad draws on Marxist ideas of ideology and applies them to popular Hindi cinema (Prasad 1998). He focuses on the 1970s period in India where he demonstrates that a change in social and political ideology was under way as part of the fragmentation of the post-independence national consensus which was brought about by shifts in political alignments. For Prasad, these shifts challenged the aesthetic conventions and mode of production of the Indian film industry of the time, causing it to split into three categories: those of art cinema, middle-brow cinema, and commercial cinema ([Prasad 1998:] 118). In terms of the latter category, commercial cinema or Bollywood, Prasad laments the status-quo affirming politics and ideology of this cinema as elaborated through practices of narrative codes and signification. Prasad's focus on Hindi cinema, then, is far from a simple celebration of Bollywood. It is more of a critique of its complicity in the social order of Indian life.

Now Prasad's viewpoint is fine up to a certain point as all popular texts have elements of the existing hegemonic social and cultural order mediated within their construction, but the best ones are often those that also challenge prevalent structures and suggest how things might be differently. This is something that Prasad lacks in his analysis of popular Hindi cinema. It is useful to hold on to Prasad's idea of the workings of Bollywood cinema as an ideology, not least extending it to think about Bollywood as espousing a predominantly heteronormative ideology. But perhaps it is a more useful formulation of ideology if we are able to think about how ideology exists and how it is able to be reworked and contested in and through the signs and codes which Bollywood cinema might offer us as constituting the language for a new form of politics (Nandy [1998]), especially one based around the queer pleasures of gender and sexuality. Furthermore, Prasad's critique of Bollywood cinema's role in hegemonic formation also operates within the realms of the nation state of India and seldom moves beyond this frame of reference. The appearance of Bollywood songs and dances in the queer spaces of the diaspora requires a careful consideration of the relationship of the homeland and its diaspora.[6]

Bollywood and diasporic mediascapes

Which leads us on to the work of Arjun Appadurai (1990; 1996). Whilst Nandy and Prasad write about the Indian context, we need to think more about how their useful ideas can be incorporated and translated in the Indian and South Asian diasporic context. This is where the cultural anthropology of Appadurai is instructive. Appadurai offers a useful perspective for understanding the relationship between cultural texts and social experience as elaborated through the concept of the imagination. To rephrase a point that I have just made, popular cultural texts (like Bollywood films) are such because they are embedded in the social worlds of its audiences, sometimes affirming the consensus of that social world and sometimes offering possibilities that suggest new worlds with different ways of being. Appadurai usefully argues that new possibilities are often suggested imaginatively through the production of, and in and through the performance of, sounds and images in texts.

Appadurai is interested in how global social flows are part of a 'disjunctive' order of economies and cultural signs which are played out between 'ethnoscapes' – the landscapes of living persons, and 'mediascapes' – 'image-centred, narrative based accounts of strips of reality' (Appadurai 1990: 298).

The availability of mediascapes for diasporic ethnic groups in their countries of settlement is especially pertinent here. Diasporic groups have undergone the experience of deterritorialisation from their places of origin and ethnic mediascapes, such as Bollywood, offer an audiovisual space for ideas of the homeland and its translations to be negotiated around the world in places of diasporic settlement (cf. Bhabha 1990).

It is the availability of the sounds and images for diasporic ethnic groups in centres of the developed world that help create a diasporic imaginary. This imaginary offers possibilities for comprehending the position of the diasporic subject in the country of settlement and the country of origin as informing each other to produce new sensibilities of being and belonging. Such sensibilities shift between local places of residence and global ideas and cultural flows. The diasporic imaginary becomes part of the everyday of diasporic subjects, as the sounds and images of mediascapes are integrated into the routines and rituals of daily life, as well as the struggles for settlement and belonging.

Appadurai's work, then, opens up the idea of the imagination and its offshoots of fantasy and desire as everyday social practices. The imagination as expressed through dream sequences, songs, music, television, film and stories offers a repertoire of possibilities to grasp the subjects' social world as it articulates with global ideas and cultural processes. This articulation allows for an engagement with the subjects' immediate sense of self, and for the contemplation of a wider set of possible lives. It is the articulation of the local and the global most notably in the cultural negotiations that are taking place between diasporic ideas about the countries of origin and ideas in the countries of settlement that I would like to draw attention to in this chapter. And in particular the imagination, as it unfolds fantasies and desires of making spaces anew for the diasporic subject particularly around the pleasures of queer gender and sexuality in and through the use of Bollywood cinema.

Nandy's cultural politics about nation building, Prasad's warnings of the workings of ideology and Appadurai's claims about the diasporic imagination can be usefully amalgamated together as a theoretical excursion in order to make sense of some of the translations of Bollywood cinema that are taking place in the diasporic urban ethnoscape of the British Asian gay and lesbian club night. Before moving on to an analysis of this site let us consider some queer readings of Bollywood cinema that have been put forward of late and that are taken up for further elaboration in this chapter as dialoguing with these three aforementioned cultural critics.

Queerying Bollywood

A special issue of the *Journal of Homosexuality* (Grossman 2000) first brought together a number of essays on queer Asian cinema. Whilst it was noted in this collection that East Asian cinemas, in particular films from Hong Kong and China, have been able to deal more overtly in aesthetic and in content with queer themes and representations, popular Indian cinema was still operating at the level of implicit queer suggestions in its aesthetics and content, or that it was at the moment of the queer audiences' rereading of the heteronormative film text that allowed for queer sensibilities to be detected and analysed. The essay by Gopinath (2000) is illuminating in this respect.

Gopinath draws on cultural theory and feminist audience studies to argue that Bollywood cinema provides queer diasporic audiences with the means by which to reimagine and reterritorialize the homeland by making it the locus of queer desire and pleasure. Gopinath is interested in tracing the possibilities of 'interpretive interventions and appropriations' made by queer diasporic audiences of Bollywood films (Gopinath 2000: 284). She employs a 'queer diasporic viewing practice' in order to see articulations of same-sex desire in particular examples of popular Hindi cinema throughout the diegesis of the film, even when the film has an orthodox heterosexual ending. Rather than attempt to look for gays and lesbians in Bollywood, she is more interested in 'looking for the moments emerging at the fissures of rigidly heterosexual structures that can be transformed into queer imaginings' [Gopinath 2000: 284]. Gopinath goes on to read the possibilities offered by images that suggest gay, lesbian and *hijra* or transgendered modes of being.

As a result of attempting such tracings, the queer diasporic subjectivity that is put forward by Gopinath is one that is created at the intersection of dominant Euro-American constructions of gay and lesbian identity that are brought into dialogue and negotiations between the spaces of multiple homes, communities and nations across the cultural registers of East and West. This is a useful formulation of the queer diasporic subjectivity as it does not privilege a European mode of understanding or performing of queer cultural identity at the cost of its Asian counterpart, but rather asks for an analysis of the communicative dialogue that is possible when the two different sensibilities interact. Whilst Gopinath [2000] posits this fascinating exchange between European and Asian queer cultural identity at a theoretical level she never really demonstrates the articulation of the two together. There is an implied tendency within the work of Gopinath to privilege the queer diaspora and readings taking place within it (i.e. as simply reformulating or re-imagining the homeland) without due consideration to the queer possibilities in the homeland, or the reciprocating social flows between the homeland and its diasporas. This is a facet of queer cultural and social phenomena that begs further discussion and analysis at the urban ethnoscape of the South Asian gay and lesbian club night and hence is offered as an addition to the work of Gopinath. The disjunctive flows (Appadurai [1996]) occurring between the homeland and the diaspora, and vice versa, are suggested in this chapter through a focus on the translations of Bollywood song and dance sequences in the queer club nights of the diaspora, and also of Bollywood cinema's increasing attention to queer themes and representations of late.

The essays by Rao (2000) and Kavi (2000) provide us with an understanding of some of the key motifs and signifying codes that feature throughout Bollywood films and how these are interpreted by its queer audiences against the grain of its ostensibly heterosexual intentions. For example, Rao describes the motifs of *yaar* (friend and/or lover) and *yaari* (friendship) as expressed in the lyrics and picturisation of song sequences as recapitulated in queer subculture as a yearning for an affectionate same-sex relationship (Rao 2000: 304–305). Kavi (2000) outlines the changing image of the male hero in Hindi films over some five decades to suggest how the contemporary male body, and in particular the semi-clad and gym-fit physique of nineties star Salman Khan, has been ambiguously paraded and eroticised on-screen whose appeal goes beyond straight pleasures and desires (Kavi 2000: 308–310). Furthermore, Rao reveals the social practices of urban Indian cinema-going that are also made queer in the dark spaces of the cinema hall patronised largely by men. Here, close physical contact and same-sex intimacy can and does occur, and as Rao describes one of his visits to the cinema, '[a]s the lights went off, the action began, so to speak, both on the screen and off it' (Rao [2000]: 304). Both, Rao and Kavi's work, then, suggest that the formulation of Indian queer identity, and gay urban Indian identity in particular, as taking shape in relation to the hierarchy of male sexuality (where men have greater access and control to public spaces over women in which to express their same-sex desires and displays, albeit implicitly) and where subversion and rereading against the grain of the heteronormative Bollywood diegesis is often a recurring strategy of existence. Extending this work, then, does the homosocial polysemy of popular film music also permit queer identifications in Bollywood's transnational circuits?

An essay by Thomas Waugh (2001), although published elsewhere, can also be considered alongside the above authors on queer Bollywood. Developing ideas of audience re-readings of same-sex sexual display and subversion in Hindi films, and by drawing on the anthropology of Lawrence Cohen's exploration of male same-sex activities in Benares, India (Cohen 1995a; 1995b), Waugh examines 'the profuse and rigidly ambiguous indigenous male-male sexual iconographies' in contemporary Bollywood cinema (Waugh 2001: 282). By exploring queer readings of male-buddy moments in films such as *Sholay* [Flames, 1975, dir. Ramesh Sippy] and *Main Khiladi Tu Anari* [I'm the Player You're the Amateur, 1994, dir. Sameer Malkan] Waugh outlines how the cultural devices of *khel* (play/playfulness) and *dosti* (friendship) between the on-screen heroes (which involves the use of sexual innuendos, phallic symbols and the close proximity of male bodies in intimate postures) can be understood as illustrating an implicit homosocial sphere that operates within and yet beyond the predominant heterosexual reel and real life ([Waugh 2001:] 292). Waugh usefully posits the devices of same-sex *khel* and *dosti* as challenging and redefining the rules of heterosexual gazes and desires as the dominant and only modes of seeing and interacting ([2001:] 293) that allow queer audiences to view themselves and their heroes and heroines as visible, invisible, polyvocal and ambiguous ([2001]: 296). Elaborating Waugh further, how does the transnational circulation of Hindi film music invest these textual ambiguities with new possibilities?

Let us now incorporate these queer readings of popular Hindi cinema within the theoretical framework of Nandy, Prasad and Appadurai as formulated above. Gopinath, Rao, Kavi and Waugh demonstrate specifically the sentiments of Nandy's hypotheses of popular Indian cinema as consisting of tacit or secret cultural politics relating to the projects of self-identity and nationhood. Such politics become further pressing and engaging as these queer readings insist that the queer in Bollywood needs to be included as part of the discussion of Bollywood cinema and its audiences. Rao, Kavi and Waugh emphasize local audiences in India and Gopinath attends to the queer diaspora. This chapter aims to tie the local and global manifestations of their implications together in a reciprocating dialogue by focusing on Bollywood's song and dance sequences in particular. Developing the work of Prasad how might we account for the reworking of the heterosexual ideology of gender and sexuality in queer Bollywood spaces? Using the insights of Appadurai, and in order to begin to understand the diasporic queer urban ethnoscape of the gay and lesbian club, to what extent are the social strategies and cultural devices as described by Gopinath, Rao, Kavi and Waugh also prevalent or translated at this site? Furthermore, is the homeland simply reconfigured in the queer diaspora (cf. Gopinath [2000]), or does the homeland also respond to the queer diaspora, or vice versa, albeit in secret ways?

The diasporic urban ethnoscape of the South Asian gay and lesbian club night

The qualitative and participant observations that I draw on and outline in this section were witnessed and experienced at a particular Asian gay and lesbian club in the UK. But the description that follows could be in any one of the growing Asian gay and lesbian club nights in Birmingham,[7] Leicester,[8] London,[9] or Manchester[10] (all UK-based), or even perhaps in New York[11] and elsewhere around the world where similar queer Bollywood activities are taking place. To think of such a club night as a diasporic urban ethnoscape (cf. Appadurai [1996]) one is drawing attention to the social and cultural interactions that manifest themselves between people and their mediascapes as drawing on signs and codes from various homelands that have travelled, metaphorically and literally, arriving at a new place of settlement and offering multiple or at least new modes of being that shift between the homeland and the place of residence. The description of the club night is offered here as a sketch or template from which to extrapolate and engage with some of the theoretical issues and queer textual readings that have been put forward earlier in the chapter.

'Live life for who u r . .' An advertising banner from the Manchester (UK) based Club Zindagi's website that draws on Bollywood aesthetics and advocates a message for social and sexual liberation.

To describe the club night as a 'gay and lesbian' one is in keeping with how those queer *desis* who regularly party-on at the club also choose to describe it as such. The term 'gay and lesbian', then, is used as a shorthand for the club's eclectic clientele along sexual lines but this is in no way to exclude its other diverse people, sexualities and personalities that also frequent the clubs. So here one is also thinking about Asian drag queens, *hijras* or transgendered people, cross-dressers, bisexuals, queer-friendly straights, straight couples, and those who might just be exploring or passing through.

The kinds of people that regularly attend this club in terms of their ethnic backgrounds include Asians (predominantly South Asians and also other Asians), Africans and Caribbeans, and Caucasians too – a metropolitan and racially diverse mixture of people. The diversity of participants here is indicative of the cultural and social exchanges and possibilities at this diasporic site of reception, a cosmopolitan nodal point on the transnational movement of Bollywood music. Thus, an understanding of queer *desi* identities in this club space needs to be located and explored through the different social registers and cultural perform- ances of race and ethnicity, gender and sexuality as articulating together.

The particular club venue under analysis has a large dance floor that is square in shape, somewhat similar to that of a high school hall. At the front of the dance hall is a raised stage. On the back wall of the stage there is a white canvas – similar to that of a small cinema screen; in fact it is the very screen upon which images from Bollywood movies are projected. Opposite the stage and on the other side of the dance floor the DJ booth is encased in a room with a large window that oversees the dance floor space. In the centre of the dance hall ceiling there is a large shiny disco ball that hangs as the centrepiece amidst the other sophisticated discotheque lighting. The club night is almost always on a Friday night, so there is a start of the weekend euphoria that is articulated with the prowess of gender and sexual pleasures. These pleasures include girls eyeing girls eyeing boys eyeing boys eyeing girls and more besides, and almost everyone is overcome with a fever to dance and exalt their bodily performances on the dance floor. One of the friends I was there with one night suggested to me that it was 'like being at an Indian wedding party after all the official ritual and ceremonies have taken place, only this is a bit more fun, more risky' – an affirmation of the secret politics (cf. Nandy [1998]) taking place at this venue if ever I had heard it. In fact there seems to be a continuity, here, as well as a new line of flight being suggested between the diaspora's appropriation of the homeland through Bollywood, and the queer diaspora's uses of the same. Bollywood movie clips and songs and dance are often used at South Asian weddings and other community gatherings such as beauty pageants throughout the diaspora. The articulation of social desires and fantasies to do with the homeland are also possibly similar – an articulation of referents from the homeland and the place of settlement professing dual or multiple cultural sensibilities. However, the issue of sexuality is often an unspoken and silent register in the enactment of cultural identities at the diasporic community events and this is where the queer desi club night offers an explicit engagement with issues of gender and sexuality. The space of the club is highlighted further as a marker of gender and sexual difference within the South Asian diaspora itself.

Gladrags are flaunted that aid the boys to look sharp and the girls sharper still. Vibrant colours and South Asian dress styles coalesce with the best of Western haute couture. The music is often a seventy percent mixture of Bollywood, bhangra, Arabic pop, rai and Anglo-Asian fusion music, and the remainder a blend of R 'n' B, ragga and hip hop, with the odd dash of pop thrown in for good measure; the tracks of Kylie Minogue often feature as pop classics in this club. These musical genres are significant not only in terms of their heralding of the club's audience's eclectic cultural identities, but also important in terms of how these genres signify certain kinds of identities that are enabled on the dance floor through a performance of the self. These can be fluid gender and sexual identities that are engaging with some of the more promiscuous melodies and lyrics of the songs from each of the genres, and at the same time urban and racialised identities being contemplated through a singing and dancing out of some of the more urban politicised lyrics and music – British bhangra, Anglo-Asian fusion, rap, ragga and hip hop being cases in point here (on the fusion and social possibilities of these music genres see Sharma, Hutnyk and Sharma 1996; Dudrah 2002). Not only, then, are South Asian gay and lesbian identities constructed and celebrated in the queer desi club space, but also they are articulated with issues of brown skins and ethnic identities that negotiate against the inequalities of racism, gender and sexuality that exist not only in heteronormative spaces but also in predominantly white gay and lesbian spaces too.[12] The queer desi club is also a safe space and its dance floor is an interesting outlet that allows these kinds of performances to take place. It signals a space for identities on the dance floor to be made mobile through a play of actual bodily movements and embodied gestures that use fantasy and the imagination to interact with the music to create a queer ambience in the club.

Amidst the performance of selves on the dance floor, one can also witness some of Bollywood's key motifs of *yaar* and *yaari* (Rao [2000]), the signifying codes of the eroticised body (Kavi [2000]) and the cultural devices of *khel* and *dosti* (Waugh [2001]) as acted out and translated in this diasporic space. In order to illustrate this performance I want to draw on three examples that I experienced and partook in at the club on more than one occasion. In the first example, I wish to recount the numerous Bollywood tracks that are often played, both in their original and remixed versions, that feature lyrics professing love for one's *yaar* or the desire to be in *yaari*. Thus, for instance, "Mera yaar bura dildaara ..." [My friend/lover is truly a braveheart], "Tu mera yaar, tu mera pyaar ..." [You are my friend/lover, you are my love], "Aaja ve mere yaar ..." [Come on my friend/lover]. Here, the notion of *yaar* and *yaari* is clearly reread and subverted from its heterosexual intentions and recast as a queer sensibility and display of same-sex affection. Moreover, this rereading of *yaar/yaari* is further complexified as it is translated amidst the fusion of different musical genres (Bollywood and bhangra beats and Afro-American rapping) and made sense of in this diaspora and cosmopolitan club space. Not only is the original heterosexual version of *yaar/yaari* changed into a queer one, the queer *yaar/yaari* is further nuanced according to its construction that takes place in the mixture of international music genres that signify new musical sounds and fluid social identities in the UK. Here, queer identities coalesce with and negotiate ethnic and racial identities too. In this way, the homosocial polysemy of popular Hindi film music permits queer identifications that are reworked and nuanced with added meaning and relevance for the lives of queer *desis* across Bollywood's transnational circuits.

In the second example, I wish to recall the movement of bodies whilst dancing and their relationship to the Bollywood images played on the white canvas on stage. On this occasion, the dance floor is packed and we are half-way through the club night. Sweating bodies are infused with cologne and decorated with colourful glitters that groove the night away. One track comes to an end and the other begins. The new track is "Chaiyya, Chaiyya" [Walk in the Shadow of Love] from the film *Dil Se ...* [From the Heart, 1998, dir. Mani Ratnam]. The crowd shouts in excitement and begins to mimic the dance steps of actor Shahrukh Khan and his gypsy-girl consort (Malaika Arora-Khan) from the film, with hips swaying, pelvics thrusting and arms waving about in the air – this is one of their queer performances to shout out to and to make their own.[13] A momentary lapse occurs between the on-screen mediascape in the club and the song playing over the club's sound system. The audio of the song is a few seconds ahead of its projected image. The *chaiyya, chaiyya* clip on-screen has also been edited and is interspersed with songs from other Bollywood movies; of note is the flashing torso of Salman Khan gyrating. The dancing bodies on the dance floor as a few paces ahead of the dancing figures in the moving image during this moment is telling of the ways in which gender and sexual pleasures are aestheticised in different yet related ways. In the film Shahrukh Khan is mesmerised after having just met his on-screen heroine, Manisha Koirala, and breaks into song and dance affirming his new found heterosexual love. In the club the crowd also register this filmic moment and yet simultaneously reclaim and acknowledge the song as one of their queer anthems. The straight aesthetics on the screen are there to be seen as part of the literal backdrop to the club's setting and also to be mimicked and performed in queer ways – the singing and dancing on the dance floor is a few paces ahead of its on-screen version both literally and symbolically. The further editing of the *Dil Se ...* film clip with images of the naked torso of Salman Khan also deliberately queers and displaces the dominant straight aesthetics of the clip to enable new pleasures around gender, sexuality and the dancing of the body. The physical use of the body in dance, here, plays with conventional and expected patterns of heteronormativity. Signifiers of perceived masculine and feminine traits are used by both genders, mingled with Bollywood, Westernised and black urban street moves and queer displays of eclectic sexual identities, thereby creating a stylised camp performance. Within this performativity a caricature of conservative heterosexual expectations of how men and women should conduct themselves as representing their sexualities is also set into play. Males on males, females on females and male and females alternate with each other playing up "butch" and "passive" body movements and dance gestures and thereby hyperbole normative gender and sexual ideologies. Through feminine and masculine screams, yells and screeches and through the repertoire of their dress and vivid colours – almost costume-like – the club revellers also exaggerate and play up their own camp performances. Caricature, in this instance, works to re-create a performance about heterosexuality and its limits in order to make way for their queer semantics, and also to render a specific performativity about South Asian queerness in the club space.

The third instance exemplifies how *khel* takes place in the club and consolidates an understanding of *dosti* that is communicative in a social cementing sense and also in terms of its queer sexual connotations. The track *Koyi Kahen* [People Will Say] from the film *Dil Chahta Hai* [What the Heart Wants, 2001, dir. Farhan Akhtar] is played which draws the dancing crowd together singing almost in unison and jumping up and down in ways that are similar to how the lead actors and actresses dance in the filmed version.[14] Boys turn to dance with boys and girls with girls as well as the exchange of other gender and sexuality combinations. The *dosti* that is forged in this *khel* is commensurate with the lyrics of the song. In the movie the singers proclaim their disavowal of rigid societal norms and elder and peer generational pressures in order to forge a new way for themselves. In the space of the queer South Asian club the translations here are quite straightforward to decipher. *Dosti*/friendships are made in the *khel*/play about being different to straight societal norms and expectations. A cultural solidarity is exhibited in and through the *dostis* that profess gender and sexual difference on the dance floor and partake in a promiscuous *khel* wherein several bodies are up close and personal – touching, sweating, and being sexually suggestive. Yet, the *khel* is promiscuous only up to a point. Like many other devices of playfulness in South Asian cultural traditions the *khel* here also works through suggestion and within its own boundary limits. Whilst there is full-on same-sex kissing and touching it very rarely becomes X-rated. The suggestion of same-sex sexual display and affection is far more titillating and provocative than going beyond it (i.e. flirtations of sexual innuendos and the close proximity of bodies in intimate postures and gestures). Also of interesting note here is that there is no dark room in the club, and this appears to be the case also for the other UK *desi* gay and lesbian clubs that I attended.[15] Whereas the heterosexual ideology of Bollywood is done away with in the *khel* of the club, the signs and codes of how heterosexuality is coded and performed in Bollywood, as imposing an order of gender and sexual conduct, is reconfigured by Bollywood's queer patrons.[16] In mainstream Bollywood one rarely sees explicit sexual exhibitionism as it is often laced with coyness, innuendos, and metaphors of suggestion. This is also the case in the South Asian gay and lesbian club. It appears that the same songs and dances in Bollywood films that are used to signify sexual effects as a way of getting around Indian censorship rules are also used in a similar way to avert the censure of heteronormativity; through bodily decorum, playfulness and same-sex sexual suggestions performed on the dance floor. And herein lies another of one the differences between the diasporic South Asian gay and lesbian scene and its white western counterpart. Public displays of sexual mores that are an exploration and illustration of selfhood are deliberately coded through Bolly-wood mores as providing a social etiquette through which to conduct oneself in the club space. This public etiquette stresses cultural difference in relation to other queer scenes at the point of sexually avant garde and liberating performances that operate within cultural codes of excess and celebration (i.e. of Bollywood), and certainly not X-rated overspill.

Just as there are differences and cultural specificities, there are also similarities to be drawn here between white gay and lesbian club culture and its use of mainstream pop songs and Hollywood film stars to express different genders and sexualities. For example, feminist readings of Hollywood have drawn our attention to a number of extra-cinematic identificatory practices (cf. Stacey 1993). These include posturing, mimicry, dressing-up, irony, exaggeration, performing oneself like a star, deploying the stars' masculine/feminine qualities, using the star's sexual appeal, and relishing in how the star has excelled at surviving the social order of the day in the reel/diegetic world on the screen, and perhaps even in real/actual life.

Equally, Bollywood has no limit to the number of its stars that have achieved demi-God status in South Asia and its diasporic societies over the years, both male and female, and who have been appropriated by different sections of Bollywood's audiences, not least its gay and lesbian audiences.[17]

In addition to these star qualities and the appropriation of Bollywood idols, central to the performance of gender and sexualities in the South Asian gay and lesbian club is a notion of pleasure that is important for sections of Bollywood's queer diasporic audiences. In particular I am drawing on the notion of pleasure as it has been widely used in the discipline of Cultural Studies where it has focused on the pleasures of the text (e.g. Regan 1992). Here, pleasures of the text have been described through the ability of the audience's cultural capital to read, partake and identify with particular forms of popular culture. It is an idea of the audience's familiarity with the text's codes and conventions that contribute to an aesthetic, emotional and, as in the case of dance as cited above, a physical enjoyment of the form. In the queer South Asian club space the pleasures of the Bollywood film text are also extended and translated in terms of queer desires and sensibilities of *yaar/yaari*, *dosti* and *khel*, and the performativity of the eroticised body.

Conclusion: is the queer re-read in Bollywood, or is Bollywood inherently queer?

Let us finally consider whether the homeland is simply reconfigured in the queer diaspora (cf. Gopinath [2000]), or whether the homeland also responds to the queer diaspora, or vice versa, albeit in secret ways? What has been proposed in this chapter is that a simple reading of Bollywood's use in the diaspora as being subverted and re-read should be resisted. Evidently, [...] there are aspects of subversion and translation of Bollywood's heteronormative boy-meets-girl romances that are taking place in the queer diaspora. Yet this is nothing unique as queer cultures, almost everywhere, often appropriate straight social texts and discourses for their own means and thereby create a new language through which to communicate and express themselves. The "newness" in the queer South Asian diaspora is its constituting of a tacit and secret politics that is in dialogue with its Bollywood sources as informing and producing each other anew. The secret politics are also becoming more visible and encoded into the workings of mainstream Bollywood that suggest a reconfiguring of the relationship between the homeland and the diaspora in a more problematic and complex way. In order to elaborate on this I want to suggest two lines of inquiry for further research and analysis.

First, the aesthetic and traditional conventions of Bollywood need to be considered further as hybrid, "queer" and "camp" from their outset.[18] In particular I am thinking of how the early development of popular Indian cinema has always been eclectic, even if it has not been acknowledged as such. The early turn of the twentieth-century films (e.g. *Raja Harischandra*, 1913, dir. Phalke) had either men playing female roles or prostitutes were hired as actresses; acting in Indian cinema of the time was considered a social taboo for "respectable" women. Such films were paradoxically used to create and confirm a social order of heterosexuality and patriarchy, but how might one also account for the early queer desires and secret politics that were enabled by such transgressions on-screen that were composed in the articulation of the "camp" and "non-camp", the "queer" and the "straight"? If such a line of thought can be developed further out of historical and contemporary inquiry, is it possible to argue that South Asian queer spaces, both in the diaspora and in the homeland, not only signify from and re-read or appropriate Bollywood, but that such queer signs are and have been pre-existing in the formation of Bollywood from its outset? Examples for further testing and elaboration could include the "camp" theatrical performances of early Hindu mythologicals where men dressed up to play women characters, and early heroines who played masculine and "butch" action roles.[19] The Parsi and regional theatres which included stories situated in the *khota* (courtesan houses and brothels) with their coexisting narratives of heterosexuality and lesbianism is another possible instance.[20] Bringing the ideas of Nandy [1998] into conversation with the queer readings put forward here, then, it is possible to argue that in a caricature of selfhood queer Bollywood is not only a matter of the "queer readings" that "queer audiences" bring to the text (as put forward by Gopinath [2000]) but rather Bollywood's investment in caricature makes it a rich cultural resource where meanings of "queer" and "camp" can be readily created and contested. Thus even the manifest heteronormative content is queered by representational excess that marginalizes questions of authenticity (of straightness for example) since both queer and straight are equally caricatured; they are re-presentations of an ordered and constructed world (i.e of heteronormativity) and its slippages that makes spaces for insights into new worlds (of queer).

The second line of thought acknowledges the shift and changes that are taking place in more recent Bollywood films in which queer themes and representations are becoming slightly more visible and perhaps more fluid, and therefore is Bollywood listening to and in dialogue with queer South Asian cultural politics both in the homeland and in the diaspora, although at an early embryonic stage? Two brief examples will suffice here. First, the queer *khel* between Aman Mathur (Shahrukh Khan) and Rohit Patel (Saif Ali Khan) in *Kal Ho Naa Ho* [Tomorrow May Not Be, 2003, dir. Nikhil Advani], set in the diasporic city of New York, that is wrongly interpreted by Rohit's housemaid that they are in a gay relationship. This film sets up a heterosexual love triangle between Aman, Rohit and Naina Catherine Kapur Patel (Preity Zinta). However, sexual innuendos between the two male characters and scenes of their bodies in close intimate proximity to each other abound in this film. The two characters also flirt with camp performativity and dance together with added suggestions of homosexuality, albeit through the use of humour as a backdrop. Even the film's climax is open to a promiscuous queer reading. As Aman lies dying on a hospital bed, the two male characters reach a compromise over their individual love for Naina, whilst holding and embracing each other closely. During this climax, Naina is seen outside of the frame of the two characters, outside of the hospital room in which Aman and Rohit make their private agreement with each other.

Shahrukh Khan (left) and Saif Ali Khan in queer Khel in the film Kal Ho Naa Ho.

Secondly, the conversation that takes place between Aman (Rahul Bose) and Chameli (Kareena Kapoor), in the film *Chameli* [Scented/Healing Flower, 2004, dir. Sudhir Mishra], while they are sheltering from the heavy rain under the same archway in Mumbai and begin to get to know each other. When Aman realises that one of Chameli's friends, Raja, is gay and is in love with a male cross-dresser, Hasina, he initially appears surprised. During their conversation, Chameli asks Aman whether he feels that there is something wrong with two men in a relationship together. Aman hesitantly responds "no" and qualifies his response saying he has other male friends who are gay. Chameli goes on to declare that there is nothing "abnormal" about gay relationships as long as there is love in them – "*bus pyar hona chayen*". Reasons for such noticeable queer representations in contemporary Bollywood cinema owe much to the rise of queer politics in India,[21] and the courting of the diaspora as an audience for Bollywood. However, what needs to be investigated further is that are genuine queer possibilities opening up here, or are they simply subsumed within the dominant heteronormative workings of Bollywood cinema?

As a way of conclusion let us return to the opening remarks made about the Selfridges celebration of Bollywood popular culture that has been juxtaposed with the diasporic ethnoscape of the queer South Asian club. The example of Bollywood film and music culture's translation at the gay and lesbian club are telling of the secret politics that the Selfridges store could only take on board in very subtle ways. The Selfridges camp and kitsch that was lifted from Bollywood was not quite right. It was not sure of how to fully deal with these aspects other than through mere suggestion, and it focused more on making a profit by trying to cater to the highest spending pound and thereby making the consumption of Bollywood safe and yet exotic. What needs to be observed and commented on is precisely how queer culture is increasingly being appropriated to market and promote consumption. Thus, what happens to camp when it turns into commodity? One is not arguing that the Asian gay and lesbian clubs are the only place for different and potentially progressive Bollywood-influenced genders and sexualities to flourish, but that they are a space in which the diasporic imaginary can shift more usefully between the place of residence or the new homeland (i.e. Britain) and the originating homeland (i.e. South Asia), and wherein both the homeland and the diaspora can be brought into dialogue with each other in ways beyond the exotica of orientalism. Furthermore, the use of Bollywood in the gay and lesbian club scene illustrates one of the internal fissures of the wider South Asian diaspora where considerations of gender and sexual difference can often be marginalized or excluded.[22] The direct enactment and performance of gender and sexuality in the queer club space interrogates the nation and its diaspora as in need of reconfiguration through an engagement with such issues. In these ways, the social interactions taking place at the gay and lesbian club also more appropriately draw on, flaunt with, and re-create the original queer and hybrid composite aesthetic and traditional forms of the popular Hindi cinema in ways that have yet to be understood more thoroughly.

Notes

1 See for instance *Life: Observer Magazine*, 7 April 2002, London.
2 Bollywood as a source of entertainment was signalled as "other", a recurrent feature of orientalism (Said 1978), and as from a faraway place, India and the East more generally, that was made available in the UK thereby playing up to notions of exotica in the contemporary present.
3 For an example of such film criticism see David Cook's (1996) *A History of Narrative Film*, p. 861.
4 The term "desi" is used by diasporic South Asians from the South Asian vernacular to refer to themselves as having socio-cultural attachments to their respective homelands.
5 Throughout this chapter, "queer" is used as an umbrella term exploring the social construction and performance of different gender and sexual identities such as gay, lesbian, bisexual, and heterosexual. It also involves a critique and displacement of heteronormative structures and predominantly straight desires. The term "camp" refers to the in-betweeness and slippages in the performance of gender and sexual identities drawing attention to the ambivalences and problematics in the performance of gender and sexual identities as not quite coherent or whole.
6 The term "diaspora" is used throughout to refer to a social condition that brings into play the co-ordinates of the place of origin and the place of

settlement and a diasporic consciousness that is created and shifts between these two places through actual and imagined cultural movements. I am less interested in nostalgic understandings of and attachments to the homeland through Bollywood cinema and am more interested in exploring the possibilities for new social and cultural formations that render problematic any simple formulations of the homeland and its diaspora. This encourages us to make a point of departure, a new line of flight as it were.

7 See the Birmingham South Asian gay and lesbian club night's website at www.saathinight.com, accessed 25 February 2004.

8 See the Leicester South Asian gay and lesbian club night's website at www.clubishq.com, accessed 25 February 2004.

9 See the London South Asian gay and lesbian club night's website at www.club-kali.co.uk, accessed 25 February 2004.

10 See the Manchester South Asian gay and lesbian club night's website at www.clubzindagi.com, accessed 25 February 2004.

11 See the New York City South Asian gay and lesbian club night's website at www.sholayevents.com, accessed 25 February 2004. Of note here, is the work of Sunaina Maira (2002) on South Asian American youth club culture in New York City. Although she acknowledges in passing the existence of separate queer desi club nights and also the existence of queer *desis* at predominantly heterosexual club events in NYC, she concurs that queer desi parties in North America exist as parallel to 'often aggressively heterosexual bhangra remix youth subculture where queerness was invisible' (Maira 2002: 47–48). The emergence of queer desi club nights in the diaspora should be understood, in part, as a call for safe spaces amidst the racism and exoticisation of brown bodies in predominantly white queer clubs, and also as a response to (male) aggressive behaviour prevalent at predominantly heterosexual Bhangra nights that were in swing since the mid to late eighties.

12 See for example the collection of essays on Asian American sexualities that discuss, amongst other things, the formation of Asian queer identities in relation to white racism in its heteronormative and queer forms (Leong 1996).

13 In the film this song is picturised on a moving train (that can be read as phallic) making its journey through picturesque virginal countryside. See Kabir (2003) for a further reading of the film's extensive use of Sufi mysticism as articulated within the film's narrative, and especially in its song and dance sequences, about the struggle for love amidst Indian state politics.

14 In the film the lead players are Aamir Khan, Akshaye Khanna, Preity Zinta and Saif Ali Khan.

15 A "dark room" is a designated area within a gay and lesbian club often separate to the dance floor where people can enter and partake in or observe numerous kinds of sexual escapades.

16 See Prasad (1994) for an account of how Bollywood songs and dancing are used in the context of Indian film censorship rules as standing in for the real thing. Prasad asserts that it is patriarchal authority that is promulgated in the scopophilia of these song and dance numbers.

17 Kavi, for example, describes the queerness of Bollywood star Dev Anand as possessing "a strange effeminacy that bordered on the child-like" and "had an innocuous sensuality about him that conspired to make his heroine into an oedipal figure" (Kavi 2000: 308).

18 I fully acknowledge here that this line of thought is brief and highly speculative and begs the need for further research to prove or disprove the claims being put forward in this instance about early Hindi cinema. Thus, by labelling the terms "queer" and "camp" in literal and metaphoric scare quotes (" ") I wish to draw attention to the possibilities in which these terms can and might not operate in ways that we understand their use in Western culture. This points towards a line of flight that requires us to think more about the similarities and dissimilarities of queer and camp cultures in South Asia and elsewhere.

19 I am thinking here of the films starring the stunt actress Nadia from the early 1930s and onwards.

20 For example, Veena Oldenburg (1989) drawing on interviews with retired courtesans in Lucknow, India, argues that most courtesans, as well as many prostitutes, practised lesbianism (*chapat bazi*), considering heterosexuality to be work and not pleasure.

21 See for instance the Gay Bombay website, www.gaybombay.cc

22 The recent history of the struggle of the New York based South Asian Lesbian and Gay Association (SALGA) to be included in the India Day Parade on the streets of Manhattan is a case in point. See Svati P. Shah, "Out and Radical: New Directions for Progressive Organizing", www.samarmagazine.org/archive/article.php?id=60, accessed 13 August 2004.

References

Aftab, Kaleem (2002) 'Brown: the New Black! Bollywood in Britain', *Critical Quarterly*, 44, 3, pp.88–98.

Appadurai, Arjun (1990) 'Disjuncture and Difference in the Global Cultural Economy' in Mike Featherstone ed. *Global Culture*. London: Sage.

Appadurai, Arjun (1996) *Modernity at Large: Cultural Dimensions of Globalisation*. Minneapolis: University of Minnesota Press.

Bhabha, Homi (1990) *Nation and Narration*. London: Routledge.

Chakravarty, Sumati (1996) *National Identity in Indian Popular Cinema: 1947–1987*. New Delhi: Oxford University Press.

Cohen, Lawrence (1995a) 'Holi in Banaras and the Mahaland of Modernity', *Gender and Lesbian Quarterly*, 2, 4, pp.399–424.

Cohen, Lawrence (1995b) 'The Pleasures of Castration: The Postoperative Status of Hijras, Jhankas, and Academics' in Paul Abramson and Steven Pinkerton eds. *Sexual Nature Sexual Culture*. Chicago: University of Chicago Press.

Cook, David (1996) *A History of Narrative Film*, 3rd edition. New York: Norton.

Dudrah, Rajinder (2002) 'Drum N Dhol: British Bhangra Music and Diasporic South Asian Identity Formation', *European Journal of Cultural Studies*, 5, 3, pp.363–383.

Dwyer, Rachel (2000) *All You Want is Money, All You Need is Love: Sex and Romance in Modern India*. London: Cassell.

Gopinath, Gayatri (2000) 'Queering Bollywood: Alternative Sexualities in Popular Indian Cinema' in Andrew Grossman ed. 'Queer Asian Cinema: Shadows in the Shade', Special Issue of *Journal of Homosexuality*, 39, 3 & 4, pp.283–297.

Grossman, Andrew, ed. (2000) 'Queer Asian Cinema: Shadows in the Shade', Special Issue of *Journal of Homosexuality*, 39, 3 & 4.

Kabir, Ananya J. (2003) 'Allegories of Alienation and Politics of Bargaining: Minority Subjectivities in Mani Ratnam's *Dil Se*', *South Asian Popular Culture*, 1, 2, pp.141–159.

Kavi, Ashok Row (2000) 'The Changing Image of the Hero in Hindi Films' in Andrew Grossman ed. 'Queer Asian Cinema: Shadows in the Shade', Special Issue of *Journal of Homosexuality*, 39, 3 & 4, pp.307–312.

Kazmi, Fareed (1999) *The Politics of India's Conventional Cinema: Imaging a Universe, Subverting a Multiverse*. New Delhi: Sage.

Leong, Russell, ed. (1996) *Asian American Sexualities: Dimensions of the Gay and Lesbian Experience*. London: Routledge.

Maira, Sunaiana Marr (2002) *Desis in the House: Indian American Youth Culture in New York City*. Philadelphia: Temple University Press.

Mishra, Vijay (2002) *Bollywood Cinema: Temples of Desire*. London: Routledge.

Nandy, Ashis (1998) *The Secret Politics of our Desires: Innocence, Culpability and Indian Popular Cinema*. London: Zed Books.

Oldenburg, Veena Talwar (1989) *The Making of Colonial Lucknow 1856–1877*. Delhi: Oxford University Press.

Prasad, Madhava (1994) 'Cinema and the Desire for Modernity', *Journal of Arts and Ideas*, 25–26, pp.71–86.

Prasad, Madhava (1998) *Ideology of the Hindi Film: A Historical Construction*. New Delhi: Oxford University Press.

Rajadhyaksha, Ashish (1998) 'Indian Cinema' in John Hill and Pamela Church Gibson eds. *The Oxford Guide to Film Studies*. London: Oxford University Press, pp.535–540.

Rao, R. Raj (2000) 'Memories Pierce the Heart: Homoeroticism, Bollywood-style' in Andrew Grossman ed. 'Queer Asian Cinema: Shadows in the Shade', Special Issue of *Journal of Homosexuality*, 39, 3 & 4, pp.299–306.

Regan, Stephen, ed. (1992) *The Politics of Pleasure: Aesthetics and Cultural Theory*. Buckingham: Open University Press.

Said, Edward (1978) *Orientalism*. London: Penguin.

Sharma, Sanjay, John Hutnyk and Ashwani Sharma, eds. (1996) *Dis-Orienting Rhythms: The Politics of the New Asian Dance Music*. London: Zed Books.

Stacey, Jackie (1993) *Star Gazing: Hollywood Cinema and Female Spectatorship*. London: Routledge.

Vasudevan, Ravi, ed. (2000) *Making Meaning in Indian Cinema*. New Delhi: Oxford University Press.

Virdi, Jyotika (2003) *The Cinematic Imagination: Indian Popular Films as Social History*. New Brunswick, NJ: Rutgers University Press.

Waugh, Thomas (2001) 'Queer Bollywood, or I'm the Player You're the Naive One: Patterns of Sexual Subversion in Recent Indian Popular Cinema' in Matthew Tinkcom and Amy Villarejo eds. *Key Frames: Popular Cinema and Cultural Studies*. London: Routledge, pp.280–297.

20

On the media assemblage of Bollywood: time and sensation in globalizing India
by Amit Rai

Introduction

The new hero of Hindi-Urdu cinema is the cosmopolitan DJ. In keeping with global cultural and economic trends, DJ culture has exploded in India since 1998. The DJ has become a ubiquitous figure creating intensities everywhere from music videos, film, art exhibition openings, to wedding receptions. How does one think of this emergence? The DJ, spinning a careful but always risky mix of old filmi favorites and club anthems, creates interfaces and intervals in the movement of bodies, the projection of aural space, and the proliferation of digital media. These are new ad-hoc media publics, marked by the politics of negotiation, but whose effects at the level of the body remain obscure because what is partially at stake in their thought is the return of the body to a level of experience before experience (thus phenomenology cannot address this contagious strata in its specificity without reducing it to forms of consciousness). As others before me have suggested, this level of experience before experience is called the virtual. Or affect.

"Ajeeb Ittafaq hai." We should consider this line so common in commercial films as a limit experience in contemporary media. It's transformation signals a threshold into a qualitatively different kind of modernity in India. So the word Ittafaq is worth lingering on. Ittafaq is derived from an Arabic compound whose semantic range includes, Accordance, Harmony, Accident, Conspiracy, Agreement, Concord, Chance, Event, Opportunity.[1]

"Ajeeb ittafaq hai" is what Inspector Shekhar (Dev Anand) says to Waheeda Rehman when, after he is wounded by her thug accomplices, he awkwardly stumbles on to her house in *C.I.D.* (1956). And so the stage is set for Waheeda's famous performance of iconic facial gestures in the song "Kahin Pe Nigahein Kahin Pe Nishana" (Gaze somewhere, Target somewhere else) as she tries to seduce the villain and allow the hero to escape.

Ittafaq is also the word General Bakshi offers to Major Ram Prasad Sharma to explain how his daughter, in desperate need of military protection, and Sharma's long-lost brother have ended up in the same elite college in a remote northern hill station in *Main Hoon Na*. The other word the General offers is *kismat* usually translated as fate or destiny. The oscillation between Ittafaq and kismat sets the stage for the digitally composited transition to the paradigmatic college song of our era, "Chale Jaise Hawayein," with its long shots, fast editing, moving cameras, digital effects, and explosive dance beats.

I am suggesting that Accordance, Accident, Agreement, Concord, Chance, Event, Opportunity – in a word, Ittafaq – have been and continue to be the order words governing the intimate passage from narrative anticipation to song/dance movement and back. The Ittafaq-image relates specific vectors or basins of attraction that energize the suspenseful transition of the body from dialogue to song. From at least the 1950s on, this passage has been represented as the advent and necessary mastery of chance through the aesthetic form of Bollywood melodrama. Indeed, as Peter Brooks pointed out long ago, part of what melodrama does as a technology of subjection is tame chance through the narrativization of coincidence. Both Ravi Vasudevan and Esha Niyogi De note that this is one of the legacies of the translation of the cultural form into popular cinema in India. More specifically, Vasudevan's work suggests how the mastery of chance in Hindi-Urdu melodrama happened through the picturization of the masculinist frontal icon.

I believe that a decisive aspect of what we are witnessing today is the rapid dissolution of the empire of signs, gestures, spatiotemporalities, and generic codes that governed this passage into and mastery of chance; the Ittafaq-image's new dispensation. In the passage from a melodramatic dialectic of Accident-Concord to the proliferation of chance as non-actualized event – a new quotidian practice of the Ittafaq-image is coming into being, a new sensorimotor circuit. I argue that a number of correlated developments have led to a qualitatively new Ittafaq-image in contemporary Hindi-Urdu cinema. The first of signal importance is the explosion of DJ culture and the specific rhythms and intensities of the audio-visual database as a patterned but unpredictable cultural form in India. Second, the displacement of the bazaar-Talkie by the Mall-Multiplex is also correlated with this emergence of new population-segmentations, risk-experiences, and chance-subjects in a globalizing economy. Third, the shift in visual style of certain commercial film genres marked by the emergence of the jump cut,[2] understood as a cut primarily in time sequence, not diegetic space, suggests the refunctioning of narrative in terms of what Gary Saul Morson has called the open time of narrativeness. Finally, crucial to this new experience of the event of chance is the regime of human security taking hold of disparate forms of work, property, value, pleasure, and life in the emergence of a Bollywood-insurance-astrology circuit between kismet and Ittafaq. All this suggests that at the level of an evolving sensorimotor schema a dissociated body accelerating with the dynamic functionality of a globalizing media assemblage has transformed the mode of address of frontal iconicity so long characteristic of commercial Indian cinema.

Loitering media

In practice, popular Hindi-Urdu cinema has always been a loitering technology. Loitering, in fact, is its mode of becoming. In malls or bazaars, loitering creates self-organizing (patterned but unpredictable) traffic – jams, interruptions, density, gazes, clusters, flows – and this is what popular media does in its non-linear circulation. Through it and in it, the body waits for incoming and ongoing connections, modulated connectivities, the movements of which have defined class, caste, and gender power, or gradients of access across technological platforms in India. First Day, First Show – a ubiquitous and decades old habituation of Bombay cinema – was an assemblage of partly loitering, partly "authorized" bodies waiting for the inaugural unfolding of a media event. The authorized bodies either held a ticket, or were going about acquiring one by standing in the queue or buying black. The loiterers are what gave First Day, First Show its carnival quality. Loiterers come mostly for the spectacle, standing, sitting, leaning, wandering – *fokat mein* – without purpose or intention, they wait and add density to the scene of exhibition. That first show, indeed the first weekend, determined the future of any given film: house full on the first weekend was the sign positive of a healthy return on investment, and the black marketeers whose money laundering schemes were the financial life of Bombay cinema breathed a sigh of relief.

This assemblage is today undergoing a qualitative change, a phase transition as indigenous financial infrastructures are completely transformed by transnational capital, Hollywood production companies, new insurance products, and the synergies of the new media. What are the coordinates of this changing media topology? *Dhoom 2* (Gadhvi, 2006) brands itself across cellphone callback tone, music video, wallpaper, Fanzine, multiplex and Talkie, nation and diaspora, and each of these platforms and spaces distributes its own system of relations and durations. In what way does the brand have consistency across these contexts? How does the brand function in piracy circuits? In globalizing India, the work of mass consumption in biocybernetic reproduction loses its aura to gain an ecology.[3] The speeds and pauses of each technological platform are thresholds and connectivities, patterned and stochastic. In turn, these connectivities become a mode through which the diaspora of Bombay cinema can participate in various media bubbles still wreathed in the discourses of the nation. There is no global cinema today without jacking-in to cyberspace, interacting with a newly plastic media, as flexible bodies-in-population form relations of motion with technologies, credit-finance, and always already pirated content. And the coils of control are in these relations of motion,[4] which is to say that the analysis of a media assemblage such as Bollywood can take no comfort in intellectual production as "resistance" retrieval.[5] The loitering mode is at once pre-colonial, colonized, and postcolonial as affective dispositions with very different histories fold into, or are nested within each other in the event of media. This means that loitering media is not a gaze reducible to a subject position, but a mechanism of connectivity, interruption, pause, lingering, stuttering; but also "time pass."

Loitering is an aesthetic and a critique of bourgeois citizenship, even though the claim of belonging that may be legible in the practice cannot found an identity. Loitering always borders the mis-fit, a practice on the edges of propriety and property. This is why all loitering media traffics in the pirated. It is the loitering nature of Indian media that has enabled the gradual but thoroughgoing refunctioning of every element of the assemblage itself: the shrinking of the average shot duration in editing practices globally, the emergence of the halting, jerky camera style in Bombay cinema, the transformation of the *Ittafaq*-image (chance-harmony becoming fate-risk), and the quotidianization of characterization in Bollywood acting form new resonances in loitering media technologies, but without resemblance or metaphoric condensation. To be more specific, each of these new aspects of Bombay cinema has emerged because there has been a change in the different durations of media, a shift in its speed, acceleration, flow, direction, a change in a given domain of validity. A modulation of duration: loitering. Each element of the assemblage has a duration all its own, an interruption specific to its looped feedback, hence an evolving ecology all its own; when the feedbacks start resonating across the assemblage new emergent properties take hold. But the aesthetic suggests another resonance, this time demographic, as hitherto excluded populations (lower caste, Muslim, queer, disabled, subaltern) find both a repre-sentative voice in the public sphere, being thus included in the liberal econos (household) of the nation (the Grand Narrative of the Secular Nation duly extended), and at the same time potentialize the spaces of the public not merely by exposing its constituent contradictions, but by opening those spaces to refunc-tioned connectivities, new temporalities, affecting bodies.[6]

Bollywood time pass

In other words, loitering is time pass: the common Indian phrase "time pass" names a historically specific social practice of cinema in India.[7] This is where an assemblage analysis of Bollywood media should begin: in practices of time, in the specific durations of a multiplicity. And this is also where politics begins: by changing the media's ontology of duration we extract experiences of the Untimely in Bollywood today. The singularity here, the durations of the media event, is a fuzzy set of correlated practices that function as a sensory-motor circuit of movie-going,[8] a strategic halting, stuttering, a pausing over and in sensation. It is this set of correlated practices (or assemblage) that is passing through a critical ridge in delirious phase transition.

There is no anticipation in time pass, it happens all at once, and not at all – when time passes loitering in the mixed streams of contemporary media you find yourself in the middle of events that exceed their actualization, waiting, wondering, the banal mixing with the monstrous. This excess, which is not representational, but mutational and virtual is the basis of a cultural politics of dominant Hindi-Urdu cinema. There is nothing but pure untimeliness in the gaps of time pass. This is also where capital derives its evolving schemes of value: *Dhoom II* wallpaper, callback tunes, and torrent are all simply time pass. And it is also something like the dead time in surrealist critiques of capital, where the linear calendrical time of capitalist standardization is literally shot dead, a bullet through the clock. Time pass derives from the middle English word "pasetyme": "A diversion or recreation which serves to pass the time agreeably; an activity done for pleasure rather than work; a hobby; a sport, a game. Also: a practice commonly indulged in"(OED). Time pass is about pleasure in killing time, a practiced art that consists in feeling time's passing so as not to feel its accretion.

Time pass signals habituations of affective open time:[9] time's divergence from itself in the act of cinema-going, as when time bifurcates, halts, or "dies" in a body's implication or folding in some media stream. Such regulated but volatile durations of media experience were central to this film culture, and these durations are now in the process of becoming something else. The new multiplex schedule of showings disrupting the long-standing 12–3–6–9 cycle suggests that these new durations have to do with maximizing space, viewers, and rental time for exhibition-wallahs.

Certain aspects of loitering media flies in the face of such utilitarianism. Let us not forget there is always something parasitic about loitering, hanging around to maximize an event's duration. In this sense loitering in Bollywood would be less about exhibition space than the becoming time of space: gaps, interruption, opening time by remapping exhibition space. Historically, such open time operated in the consuming or "partaking" of extra-diegetic star auras, the renewed past of cinema unfolding activated the memories of viewers who in turn rendered that memory audible in shouts of acknowledgement for heroes, heroines, songs, scenes, or intertextual allusions. Time pauses as an immediate memory contracts the image-sound in the timespace of the media event, viral memory as a kind of interactive repetition of indices, or attention-attractors, distributed throughout the media ecology, and finding resonances in the feedback of active audiences. The time of cinema opens as well in anonymous hoots of displeasure for power outages, audio-visual failures, broken fans, bad dialogue, or zealous ticket-checkers and ushers (an active antagonism between the managers and workers of exhibition spaces and working class and youth audiences). More, the notion of time pass has often been integrated into the idea of its pleasurable return, that is, in the future of repeat viewings, cinema-going as pastime, as a way of killing time, is not its dissolution, but the rendering of time into a repeatable packet of memory. Here in the openings of filmi time pass, the fragmented present of cinema-going (so well analyzed by Lalitha Gopalan)[10] seems infinitely divisible, re-functioned as it were, in the form of talk back, sing alongs, crying, bathroom breaks, diegetic gaps, waiting in line, forced scene/song replays,[11] and of course the ubiquitous intermission.

These differently experienced aspects of Bollywood's temporalities break apart the discreet packet of time that defines the pedagogies of film culture in the West (although one could show that specific elements of fragmentation and interruption differently structure cinematic temporalities in the West).[12] In that sense, analyzing time in media assemblages suggests a method that first and foremost problematizes the timescales of an event – at what border of a phase transition, in terms of what durations, can we locate the limits of the event, that bubble of resonance that Ilya Prigogine and Manuel Delanda have explored in their different ways?

A media assemblage analysis of Bollywood would focus on the changing timespaces of media events. Thus, time pass films, despite their generally acknowledged formulaic mediocrity, were social events that integrated the specific theatre into the body's social passage; in that sense the singularity of the event was indissociable from the specificity of a theater's space. Time pass films could become a time pass event only in certain talkies, only at certain times. This specificity is transformed in the globalized malltiplex into a space with no outside, like the Benjaminian dream: "Arcades are houses or passages having no outside – like the dream."[13] Benjamin's method and project in his study of the Paris arcades is peculiarly suited to understanding the hybrid temporalities of the contemporary malltiplex in India, and I will suggest some relevant connections here. Commenting on "the panorama of gaiety and tears passing before us like the dust of the rails before the windows of the coach" (Benjamin Gastineau, *La Vie en chemin de fer* [1861]), Benjamin wrote,

> Rather than pass the time, one must invite it in. To pass the time (to kill time, to expel it): the gambler. Time spills from his every pore. – To store time as a battery stores energy: the flâneur. Finally, the third type: he who waits. He takes in the time and renders it up in altered form – that of expectation.[14]

To kill, expel, store, spill, and render time: loitering. Divergent pasts and futurities fold into the act of cinema-going. They name different strategies of cinema-going in India, aggregated in the phrase "time pass." To kill, expel, store, spill, and render time are also different aspects of the rhythms of film culture's media *duration*: time pass is an emergent quality of sensation in the interactions of Indian cinema's media assemblage, and it is that experience of duration-pleasure that is being transformed today through new media intervals.

And it is here, in the immanent duration of the media event, where sexuality becomes pre-individual and potential. (We should recall that the level of the preindividual suggests a timespace in the body that is singular, immediate, populational, and stochastic.)[15] This is because an analysis of sexuality *in* Bollywood, rather than taking on the paradoxical ambitions of a representational critique (*"is this a masculinist frame?" "is this narrative queer(able)?"*), would follow the movements of sensation becoming habit and mutation in an entire *ecology of sensation*. Sexuality is where the body and populations meet, says Foucault. More specifically, sexualization in ecologies of sensation unfolds through changing relations of affect (capacities to affect and be affected), relations that are probabilistic and populational. Thus the timescale for apprehending sexuality would necessarily be as broad as the virtual-material arc needed to create a set of functional affordances or sensorimotor circuits at the threshold of a body and its populations: what a body can and cannot do in relation to the material substrate that it is connected with would be its sexuality, its evolving regime of sensation. In this sense we can speak of the specific charge of an attractor which would have numerous and changing dimensions, let us call him Shah Rukh Khan for the moment. I had a great conversation with a fan about SRK a few years ago – it would have to be updated for his newfound washboard abs, prominently on display in the publicity for *Om Shanti Om*. She had come to New York city as a college graduate in her twenties, a transplant from the small immigrant Hindu community in Minnesota. She remarked that New York provided the fan with so many more "outlets" to connect to Bollywood. For this fan, the internet was a mode of connecting to the oceans of information on Hindi film, to fanzines, and finally to the affecting body of Shahrukh:

Q: How have you found that experience of Bollywood on the Web?

A: I think it's great. There's just, there's a lot out there, you know. There's, there's almost too much out there, to a point where do you want to read about the stars, do you want to read about their love life ... I feel like you can just read everything now. Um, you can have chat room discussions if you want, though I've never done that. But it's like a whole new level that they've taken it to. Bollywood's definitely ...it's, it's kinda become like a lifestyle rather than a trend. Like, people are doing everything [through it]. You know, I subscribe to Stardust. (Q: You do?) (Laughs.) Actually I don't subscribe to it but, because I've been called such a FOB [Fresh off the Boat] it was my birthday present from a friend of mine. (Q: Ah, but you kept it.) But I kept it. (Q: And you read it.) Um, the whole subscription ... So I get it every month now ... I mean, you can see all the pictures and the, you know, the photo shoots and, and whatnot. But, um, I was recently an extra in the *Kal Ho Na Ho* movie ... the Karan Johar's movie with Shahrukh Khan, I did three scenes with them ... mind you, I don't think a lot of people would because they pay you nothing for an all-day thing in which all you do is, like, sit around and wait. You know, I don't know if you've ever done that thing, but you seriously just wait, and I was ... just there because the whole, like, aura of being around Shahrukh Khan was so amazing. He is one of the most intense people I've ever been around. Seeing him is definitely an experience. Like, you can see him on film, but to see him act in real life is, is definitely something. (Q: He's a great actor.) He is. He's a great actor and has, like, his expression, and not only just his face but, like, his whole body expression. He's really intense. You know and even just watching him, he makes you just feel, like, feel what he's feeling. You know, like, there's a scene where he's sad about it and he's just crying and you want to go up to him and tell him that it's gonna be okay 'cause he just looks so sad.[16]

We could consider these moments: internet, Stardust, movie set, Shahrukh, affection – not as sequential stages, or lines of a narrative, but as implicated in one another, infolding continuously – taken to a new level of intensity, and in moments we glimpse the outlines of a phase transition to come. The meeting, for instance, of Internet-friendly digital cinematography (which would include within its own assemblage both technology and brand logo of T-1 lines, Lucasfilm THX and miniDV) and Bollywood melodrama has produced many skins, many relations of motion, many affects. Its diagram will be a sensorimotor schema. In one way or another it signals the death of Bollywood – which is not to say the end of Bollywood: both Benjamin and Derrida remind us that what is dead wields a very specific force: the force of becoming.[17] The futures of Bollywood are being born within the different fetishisms specific to this cinema – that is, its own fetishes (in no particular and non-exhaustive order: light-skinned virgins, Switzerland, muscular *jawans* [male youths, soldiers], colonial nature, the workerless City, cosmopolitan consumer, and the global Logo) and the fetish that it is turned into in the West (middle-class European Americans were dancing "authentic" bhangra in the aisles during the screening of *Lagaan* [dir. Ashutosh Gowariker, 2001] at the artsy FilmForum in Manhattan) – the proliferation of these fetish surfaces – the skins of an assemblage – guarantee a mutational future, monstrous or not. Thus, the body's ability to co-emerge with the technologies it interfaces with obliges us to situate the question of sexuality in a preindividual plane of potential mutation.

Why is this diagramming of assemblages any different from a representational critique? I take seriously Deleuze's famous warning about representational thought, to wit, that the idealization of images (as discursive practice, as performative repetitions, or resistant identities) constrains thought within the narrow range of analogy, contradiction, identity, and sameness. Such an idealization values consciousness as product over the intensive processes that constitute an ecology of sensation. To return to our initial point of departure, loitering media, which is what Bombay cinema is today, allows different temporalities of the body to assemble on the same plane of becoming: intercalated interruptions. At the level of the incipience of perception, where sensation feeds back and forward in a time loop of potentiality, the rush of life contracts and expands, the body waits, populations interface, and the event bubble of media forms, self-organizes, and resonates. More specifically, when time is killed, expelled, stored, spilled, and rendered what happens at the level of the body is the modulation of its durational connectivities, a change in its self-relation, the opening of the body to new and old populations already within it. Habit (which is no longer discursive or analogical) and mutation (patterned but unpredictable) happen in the evolution of sensation's ecology.

How is it possible to think Bombay cinema today without the malltiplex boom? Consider: this is how one Indian filmmaker and cinephile, Ravi Deshpande, describes the urban cinema-going experience in the wake of new technologies associated with the multiplex.

> Look at the way you go to the movies in any of the metros today – You've logged in & checked the reviews, you've zapped into the slickly made promos, which in turn, have been made out of slickly shot songs somewhere out there – on the prairies, the mountains, the clean & nice streets – but almost always "phoren" [foreign], & at other times with lavish sets, costumes & at very ethnic-Indian locales; you have heard the new music that is familiarly a rehash from a groove sampled from a CD – again from "phoren"; you've found time, you've called amidst stressed city travel & connected cellularly to other stressed but "wanting-to-check-out-the-film" friends, you have found the money for that Dolby/DTS experience with non carbon arc "xenon lamp" projection, you have left the sweat-n-smell land & entered the cool-n-clean theatre. The lights dim & you settle to view a crisp positive on the new "Vision" (Kodak stock-stunning skin tones & cinematography).[18]

These are the elements of a continuous multiplicity – cell phone exchange, internet research, and the digitized cool of the multiplex are synaesthetically co-implicated in the modular body of today's media assemblage, these are the media intervals that are intercalated in the enfolded sensorium of this ecology. The new Bollywood-media interface has changed the very nature of cinema-going, but has also defined particular trajectories for the commercialization of the human-computer interface in India. The multiplex is central to this transformation.

This diagrams an emergence: a news report on cinema-going in India from April 30, 2004 announced that Bollywood revenues would more than double by 2008, to $2.3 billion, supported by "a boom in multiplex building and the deployment of digital cinema to speed distribution."[19] But new digital technologies do not merely speed up distribution, since the interface between broadband and BitTorrent (or some other peer to peer protocol) will most likely transform the entire field of distribution itself; so these revenue forecasts remain in the realm of "science fiction." From First Day, First Show frenzies at single screen talkies to the new multiplex boom, the globalizing media assemblage of contemporary Bollywood is emerging through its new connectivities: digital images, spaces, sounds; cross merchandized consumption; population re-segmentation; immersive experiences focused on the autonomous life of the sensations.

The malltiplex is not an ecology a priori, but there is something nonlinear about its dynamical interactions. Now, my argument here is that to loiter (to kill, expel, store, spill, and render time) is the general condition of affectivity of the media assembling body in the contemporary malltiplex. This parceling of time, its divisibility, its continuous rhythms act on the body directly producing both new habituations as well as potentially new assemblages. Loitering is the very condition of evolution in media assemblages. The potential multiplexing of the body-technology assemblage is also a marketing gimmick. Brian Massumi suggests that potential is singular: a multiple in- and unfolding into each other of "divergent futurities, only the *divergence* of which is reproducible." The particular nature of each divergent conjunction in the series is what is problematic. "Multiple in- and unfolding: singularity is multiplex." Massumi means something different with this term than how I am using "malltiplex," however. The multiplex divergence of the singular, writes Massumi, is not to be confused with the "disjunctive simplicity" at the basis of a "system of possibility" (malltiplex). The multiplex mutually includes. Possibility develops disjunctively, one might even say quantitatively, toward the extension of a next actual step. "Multiplex potential envelops, around an intensely suspended (virtual) center."[20] The disjunctive simplicity at the basis of an audio-visual system of digitized possibility is how the machinic evolution of contemporary multiplexing captures the singular affectivity of the body and renders time through a specific organization of interruptive, quantified *bits of pleasure*. Malltiplexes aim to divide film's interruption in time through a highly selective, but also partly arbitrary refunctioning of the body-image-duration-space-pleasure-commodity topology. This entails the commodification or value-generating capture of potential connections that the body can make in the present moment: through food-thirst-hunger, through a certain appetite for star-aura, or by attending to, and consuming visual and aural affects less and less centered on the auditorium itself, attention as continuous distraction. Always, the malltiplexed body is drawn into a presentist temporality of total immersion that functions through an always changing, and seemingly expanding combination of sensation: but never to the point of excess (no fainting, heart attacks, or extreme sports-like viscerality, hopefully). Simply, this mutliplexed presentism both solicits and controls potentializing excess. Loitering bodies in today's malltiplex (consider Forum Mall in Bangalore on a Saturday afternoon), by the differentiated nature of their waiting, anticipation, boredom, or excitement – kinesis – are implicated in the duration of media streams and are the catalysis for its mutation.

In sum, I have presented some coordinates of a phase transition in contemporary Bollywood. The aim here has been to de-fetishize popular Indian cinema and its cultures, situate film within a broader mediascape, and specify the nested timescales of its practices. Today, Bollywood media does other things than what it was capable of during its various Golden Ages. What a media becomes is partially determined by the emergent properties it makes functional in the assemblages it self-organizes through. An assemblage analysis of globalizing popular media would diagram emergent capacities as the very conditions of habituations and mutations that as yet have no name.

Notes

1 See *Oxford Hindi-English Dictionary*.
2 A jump cut is a cut to later action from one filmed scene to the next, creating an effect of discontinuity or acceleration.
3 See Mitchell, W. J. Thomas, "The Work of Art in the Age of Biocybernetic Reproduction", *Modernism/modernity*, 10.3, September 2003, 481–500. The term "ecology" comes from many sources, but my most direct reference here is Manuel Delanda's *Intensive Science and Virtual Philosophy* (New York: Continuum, 2002); the analysis of a continuous multiplicity with phase transitions, critical edges, singularities, basins of attraction, and nested timescales is, to my mind, the clearest method for diagramming an ecology.
4 See Gilles Deleuze, "Postscript on Societies of Control," *October*, 59, Winter 1992, MIT Press, Cambridge, MA, pp. 3–7; www.n5m.org/n5m2/media/texts/deleuze.htm, accessed 20 December 2007.
5 Spivak once warned us about "information retrieval" and today we must be equally suspicious of "resistance retrieval." See Gayatri Spivak, "Can the Subaltern Speak," and "Deconstructing Historiography."
6 This seems to me the radical implications of Shilpa Phadke's work on gender, caste, and loitering in Mumbai's public sphere. See Phadke, Shilpa, "Dangerous Liaisons: Women and Men: Risk and Reputation in Mumbai," *Economic and Political Weekly*, 28 April 2007, www.epw.org.in/epw/uploads/articles/10544.pdf.
7 Although I was not able to see the movie, a film titled *Time Pass* was playing for a couple of weeks in the summer of 2000 in Bhopal. It was a kind of running joke between patrons and theatre staff, a code word for sheer useless expenditure. Moreover, the phrase kept returning in my interviews with cinema goers: going to see a movie was nothing other than time pass, it was

just the quality of that passage that differed from one movie to the next, from one movie hall to the next. More recently, a very odd, grotesque even, film by the same title was released (2004, dir. Chander Mishra); it narrates the story of a Hindu college boy trying to seduce a Christian girl amidst Hindu–Muslim riots in Bombay.

8   Fuzzy sets are defined as sets whose elements have degrees or gradients of membership.

9   For the notion of open time in narratology see Gary Saul Morson, "Narrativeness," *New Literary History*, 34.1 (2003): 59–73. He writes:

   And what gives a moment presentness? In a phrase, open time. For a present moment to matter, to have real weight, more than one thing must be possible at the next moment. We may define open time as the excess of possibilities over actualities. For a determinist, one and only one thing can happen at any given moment; what did not happen could not have happened. In open time, at least one thing that did not happen could have. Think of the moment in *War and Peace* when Rostov, with "his keen sportsman's eye," realizes that if he and his men charge the French at this moment, they will rout them, but if he waits, the configuration of the French troops climbing the hill will change and the opportunity will be lost. Rostov may charge or not, and his choice matters. Or consider Dmitri Karamazov holding a pestle over his father's head and trying to decide whether to kill him. He could do either, that is the whole point. The examples are endless.

10   See Lalitha Gopalan, *Cinema of Interruptions* (London: British Film Institute, 2001).

11   Almost every movie theatre owner I spoke with in Bhopal had some story to tell about students commandeering the projection room, and demanding the rescreening of key songs.

12   Considering this experience of open time in Bollywood cinema going it would be useful not only to provincialize the Hollywood dominant, but also to question if Hollywood's temporal pedagogies were ever that total in the first place even in the West. Consider in this regard some "temporal strategies" of everyday life used by the Surrealists and the Situationists to interrupt the dead time of capitalist alienation.

   An example of this kind of temporal interruption can be found in Breton's Second Manifesto of Surrealism, "the simplest Surrealist act consists of dashing down into the street, pistol in hand, and firing blindly, as fast as you can pull the trigger, into the crowd". Paul D. Miller identifies this as a "psycho-social critique" of the regimentation of time and culture in industrial society. The Surrealists parodied the monotony imposed by the industrialization of time through the activity of crétinisation, where "hours and hours going round in loops on city trams" aimed at disalienation from the very empty repetition it mimicked. This activity of dérive, or drift, "has an immediate shattering effect on calculated time". Through the shards of clock-time, another temporality appears, marked by "oneiric continuity", as opposed to the fragmented state of Debord's "commodity time" (p. 200).

See Conrad Russell, "Against Dead Time," *Time & Society*, 11. 2/3 (2002), pp. 193–208; see also Mary Ann Doane, *The Emergence of Cinematic Time* (Cambridge, MA: Harvard University Press, 2002).

13 Walter Benjamin, *The Arcades Project*, trans. Howard Eiland and Kevin McLaughlin (Cambridge, MA: Belknap Press, 1999), p. 406.

14 Benjamin, *Arcades*, p. 107.

15 The concept "preindividual" was first developed by Gilbert Simondon, elaborated by Gilles Deleuze, and taken up again by Brian Massumi.

16 Interview with "Anjali," *October*, 2003, New York City.

17 See Jacques Derrida, *Positions*, trans. Alan Bass and Henri Rense (Chicago: University of Chicago Press, 1981), p. 6; Benjamin, "Paris, The Capital of the Nineteenth Century," trans. Howard Eiland, in *Selected Writings, Vol. 3* (Cambridge, MA: Belknap Press, 2003) pp. 40–41.

18 Ravi Deshpande, "A Taste of Technology," *Expressions*, August–November, 1999 (3), www.abhivyakti.org.in/expression/tech.htm, accessed 1 October 2006.

19 Dodona Research, www.dodona.co.uk/news61.htm, accessed 1 October 2006.

20 Massumi, *Parables*, p. 113.

Select keywords
by Rajinder Dudrah and Jigna Desai

The following keywords, listed in alphabetical order, are provided as a starting point to aid in the viewing and critical reading of Bollywood films and scholarly writings on the subject. In a few cases we suggest films for viewing due to their continued popularity beyond their initial box-office release and critically acclaimed success, or that they make for interesting viewing as indicative of the predominant genre to which they might be broadly categorized by. We also elaborate on some of the keywords that appear throughout this reader, either in the contributions by the editors or in the collected seminal chapters by some of the authors.

Angry young man

The name given to the character persona of Vijay, played by actor Amitabh Bachchan. Bachchan rose to stardom in the 1970s as the angry young man of commercial Hindi cinema in his role as the wronged everyman who turns vigilante. This role, scripted by duo Salim-Javed, was exceptionally executed in the film *Zanjeer* (The Chain, 1973, dir. Prakash Mehra) amidst India's turbulent social and political climate of the 1970s. Other films where the persona of this character is broadly developed can be seen in *Deewaar* (The Wall, 1975, dir. Yash Chopra), *Trishul* (Trinity, 1978, dir. Yash Chopra) and *Kaala Patthar* (Black Stone, 1979, dir. Yash Chopra).

Ashok Chakra/wheel of independence

This is the wheel that sits prominently in the centre of the Indian national flag, where it is blue in colour. The wheel can be seen to have a number of different interpretations, not least being developed from the image of the handloom, a symbol of self-dependency and hard work, from Gandhi's *swadeshi* movement; or much earlier from the Hindu and Buddhist symbols of the wheel of life – as in the Ashok Chakra. The wheel has often been used as a motif in popular Indian cinema, particularly in post-independence social dramas, to mark the progression of time (i.e. as in the wheel turning or moving forwards); to signal an issue between the rural and the city (e.g. the wheels of a bullock cart versus the wheels of a car); or when the wheel is mangled or becomes undone to signal a break in the nation's progress.

Assemblage

This idea has perhaps been more fully developed in the cultural theory of Gilles Deleuze and Felix Guattari. It is used by Dudrah and Rai (see Readings 19 and 20) to draw attention to its application to Bollywood cinema as moving away from exclusive text- and representational-based studies of popular Hindi cinema, and moving towards examining the articulated processes and aesthetics of text, audiences and cultural industries simultaneously. 'Assemblage', then, draws our attention to the production of desire in audiences through the filmic text and the cinematic process as a convergence of technologically mediated productions and experiences with the interactions of a socio-cultural and biological body of spectators.

Bollywood

The term arises as a portmanteau of Bombay (the former name of Mumbai) and Hollywood. Bollywood is the common and sometime controversial term for the large popular film and culture industry centred in Mumbai. See the Introduction, as well as Rajadhyaksha's contribution (Reading 15), for further discussion.

Censorship

Films in Indian must pass the Central Board for Film Certification, the regulatory body that requires cuts and edits as well as provides ratings. The censorship guidelines were first created by the British colonial state which attempted to prevent offensive images of disrupting colonial relations. Contemporary censorship codes focus on issues of obscenity (including sex, nudity, violence, and sedition). Censor laws have been applied to films whereas directors are asked to make multiple cuts in order to release their films. Usually understood as regime of repression practiced by the state, censorship can also be thought of as the ways in which the State often creates policy that simultaneously forecloses and produces certain kinds of representations, aesthetics, and narratives.

Diaspora

A term used widely in the contemporary arts, humanities and social sciences referring to the social condition and triadic socio-cultural relationship of migration from a place of origin (usually known as the homeland), to new places of settlement and the diasporic consciousness that arises which shifts between the these multiple coordinates through the movement of people, objects, images, sounds, memories, and histories. When applied to the study of Bollywood cinema, the Indian and South Asian diasporic audiences are often implied. The millions of diasporic South Asians who may partake in Bollywood film viewings and related Bollywood popular cultural activities can be seen to have a relationship of contemplating on established identities (as in Indian), the formation of new ones (e.g. British Asian, South Asian-American etc.) which have the possibility to circumvent fixed ideas of race and nation, through an engagement with Bollywood cinema. In this view, cinema and its popular cultures are also socially reproduced anew in the diaspora, for instance, through examples of Bollywood film music remixed with African-American R 'n' B, British Bhangra music, and hybrid fusion cinema as seen in the works of filmmakers Gurinder Chadha and Mira Nair.

Director

Within filmmaking, the person who controls the aesthetic, performative and technical aspects of the film. The director guides the technical crew as well as the actors in achieving the overall vision of the film.

Distributor

Distribution, of course, has been critical to the success of the Indian film industry. Main distributors generally divide India into five main territories with the overseas/foreign market counting as the sixth territory. The cost of the film per territory is set by factors such as star appeal, the popularity of its music, and the previous success rate of the director and producer. In general, a film is expected to recoup double its distribution costs.

Exhibitor

The exhibitor has also been critical to maintaining the film industry within India. Exhibition practices have changed radically over the last few decades. The proliferation of media and technologies created the means by which many middle class audiences withdrew to their living rooms watching television and film via satellite and video and abandoned the movie theatres. Since 1998, along with the other transformations in Indian urban spaces, the phenomenon of the multiplexes has altered the processes and conditions of film consumption in metropolitan areas. Multiplexes have proven to be profitable and changes the ways in which profit can be earned without turning to villages and small towns and cities for returns on investments.

Historicals

These films were particularly pertinent in the pre-1947 independence period where a focus on actual Indian historical figures was laden with messages about foreign British rule, for instance *Ghulami Nu Patan* (The Fall of Slavery, 1931, dir. Shyam Sunder Agarwal) and *Puran Bhakt* (The Devotee, 1933, dir. Debaki Bose).

Indian cinema

Bollywood or popular Hindi-Urdu commercial films from Mumbai are only one cinema from India. Other regional cinemas which collectively make Indian cinema the largest in the world with an approximate output of 900–1000 or more films each year include Assamese cinema, Bengali cinema, Bhojpuri cinema, Gujarati cinema, Kannada cinema, Malayalam cinema, Marathi cinema, Oriya cinema, Punjabi cinema, Rajasthani cinema, Tamil cinema, and Telugu cinema. In addition to these aforementioned major language cinemas the 'minor' language cinemas of Kashmiri, Tulu, Konkani, Haryanvi, Khasi and Maithili also exist.

Masala

Literally meaning mixture, the term also refers to the all-encompassing genre which features drama, comedy, song and dance, and action that have been characteristic of much of popular Hindi cinema. See the Introduction for further elaboration.

Muslim socials

These films are perhaps best considered as a sub-genre of the Social Films. These were especially popular in the 1970s and 1980s and inspired by stories from Urdu love poetry, whose appeal crossed religious boundaries. Two memorable and critically acclaimed films include *Pakeezah* (Pure Heart, 1971, dir. Kamal Amrohi) and *Umrao Jaan* (Umrao Jaan, 1981, dir. Muzzafar Ali).

Mythologicals or devotional films

These recount or rework epic stories from the *Ramayana* or the *Mahabharat* as well as other religious traditions within the Indian subcontinent. Examples include *Raja Harischandra* (King Harischandra, 1913, dir. D. G. Phalke), *Shri Krishna Janma* (The Birth of Shri Krishna, 1918, dir. D. G. Phalke) and *Sampoorna Ramayana* (The Ramayana, 1961, dir. Babubhai Mistri).

Non-resident Indian or NRI films

Films under this grouping have been on the rise since the mid-1990s and represent the relationship of the overseas Indians to the homeland through the particular lens of Bollywood cinema. Examples include *Dilwale Dulhaniya Le Jayenge* (DDLJ or The Braveheart Will Take the Bride, 1995, dir. Aditya Chopra), *Pardes* (Foreign Land, 1997, dir. Subash Ghai) and *Namastey London* (Greetings London, 2007, dir. Vipul Amrutlal Shah). Actor Shahrukh Khan, since the film DDLJ (above), has emerged as the premier global Bollywood box office superstar of late, regularly playing the urban Indian and diasporic hero.

Partition

The official separation of colonial India into the postcolonial nation states of Pakistan and India: 14 August 1947 marked the official transfer of British colonial power to Pakistan as a free independent state, with Muhammad Ali Jinnah as first Prime Minister, and 15 August 1947 marked Indian independence, with Jawaharlal Nehru as its first Prime Minister. Millions of people were displaced amidst mass communal violence. Partition also marked the separation of the regional pre-partition Indian film production centres along the new nation-state lines. Popular Indian cinema did not explicitly deal with the violence and trauma of partition in its films made immediately after independence. It was not until the late 1990s and early 2000s that the issue of partition and the Indo-Pak border started to feature in a sustained and varied manner in popular Hindi films.

Playback singers

Within Bollywood films, songs are pre-recorded by professional playback singers. Actors then lip-synch the words while dancing along. Playback singers are often well known in their own right – such as Lata Mangeshkar and Asha Bhosle – and can have their own fans and followings.

Postcolonial India

Cinema has been critical to the conceptions of modernity, sovereignty and independence within India. While cinema made contributions to the anti-colonial nationalist struggle, it was not recognized by the state as an official industry upon the nation's independence. In fact, the industry was often derided for being a corrupting influence and attempts were made to marginalize its presence. The film industry is still under the purview of state regulation through censorship, ratings, and economics. All of this has impacted production and consumption practices and the films themselves.

Producers

Historically, filmmaking has relied on the informal sectors of the economy for its funding as the state has been reluctant to recognise the industry. Because of this lack of assistance in acquiring funding, investments in film have involved high risk and speculative loans with some funding coming from illegitimate sources. Under these conditions, producers have been in a vulnerable position of having the possibility of high returns as well as likely failures.

Queer Bollywood

This term refers to recent academic research, activist work and fanzine activities into how Bollywood cinema and popular culture is used, appropriated, invested with, and even influenced by, particularly in contemporary filmmaking aesthetics, by queer gender and sexual patrons. Areas for discussion and analysis include, among others, Bollywood's hetero-normative boy-meets-girl love stories as being reread with queer gender and sexual possibilities, same-sex desire in and through the representations of Bollywood films, and queer South Asian popular cultures both in the homeland and in the diaspora that recode original Bollywood sources and question the assumption of heteronormativity in general.

Romantic films

This genre depicts the universal boy-meets-girl love story and the numerous social obstacles that they face along the way, for example *Bobby* (1973, dir. Raj Kapoor), *Love Story* (1981, dir. Rajendra Kumar), *Maine Pyar Kiya* (I Have Loved, 1981, dir. Sooraj R. Barjatya) and *Veer Zaara* (2004, dir. Yash Chopra). Often, the crucial moment of declaration, where the lovers make clear to themselves and to the audience their unrequited sentiments for each other, these are dramatically spoken through the English words, 'I love you'.

Social films or topicals

These films were often social-conscious evoking melodramas that engaged with the hopes, ideals and broken promises of India as it emerged as a young independent nation, post-1947. Popular examples here include *Awaara* (The Vagabond/Tramp, 1951, dir. Raj Kapoor), *Pyaasa* (The Thirsty One, 1957, dir. Guru Dutt) and *Mother India* (1957, dir. Mehboob Khan).

Song and dance

Seen as a key component of Bollywood films, the sequences involve lip-synching actors who dance along to pre-recorded songs. The song and dance often interrupts the narrative transporting characters to locations which are sometimes separate from and unrelated to the plot. Moreover, the song and dance sequences, while derided as being extraneous and merely spectacle by some, have also been defended as critical to the possibility of film itself (see Gopal and Sen, Reading 12).

South Asia

A large and diverse area of geography and people stretching across the Indian subcontinent, including the countries of Bangladesh, Bhutan, the Chagos Islands, India, Maldives, Nepal, Pakistan and Sri Lanka.

Supernatural or horror films

This genre of films draw on adaptations of religious stories, myths, eerie folk tales, suspense, and urban legends from India's oral and popular cultures. Examples include *Nagin* (The Female Cobra, 1954, dir. Nandlal Jaswantlal), *Jaani Dushman* (Beloved Enemy, 1979, dir. Rajkumar Kohli), *Guest House* (1980, dirs. Shyam Ramsay and Tulsi Ramsay) and *Bhoot* (Ghost, 2003, dir. Ram Gopal Verma).

Indian cinema: select timeline of some key events
by Rajinder Dudrah and Jigna Desai

As with any brief and select timeline, what is omitted is just as important as what is included. Here, we offer this disparate chronology to indicate the growth of popular Indian cinema, from its hybrid Western and domestic media roots, to its rise and expansion across the South Asian subcontinent and beyond, to its appeal among non-Indian overseas audiences (such as the former USSR), and in the contemporary 2000s, the growing interest – predominantly in its Bollywood variety – that it has generated and is eager to capitalise on, especially amongst Western international media and cultural industries. For a fuller encyclopaedic timeline of Indian cinema spanning 1896 to 1996, see Rajadhyaksha and Willemen (1999).

1896 First film screening at Watson's Hotel Bombay, on 7 July, by the French Lumière brothers' cameraman Marius Sestier.

1897 First films shown in Calcutta and Madras. These were imports of Western shorts, and part documentary and part early-home video in style.

1912 *Pundalik* (Saint Pundalik, 1912, dir. P. R. Tipnis), probably In-

dia's first feature film that was religious and mythological in its content.

1913 *Raja Harischandra* (King Harischandra, 1913, dir. D. G. Phalke), India's first commercially released feature film, a religious and mythological early spectacle.

1918 Indian Cinematograph Act enforced as law by the British colonials in India regulating the terms of censorship and cinema licensing.

1931 *Alam Ara* (Alam Ara, 1931, dir. Ardeshir Irani), India's first sound film featuring seven songs.

1947 Independence of Pakistan (14 August) and India (15 August) from British colonial rule and Partition of South Asia into Pakistan, India and then later (1971) into Bangladesh. The inception of the formal separation of the subcontinent's film industries into India, Pakistan and Bangladesh.

1951 *Awaara* (The Vagabond/Tramp, dir. Raj Kapoor) starring Raj Kapoor and Nargis is a huge success and launches their popularity as major stars in parts of the former USSR, Africa, and in parts of the middle East.

1952 The first Indian International Film Festival of India held in Bombay, Madras and Calcutta.

1952 West Pakistan (now Pakistan) bans Indian films.

1955 *Pather Panchali* (Song of the Little Road, 1955, dir. Satyajit Ray) has its world premiere at the Museum of Modern Art, New York.

1957 *Mother India* (dir. Mehboob Khan) is released. India's first-ever official Oscars Awards entry.

1962 East Pakistan (now Bangladesh) bans Indian films.

1964 The National Film Archive of India is founded in Pune.

1973 *Zanjeer* (The Chain, dir. Prakash Mehra) is released and launches

Amitabh Bachchan's star persona as the 'angry young man' of Hindi cinema.

1975 *Sholay* (Embers, dir. Ramesh Sippy) is released.

1988 *Qayamat Se Qayamat Tak* (Until the End of Eternity, dir. Mansoor Khan) is released, a hugely popular Romeo and Juliet-style tragic romance.

1993 *Bhaji on the Beach* (dir. Gurinder Chadha) is released blending British, American and popular Hindi cinema styles together.

1995 *Dilwale Dulhaniya Le Jayenge* (The Braveheart Will Take the Bride, dir. Aditya Chopra) is released and marks the arrival of the non-resident Indian (NRI) or diasporic hero, played successfully by Shahrukh Khan.

1998 *Dil Se* (From the Heart, dir. Mani Ratnam) is released and officially tracked and listed in the UK top ten box office releases, ahead of several mainstream British and Hollywood cinema releases.

1998 Announcement is made of Indian cinema being granted official industry status by the Indian government led by the Bharatiya Janata Party. Three years later in 2001 this process is formalized.

2000 IIFA (International Indian Film Academy) Awards held at the Millennium Dome in London, UK.

2001 *Lagaan* (Land Tax, dir. Ashutosh Gowariker) is released and is India's official Oscars Award entry in the following year. *Gadar: Ek Prem Katha* (Revolution: A Love

Story, dir. Anil Sharma) becomes one of the highest grossing films in Indian film history making Rs 700,000,000. It is also a controversial anti-Pakistani film.

2002 *Bombay Dreams*, Andrew Lloyd Webber's musical, opens at London's Apollo Victoria Theatre in June. The third version of *Devdas* (dir. Sanjay Leela Bhansali) starring Shahrukh Khan, Madhuri Dixit and Aishwarya Rai is one of the most expensive films made costing about Rs 500,000,000.

2003 *Munnabhai M.B.B.S* (dir. Rajkumar Hirani) is released. It is followed three years later by the equally successful *Lage Raho Munna Bhai* (Carry on Munna Bhai, 2006, dir. Rajkumar Hirani). Both films star Sanjay Dutt as an underworld character who sees and becomes guided in his actions by the figure of Gandhi. Practising this belief system of *gandhigiri* becomes a buzzword in India as various groups deploy it in their social protests. Both films' popularity is recognized in-

ternationally and the latter is the first Hindi film shown at the United Nations in 2006.

2004 Gurinder Chadha attempts a crossover Bollywood film *Bride and Prejudice* for Western audiences loosely based on Jane Austen's novel.

2006 *Rang De Basanti* (Colour Me Saffron, dir. Rakesh Omprakash Mehra) a film focused on youth violently fighting corruption in India also inspired social action against the acquittal of the culprits in the murder of Jessica Lal as well as anti-reservation protests.

2007 IIFA Awards held at the Sheffield Arena, Yorkshire, UK.

2008 Following on from the success of the animated feature *Hanuman* (dirs. V. G. Samant and Milind Ukey, 2005), several animated films are due for release in the summer by big banner production companies with co-production finance and ideas from transnational media companies (e.g. Walt Disney and Time Warner).

Reference

Rajadhyaksha, Ashish and Paul Willemen (1999) *Encyclopaedia of Indian Cinema*, 2nd edition. London: British Film Institute.

Further reading

Alessio, Dominic and Jessica Langer (2007) 'Nationalism and Postcolonialism in Indian Science Fiction: Bollywood's Koi Mil Gaya (2003)', *New Cinemas: Journal of Contemporary Film*, 5(3): 217–29.

Banaji, Shakuntala (2006) *Reading 'Bollywood': The Young Audience and Hindi Films*. Basingstoke, UK: Palgrave Macmillan.

Barnouw, Erik and Subrahmanyam Krishnaswamy (1980) *Indian Film*, 2nd edition. New York: Oxford University Press.

Bhowmik, S. (1995) *Indian Cinema, Colonial Contours*. Calcutta: Papyrus.

Bose, Derek (2006) *Brand Bollywood: A New Global Entertainment Order*. New Delhi: Sage.

Bose, Mihir (2007) *Bollywood: A History*. New Delhi: Lotus Collection, Roli Books.

Chakravarty, Sumita S. (1993) *National Identity in Indian Popular Cinema, 1947–1987* (Texas Film Studies Series). Austin, TX: University of Texas Press.

Chopra, Anupama (2004) *Dilwale Dulhania Le Jayenge: The Making of a Blockbuster*. New Delhi: HarperCollins.

Das, Veena (2000) 'The Making of Modernity: Gender and Time in Indian Cinema', in T. Mitchell (ed.) *Questions of Modernity*. Minneapolis, MN: University of Minnesota Press, pp. 166–88.

Derne, Steve (2000) *Movies, Masculinity, and Modernity: An Ethnography of Men's Filmgoing in India*. Westport, CT: Greenwood.

Desai, Jigna (2004) *Beyond Bollywood: The Cultural Politics of South Asian Diasporic Film*. New York: Routledge.

Desai, Jigna (2005) 'Planet Bollywood: Indian Cinema Abroad', in Shilpa Davé, LeiLani Nishime and Tasha Oren (eds) *East Main Street: Asian American Popular Culture*. New York: New York University Press, pp. 55–71.

Desai, Jigna (2006) 'Bollywood Abroad: South Asian Diasporic Cosmopolitanism and Indian Cinema', in Gita Rajan and Shailja Sharma (eds) *New Cosmopolitanisms: South Asians in the US*. Stanford, CA: Stanford University Press, pp. 115–37.

Dissanayake, Wimal (ed.) (1988) *Cinema and Cultural Identity: Reflections on Films from Japan, India, and China*. Lanham, MD: University Press of America.

Dudrah, Rajinder (2002) 'Vilayati Bollywood: Popular Hindi Cinema-Going and Diasporic South Asian Identity in Birmingham (UK)', *Javnost: Journal of the European Institute for Culture and Communication*, 9(1): 9–36.

Dudrah, Rajinder (2006) *Bollywood: Sociology Goes to the Movies*. New Delhi: Sage.

Dudrah, Rajinder (2008) 'Borders and Border Crossings in *Main Hoon Na* and *Veer Zaara*', in Meenakshi Bharat and Nirmal Kumar (eds) *Filming the Line of Control: The Indo-Pak Relationship through the Cinematic Lens*. New Delhi: Routledge, pp. 40–55.

Dudrah, Rajinder and Amit Rai (2005) 'The Haptic Codes of Bollywood Cinema in New York City', *New Cinemas: Journal of Contemporary Film*, 3(3): 143–58.

Dwyer, Rachel (2000). *All You Want is Money, All You Need is Love: Sexuality and Romance in Modern India*. London: Cassell.

Dwyer, Rachel and Divia Patel (2002) *Cinema India: The Visual Culture of Hindi Film*. New Brunswick, NJ: Rutgers University Press.

Dwyer, Rachel and Christopher Pinney (eds) (2001) *Pleasure and the Nation: The History, Politics, and Consumption of Public Culture in India*. New Delhi: Oxford University Press.

Gandhy, Behroze and Rosie Thomas (1991) 'Three Indian film stars', in Christine Gledhill (ed.) *Stardom: Industry of Desire*. London: Routledge, pp. 107–31.

Ganti, Tejaswini (2004) *Bollywood: A Guidebook to Popular Hindi Cinema*. New York: Routledge.

Garga, B. D. (2005) *The Art of Cinema: An Insider's Journey through Fifty Years of Film History*. New Delhi: Viking.

Garwood, Ian (2006) 'The Songless Bollywood Film', *South Asian Popular Culture*, 4(2): 169–83.

Gokulsing, K. and Wimal Dissanayake (1998) *Indian Popular Cinema: A Narrative of Cultural Change*. New Delhi: Orient Longman.

Gopalan, Lalitha (2002) *Cinema of Interruptions: Action Genres in Contemporary Indian Cinema*. London: British Film Institute.

Govil, Nitin (2005) 'Hollywood's Effects, Bollywood FX', in Greg Elmer and Mike Gasher (eds) *Contracting out Hollywood: Runaway Productions and Foreign Location Shooting*. Lanham, MD: Rowman & Littlefield, pp. 92–139.

Jaikumar, Priya (2006) *Cinema at the End of Empire: A Politics of Transition in Britain and India*. Durham, NC: Duke University Press.

Kapur, G. (1987) 'Mythic material in Indian cinema', *Journal of Arts and Ideas*, 14(15): 79–107.

Kaur, Raminder and Ajay J. Sinha (eds) (2005) *Bollyworld: Popular Indian Cinema through a Transnational Lens*. New Delhi: Sage.

Kazmi, Nikhat (1998) *The Dream Merchants of Bollywood*. New Delhi: UBS Publishers' Distributors.

Majumdar, Neepa (2001) 'The Embodied Voice: Song Sequences and Stardom in Popular Hindi Cinema', in Pamela Robertson Wojcik and Arthur Knight (eds) *Soundtrack Available: Essays on Film and Popular Music*. Durham, NC: Duke University Press, pp: 161–81.

Mazumdar, Ranjani (2007) *Bombay Cinema: An Archive of the City*. Minneapolis: University of Minnesota Press.

Mishra, Vijay (2002) *Bollywood Cinema: Temples of Desire*. New York: Routledge.

Nandy, Ashis (ed.) (1998) *The Secret Politics of our Desires: Innocence, Culpability and Indian Popular Cinema*. New York: Oxford University Press.

Pendakur, Manjunath (2003) *Indian Popular Cinema: Industry, Ideology, and Consciousness*. Cresskill, NJ: Hampton Press.

Pfleiderer, Beatrix and Lothar Lutze (eds) (1985) *The Hindi Film: Agent and Re-Agent of Cultural Change*. New Delhi: Manohar.

Prasad, M. Madhava (1998) *Ideology of the Hindi Film: A Historical Construction*. New York: Oxford University Press.

Rajadhyaksha, Ashish and Paul Willemen (1999) *Encyclopaedia of Indian Cinema*, 2nd edition. London: British Film Institute.

Rao, Shakuntala (2007) 'The Globalization of Bollywood: An Ethnography of Non-Elite Audiences in India', *Communication Review*, 10(1): 57–76.

Sharma, Ashwani (1993) 'Blood, Sweat and Tears: Amitabh Bachchan, Urban Demi-god', in Pat Kirkham and Janet Thumim (eds) *You Tarzan: Masculinity, Movies and Men*. New York: St Martin's Press, pp. 167–80.

Torgovnik, Jonathan (2003) *Bollywood Dreams: An Exploration of the Motion Picture Industry and its Culture in India*. London: Phaidon.

Uberoi, Patricia (1999) 'The diaspora comes home: disciplining desire in DDLJ', in V. Das, D. Gupta and P. Uberoi (eds) *Tradition, Plurality and Identity*. New Delhi: Sage, pp. 164–94.

Vasudev, A. and P. Lenglet (eds) (1983) *Indian Cinema Super Bazaar*. Delhi: Vikas.

Vasudevan, R. (1995) 'Addressing the Spectator of a "Third World" National Cinema: The Bombay "Social" Film of the 1940s and 1950s', *Screen* 36(4): 305–24.

Vasudevan, Ravi (ed.) (2000) *Making Meaning in Indian Cinema*. New Delhi: Oxford University Press.

Virdi, Jyotika (2003) *The Cinematic imagiNation: Indian Popular Films as Social History*. New Brunswick, NJ: Rutgers University Press.

Index

RETHINKING DOCUMENTARY

New Perspectives and Practices

Thomas Austin and Wilma de Jong

From a boom in theatrical features to footage posted on websites such as *YouTube* and *Google Video*, the early years of the 21st century have witnessed significant changes in the technological, commercial, aesthetic, political, and social dimensions of documentaries on film, television and the web.

In response to these rapid developments, this book rethinks the notion of documentary, in terms of theory, practice and object/s of study. Drawing together 26 original essays from scholars and practitioners, it critically assesses ideas and constructions of documentary and, where necessary, proposes new tools and arguments with which to examine this complex and shifting terrain.

Covering a range of media output, the book is divided into four sections:

- Critical perspectives on documentary forms and concepts
- The changing faces of documentary production Contemporary documentary: borders, neighbours and disputed territories
- Digital and online documentaries: opportunities and limitations

Rethinking Documentary is valuable reading for scholars and students working in documentary theory and practice, film studies, and media studies.

Contents: *Part 1: Critical perspectives on documentary forms and concepts – John Corner – Bill Nichols – Michael Renov – Thomas Austin – Silke Panse – Mike Wayne – Paul Basu – Erik Knudsen – Michael Chanan – Part 2: The changing faces of documentary production – Wilma de Jong – Jerry Rothwell – Marilyn Gaunt – An interview with John Smithson by Wilma de Jong and Thomas Austin – An interview with Ralph Lee by Wilma de Jong – Ishmahil Blagrove, Jr – An interview with Ai Xiaoming by Sue Thornham – Part 3: Contemporary documentary: borders, neighbours and disputed territories – Paul Ward – Craig Hight – Annette Hill – Su Holmes and Deborah Jermyn – Jon Dovey – Nick Couldry and Jo Littler – Part 4: Digital and online documentaries: opportunities and limitations – Ana Vicente – Danny Birchall – Patricia R. Zimmermann – Alexandra Juhasz.*

2008 376pp

978-0-335-22191-2 (Paperback) 978-0-335-22192-9 (Hardback)

THE TABLOID CULTURE READER

Anita Biressi and Heather Nunn (eds)

- What is tabloid culture?
- How do tabloid media prompt debates about values and ethics?
- Can we respond positively to the 'tabloidization' of culture?
- What is so appealing about the rhetoric, attitude and posture of tabloid culture?
- Which theories and concepts can help us analyse and understand tabloid media?

This wide-ranging and accessible Reader provides a useful introduction to the historical and contemporary debates about the values, ethics and pleasures of tabloid news, entertainment and culture.

Arranged thematically, the book addresses definitions and debates, values and ethics, carnival and excess, celebrity, gender and sexuality, production and the audience. With specially written introductions to the volume and to each section, the Reader features key writings from leading scholars in the field. Essays explore the history and origins of tabloid culture and concepts such as the press, magazines, shock-jocks, the public sphere, reality and talk show television, photojournalism and voyeurism, and examples used include:

- *heat* magazine
- *Loaded* and men's lifestyle publications
- Jackass
- The tabloid life of O.J. Simpson
- Big Brother's Jade Goody

Each section is followed by recommendations for further reading.

Contributors: *Mark Andrejevic, Feona Attwood, Karin Becker, S. Elizabeth Bird, Anita Biressi, Frances Bonner, Kate Brooks, Martin Conboy, Mark Deuze, John Fiske, Bob Franklin, Des Freedman, Kevin Glynn, Laura Grindstaff, Jostein Gripsrud, Bridget Griffen-Foley, Su Holmes, Patricia Holland, Leon Hunt, A. M. Jönsson, Jason Kosovski, P. David Marshall, Victoria Mapplebeck, Heather Nunn, Henrik Örnebring, Mark Pursehouse, Graeme Turner, Pamela Wilson.*

Contents: *List of contributors – Acknowledgements – Publisher's acknowledgements – Foreword by Martin Conboy – Introduction – Part 1: Debates, concepts, theories – Section 1: Origins, definitions and debates: talking about the tabloids – Section 2: The values and ethics of tabloid media – Section 3: Carnival, spectacle and excess – Part 2: Aspects of tabloid culture – Section 4: Celebrity – Section 5: Gender and sexuality – Part 3: Tabloid culture, production and consumption – Section 6: Producing tabloid culture: behind the scenes – Section 7: Tabloid audiences – Bibliography – Index.*

2007 400pp

978-0-335-21931-5 (Paperback) 978-0-335-21932-2 (Hardback)

FEMINIST TELEVISION CRITICISM

A Reader

Charlotte Brunsdon and Lynn Spigel (eds)

The first edition of this book immediately became a defining text for feminist television criticism, with an influence extending across television, media and screen studies – and the second edition will be similarly agenda-setting. Completely revised and updated throughout, it takes into account the changes in the television industry, the academic field of television studies and the culture and politics of feminist movements.

With fifteen of the eighteen extracts being new to the second edition, the readings offer a detailed analysis of a wide range of case studies, topics and approaches, including genres, audiences, performers and programmes such as 'Sex and the City', 'Prime Suspect', Oprah and Buffy.

With a new introduction to the volume tracing developments in the field and introductions to each thematic section, the editors engage in a series of debates surrounding the main issues of feminist television scholarship. They explore how television represents feminism and consider how critics themselves have created feminism and post-feminism as historical categories and political identities. Readings consider women who are engaged in various aspects of television production on both sides of the camera and examine how television targets and imagines its female audience, as well as how women respond to and use television in their everyday lives.

Feminist Television Criticism is inspiring reading for film, media, cultural and gender studies students.

Contributors: *Ien Ang, Jane Arthurs , Sarah Banet-Weiser ,Karen Boyle, Marsha F. Cassidy, Geok-lian Chua ,Bonnie J. Dow, Joanne Hollows, Deborah Jermyn , Annette Kuhn, Elizabeth MacLachlan, Purnima Mankekar, Tania Modleski, Laurie Ouellette, Yeidy M. Rivero, Lee Ann Roripaugh, Beretta E. Smith-Shomade, Kimberly Springer, Ksenija Vidmar-Horvat, Susan J. Wolfe.*

Contents: *Introduction – Introduction to Part One: Programmes and Heroines – The Search for Tomorrow in Today's Soap Operas: Notes on a Feminine Narrative Form – "Sex and the City" and Consumer Culture: Remediating Postfeminist Drama – Women with a Mission: Lynda La Plante, DCI Jane Tennison and the Reconfiguration of TV Crime Drama – Divas, Evil Black Bitches, and Bitter Black Women: African-American Women in Postfeminist and Post-Civil Rights Popular Culture – "Ellen", Television and the Politics of Gay and Lesbian Visibility – You'd Better Recognize: Oprah the Iconic and Television Talk – "Take Responsibility for Yourself" Judge Judy and the Neoliberal Citizen – Feeling Like a Domestic Goddess: Postfeminism and Cooking – Feminism Without Men: Feminist Media Studies in a Post-Feminist Age – Girls Rule! Gender, Feminism, and Nickelodeon – The (In)visible Lesbian: Anxieties of representation in the L word – Introduction to Part Two: Audiences, Reception Contexts, and Spectatorship – Women's Genres: Melodrama, Soap Opera, and Theory – Melodromatic Identifications: Television Fiction and Women's Fantasy – National Texts and Gendered Lives: An Ethnography of Television Viewers in a North Indian City – Defining Asian Femininity: Chinese Viewers of Japanese TV Dramas in Singapore – The Globalization of Gender: Ally McBeal in Post-Socialist Slovenia – The Performance and Reception of Televisual 'Ugliness' in "Yo soy Betty la Fea" – Sob Stories, Merriment, and Surprises: The 1950s Audience Participation Show on Network Television and Women's Daytime Reception – Bibliography.*

2007 384pp

978-0-335-22545-3 (Paperback) 978-0-335-22544-6 (Hardback)

THE CULT FILM READER

Ernest Mathijs and Xavier Mendik (eds)

'A really impressive and comprehensive collection of the key writings in the field. The editors have done a terrific job in drawing together the various traditions and providing a clear sense of this rich and rewarding scholarly terrain. This collection is as wild and diverse as the films that it covers. Fascinating.'
Mark Jancovich, Professor of Film and Television Studies, University of East Anglia, UK

'It's about time the lunatic fans and loyal theorists of cult movies were treated to a book they can call their own. The effort and knowledge contained in **The Cult Film Reader** *will satisfy even the most ravenous zombie's desire for detail and insight. This book will gnaw, scratch and infect you just like the cult films themselves.'*
Brett Sullivan, Director of Ginger Snaps Unleashed and The Chair

*'***The Cult Film Reader** *is a great film text book and a fun read.'*
John Landis, Director of The Blues Brothers, An American Werewolf in London and Michael Jackson's Thriller

Whether defined by horror, kung-fu, sci-fi, sexploitation, kitsch musical or 'weird world cinema', cult movies and their global followings are emerging as a distinct subject of film and media theory, dedicated to dissecting the world's unruliest images.

This book is the world's first reader on cult film. It brings together key works in the field on the structure, form, status, and reception of cult cinema traditions. Including work from key established scholars in the field such as Umberto Eco, Janet Staiger, Jeffrey Sconce, Henry Jenkins, and Barry Keith Grant, as well as new perspectives on the gradually developing canon of cult cinema, the book not only presents an overview of ways in which cult cinema can be approached, it also re-assesses the methods used to study the cult text and its audiences.

With editors' introductions to the volume and to each section, the book is divided into four clear thematic areas of study – The Conceptions of Cult; Cult Case Studies; National and International Cults; and Cult Consumption – to provide an accessible overview of the topic. It also contains an extensive bibliography for further related readings.

Written in a lively and accessible style, *The Cult Film Reader* dissects some of biggest trends, icons, auteurs and periods of global cult film production. Films discussed include *Casablanca, The Rocky Horror Picture Show, Eraserhead, The Texas Chainsaw Massacre, Showgirls* and *Ginger Snaps*.

Essays by: *Jinsoo An; Jane Arthurs; Bruce Austin; Martin Barker; Walter Benjamin; Harry Benshoff; Pierre Bourdieu; Noel Carroll; Steve Chibnall; Umberto Eco; Nezih Erdogan; Welch Everman; John Fiske; Barry Keith Grant ; Joan Hawkins; Gary Hentzi; Matt Hills; Ramaswami Harindranath; J.Hoberman; Leon Hunt; I.Q. Hunter; Mark Jancovich; Henry Jenkins; Anne Jerslev; Siegfried Kracauer; Gina Marchetti; Tom Mes; Gary Needham; Sheila J. Nayar; Annalee Newitz; Lawrence O'Toole; Harry Allan Potamkin; Jonathan Rosenbaum; Andrew Ross; David Sanjek; Eric Schaefer; Steven Jay Schneider; Jeffrey Sconce; Janet Staiger; J.P. Telotte; Parker Tyler; Jean Vigo; Harmony Wu*

Contents: *Section One: The Concepts of Cult – Section Two: Cult Case Studies – Section Three: National and International Cults – Bibliography of Cult Film Resources – Index.*

2007 576pp

978-0-335-21923-0 (Paperback) 978-0-335-21924-7 (Hardback)

THE MOVIE BUSINESS BOOK

International Third Edition

Jason E. Squire (ed)

Drawing on the knowledge of a full spectrum of industry experts including producers, independent filmmakers, managers and financiers, the third international edition of *The Movie Business Book* offers a comprehensive, authoritative overview of the film industry. It features a preface written especially for the international edition, which contextualizes this definitive, state-of-the-art sourcebook for readers in the expanding global entertainment business.

A must-read for anyone working in the film and entertainment industry, it covers the nuts-and-bolts of financing, revenue streams, marketing, DVDs, globalization, the Internet and new technologies. Using actual examples and advice from practitioners, this edition includes contributions from key industry players such as David Puttnam; Tom Rothman, chairman of Fox Filmed Entertainment; Benjamin S. Feingold, President, Business & Operations, Columbia TriStar Motion Picture Group (a division of Sony Pictures Entertainment); Sydney Pollack; and Mel Brooks.

The Movie Business Book: International Third Edition is an essential guide for anyone wanting to launch or advance a career in the growing media marketplace.

Contents: *The Creators – The Property – The Money – The Management – The Deal – Production – Marketing – The Revenue Streams – Theatrical Distribution – Theatrical Exhibition – Home Video – Consumer Products – International – The Future.*

2006 584pp

978-0-335-22002-1 (Paperback) 978-0-335-22003-8 (Hardback)

CONTEMPORARY AMERICAN CINEMA

Linda Ruth Williams and Michael Hammond (eds)

"One of the rare collections I would recommend for use in undergraduate teaching – the chapters are lucid without being oversimplified and the contributors are adept at analyzing the key industrial, technological and ideological features of contemporary U.S. cinema."

Diane Negra, University of East Anglia, UK.

"*Contemporary American Cinema* is the book on the subject that undergraduate classes have been waiting for ... Comprehensive, detailed, and intelligently organized [and] written in accessible and compelling prose ... *Contemporary American Cinema* will be embraced by instructors and students alike."

Charlie Keil, Director, Cinema Studies Program, University of Toronto, Canada.

Contemporary American Cinema is the first comprehensive introduction to American cinema since 1960. The book is unique in its treatment of both Hollywood, alternative and non-mainstream cinema. Critical essays from leading film scholars are supplemented by boxed profiles of key directors, producers and actors; key films and key genres; and statistics from the cinema industry.

Illustrated in colour and black and white with film stills, posters and production images, the book has two tables of contents allowing students to use the book chronologically, decade-by-decade, or thematically by subject. Designed especially for courses in cinema studies and film studies, cultural studies and American studies, *Contemporary American Cinema* features a glossary of key terms, fully referenced resources and suggestions for further reading, questions for class discussion, and a comprehensive filmography.

Individual chapters include:

- The decline of the studio system
- The rise of American new wave cinema
- The history of the blockbuster
- The parallel histories of independent and underground film
- Black cinema from blaxploitation to the 1990s
- Changing audiences
- The effects of new technology
Comprehensive overview of US documentary from 1960 to the present

Contributors include: Stephen Prince, Steve Neale, Susan Jeffords, Yvonne Tasker, Barbara Klinger, Jim Hillier, Peter Kramer, Mark Shiel, Sheldon Hall, Eithne Quinn, Michele Aaron, Jonathan Munby.

Contents: Introduction: *the whats, hows and whys of this book –* **The 1960s** *– Introduction – The American New Wave, Part 1: 1967–1970 – Debts Disasters and Mega-movies: the studios in the 1960s – Other Americas: The underground, exploitation and the avant garde – U.S Documentary Cinema in the 1960s – 'The Last Good Time We Ever Had'?: Revising the Hollywood Renaissance – Suggested Further Reading – Essay Questions –* **The 1970s** *– Introduction – The American New Wave, Part 2: 1970–1975 – New Hollywood and the Rise of the Blockbuster – Blaxploitation – U.S.*

2006 584pp

978-0-335-21831-8 (Paperback) 978-0-335-21832-5 (Hardback)